THE SCANDAL OF CONTINUITY IN
MIDDLE EAST ANTHROPOLOGY

PUBLIC CULTURES OF THE MIDDLE EAST AND
NORTH AFRICA

THE SCANDAL OF CONTINUITY IN MIDDLE EAST ANTHROPOLOGY

Form, Duration, Difference

Edited by
Judith Scheele and Andrew Shryock

INDIANA UNIVERSITY PRESS

This book is a publication of

Indiana University Press
Office of Scholarly Publishing
Herman B Wells Library 350
1320 East 10th Street
Bloomington, Indiana 47405 USA

iupress.indiana.edu

Manufactured in the United States of America

Cataloging information is available from the Library of Congress.

ISBN 978-0-253-04376-4 (hardback)
ISBN 978-0-253-04379-5 (paperback)
ISBN 978-0-253-04378-8 (ebook)

1 2 3 4 5   23 22 21 20 19

CONTENTS

ACKNOWLEDGMENTS

THIS BOOK IS THE RESULT OF A TWO-DAY workshop, "People versus Human-kind," held at All Souls College, Oxford, to which thanks are due for its hospitality and funding. Additional support was provided by St John's College and the Institute for Social and Cultural Anthropology, both also at Oxford. The workshop was instigated by Morgan Clarke, Walter Armbrust, and Judith Scheele, to mark Paul Dresch's retirement from Oxford by a gathering of his advisees, colleagues, and friends; it could not have taken place without the help and advice provided by Melinda Babcock. Additional thanks are due to Nick Allen, Elizabeth Ewart, Tim Jenkins, and Tom Lambert, who provided invaluable feedback as discussants at the workshop. We are also grateful for the commentary provided by two anonymous reviewers of the original manuscript, and to Dee Mortensen, our editor at Indiana University Press.

If not a Festschrift of the traditional kind, this volume is intended to engage with and celebrate the work—and the inspirational teaching—of our common mentor, Paul Dresch. His aversion to limelight is now legendary, so we thank him for indulging our efforts. In the end, the ideas and the personal influence were harder to tell apart than we thought they would be. We thank Paul for that, too. In whichever way we came to be "Dresch students," wherever it led us, and whatever we took away from it, it was an experience that changed our lives.

MAP

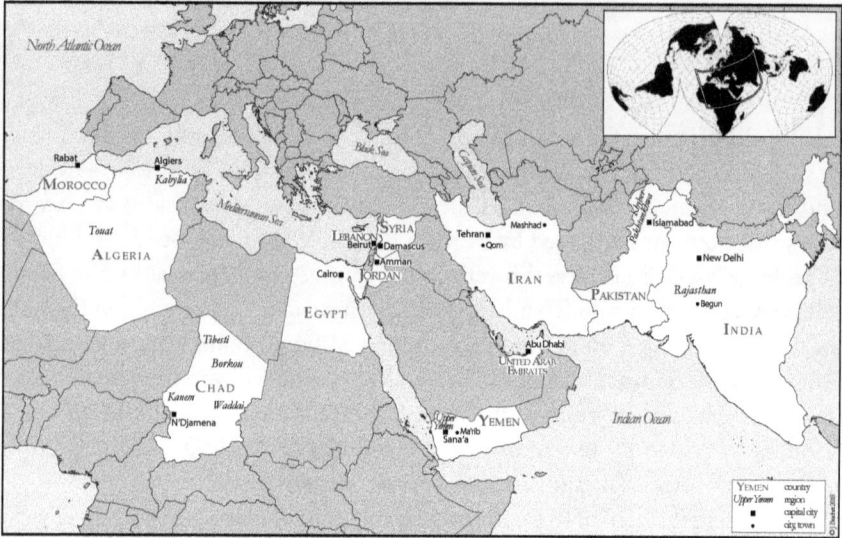

Map 0.1. Places and regions mentioned in this book. This map echoes al-Idrisi's (1154), used as a cover image.

THE SCANDAL OF CONTINUITY IN
MIDDLE EAST ANTHROPOLOGY

INTRODUCTION

On the Left Hand of Knowledge

Judith Scheele and Andrew Shryock

As an anthropologist one tries to make intelligible, to oneself and others, forms of human life. These are complex, for they conjoin many subjectivities and by definition no one account is adequate; yet they possess a certain objectivity despite this, for, at the least, there is a choreographed circulation of words, images, made things, formulae of interaction . . . in which people build some enduring sense of shared position. Whether clustered in a village or spread across the internet or family visits, the imageries that characterise such particular lives involve currencies of reference held partially in common and forms of interaction which are, as the saying goes, second nature. (Dresch and James 2000, 7)

If theory is active, fieldwork is also rich in theory, because it produces what might be called moral knowledge, both ordering and revisable, intervening and reflecting, acting and comprehending. (Jenkins 1994, 452)

IT IS NOTORIOUSLY DIFFICULT TO DESCRIBE WHAT ANTHROPOLOGISTS do. Under pressure, we often tell curious interlocutors that we study "customs and traditions" or that we "live with people to learn about their culture." We cringe as we speak these words. The truth is much harder to explain; it would take too much time, and it would probably make less sense. Besides, we hardly agree among ourselves about what we do or why. We go into the field looking for many things. What is surprising about fieldwork, as method and experience, is the remarkable degree to which it has remained, over the history of the discipline, a reliable way of producing anthropological knowledge, however contested that knowledge might be. In this volume, we make the case for a particular way of constructing knowledge that derives its strengths from an old and ongoing encounter of scholars, a discrete set of ideas, and a region of the world. It draws on early twentieth-century French social theory, the Oxford anthropology of the 1960s and 1970s, and a diverse body of ethnographic work located mostly in the Middle East, in Muslim societies, and in the political contact zones around and within them.

The Middle East is a world of part-worlds, of polities and economies that are internally differentiated and arrayed in elaborate hierarchies of interdependence. It long has been so. This might be one of the reasons why the anthropology of the Middle East tends to feel marginal to a discipline that historically drew strength from its embeddedness in worlds that seemed coherent and freestanding. Anthropology has turned away from these worlds, noting that, although images of self-sufficiency and stasis might at times correspond to local self-perceptions, they had little historical and have even less contemporary reality. This recognition was overdue but also troublesome. Arguably, it has undermined the intellectual confidence of the discipline—what, apart from "local knowledge" and ethnographic fieldwork, makes us special? More importantly, it has handicapped us in relation to our traditional interest in "ordering principles," the constructs that make human life intelligible, give it regularity and form, and help us understand how it changes over time. In this volume, we argue that Middle East anthropology, which is undertaken in societies that are highly distinctive yet seldom neatly bounded—where part-worlds, assertions of autonomy, widely shared ordering principles, and crosscutting patterns of inclusion and fragmentation in fact go together—might hold lessons for the discipline as a whole.

In 1951, Evans-Pritchard, who emphatically was *not* a Middle East specialist, wrote that an anthropologist "must have, in addition to a wide anthropological knowledge, a feeling for form and pattern, and a touch of genius" (1951, 82). More modestly, we argue that renewed attention to patterns of continuity, both temporal and spatial, will allow us to develop a more sophisticated and deeply historical approach to worlds that are filled with "form and pattern" but have never been self-contained. It will also encourage a much-needed reconsideration of how metropolitan categories of thought interact with local concepts, categories, and forms of action—a process that itself may produce, as Dresch and James suggest, an "enduring sense of shared position" (2000, 7). In the end, what we call for is not a particular approach to theory or method but a mode of analytical engagement that moves constantly beyond its own privileged categories and into the world.

The Modern Imperial Frame

David Pocock (1961, 105) captured this sensibility when he wrote that anthropology is a dialogue of three: the anthropologist, the discipline, and the society studied. The subject matter of this exchange is not limited to local knowledge, or theory, or the analyst's position. Rather, the dialogue grows out of assumptions, often unspoken at first, that slowly become intelligible as the parties to this conversation interact in depth and across difference. Whether they happen in remote field sites, at home, or in the archives, such conversations lead to the recognition of ordering principles: shared ideas, meaningful patterns of action and comprehension, recurrences, durable trends, and what earlier generations of anthropologists called "structure."[1] The word has since fallen out of use, mostly due to associations with functionalism and stasis. Nonetheless, it is clear that fieldwork is not simply a collection of "data," as one might pick apples from a tree; it is more about figuring out the categories and frames that make things appear as data in the first place. "One must reflect in order to measure, not measure in order to reflect," wrote Bachelard (1938, 213), famously, though hardly with anthropology in mind. It follows that ethnographers must constantly step back from their conversations—those happening across the discipline and in fieldwork settings—to take in what is being said, a complicated maneuver that requires the creation of reflective spaces that feed back into the dialogue. The point is not simply to participate in a conversation or observe it, but to analyze it, to make extra sense of it. The "structure" that emerges is as much a product of this interpretation as it is of things experienced directly "in the field." Distinguishing cleanly between these two realms is impossible; the "meta" is built into empirical analysis, and vice versa. Evans-Pritchard assumed as much, long ago, when he said that "the theoretical conclusions will . . . be found to be implicit in an exact and detailed description" (1973, 3).

Contemporary anthropology, however, has little interest in "implicit" theory. Theory is declarative; it signals allegiance and innovative capacity, and its value in the intellectual marketplace plummets when it is buried in ethnographic detail.[2] "Topping and tailing one's account with long mentions of other anthropologists"—an exercise Dresch (1989, ix) in the late 1980s judged "mischievous"—has thus become a necessary marker of one's active membership (real or aspirational) in the profession, one moreover that is mandatory for publication in many journals. If Pocock's "dialogue of three" worked as a set of checks and balances, keeping the ethnographer from falling "back into the collective representations of his own or the other society" (1961, 105), then we should expect the emancipation, or rather exteriorization, of theory to have distorting effects. Today, da Col and Graeber observe with regret, "anthropologists take their concepts not from ethnography but largely from European philosophy" (2011, x). Patterns and durable forms that arise from the local, from "the field," are treated with suspicion; they restrict our ability to apply or invoke metropolitan concepts. But at the same time, "no one really cares what we have to say about" metropolitan concepts; "and as a result, we have become a discipline spiralling into parochial irrelevance" (da Col and Graeber 2011, x).

The specter of parochialism notwithstanding, more fundamental points are at issue here: namely, a growing inability to recognize social reality as inherent in anything but individual agency, a distaste (dating back to Malinowski) for rules and abstraction, and a pervasive uneasiness with cultural difference. Combined, these trends lead ethnographers into "a commonsensical world of calculating individuals in local fancy dress" (Dresch and Scheele 2015, 20). It is hard to tell which is worse: "othering" the people we describe (by noticing their fancy dress), or "mainstreaming" them (by turning them into citizen consumers, rational actors, or rights-bearing subjects). Ethically, either course is likely to be criticized as a kind of cultural bullying. Philosophically, each lays us open to charges of naivety: as Searle points out, "social facts" are "institutional facts" and depend on "prior *assignments* of value" and on constitutive rules that "create the very possibility of certain activities" (1995, 15, 27; emphasis in original). A focus on agency and choice making, prescribed as the antidote to deterministic notions of structure, will inevitably smuggle ordering principles back into analysis. This is so because meaningful action, whether we treat it ideologically as sameness or difference, can be meaningful only when larger interpretive frames allow us, as actors or analysts, to recognize it as such.

It is barely an exaggeration to say that anthropologists no longer have the terms they need to describe ordering principles, underlying or overarching. We discard one term after another: mentality, habitus, culture. Ontology will be next. Kinship has become sentiment rather than structure, process and practice rather than system;[3] social rules—of law, ethics, or religion—are treated no longer as norms habitually embraced but as arenas of self-fashioning, governmentality, and expertise.[4] This shift in perspective has produced some good ethnography. Yet it draws our attention away from comparison, and a diminished interest in formal likenesses has made it harder to grasp (or even to perceive) phenomena that an older anthropology was once keen on. How does one explain the recurrence of kinship patterns—certain kinds of genealogy, say, or preferences for close-range marriage—over large areas that have never been politically united (Pitt-Rivers 1994)? How does one account for the continuity over time not so much of social organization but of categories within which action makes sense, like "house," "host," and "guest," which correspond to notions of hospitality that are demonstrably ancient (Shryock 2008)? How can one make sense of systems of moral legitimation, like notions of "honor" or ways of inheriting mobile and immobile wealth that lack centralization or even a literate tradition, but prove nonetheless resilient for centuries (Hann 2008)? If communities in parts of North Africa define themselves as unique, yet all do so in the same way (Scheele 2014), is this mere contingency? The problem is not that researchers are unaware of these configurations but that they too easily take them for granted; treat them as alienating or othering; dismiss them as illusions of an older, less sophisticated scholarship; or avoid discussing them altogether. As a result, larger ordering principles are left to be explained by other disciplines as "context" (economic, historical, ecological, political), often in starkly unsatisfactory terms.

Scandals of Continuity

This distrust of pattern has fed an appetite for epistemological breaks, invented traditions, and constant, contingent change. Of course, fluidity can itself be patterned, even predictable, but for many contemporary anthropologists, "historical continuity" is an awkward pairing of terms. If history is about change—it might not be, but most readers assume it is—then continuity would appear to be an ideological commitment, a political claim made to speed up or slow down the inevitability of change. Things that have the look of antiquity, from caste systems (Dirks 2001) to "authentic" religious practices (Deeb 2006) to national and ethnoracial identities (Mamdani 1996), are typically analyzed so as to show how they fit within, or emerge in resistance to, a larger world system or an encompassing colonial power. Richard Reid's lament about the "hegemony of the modern" in African history is thus familiar: "The growing conviction that the colonial experience had engendered identities and processes that were not connected—or only tenuously so—to anything that had gone on before meant that the deep past was increasingly relegated to mere prologue. Since the 1980s, what began as a series of legitimate lines of scholarly enquiry has become a dominant intellectual worldview; the obsession with the modern has led to the marginalization of the deep past, which means in effect that historians are increasingly fixated with the tip at the expense of the iceberg" (2011, 147). The analyst can certainly advocate for social actors who represent "the local," but the interpretive orientation overall gives precedence to a modern, imperial frame. Attempts to connect extant social forms to precolonial ones are portrayed as impractical—reliable data, alas, are not at hand—or the focus itself as politically suspect, as it encourages primordialism and deflects attention from an oppressive global political economy (e.g., Asad 1973a, 270). For metropolitan anthropologists, this stance requires us to impose our own terms of debate, our own moral fixations, all in the hope of unsettling them.

Yet the people we work with do not always feel edified when we de- and reconstruct their identities. We like to pretend otherwise, but ethnographers (historically inclined ones especially) are tactical when they say "the native is never wrong." The beliefs and practices we encounter in fieldwork are often indeed quite old—bridewealth payments, religious pilgrimages, forms of bodily modification, ways of naming people or places—and our research subjects would like us to acknowledge this, whether anthropological fashion rewards us for it or not. That local Bedouin tribes predate the modern nation-state in which they live is a politically sensitive fact in Jordan (Shryock 1997), as is the documented existence, long before the British arrived to invent them, of "criminal castes" in India (Piliavsky 2015). Whether such cases are endorsed as "indigeneity" or denounced as "backwardness" is itself part of the ethnography, and the relationship between old social forms and "the colonial rule of difference" (P. Chatterjee 1993) that stigmatizes and privileges them is not straightforward. All of these problems correspond to a more basic condition: history and continuity are measures of value; they constitute moral spaces that do not simply persist but are seen to do so in ways good or bad, safe or dangerous, welcoming or inhospitable. Indeed, how a moral space reproduces itself, as an institution, an identity, or a set of practices, is often a matter hotly contested by those who inhabit the space and by those defined as outsiders to it.

Temporality is a crucial register in which these contests unfold. The quality of history—its reliability and richness, but also its formal properties (Sahlins 1983)—is determined by how history makers relate to, and how they move into and out of, the moral spaces they describe. Continuity answers to the same logic of belonging and mobility, and the extent to which we perceive continuity will depend on our ability to connect moral spaces across time. The centrality anthropologists now give to "history" has an odd, generally unpondered relationship to this dynamic. In one way of seeing things, continuity—or too much of it at least—takes people out of history. The assumption was prefigured in Lévi-Strauss's (1966, 233) famous distinction between hot and cold societies, which suggested that modern societies were all about change, which made them historical, while certain others were all about reproduction without acknowledging change, which made them ahistorical. The claim quickly evolved into a double caricature (Palmié and Stewart 2016, 211; Gow 2001, 14–19). Patterning and change are present in all human societies, as Lévi-Strauss well knew. It is impossible to define one without the other, but it is possible, and entirely appropriate in certain contexts, that one concept will be marked, or privileged, in analysis: "all societies are equally historical, but some frankly admit to it, while others are averse to it and prefer not to know" (Lévi-Strauss 1983a, 1218). The problem is not that different societies admit to their own history in different ways; it is the claim that they are all "equally historical," an idea that facilitates the absorption of all people into the time frames imposed by Western societies.

To a long list of imperial gifts, we can now add the dubious privilege of "co-evalness" (Fabian 1983).

Today, all human societies are supposedly "hot." They are also open, fluid, and connected, in a world that, like time, is conceived to be, if not frictionless (Tsing 2005), then at least morally neutral. Anthropologists must now routinely emphasize tensions between the local, the national, and the "global," but very little intervenes between these terms to make them distinctive. Area studies have dropped out of fashion (but see Mintz 1998; Slocum and Thomas 2003); we do fieldwork, Appadurai argues, in "a world in which points of arrival and points of departure are in critical flux, and thus the search for steady points of reference, as critical life choices are made, can be very difficult" (1996, 44). The movement of people and things is portrayed as fluid and therefore inexplicable in localizing terms. Appadurai depicts localizing terms as old-fashioned, even when updated as "practice theory": "It is in this atmosphere that the invention of tradition (and of ethnicity, kinship, and other identity markers) can become slippery. . . . As group pasts become increasingly parts of museums, exhibits, and collections, both in national and transnational spectacles, culture becomes less what Pierre Bourdieu would have called a habitus (a tacit realm of reproducible practices and dispositions) and more an arena of conscious choice, justification, and representation, the latter often to multiple and spatially dislocated audiences" (1996, 44). The cultural products of "globalization" are akin to commodities and should be evaluated as such: they are old or new, good or bad, appealing or not, and issues of "power" tend to enter and exit analysis as foregone conclusions. (Prosperous transnational intellectuals even mistake the position of migrant laborers for their own, as if freedom of movement were a given.) Identity claims, meanwhile, are increasingly built out of mass-mediated, remarkably thin materials of the sort that can in fact be readily displayed in popular museum exhibits or culture shows (Shryock 2004a, 306–7).

Multisited fieldwork has not delivered the promised corrective. Instead, it has evolved into a "research imaginary" that either is logistically impractical or, in practice, functions much as bounded, self-contained field sites once did. Candea (2007, 178) thus speaks of "the paradoxical reconfiguration of holism implicit in the multi-sited imagery" that aims to "grasp whole systems." "If post-modern ethnography posited wholes by showing their fragments," he writes, "multi-sited ethnography . . . tries to follow and encompass these wholes" (179). Unboundedness remains difficult to grasp, and as our articulatory efforts proceed, or flounder, regions of long-standing connectedness (once called "culture areas") become analytically invisible, or else are reinterpreted as external impositions devised to further the interests of colonial overlords, who resemble ethnographers in their willingness to unsettle and reconnect.

People locally are left in much the same position as Scott's (1998, 316) apocryphal fisherman or peasant, relying uniquely on half-conscious local knowledge or *mètis*, which varies from village to village, or even family to family, and thus remains necessarily opaque. Yet in practice, the older world ecumenes—whether they are marked by shared languages, internal oppositions, legal or political traditions, common mythology, kinship patterns, or similar ways of preparing foods or approaching gods—matter greatly to most people. They constitute interactional sets through which "globalization" tends to be refracted.[5]

Actor-network theorists, meanwhile, have attempted to draw larger connections on different terms. However, their emphasis on the processual articulation of networks and assemblages produces models of the social that are oddly flat. Anthropology, writes Latour (1988, 149), "first had to study symmetrically all the logical systems, those of the Alladian witch doctors as well as those of the Californian biochemists or the French engineers. But in gradually discovering what made up the logical systems and paths, anthropology finally collapsed." Latour's conclusion is eye-catching. One can hardly ignore the claim that our discipline is in ruins and we are free at last to study, unhindered by localized cultures, "the world"! But what, for Latour, is a selling point, should perhaps make us pause for thought: the moral evaluations and hierarchies that ensure that Californian biochemists and Alladian witch doctors can be distinguished from each other are in fact what defines our subject matter.

Anthropology East and West

The syndrome we are describing is general, but not all anthropologists would find it debilitating. Where one does ethnography is important. In regions that once offered the ethnographer "bounded communities" in which to work, where life supposedly transpired in "local moral worlds" (Dresch 2000a, 115), a decisive break with insularity can produce liberating sensations. The Middle East, however, has never been one of these regions. It has known coins, trade, scriptural religions, and states for millennia. Here, societies are not "total" in the Maussian sense, and notions of bounded community rarely hold. Indeed, even anthropology's fascination with exchange must often be treated cautiously, for "there is no determinate set in which to calculate loss and profit as participant or analyst" (Dresch 1998, 115). In such a world, sociality cannot be reduced to the local or indeed to the contemporary: history itself, often conceived as a narrative of permanence rather than change, is central to local discussions of rightful order, proper social interactions, and causality on all levels (Lindholm 1995, 809). People claim relatedness to others whom they have never met ("We are all sons of Adam") while denying all ties with their neighbors ("They are trouble, and they have no origins"). Horizons are broad, stretching as far as there are Muslims, or Arabs, or Turks, and each of these identities is as transregional as it is local; notions of "ethnicity" cannot contain them. Continuities, both temporal and spatial, are strong, intrinsically relevant, and beyond ethnographic control. An unsettling parallel is evident between this reality and the explanatory inadequacy of the single place, a predicament now generalized in contemporary anthropology; yet in the Middle Eastern case, the predicament comes with a heightened sense of duration and form, not a lessening of it. In villages, cities, and the multiple diasporas that suffuse and extend beyond the Middle East, people are convinced that they belong to societies and civilizations that are historically durable and widespread.

Although different regions create different ways of "doing anthropology" and distinctive ways of defining one's place as an outsider, such differences are rarely analyzed explicitly.[6] Instead, they form part of anthropology's "cultural intimacy," alongside awkward tales of fieldwork gone wrong. "To suggest that some areas are more difficult than others, or less transparent, is uncomfortable in ethnographic company" (Dresch 2000a, 113). But more is at stake here than competitive shoptalk: the place given (or denied) to the visiting ethnographer itself produces a certain type of knowledge. It indicates broader social patterns that are—or ought to be—of primary interest. Intimately connected to the wider world, Middle Eastern societies have long developed a "stranger slot" that, because it is part of local sociality, anthropologists often find difficult to escape. There are no stories of "first encounters" with White Others on the beach. The Others are always potentially there, and it is always possible for them to become local. As a result, the "authenticity" of social categories is contested, and reliable knowledge about them is assumed, by scholars and laypeople alike, to be partial. The role played by anthropologists is, in Ardener's terms (1989, 215, drawing on Althusser 1969), "overdetermined." Field-workers have to submit to the social formations available and thereby put themselves at risk. They cannot heedlessly impose their own agenda but have to trust their interlocutors. Hence, interpretation is a shared project—not a "method" used by the ethnographer but something the ethnographer does with willing partners in the field.

More generally, the absence of bounded locality, the importance of far-flung connections and historical frames of reference, shapes knowledge in and of the region in peculiar ways. One cannot just pluck knowledge of Islam, or tribal dispute resolution, or Egyptian movies for that matter, from moments of observation or even from sustained participation. Authoritative knowledge is often located, by locals themselves, elsewhere. It is of its nature suspect, and there is always someone who has more of it. The terrain of knowing is sharply moralized; it is often defined by durable oppositions, and certain kinds of knowledge can be had only with proper escort, which is given only to people who need it, who are vulnerable, and who seem to want help in navigating toward "truth." Yet truth is by definition unobtainable, contested, or else unpublishable, in a context where "privacy is highly structured and integral to the definition of social groups" (Dresch 2000a, 111). Lying, trust, and distrust are thus part of any ethnographic enterprise, much as they are central to everyday social interactions (Gilsenan 1976). It is hard to write about such things. They are based on acrimonious assumptions, and they sometimes produce troublesome accounts. Yet they also, paradoxically perhaps, open up spaces for a certain type of inquiry. "If, to take an old formulation, oppositions are 'nested', a structure will be found in whose nodes and interstices fieldworkers from elsewhere might thrive in distinctive ways" (Dresch 2000a, 111).

More so than other anthropological "regions," the Middle East poses conceptual and ethical challenges to the West. Too historical, literate, complex, and self-confident to be turned into ordinary anthropological subject matter, the Orient tends to look like a bad reflection of the Occident, uncannily similar, but where key moral evaluations are ignored or turned on their head. The Muslim empires rivaled European power into the nineteenth century, and much that is nowadays deemed modern, progressive, and advanced came to be understood as such, in the West, through explicit comparison to these societies. What Edward Said (1978) called "Orientalism" was a result of struggle with and domination over non-European regimes. Yet the critique of Orientalism, so appealing as a weapon against imperial racism and claims to superiority, had the effect of further marginalizing the anthropological study of Middle Eastern societies: first, because anthropology was easily depicted as white mischief dedicated to the knowing of "primitives"; and second, because anthropologists seemed always to be interested in difference, and difference was the top bogey of any anti-Orientalist stance. "Insofar as one can make a sweeping generalization," Said wrote, "the felt tendencies of contemporary culture in the Near East are guided by European and American models" (1978, 323). It is not surprising that anthropologists, ever sensitive to the geopolitics of cultural representation, have so far drawn mostly negative conclusions from Said's critique; many have become "increasingly and sometimes cripplingly self-conscious about their work" (Lindholm 1995, 808; see also Varisco 2005, 2007).

One might argue, however, that it is precisely the rivalrous politico-ethical intimacy of East and West that should grant the Middle East a more prominent position within anthropology. A quick nod to one of the great underutilized classics, Hertz's (1909) "Pre-eminence of the Right Hand," might suggest what is at issue. Hertz argues that the human body and human society are models of each other, and it follows that much of social life is left-handed—that is, persistently stigmatized, or negatively marked. The left hand is "despised and reduced to the role of the lowly assistant; by itself it can do nothing"; it is the symbol and model of "the rabble" (1909, 553). In much the same way, any social field made by humans will have a problematic side, a left dimension that keeps the morally upright in place. Hertz shows that there are periodic and predictable attempts to recuperate the left hand, to give it newer and nicer names. But it usually reverts to its unwashed state. It is easy to show how this happens with the labels applied to minority groups in contemporary society. But, in keeping with tradition, this is a gross underutilization of the concept's powers. It takes our attention away from the genuine uniqueness of the left hand and all it grasps.

Anthropology itself is a left-handed discipline, designed to explore the "savage slot" (Trouillot 1991). Anthropologists are aware of this, and we try constantly to fix it. The entire discipline is thus castigated—by ourselves, mostly—as prone to exoticism, as a handmaid of colonialism, as a solipsistic projection of Western fixations onto Others, and so on. As soon as we accept a critique of this kind, however, it immediately begins to feel inadequate. New confessions are soon to follow. The process is internally ramified, endless, but always of the same kind. Entire topics and theoretical approaches, once acceptable, start to look left-handed: kinship, tribal societies, witchcraft, assertions of cultural coherence, the ethnographic present, the godlike power of the ethnographer to fathom Otherness, and—as was bound to happen—the concepts of society and culture themselves. To describe these problem zones as simply wrong or bad misses the more important point: they correspond to something necessary, something generative in the anthropological enterprise. Hastrup (2007) calls it the "call of the unknown," da Col and Graeber (2011, vii) the "exotic," Ardener (1989, 211–23) the "remote." This quality keeps anthropology on the wrong side of metropolitan standards; it is appealing to non-anthropologists, much to our chagrin; it is highly durable; and it seems to have formal properties that generate change in the discipline.

If there is now a familiar choreography to Middle East anthropology, one of its favorite steps is the once-every-generation summing up of the state of the field: Fernea and Malarkey in 1975, Abu-Lughod in 1989, and Deeb and Winegar, Slyomovics, Inhorn, and Joseph in 2012, 2013, 2014, and 2015. The post-Saidian versions of this dance almost always contain a comment on the left-handed quality of work in the region. Is it more or less marginal than before? More or less Orientalist? The most popular topical and theoretical approaches are then lined up and assessed, followed by predictions of what trends will, or ought to, come next. The routine is so well rehearsed that Slyomovics calls out the genre as she reproduces it in her recent "state of the field" essay, noting that it invariably "begins by and depends on reciting a litany of failures attributed to Middle East studies and the social sciences of the region" (2013, 4).

What is most revealing about such essays is their double duty as litera-ture review and remedial therapy. Not only do they identify the abandoned and proclaim the ascendant, they also trace the outline of all that is too left-handed in this most familiar yet most immediately Other of "culture areas." There is lingering uncertainty about how far the discipline should move left or right and what the effects might be. Whereas Abu-Lughod (1989, 279) be-moans the absence of urban studies and overemphasis on tribal hinterlands, Deeb and Winegar (2012, 540) note the growing neglect of the rural and the poor in favor of urban middle classes, NGO offices, and what are, for many ethnographers, cosmopolitan comfort zones. Beyond this to-ing and fro-ing, however, the same topics are cited again and again, most of them related to gender, Islam, and politics. Inhorn (2014) starts her own review with the claim that Middle East anthropology is "still operating within narrow geographical 'prestige zones' and limited conceptual 'zones of theory'" akin to those iden-tified by Abu-Lughod a generation earlier (2014, 64–65). The innovations in theory and practice that would finally usher Middle East anthropology toward the disciplinary center remain, like unicorns or occulted imams, elusive. Until they are found, the literature reviewers urge us to move regional scholarship to-ward research agendas that dominate the rest of anthropology: infrastructure, ontology, science and technology studies, intersectionality, environmentalism, racialization, citizenship, human rights, violence, nation/state politics, youth cultures, and popular media. The fact that Middle East anthropology has con-tributed vitally to all these topics does not, in the end, overwhelm the prevail-ing sense of marginality and stasis.

The left-right sorting principle that drives these rituals of review is not dir-ectly visible, but a bit of dusting reveals it. The field is continually marking and moving away from stigmatized difference. But toward what? The modern? The cosmopolitan? The relevant and politically important? The inclusive and so-cially just? One suspects that, yes, it is all of these things, and that anthropolo-gists are limited in their ability to move comfortably in these directions by their own critical perspectives. The latter have been shaped by the commitments, the actual beliefs and ways, of the people we study, who often have understandings of gender, religion, politics, kinship, and sexuality that do not conform to, and are sometimes flagrantly at odds with, European and American models. These ethical alternatives snag us between moralizing and mainstreaming agendas. This is not an unusual predicament for an anthropologist (one would guess that the average male Melanesian opinion on women and violence is hardly palat-able to metropolitan tastes), but in this case the contradictions are intensified by the close historical and contemporary relationship between Middle Eastern and European societies and by the "strong models" of identity and collectivity that give these regions their specific character—ideas of prophetic authority, genealogical authenticity, the moral opposition of city and countryside, the patriarchal family, and the tension between divine law and custom, between literate and unlettered traditions, between dynasty and insurrection, between protected domestic spaces and the uncertain worlds beyond them. Each set of ideas corresponds, in Said's apt wording, to "felt tendencies," and each belongs to long-standing, transregional historical formations. One could even argue that these are key points of mutual recognition between East and West. They have the potential to upset stereotypical images of tradition and modernity, Self and Other, precisely because they exist in spaces of overlap, where comparison and contestation are possible as each moral world struggles to encompass the other.

This state of play brings to mind Dresch's claim that "anthropologists, in the nature of the job and whomever they work with, deal with persons who retain autonomy" (2000a, 124)—autonomy in relation to the ethnographer, if not in relation to larger political and economic systems. Yet anthropologists at work in the Middle East have a vexed relationship to autonomy, a concept they are compelled to moralize in contradictory ways. They want greater inclusion for their subjects and subject matter in anthropology generally, but this desire is persistently denied, intellectually and politically, because the region is in fact the site of intense, long-standing efforts to marginalize, control, incorporate, and govern its people and their sensibilities. This effort is exerted by Western powers and by political actors internal to the region. Autonomy, expressed locally in "strong models of . . . moral worth" (Dresch 2000a, 124), is very much at stake. As we shall argue in chapters to come, the presumed integrity and alterity of Middle Eastern societies, when combined with their historically recent encompassment in Western hierarchies of value, serve only to intensify their left-handed quality, both within the region and in transregional contexts. It gives them a capacity to decenter that complicates analysis. This quality need not culminate in dysfunction; rather, it is formative. It will work its way into, and improve, any careful ethnographic account. Through engagement with strong models—we might even call them "discursive traditions," of which Islam (in Asad's formulation [2009, 20–24]) is but one—we can form interpretive alliances that effectively push back against the orthodoxies of the antistructural age.

The Oxford Tradition

In taking this approach, we follow Paul Dresch, whose ideas we have already mentioned. Dresch's career is itself a series of hard left turns: he is an anthropologist, a Middle Easternist, and a specialist in the study of Yemen, a country that, to most observers, looks peripheral and tradition-oriented. Dresch is best known for his work on tribalism, the politics of the Zaydi Imamate, customary law, and the forms of historicity associated with them. Insofar as good ethnographers become, over time, isomorphic with the contexts in which they work and write, a close reading of his work and its intellectual background offers insights into what a resolutely left-handed approach to the region might entail.

Dresch's career is closely associated with the Institute of Social and Cultural Anthropology at Oxford. He went to Oxford to study Human Sciences as an undergraduate, and then Social Anthropology beginning in 1975. Oxford then was an exciting place. Evans-Pritchard had retired in 1970 and died in 1973, but his spirit was still very much alive; Dumont had lectured there, and he often visited; French intellectuals were read and appeared to matter; people argued about fundamental conceptual questions and cared deeply about them. Leafing through early editions of the *Journal of the Anthropological Society at Oxford*, edited and printed by graduate students at the time, one can feel the excitement. The hand-typed, oddly formatted pages, printed in small runs, convey a sense of urgency and a willingness—indeed, a felt need—to engage with larger questions, with a world to be remade.[7] Edwin Ardener, Dresch's doctoral supervisor, had announced in 1971 that "there has occurred an epistemological break . . . of an important kind. . . . The field of social anthropology is totally restructured: the old field and the new field form different conceptual spaces" (Ardener 1989, 46). In his reading, structuralism, which in itself had played havoc with the "old" anthropology, had been replaced by something new, equally sophisticated intellectually, and perhaps unique to Oxford (Benthall 2007). Despite this intellectual effervescence, the students produced at that time now tend to be represented as a "lost generation" who paid the price of the Thatcher years and the genuine disenchantment of the world that followed (see Chapman 1989, xix; Rivière 2007; Jenkins n.d.). Funding was in fact brutally interrupted. Many students were forced to choose circuitous careers, leave the discipline altogether, or radically downscale their intellectual agendas. "Within the harsher climate," as Rivière (2007) notes, "the search for [practical] relevance became important again." The audience for anthropology was changing as well. By the time Dresch's generation had finished their doctoral research, mostly in the first half of the 1980s, the discipline had moved from being a minority subject to something almost mainstream, open to diverse forms of postcolonial critique and redirecting its attentions to more recognizably metropolitan concerns.

Key aspects of the earlier tradition persist, however. A definite sense of familiarity stretches from Evans-Pritchard and his students via Edwin

Ardener and people like Dresch to their own students, a kinship that, as Dresch would have it, involves a constant effort to avoid "the asking of faulty questions" (1989, vii), an engagement with history and texts as well as with fieldwork, and an attentiveness to philosophical concerns that leaves room for the marginal and that remains implicit rather than loud. This tradition has rarely been summed up by its adherents, and Dresch himself refused, in the preface to his 1989 *Tribes, Government, and History in Yemen*, to spell things out in formulaic terms, despite the risks of misrecognition he knew he was taking: "As I know from experience with published articles, there will be those who read the present book and, despite what they read, will believe it is all to do with 'lineages'; there are others who will think it structuralist, others who will think it functionalist, others still who will label it as part of some other -ist or -ism with which they think they disagree. It is contrived, in fact, to be none of these" (xviii). "Contrived" might be the operative term here, and the style is deliberately evasive. Let us try nonetheless to explain what people who work in this tradition are attempting to do.

Peter Winch famously wrote that social life, like language, could not exist without certain rules or shared assumptions, be they implicit or explicit. "All behaviour which is meaningful (therefore all specifically human behaviour) is *ipso facto* rule-governed" (1958, 52).[8] Social relations are themselves "expressions of ideas about reality" (23), and an analysis of the social thus requires the understanding of human actions rather than observation of statistical regularities. "Actual men do not *behave*, they *act* with an idea in their heads" (Dumont 1970, 6; emphasis in original). Collingwood (1946) had earlier argued something similar when he distinguished historical knowledge from that produced by the natural sciences, the latter being concerned with the external observation of processes, the former with the need to understand "internally" the roots of human action. Evans-Pritchard presumably had read Collingwood when he claimed that societies needed to be studied as "moral" rather than as "natural" systems" (1962, 26). "Theory," in any case, cannot properly be external to analysis. "Explanations . . . will be found embedded in my descriptive account and not set forth independently of it. My interpretations are contained in the facts themselves, for I have described the facts in such a way that the interpretations emerge as part of the description" (Evans-Pritchard 1937, 5).

What Pocock (1961, 72) had called a "shift from function to meaning" was reworked by Ardener as a shift of analysis from "syntagmatic" to "paradigmatic" structures. The former deal with events on the level of observation, the kind of thing one might render statistically; the latter draw attention to the categories and principles that underlie human action. A traditionist in his own way, Ardener explicitly related this to Evans-Pritchard's classic ethnographies: "*Witchcraft, Oracles and Magic* was about knowing. The structures were paradigmatic. Yet the contribution was seen by most anthropologists as syntagmatic: as about 'social control' and the like. Again, the Nuer proposed a model for the opposition of segments in a system of segments. This was a paradigmatic statement: a truly Saussurean vision, but 'opposition' in a paradigmatic statement was apprehended as 'conflict' in a syntagmatic statement" (1989, 55). In Ardener's own formulation, the careful recording of footfalls and the movement of chairs in a room tells us little unless it is accompanied by the statement *this is a dining room* (1989, 48). Dresch recasts the point in terms of a "distinction between analysing types of event and the course of events" (2012a, 10n). In order to unearth "paradigmatic structures," or indeed to understand what one sees or hears, "one is listening for the unsaid," for "tacit spacers and assumptions" (Dresch 2000a, 122–23).

Anthropology of this kind may be described as, in Pocock's (1988, 203) phrase, "empirical philosophy." It differs from (and, in Ardener's view at least, surpasses) structuralism in that structure has no separate existence from action, whereas the problem with structuralism was that it "floats, as it were, attached by an inadequate number of ropes to the old empiricist ground beneath" (Ardener 1989, 159).[9] Ardener was at pains to refute accusations of "idealism" (Chapman 1989, xxxi) and insisted on the empirical grounding of his research throughout, arguing for what he called "semantic materialism" (Ardener 1989, 173).[10] "Conceptual finesse . . . could only legitimately grow out of serious involvement with empirical detail. . . . Conceptual advance and empirical advance would come together, not necessarily predictably and comfortably, but always inalienably joined" (Chapman 1989, xxxii). Or, as Dresch put it even before he set off to Yemen, "The unique structuring of a particular social formation can only be approached through its own terms, terms which control and define their context" (Dresch 1976, 69). Yet "the *distinction* between structure and event is of the analyst's making, and one must not pretend otherwise" (Dresch 1989, 37; emphasis added). "Theory," then, cannot properly be external to ethnography or understanding; instead, it translates into an attention to internal patterns and reasoning and to detail, especially the kind of detail that initially does not seem to "fit."[11] The anthropologist's main enemy is not so much power or Western hegemony but their subtler and infinitely more invasive counterpart, common sense.

This approach is evident in discussions of segmentation. As early as 1984, Dresch—then rather a lonely voice—was an avowed Evans-Pritchard fan: "It is difficult to make any progress at all in describing Yemeni tribes without constant recourse to the ideas first set out in *The Nuer*" (1984, 45). Notions of "power" (or, in Dresch's terms, "politics"; see ibid., 38) are not equivalent to those of order. "The structure of tribes and the features which make up political history need to be clearly distinguished," as "the tribal structure consists primarily in the opposition of tribal names to tribal names and of section names to section names. It is to be understood more as providing the context in which politics of a certain kind is pursued than as a causal determinant of the course of politics" (1984, 32–33, 38). "Lineage theory and segmentation are not at all the same thing; indeed, they represent two different types of anthropology. The first deals with sequences of events at the level of observation (and in particular with the appearance of groups), while the second deals with formal relations that characterize the types of events possible" (Dresch 1986, 309). Structures, in such a reading, do not "emerge" from actions, but rather actions presuppose structures: values are prior to political relations (312, 318); they make action possible in the first place. Nor can they be reduced to "ideology," for "the actor is constituted in accord with the same structural principles as the categories with which he works and the forms of action available to him" (319). Change is of course possible, as are alternative structurings of the same moral space, and simple extrapolation from the past is risky. In Ardener's terms, "syntagmatic models 'work' until a paradigmatic change occurs" (1989, 56).

This is plainly an evaluative as well as a descriptive statement: the insistence on "patterns that outlast events" is really about the possibility of social analysis. But it has immediate practical implications. First, knowledge of one analytical location is rarely sufficient to capture an "idiom" or "principle" of the kind that "survives and recurs in quite different settings," including sacred texts (Dresch 1988, 54). "Tribalism," for instance, is necessarily beyond individual experience and resembles in this sense (as well as in the language it often adopts) the "great literate traditions" (52), in which authority and "truth" cannot be limited to a single place or time: they are always partially here and elsewhere. "It became obvious that a 'village study' would leave one in the position of the wise men with the elephant: one might get a trunk or a leg, but not the shape of the whole beast" (Dresch 1989, xii). Second, history is crucial, as it appears not only explicitly in local literate traditions but also in the gaps and assumptions that are part of those traditions. This approach (like anthropology at its inception)[12] thus has great affinity with the written word, and it is clear that fieldwork alone is not sufficient but needs to be combined with texts and archives.[13] Yet, as seen above, history takes a particular shape in particular places—hence Dumont's observation that "history is the movement by which a society reveals itself as what it is" (1964, 43). History of the kinds made by Yemeni tribespeople or sayyid chroniclers is rooted in temporal regimes that assume a kind of continuity that baffles modern historiography, which is typically concerned to explain the differences between past and present and, more centrally, to stress the novelty of recent times (Smail and Shryock 2013).[14] In Dresch's work, by contrast, the past (both of northern Yemen and of Western intellectual endeavor), as genealogically reconstituted and left-handed as it might be, pervades the present. The scandal of continuity, both spatial and temporal, is at the heart of his anthropology and makes it possible.

Today, this approach is unfashionable. But most analysts know that the current emphasis on change and flux hides considerable continuities. Jenkins, for instance, points out the cyclical nature of much internal history-making in anthropology, including the mythical construction of a once-in-every-generation "epistemological break," when he describes anthropology at Oxford in the 1970s:

> We were in fact returning to the concerns and style of publication of an older anthropology (the *Année sociologique* school, or Weber, or Simmel), which produced works simultaneously of a greater generality and a greater insight. We might have supposed we were coming to the end of a particular interlude, one in which empiricist, positivist thinking had predominated, and which might be dated, say, from 1920 to 1950. Though, looking from fifty years later, we might conclude that Positivism has not gone away. Another way of looking at the issue is to suggest that it [empiricist thinking] always threatens to predominate in the modern period, but that, at intervals, more interesting forms of thought gather energy to challenge its dominance. (Jenkins n.d.)

Jenkins sets this insight aside with the truism that "intelligent criticism has only a small role to play in the life of social formations, even in Universities," but he also insists that empiricism and the functionalism that often accompanies it "are themselves collective representations of an enduring kind—moral accounts of the world or theodicies—and relate in partial and obscure ways to the manifold of effects that organize our lives" (Jenkins n.d.). In Ardener's terms, "metaphysical positivism . . . feels right": a 'positivist religion', if not that of Comte, has certainly won the compulsorily educated masses" (Ardener 1989, 59).[15]

When Abu-Lughod (1989, 279) referred dismissively to "the general romanticism of anthropology," Dresch and the intellectual tradition he represents were among her principal targets. But insofar as romanticism provides a counterweight to "metaphysical positivism," its role in sociocultural anthropology is vital. Romanticism implies a readiness to be overwhelmed, if only briefly so; it implies a skeptical stance toward the calculating rationality that dominates both the academic institutions in which anthropologists work and the commonsense notions—of polity, self, and shared humanity—that metropolitan actors and institutions foist upon the world. Abu-Lughod's rejection of romanticism is itself part of a tradition, one that sees romantic sensibilities as endemic to the process of "othering". Yet Dresch, like many anthropologists, has never been ashamed to say that difference is what interests him. He is also aware that, while Amazonia and New Guinea were once safely characterized as exotic (and had to be "domesticated" for uninformed readers), the problem with the Middle East is quite the opposite. Western readers are likely to mistake it for a warped, heretical version of their own society. "False resemblance is as much a problem as exoticism ever was" (Dresch 1992, 28). This observation is not sentimental. It describes an intellectual orientation, a decision to pursue alternative forms of knowledge and to insist on their value as tools for thinking beyond shared sensibilities anywhere. With this agenda comes a critical concern for diversity, unboundedness, and forms of mutual respect that go beyond "the anomie and enforced uniformity that seem sometimes the only modern alternative to a stifling conception of rank" (Dresch 1989, 395).

Into the Field

This volume gathers contributions made by Dresch's students, who, each in their own way, continue the tradition outlined above. What lends coherence to the essays is not so much their attention to field sites that are geographically peripheral to the dominant Middle Eastern culture zones—quite as many contributions deal with cities as with tribal areas, and settings range from Morocco via Chad to Egypt, then to Iran, and finally to northern India. Rather, the binding thread is a certain stance in relation to the "field"—a fateful relationship between our work, a region, and a point of view or style. Historical materials and sensibilities are prominent in several of the essays, as is an awareness of a hegemonic cultural tradition or political center. The metropolitan and cosmopolitan are never far from view. We are repeatedly drawn, nonetheless, to the defining margins of the contexts we study, to "remote areas," whether these are filled with elite or subaltern social types, and whether they are located in oasis villages along trans-Saharan trade routes or in Damascus neighborhoods, where film crews produce the latest Arabic-language TV serials.

We all recognize that field-workers are and must be vulnerable and that our work should be grounded in local concerns, which often grate against disciplinary trends. The whole point is to find out what local terms are compelling. This can be done across multiple topical fields, using a mix of theoretical and methodological toolkits, but the approach will fail if we impose our own intellectual, political, or ethical concerns on "the society studied," to invoke again Pocock's triad. As a result of these commitments, the topics considered here often have a scandalous continuity. They are scandalous because they are old—many go back to analytical terms and problems forged by the *Année sociologique*, whose leading figures were fascinated by moral systems, classification, identification and mutual recognition, modes of solidarity, personhood, and other facets of community formation that, in their view, imbued social life with a deeply structural character. These are human fixations, not merely academic ones. Their Middle Eastern variants pull us toward issues that predate the region as an object of area studies and transcend it even today—problems of authority (divine and human), family and kinship, authenticity and power, the role of texts and literate expression in social life, the city as a protected and privileged space, hierarchy and equality, relations between men and women. This subject matter is scandalous, too, because it takes up ethnographic business that is nowadays pushed aside—typically, because it calls the normative modernity of our subjects into question—only to reappear in oddly refracted forms. Amid national and Islamist politics, neoliberal market forces, mass-mediated technological change, and popular uprisings, our essays return inevitably to issues of revelation and concealment, oppositional identities, truth claims, honor, modesty, and the integrity of domestic spaces.

The volume opens with reflections on fieldwork in various Middle Eastern settings: the ways in which it can and cannot be done, the patterns of public and private thereby implied, and how the place allotted to strangers is crucial to the knowledge ethnographers produce. As Andrew Shryock demonstrates in his paper on escort and tribal history-making in Jordan, customary ways of moving through physical space are important preconditions for research. They act as "hidden replicators" of diverse social forms, reproducing tribal geographies and giving shape to historical knowledge itself. Relations of escort and protection determine how an outsider can know Bedouin worlds in Jordan, where control over space and access to "truth"—of the sort conveyed by authentic genealogical links to the speech, blood, and deeds of ancestors—combine to give local sociality and notions of moral personhood their distinctive quality.

Morgan Clarke's essay shows how similar principles apply in the elite quarters of religious scholarship—specifically, among Lebanon's actual and aspiring mujtahids, who claim the ability to apply and interpret Islamic law correctly. In this domain of bookish expertise, uncertainty and skepticism flourish. Who exactly is a mujtahid? Are their credentials real? Can their decisions be trusted? These questions are hard to answer definitively, and Clarke suggests that the remaining nodes of doubt are not leftovers in a secure hierarchy of religious authority. Instead, they serve as essential pivots that allow a genealogical system to persist, despite occasional failures in the legitimate transfer of learning from one mujtahid to the next, by locating ultimate knowledge (and best practices) in other places, in the past or future, or with God. Fieldwork in these settings consists of a technical apprenticeship in how to move through space and time, an apprenticeship that does not yield "objective knowledge"—despite prevailing obsessions with "truth"—but fosters an ability to interpret the connections between highly contested knowledge claims.

Christa Salamandra's essay, which unfolds across two decades of ethnography in Damascus, sums up the challenges of following such an approach in conspicuously elite and urban spaces, where metropolitan social theory and cosmopolitan culture makers—urban planners, heritage experts, and TV serial producers—continually draw the ethnographer's attention to aspects of personhood, gender, sectarianism, and kinship that are contested as signs of modernity and "traditional culture." Salamandra argues that there is, in fact, no way to represent these topics that will avoid provoking criticism, in large part because Damascenes are themselves a "community of disagreement." In an authoritarian polity that insists on uniform support for its leadership and national culture, Salamandra's insights are intensely problematic, but the reality of incessant social critique—and the right to make social criticism a protected aspect of public media culture—remains crucial to the construction of Syrian modernities, especially now, as the country is torn apart by war.

Because of the salience of patterns of knowability and secrecy in the Middle East, the reaction to any "gaze," that of the empire or that of the neighbors next door, might easily be the assertion that there is "nothing to see here"; the observer is actively encouraged to look in other directions. Fieldwork thus becomes a "trade in secrets" (Dresch 2000a, 109), and the simple observation that the truth lies elsewhere can be expanded—in segmentary fashion, one is tempted to say—from domestic matters to those of international relations, as Ammara Maqsood demonstrates in her paper on who is, or might be, Taliban in Pakistan. The apparent lack of reliable "data," and indeed the impossibility of neatly defining the categories to which such data would refer—Talib, Pashtun tribesman, soldier, insurgent, foreign spy, collaborator—is itself a "social fact" that shapes perceptions of insecurity and divided loyalties in contemporary Pakistan, sentiments that permeate folk theories about the country's internal and external relations. Maqsood's interlocutors, Pashtun migrants in Lahore, have complicated relationships to geopolitical spaces that government forces cannot easily enter and do not fully control. They use the "remoteness" of Pakistan's tribal areas—their "imperfect attachment" to the center and overdetermination by outsiders (Ardener 1989, 221–22)—to "deflect the truth" of their own involvement with the Taliban. Yet some of Maqsood's informants admit that they once belonged to the movement, or suggest that other families or factions do so now, thereby inviting her into a zone of protected knowledge that is bounded, ethically, by the same patterns of "deflected truth" that define all talk of the "war on terror" in Pakistan.

Anastasia Piliavsky's essay deals with comparable patterns of knowability among Kanjars, a caste of professional thieves in Rajasthan. Their stealth, magical acumen, and astonishing longevity are "secret attributes" known, iron-ically, to everyone, while mundane knowledge of how Kanjars operate and who they work for is sensitive and must be hidden from public view. Experts in "dis-appearing acts," break-ins, and other penetrations of intimate, domestic spaces, the Kanjars facilitate interaction between social categories—criminals and the state, sisters-in-law and brothers-in-law, patrons and the poor—that are nor-mally defined by mutual distinction and avoidance. Piliavsky shows that the Kanjars, as a named group, are centuries old, and so is the dirty work they do: impeccable reputations need invisible thugs to prop them up, just as the right hand needs the left.

Threats to the integrity of private space are likewise the focus of Mary Montgomery's essay on domestic servants in urban Morocco, where interstitial patterns of moral guardianship, similar to the protocols of escort described by Shryock in Jordan, make it possible to bring total strangers into the most secret (and often most banal) of settings: the household. In Montgomery's case, how-ever, they are admitted as servants, cooks, and nannies rather than anthropolo-gists. Playing off a mythical narrative of a golden age in which all domestic labor was performed by kin, who were trustworthy, grateful, and just like "daughters of the house," Montgomery shows how even the most profound socioeconomic changes—in Rabat, the emergence of an anonymous labor market—are dealt with, or at least tentatively moralized, through long-standing patterns of incor-poration. Unknown domestic workers are redefined either as "kin" (with all the disappointment that necessarily ensues from purposeful misrecognition) or as "known," through mostly fragile, even dubious links. "Strong moral models" are clearly in evidence, as is a sense of responsibility for domestics, but state regulation of these new labor relations would do away with the moral ambigui-ties that pervade kinship and host-guest ties and is thus rejected by all.

Zuzanna Olszewska's essay addresses similar tensions between the inti-mate and the public as expressed in changing models of personhood among Afghan poets in Iran. Ethnographers have characterized personhood in the Middle East in contradictory ways, putting weight on either individualistic or relational values. For Olszewska, this is a false debate, as both individualism and relationality have long coexisted in the region, for men and women alike, and both inform personal life histories and struggles for recognition today. Distinguishing between two aspects of individual personhood that tend to be conflated in Western academic rhetoric—moral autonomy and the recognition of one's unique attributes, talents, or virtues—Olszewska argues that the Af-ghan case shows how one can be achieved without the other and that individual self-assertion does not necessarily imply a break with collectivist moral propri-eties, even when these are of a hierarchical nature.

Judith Scheele's paper, based on material drawn from North Africa and the Sahara, argues that by limiting its subject matter to state formations and state politics, contemporary political anthropology evades questions that are in fact central to it. Although one could easily demonstrate that today large parts of the world's population, willingly or not, live unencompassed by states, Scheele makes a more fundamental claim: namely, that "politics," beyond definitions of power and its distribution, is about the possibility of imagining different forms of sociality. These alternatives might be located at the margins of state systems or fully within them, but they touch on notions of moral autonomy and personhood that cannot be subsumed in state rhetoric or generated in response to statist claims; in many cases, moreover, they demonstrate astonishing historical and regional depth.

Approaching political anthropology from a radically different angle, Walter Armbrust concentrates on recent events in Egypt, where local and international models of "revolution" have produced a new political climate, unsettled between radical change and a "new normal," in which "tricksters" thrive. Drawing on the work of Victor Turner and Arnold van Gennep, Armbrust explores the liminal spaces that open up within moments of political transition. In contemporary Cairo, authoritarian and neoliberal trends converge to produce leaders—like the newfangled dictator, Sisi, and the regime-supporting media pundit, Taufiq 'Ukasha—whose similar talents for hoodwinking, intimidation, and breaking and making rules are chillingly obvious, although one of these men commands a modern army while the other hosts a popular television program. Armbrust and Scheele work in very different settings, yet the oddness of contemporary state arrangements, and the structural violence on which they are based, are paralleled in both essays by a persistent desire to undermine the state, co-opt or blunt its powers, and drain its resources—whether from its heart or from its edges.

Conclusion

All of these papers are careful to engage closely with local terms and relations, but they also listen for the unsaid. They pay attention to patterns that are discernible over long stretches of time and that seem, quite literally, to predate and outlast events; they assess contested knowledge claims; and they move incessantly between the right and left hand of knowledge, between the proper and the less so. This is vividly apparent when, among adept practitioners of Islamic law in Beirut, claims to high-minded expertise are mixed with (and sometimes produce) suspicions of immoral conduct and juridical fraud, or when elite families in Rajasthan deploy Kanjars as mercenaries and mediators in their political disputes. It is evident among Afghan poets, male and female, who explore modernist notions of expressive freedom in their verse and marital choices but craft careers that uphold the moral integrity of domestic spaces that, because they protect the modesty of women, resist certain forms of mass-mediated celebrity. It is true of the "war on terror" in Pakistan, where local conspiracy theories, village gossip, and the practicalities of the regional fruit trade are part of geopolitical contests that involve hypermodern weapons, espionage, and propaganda campaigns mounted by global superpowers. In all of these cases, the "left hand" is intrinsic to social life and its proprieties, a fact that is troublesome only when it is discussed too loudly and openly, as if transparency (not deft opacity) were a virtue.

How then should we appropriately engage with the left hand as such? We know that it is not invariably residual, or weak, or a zone of stigma. It is everywhere. It is remote yet coextensive with the center. It is marginal yet part of the mainstream. It can be backward and trendy, incorrect and preferred. For easy proof, consider the Arab Gulf States, where millions of people are wealthy and highly educated, live in gleaming new cities, and have conspicuously crafted tribal identities, which they express in nationally televised poetry contests, in electoral contests and legal practice, in heritage tourism, in genealogical research, and in the display of "traditional" material culture in domestic and public spaces (Dresch 2005; Cooke 2014; Samin 2016). How one sees societies of this kind is itself diagnostic: are they a study in continuity or transformation; are their traditions invented or authentic; is the persistence of tribal formations in these countries evidence of cultural resilience or a new form of institutional racism? However one might answer these questions or rephrase them, it should be apparent that we are not necessarily talking about country folk, the oppressed, or the primitive when we talk about left-sided cultural spaces. The spaces we have described in this volume belong to another kind of interactive milieu, one that is pervasive but is not designed to admit everyone. Often, this milieu is valued precisely because it is alternative to the modern, the Western, the progressive, the properly democratic, the correctly gendered, or the respectably Muslim. Insofar as anthropologists aspire to unsettle hegemonic assumptions about how people should live, the left side of experience will be a space in which our projects can thrive, fed by the moral uncertainties we encounter in fieldwork, and expressed in the new languages we create as we try—with the help of our subjects, our colleagues, and our own intellectual traditions—to grasp durable forms of human life.

JUDITH SCHEELE is Directrice d'études at the Écoles des hautes études en sciences sociales (EHESS) in Paris. She has carried out research in Algeria, northern Mali, and Chad. She is author of *Village Matters: Politics, Knowledge and Community in Kabylia* and *Smugglers and Saints of the Sahara: Regional Connectivity in the Twentieth Century*, and co-author of *The Value of Disorder: Autonomy, Prosperity and Plunder in the Chadian Sahara*.

ANDREW SHRYOCK is Arthur F. Thurnau Professor of Anthropology at the University of Michigan. He studies political culture in the Middle East, Arab and Muslim immigrants in North America, and new approaches to history writing. His recent books include *Deep History: The Architecture of Past and Present*, *Islamophobia/Islamophilia: Beyond the Politics of Enemy and Friend*, and *From Hospitality to Grace: A Julian Pitt-Rivers Omnibus*.

Notes

1. "Structure" has had many definitions and applications, several of them mutually contradictory. No less a structuralist than Lévi-Strauss argued that "the term 'social structure' refers to a group of problems the scope of which appears so wide and the definition so imprecise that it is hardly possible for a paper strictly limited in size to meet them fully" (1963, 277). The study of social structure, therefore, is not a topic in and of itself, but "rather a method to be applied to any kind of social studies, similar to the structural analysis current in other disciplines" (279).

2. The sentiment was already in place in the 1950s, when Edmund Leach announced in print what many of his colleagues clearly felt: "When I read a book by one of my anthropological colleagues, I am, I must confess, often bored by the facts" (1970, 227). Leach called for a focus on "principles" rather than theory per se.

3. For an assessment of "new kinship" studies that neatly links their strengths and weaknesses to the concerns of this volume, see Clarke (2008).

4. The list here is potentially long: for an overview of the new "ethical turn" in anthropology, see Laidlaw (2013); for critical comments, see Fassin (2014a) and Ortner (2016). Mitchell (2002) has done exemplary work on "experts," as has Mahmood (2005) on self-fashioning.

5. For a recent analysis of how the politics of "region formation" and well-established metaphors of kinship and marriage continue to make the Mediterranean a compelling identity space for Italians and Tunisians, see Ben-Yehoyada (2014); also Bromberger (2006).

6. A notable exception here is Fardon (1990).

7. "During the winter power-strike the stencils were typed by candle-light, which meant practically blind, and corrections were difficult" (Ardener 1980, 125). Veterans of the period say that *roneotype* is a term now quite unknown and that the pages came off the stencil machine smelling oddly of vegetables. The whole thing was of its time.

8. Winch draws heavily on Wittgenstein. An alternative genealogy would refer to Durkheim, who had anticipated Wittgenstein's argument that concepts necessarily presuppose a social milieu (Steven Collins 1985, 51; see especially Durkheim 1991, 61). In fact, this is perhaps the most enduring argument of the *Année sociologique* (see also Durkheim and Mauss 1903; Allen 2000, 104).

9. In Sahlins's terms (which he ascribes to Lévi-Strauss himself), structuralism was concerned with superstructure, not infrastructure. Sahlins went on to claim, as did Ardener, that the distinction between these levels is artificial and ought to be collapsed (2010, 374).

10. Ardener carried out more fieldwork than most: he was in Cameroon from 1949 to 1963, and he followed this with years of lengthy annual visits, always to the same field site (Chapman 1989, xvi–xviii).

11. "It is obvious that the best model will always be that which is *true*, that is, the simplest possible model which, while being derived exclusively from the facts under consideration, also makes it possible to account for all of them" (Lévi-Strauss 1963, 281). For fieldwork implications, see Jenkins (1994).

12. Mauss and Durkheim were first and foremost textual scholars and steeped in the Mosaic traditions (Dresch 1988, 52). If the Middle East, since then, has mostly been marginal to the production of metropolitan anthropological theory, it was nonetheless crucially present at its inception.

13. Dresch has spent much time and energy editing and translating vernacular texts. See, e.g., Dresch (1987, 2003, 2006b).

14. "Academic history . . . seeks to keep the past in the past" (Palmié and Stewart 2016, 220), and the same can surely be said of sociocultural anthropology, which increasingly locates itself in colonial and postcolonial worlds that are rarely more than a few centuries deep (Shryock and Smail 2011).

15. "The spectacle all around us of empiricism confirming its assumptions at the expense of connected thought is sobering" (Dresch and James 2000, 11).

1

DIALOGUES OF THREE

Making Sense of Patterns That Outlast Events

Andrew Shryock

What was it? A mass of material accumulated over ages, originating as oral history, some of it the same but written down later, all purporting to deal with the earliest record of us.... It was a cumbersome, unwieldy mass and more than one hopeful historian had been defeated by it, and not only because of its difficulty, but because of its nature. Anyone working on it must know that if it ever reached a stage of completion where it could have a name, and be known as a product of scholarship, it would be attacked, challenged, and perhaps be described as spurious.*

—Doris Lessing, *The Cleft*

SINCE HIS EARLY WORK ON TRIBALISM IN YEMEN, Paul Dresch has been fasci-nated by cultural patterns that endure over very long periods of time. Most notable of these is the ancient division between the Hashid and Bakil tribal blocs, but related topics include facets of customary law, statecraft, and durable ways of defining identities and relating them to persons or spaces. It is hard to tell how much of this interest derives from prior commitments to structural-ist analytics and *longue durée* historicism. Dresch traveled to Yemen with a healthy supply of Evans-Pritchard in his knapsack, and if he was not yet carry-ing Braudel, he certainly had R. B. Sergeant. Yet these predispositions, however strong they might have been, could not have found more fertile ethnographic soil in which to grow. In the northern highlands, Dresch encountered political systems that, for many centuries, had been held together and enhanced by ideo-logically contrastive principles. One system, still functioning around him, was based on moral equivalence, segmentation, and a language of honor. It pro-duced tribes and their laws. The other, only recently eclipsed, was based on divine revelation and unified moral truths. It produced the Zaydi imamate, a state-like tradition in which Islamic law, scholarship, and prophetic descent were essential to legitimate rule. In numerous essays[1] and in his foundational monograph, *Tribes, Government, and History in Yemen* (1989), Dresch shows how these worlds were joined in practice to produce a dynamic polity with im-mense staying power, both in its parts and as a whole. The Zaydi Imams enter Yemeni history in 879 CE and do not leave it until 1962. The tribes have an even deeper history. Hashid and Bakil existed as named groups before Islam, and they are vitally engaged in Yemeni politics today.

Dresch often suggests that this antiquity has a troubling quality, that it poses analytical and moral challenges the modern scholar cannot easily ad-dress. It is not the durability of the Zaydi Imamate that produces this sensation, although Yemenis fought a bloody civil war to dispose of it. Dynasticism, as a cultural form, is meant to go on and on, and moderns have found several ways to include it in their republics and parliamentary democracies. Rather, it is the persistence of tribalism that seems especially scandalous, and the ob-servers who might draw this conclusion do so from diverse points of view. For centuries, Zaydi imams colluded and collided with tribes, commanding them as "our servants"—never, Dresch notes, as allies or equals—denouncing them as "the fang of a cur in a cur's head." Modernists of Arab and Western vintage see tribalism as backwardness, plain and simple; and Yemeni nationalists, even when they portray "their" tribes as essential to Yemeni identity, will argue in the same breath that tribes are a source of political discord and that progress will inevitably wear tribalism away. Across these interpretive positions, tribal-ism is (at best) a deficient moral space that generates many problems and few solutions. Analysts who linger in this space, as Dresch has done throughout his career, will draw the critical attention of those who oppose "tribes" as a term and a tradition.[2]

As a student of tribalism in Jordan, I deal with similar trends, but the tem-poral scale is more compact. Hashemite dynasticism, its prominent tribal back-ers and opponents, and the local geography of state-like and tribal identities in Jordan all seem shiny and new by Yemeni standards. The 'Adwani and 'Abbadi tribal confederations among whom I have done the bulk of my fieldwork took shape in the seventeenth and eighteenth centuries, after the collapse of the Mi-hadia shaykhdom, a complex alliance of local tribes that exists today only in the stories told of its demise.[3] There was no pre-Hashemite political tradition that resembled the Zaydi Imamate, and the tribal system itself was based on high rates of turnover. In the Balga of central Jordan, tribes routinely displaced each other, and newcomers aligned with older groups, sometimes coming to dominate and absorb their hosts. In Yemen, the boundaries of Hashid and Bakil have shifted surprisingly little for centuries, despite political conflict and population movements within and across these blocs. Tribal sections are apparently equal to each other, oriented serially, and defined by oppositions that work synchronically; the average tribesman cannot, off the top of his head, produce the name of his own great-great-grandfather. It is not possible for a tribe or section to describe its own past from an internal perspective; its particularity can be defined only in balanced contrast to other tribes and sections. "A great deal happens," Dresch says, "but little is conceived to change" (1989, 179).

In Jordan, the tribal system is oriented toward inequality and diachrony. It is replete with client and follower tribes, weak and strong tribes, fragmented and unified tribes. Groups like 'Adwan and 'Abbad are opposed to each other, but it would be hard to argue that they are morally or politically equivalent, and oral tradition is dedicated to proving their conflicting claims to distinction. Genealogical knowledge is robust among Balgawis, who must know the names of at least four patrilineal ancestors to participate in tribal law cases that involve homicide or personal injury. My 'Adwani informants could often name up to twelve. In the Balga, one might even say that men, events, and collective attributes define tribal sections, and entire tribes, from the inside out. The Bani X are known for having fertile daughters; the Bani Y are generous to a fault; the Bani Z have betrayed their allies many times (and probably will again). Each of these groups tells stories about where its first ancestor came from, and the value of each is enhanced, or diminished, by the deeds of its shaykhs. In the Balga, tribes are not defined simply by way of balanced opposition, like the white and black squares on a Saussurean chessboard.

What I find most interesting about these contrasts is, in a sense, how little they matter. In both systems, tribes claim to be old, and their durability is problematic. The literal amount of durability in a tribal system—is it two hundred years or one thousand years?—is of less importance than the social boundaries that are defined and transgressed by this durability. The literate historicism Dresch locates in the Zaydi half of his Yemeni reality is present, in my work, among tribal historiographers themselves, who are busily adapting their oral traditions to print. These men see their work as controversial, even dangerous, not simply because oral histories are contentious but because local tribes preexisted the Hashemite state and therefore represent (potentially) alternative frames of political loyalty. In short, the persistence of a tribal system in Jordan is considered a challenge in much the way it is in Yemen. Tribes carry a "still/even" stigma. Bedouin heritage can be redeemed as national decor perhaps, but for many Jordanians it is shameful that tribes *still* exist today, corrupting bureaucracy and national elections with their clannish habits. For critics who have attained postcolonial sophistication, it is wrong to say that Jordan is *still* beset by tribalism, since this assumes that the tribes of today existed *even* then, before the British arrived to administer and reinvent them, before the Hashemite state co-opted them to the task of creating a national culture that casts Palestinians as nontribal, as outsiders, and therefore as second-class citizens. All of these claims can be argued on an evidentiary base, and they correspond to legal and policy issues that are pressing in Jordan, but they carry a rather obvious bias against political actors who define themselves in explicitly tribal terms. Giving attention to tribes is quickly assimilated to a language of advocacy or affront.[4]

Why should this be so? We know that tribal structures are patterns that outlast events, but why is their durability a problem, and how does it become a moral and political problem? In thinking about these issues, I want to move away from the familiar idea that tribal populations are not neatly contained within states (because often they are), that they are points of resistance to centralized polities (because often they are not), or that they preexist the national cultures they inhabit (because, for the most part, they are *in* and *of* those cultures now). Rarely are Arab tribes treated as "indigenous people" on the Amazonian model, and scholars of the Middle East whose politics are self-consciously progressive— who are warm to indigeneity as a platform for inclusion or autonomy in other parts of the world—are not always sympathetic to tribal people, much less tribalism, in Middle Eastern contexts.[5] The study of these populations is nowadays widely considered retrograde. Deeb and Winegar, in their recent summing up of anthropology in Arab-majority societies, put it bluntly: "Tribal social organization has practically vanished as a topic of concern for scholars, though not for policy makers, right-wing analysts, and anthropologists embedded with the U.S. military, many of whom persist in using stereotyped notions of tribal structures to explain political violence" (2012, 540).

Of course, the trending topics of Arab world anthropology (gender, Islam, politics and popular culture, and reform-oriented social movements) are also of interest to policy makers, right-wing analysts, and military types. If a critical take on US power in the region is an intellectual goal, then ethnographers should be flocking to the tribal zones, where some of the most visceral, ideologically driven, and technically complex encounters between Western imperialism and Arab (and Pakistani, and Somali, and Afghan, and Kurdish) societies are happening. Tribal social forms are crucially entangled, and disproportionately so, in the making and breaking of the political structures on which global security, human rights, and national identification are based. The tribal zones are often dangerous places, but as Dresch reminds us, they are oddly accommodating as well. They are filled with structures "in whose nodes and interstices fieldworkers perhaps might thrive"—alongside the Islamist militants, journalists, aid workers, prophets, descendants of prophets, colonial officers, oil company engineers, and cigarette smugglers—"and so they do, in distinctive ways."[6]

The Name/Space

The moral challenge of tribalism is situated precisely here, in an alternative model of secure space. It is a simple model, and Dresch has defined it for us clearly on many occasions. "Were one looking for a single attribute that characterized tribalism," he writes, it would be "moral reciprocity that turns on protection" (1990, 255). The idea of "social organization" is not adequate to capture what is at stake.

> Far from tribes cohering unthinkingly as wholes around men at odds, men are constantly being moved back and forth through the system and being "covered" for a time from the view of their antagonists: the verb commonly used to describe this action is *tahajjaba*, from the same root as the word for a veil or for an amulet that covers someone from envious eyes. The tribal answer to men's general vulnerability is often temporary refuge. Similar concepts of covering pervade the whole ethnography [of Yemen] and relate directly to a language of honor that applies to collective identities and to persons equally. (ibid., 255–56)

This system is durable, yes, but the zones of protection it creates are fragile and impermanent, as if by design. Dresch calls the system a "half-world." It seems too simple to generate the complex political events that surround it; hence, it leaves scholars (and politicos) with too much or too little work to do. It is geographically widespread, yet it delimits regions and identities wherever it travels; hence, it facilitates othering as much as incorporation. The phrase "language of honor," for instance, will set off alarms. Finally, this system is old, very old, but hardly peripheral. It pervades the literate and scriptural traditions of the same "high cultures" that stigmatize and marginalize tribal populations; hence, it both encourages and blurs the self/Other distinctions on which ambient notions of "civilization" and "the primitive" depend. One suspects that all these ambiguities are essential to how covering and refuge operate, and I have recently argued that tribal storytellers in Jordan, European philosophers like Kant and Derrida, and social theorists like Mauss use similar ideas of protection—ideas of house and hospitality—in explaining human sociality and in moralizing about it (Shryock 2008, 2012). Whether the issue is gift giving, citizenship, or the respect owed even to hostile or offensive guests, the context of moral evaluation is always a "name/space" somehow marked as vulnerable.

Dresch is reluctant to generalize about the name/space, despite its ubiquity, and he refuses to explain its durability in ecological or economic terms. His preferred strategy is to characterize it as a set of relations, show how it works through examples, note its impressive age or spatial distribution, and then delicately back away, as if saying anything else would put him at risk. This maneuver, which creates a feel of mystery, even taboo, is on display in several of Dresch's best essays. In "Mutual Deception" (1998), he explores how Maussian concepts of exchange differ from Abrahamic ones, to which the name/space is essential. Working through a diverse range of cases, Dresch shows how Middle Eastern materials are organized around notions of autonomy; endogamy; unbalanced, irregular exchange; and debilitating generosity, all of which enhance the reputation of the name/space, often at the expense of the socially conscious giving endorsed by Mauss. "We have moved," Dresch observes, "from the Qur'an to the 'age of ignorance', to Arabia a millennium and a half later, and from there to stories of nineteenth-century Baluchistan. *There may be a real coherence. That point I shall not argue (not here at least)*" (1998, 116; emphasis added).

The same dodge appears in "Aspects of Non-State Law" (2012b) where Dresch analyzes Yemeni legal traditions that go substantially unchanged for centuries at a time. It is hard to determine exactly how this continuity is reproduced, he claims, but what "we do know is that every time we gain a glimpse of tribal affairs, through a document-find or through anecdotes in a chronicle or learned biography, we find much the same logic of mutually-recognized protection" (2012b, 171). In a tantalizing footnote, Dresch suggests that a hidden replicator is at work: "Texts provide our evidence, but one doubts that texts alone explain continuity. Nowadays in Yemen one finds not only copying back and forth of documents, but people who quote word for word early texts they could not possibly have read and have not heard of. Yemen at least has texts; so perhaps does Oman (Schacht 1964: 77). But resemblances become deeply unsettling when, in the absence of any institutional or documentary connection, one finds sometimes the same turns of phrase in Sinai, the Egyptian desert, or North Africa. Contemporary anthropology and history seem ill-equipped to describe this" (171n).

The descriptive toolkits nearest to hand are those designed for work on "invented traditions," but the problem Dresch pinpoints here has little to do with the realization that nation-states are not in fact ancient or that ancestral Scottish kilts are in fact new.[7] The persistence of customary law, for which there is abundant empirical evidence, must be explained by entering the world of tribal knowledge production and working out logics of transmission appropriate to it. That is the underlying problem. The durability of this world—its location before, within, and possibly after the universal claims of empire, Islam, secular democracy, the market economy, or modernity at large—is itself a kind of trespass. Surely it is a kind of history as well, not simply a lack thereof, yet even Dresch sees this alternative historicity as horizontal in configuration and concerned with the (balanced) opposition of moral equals. Historical accounts of tribal worlds must be pieced together using data found outside them, he concludes, because tribal actors "have no unified story to tell, only the indefinitely fragmented body of heroic tradition" (1990, 258).[8] I think this conclusion is problematic in several ways, and it is the utility of Dresch's analytical concepts, their rightness in the ethnographic contexts I know best, that makes me think so. In the remainder of this chapter, I would like to show how the name/space is itself an effective means to historicize patterns that outlast events. The ethnographer's passage through tribal space, if it is correctly routed through name/spaces, will produce the continuities and the evidence of connection that "texts alone" cannot explain.

Escort Service

The choreography of published work is often misleading. Dresch, the essayist and ethnographer, prefers a discrete set of analytical moves, but Paul, my advisor and teacher in the realm of fieldwork, introduced me to a much broader range of steps. Something like "method" was at stake. It was not the method of specific data-gathering techniques, about which Paul taught me almost nothing. Rather, this training was done remotely, as a kind of experimental replication of key relationships and terms discovered in fieldwork, which themselves would make a certain kind of fieldwork possible. Paul has since confessed that he was not sure what would happen to me as I followed his instructions, but if his ideas about shaykhs, protection, and escort were wrong, my early misadventures in tribal space might have been more traumatic, and less comical, than they were.

When I traveled to Yemen for the first time, in 1986, Paul sent me into the northern highlands with a bevy of helpful anecdotes—the kind he told the world he would not divulge in print, so I will not repeat them here—a list of telephone numbers and addresses of his most reliable contacts, some good things to see and do, notes on Yemeni dialect, and tips on how to go to places that were officially off limits. He did not buffer me from surprises, which meant I had no idea how to be manly or modest in a skirt, or how to use a Yemeni toilet, or how to respond (while stoned on qat) to intense questioning about the sexual positions preferred by the French, Germans, Americans, and other northern peoples. As prep for my visit, Paul instead gave close attention to producing letters of introduction, each sealed in a light-blue par avion envelope, the recipient's name written in Paul's neat Arabic script on the outside. All of these gifts, including the silence on matters of wardrobe, toiletry, and sex talk, turned out to be immensely helpful to a rookie ethnographer, and they have produced some of my best shtick for college teaching. The letters of introduction, however, were a very special tool. When I showed them to one of Paul's lawyer friends in Sanaa, the man gave me a sly look, immediately took the stack away from me, promised to store it safely, and advised me not to carry around more than one of these letters at a time: "People will think you are planning a coup!" The names on the envelopes included several heavy hitters, big shaykhs from Hashid, Bakil, and Murad—in short, men who could very well attempt a coup, if they so desired.

The power of these men became apparent to me when I traveled to see them, letter of introduction in hand. People in Sanaa advised caution. My camera, my money, and my wife, Sally, would be at risk, they were sure. The lawyer gave me my letter to a prominent shaykh of Bakil, suggested that Sally should stay in Sanaa and visit with his wife—a kind offer we refused—and then wished us well. As we moved into the northern and eastern countryside, not always knowing exactly where we were going, I would show people the envelope and ask directions. As soon as the name of my future host was known, we were given the best hospitality. People fed us and drove us great distances in directions they were not originally headed. A smuggler who worked the areas beyond Jabal Barat, in the extreme northeast, insisted that we spend the night in his home. When I tried to pay him the next day, he lifted the back seat of his Land Rover to reveal his personal currency exchange—rolls of dollars, pounds, marks, and riyals. Did he need money, he asked me? No. In fact, he would give me money. He pressed a few bills into my shirt pocket and told me to send his greetings to Shaykh Hasan Daris when I arrived. "Say to him that his American guest was treated well by his friend, Fulan bin Fulan."

As long as a letter of introduction was in my hand, we were treated like dignitaries. After staying with a shaykh for a few days, we would return to Sanaa without the letter, and we would become different people. In one case, the shaykh's own driver confiscated the wad of cash his boss had given me as traveling money and then dumped us miles from where he was told to take us. Another driver left us at an army post, where friendly soldiers attempted to secure a ride for us in one of the heavily armed motorcades of passing shaykhs. We were accustomed to traveling in these paramilitary fleets. But now the shaykhs consistently refused. As darkness set in, the soldiers ordered two rough-looking men to take us to Amran. On the way, a tire blew out. My modern standard Arabic was feeble and never of much use, but I could make out some of their angry talk: "This is what comes of giving rides to Christians." One of the men wanted to abandon us. The other said it would be shameful to do so. As a compromise, they let us off at a dirty flop house at three in the morning. The Yemen we experienced while carrying the letters of introduction was not the one we moved through in our exposed, generically touristic state. I cringe now at these stories. They remind me of my reaction when I hear tales of misfit travel in Jordan, which are entirely at odds with my experience of moving through Bedouin terrain, where I can activate hospitality protocols easily (but the two British women who decide to picnic on the hill above the village are harassed by the same young men who politely pour my tea). In Yemen, the name/spaces of powerful shaykhs held protection, favor, and respect. These spaces, which I entered and exited one letter at a time, belonged to a privileged geography of security and access. It resembled very closely the world Dresch had written up.

If a cultural system lasts for a thousand years, or even a century, it must reproduce itself over much shorter spans of time. With Paul's help, I was contributing to the durability of name/spaces by activating them, by deepening them as channels of personal and intellectual movement. Had I stayed in Yemen and done research there, I would ultimately have produced knowledge within these channels, re-creating a very peculiar perspective. I would have wandered into other name/spaces, producing local variations in point of view, but I would not have been entirely free to do so. Continuity is not possible without precedent and constraint. The rites of escort, as Dresch has amply shown, are rich in both. Their shaping power becomes evident when the ethnographer realizes that he is himself configured and reproduced within these structures, although the replication might be a sorry one. When I visited the shaykhs of Murad, they told me flattering stories of Paul, whom they called Abu Zayd. When he spoke Arabic, it was like poetry. He knew everything about tribal customs and traditions. All true, I'm sure. But then the bar was raised. "He could shoot a cigarette from a man's fingers at one hundred paces!" This was news. And demoralizing. Would I live on in local legend as the one who shot off the fingers of the man holding a cigarette at fifty paces? Luckily, I could never secure a research permit in Yemen. I went off to Jordan, where Abu Zayd's skills as a marksman were unknown.

Dialogues of Three

Most ethnographers encounter an exemplary predecessor in the field. It is a likeness that lends historicity and local grounding to Pocock's "dialogue of three," a special conversation that, as Dresch argues, helps maintain reliable perspective in fieldwork accounts. The three are the ethnographer, the society studied, and fellow scholars. It is by keeping up this dialogue that "the objectivity peculiar to [the ethnographer] is preserved.... It is clear that if he eliminates any one of the partners . . . the dialogue is broken and he falls back into the collective representations of his own or the other society" (1961, 105, quoted in Dresch 1989). One assumes the conversation is taking place in the present and that the participants are coeval in Fabian's (1983) sense, but the dialogue becomes much more interesting if we use it to travel in time. Members of "the society studied" do this when they liken new ethnographers to their predecessors in the field. Scholars do it when they historicize their literatures or the societies they study. It is very easy to use the dialogue of three to edge our way into the past or even to leap over massive amounts of space-time. The tribal continuities Dresch identifies in Yemen, remember, are verified by reference to Zaydi records, but ultimately they are grounded in an ancient dialogue of three between al-Hamdani (who wrote in the tenth century and can be read today), Hashid and Bakil (who existed then and still do), and other historians of Yemen (who wrote before and after al-Hamdani). *Tribes, Government, and History in Yemen* would lose much of its analytical traction without its constant invocation of this ancestral triad, which is license and mandate for the *longue durée* models of Yemeni society Dresch creates.

It is not necessary, however, to transect so much time or space at once. The chain that starts with al-Hamdani ends eventually with Abu Zayd, the sharp-shooter, who brought me into this dialogue of three by way of epistolary introductions and the structures of protection and escort they engendered. When I relocated my research to Jordan, Paul once again made a fateful introduction, this time to Dr. Ahmad Oweidi al-'Abbadi, a Bedouin anthropologist with a PhD from Cambridge. Paul was his external examiner. My plans to live and work among the Bani Sakhr, one of Jordan's prominent Bedouin tribes, were immediately scuttled by Dr. Ahmad, who told me that "too much research has been done on them already." With the aplomb of a veteran kidnapper—I cannot quite remember how all of this happened; it was fast and shocking and oddly reassuring to a young ethnographer adrift in a new country—Dr. Ahmad carried me off to 'Abbad, his own tribe, settled me in his home village, and had me paying rent to his cousins within a few days of my arrival in Jordan.

In the late 1980s, Yemen was an anthropological "prestige zone,"[9] and my tribal hosts generally had a good understanding of what an anthropologist does. Jordan, by comparison, was a backwater. Little ethnography had been done there, and people were not sure what to make of an anthropologist. In addition to seeing me as a spy, most 'Abbadis likened me at first to Glubb Basha, the legendary British military officer who led Jordan's Bedouin-dominated Arab Legion from 1939 until King Hussein kicked him out of the country in 1956. I was not comfortable with this comparison, although most 'Abbadis and other tribal Jordanians respected Glubb for his knowledge of Arabic and tribal custom. The quick link my hosts made between me and a white conquering imperialist was unnerving. It constantly reminded me that my status in Jordan was part of a legacy of colonial rule, Bedouin romance, militarism, and covert operations. Dr. Ahmad, for one, assumed that I might have useful connections in the American embassy that could help him with his political career. When he was elected to parliament in 1989, several of Dr. Ahmad's supporters thanked me personally for engineering his victory. The fact that I might just be a twenty-something American doctoral candidate with no political influence, who came to Jordan to study the rise and fall of shaykhly families, seemed the least likely account of who I was. As I would soon realize, however, my vexed position as ethnographer, as an outside observer whose intentions are unclear but who is taken in and protected nonetheless, is part of a dialogue of three that has (and continually remakes) its own history in the Balga of Jordan. It predates the colonial and Hashemite configurations in which Glubb Basha is my exemplary double.

Sanctuary

Early in my Jordanian research, I committed myself to recording oral histories and interpreting them in relation to new and old traditions of literate historiography. The method was unusual at the time—not because it fixated on poetry, genealogy, and stories, which had been studied by ethnographers before. The unusual part was my insistence on treating these sources as the building blocks of a distinctive historical sensibility. Other ethnographers had treated these materials as verbal arts, or as ways of organizing space using an idiom of descent, or as self-contained heroic tales.[10] Insofar as I could claim that I was doing otherwise—that I was treating the oral traditions of the Balga tribes as history-making traditions in their own right—I could reduce my Pocockian dialogue with "other scholars" to a tactical minimum. I was busy engaging with "the society studied," especially that section of it that specialized in remembering the past. I sat with old men, recorded their testimony on cassette tapes, and learned to speak with an old man's tongue. I found natural allies (and rivals) among a small group of younger tribesmen who collected oral history, much as I did, with the intent of writing it up in books. The similarity ended there, however. Dr. Ahmad, my original sponsor, was just as likely to obliterate as to preserve the oral traditions he gathered. His binary intent was to solidify the links between Jordan and its "native" tribal populations (at the expense of Palestinians) and to overhaul the reputation of his own group, the Sikarnah, an 'Abbadi clan who, he adamantly claims, are not descended from a West Bank Bedouin tribe but are Hijazi in origin and, better yet, descendants of the Prophet Muhammad. To bolster this new vision of the past, Dr. Ahmad was compelled to find evidence outside local oral traditions, traveling to England and Saudi Arabia in search of genealogical data and other forms of documentary proof; he also made a point of ignoring, in his books, influential shaykhly families and powerful tribes that loomed large in the stories I recorded from the old men who knew tribal history best.

In the local world of protection, I lived and did research in the name/space of Dr. Ahmad's kin, but as I collected oral histories, I was constantly introduced to other groups—more precisely, to their ancestors—as characters in historical accounts. Visiting these groups and recording stories from their principal narrators was often a delicate procedure, but one for which I discovered handy local rules. Using well-established conventions of sanctuary and escort, I would sometimes go directly to the house of a man who was said to know history, visit with him, and ask to record him. Or, more often and more successfully, I would meet young men at communal events (at weddings and funerals), and they would arrange a visit to their preferred historical source, who was often their father or grandfather. These escorts usually sought me out, and they were eager to improve and correct my data. I gradually learned that the best way to be granted sanctuary in a new name/space was to pose as the research equivalent of a *dakhil*, a refugee in need of help or cover. I could do this simply by telling my hosts a bit of what other families had said about the past. Because tribal histories are intensely oppositional, my hosts almost always accepted the challenge of giving me their view, which was "the truth," unlike what I'd been told by others, which was clearly "lies." This transfer worked best when I entered a name/space unaccompanied by members of the name/space I was escaping. My only experiences with "bad hospitality" came when my escort and my new protector belonged to groups that told contradictory versions of the same historical events. In these situations, where jurisdictions blurred, arguments or evasive talk were common; neither was conducive to recording on tape. My movements, both through space and through the time of historical accounts, were shaped by the integrity of name/spaces, by the oppositions ingrained in historical narrative, and by the possibility of getting into one space and out of another cleanly. Where there was no protection, no means of seeking or gaining refuge, and no way to temporarily insulate one authoritative speaker from his rivals, there was likewise no practical way for me to gather history.

Into the Past

So began my yearlong journey into the Balga past, which had a destination, a kind of temporal looping point, at which my true historical doubles were awaiting my arrival. I began with Dr. Ahmad's clan, the 'Uwaydi, worked my way through several other clans of the Afgaha section of ʿAbbad, and then found narrators among the neighboring Zyudi sections. The stories I recorded were rich in local content, but they were organized around a long-standing conflict with another tribe, the ʿAdwan, whose shaykhs, even in ʿAbbadi accounts, were described as the strongest in the region. To record ʿAdwani narratives, I had to leave ʿAbbadi territory altogether, since my ʿAbbadi hosts could not (or, in Dr. Ahmadʾs case, expressly would not) provide escort into ʿAdwani space. I relocated to Salihi, the village of Yasser Mannaʿ Abu al-ʿAmmash, an ʿAdwani professor I met at Yarmouk University. Yasser belonged to the Kayid, one of the three main sections of the ʿAdwan. Among his uncles were outstanding poets, genealogists, and storytellers, but the Kayid had never controlled the ʿAdwani shaykhdom, and their narratives always culminated in the dominance of the Nimr and Salih clans, who were based in the Jordan Valley. To get Nimr and Salih accounts, I had to relocate once again. This time, I was introduced to a Nimr lawyer who worked for a Kayid shaykh. With an eye toward keeping his clients and his kin apart, the lawyer passed me into the custody of a Nimr relative, who drove me down to the valley to visit with ʿAli Barakat, a renowned Nimri storyteller.

After two days of continuous recording, ʿAli Barakat took me to visit the Salih, the family who had produced paramount shaykhs of the ʿAdwan for seven generations. It seemed that ʿAli Barakat was dangling me as a prize in front of Shaykh Nawfan Saʿud, a retired member of the Jordanian Upper House of Parliament. Although he was well over eighty years old and had witnessed key events in the transition from Ottoman to Hashemite rule, Shaykh Nawfan deflected all my questions about tribal history, which he found an irritating topic. He spent most of the evening receiving guests and passing their requests to his attendants. A grandson of the old shaykh said that I should come back another time, and perhaps the Hajj would talk to me. Until then, I should talk to Muhammad Hamdan, a fellow member of the Salih clan who was writing a history of the ʿAdwan.

"Where can I find him?" I asked.

"He is sitting right there," the grandson replied.

Muhammad came from the far end of the patio to sit beside me, intentionally blocking out ʿAli Barakat, who smoked distractedly as we chatted. Muhammad arranged to visit me at ʿAli Barakatʾs house the following day. While we ate ʿAliʾs *mansaf,* Muhammad made clear that he could provide me with the best sources of ʿAdwani history: "Anything you have recorded from ʿAli Barakat is already present in my notebooks." He asked me to return to the valley for another visit, during which he convinced me to relocate to Shunah, where he lived, and not to Kafrayn, home ground of the Nimr. This was a rather artful steal. Soon, I was spending several hours a day taking dictation from Muhammad, who read to me aloud from his book manuscript. As I settled into Shunah, I was approached by Faris Salih al-Nimr, a close relative of 'Ali Barakat. Faris immediately attempted to regain custody of me for the Nimr, visiting me often and taking me to see his favorite narrators. He assured me that I would eventually tire of Muhammad Hamdan, whose historical accounts were fixated on the Salih. The Nimr, he said, had produced some of the most distinguished shaykhs of the 'Adwan, including Nimr, Father of Poems, and Goblan, "who is mentioned many times in the writings of the Orientalists who visited the Balga in the time of the Turks."

Faris was, in fact, a descendant of Goblan through his mother, whose father, Hajj Khalaf al-Fahid, was the patrilineal grandson of Goblan, who was himself the grandson of Nimr, Father of Poems. 'Ali Barakat was the grandson of Goblan's brother, Filah. Some of the most famous nineteenth-century travelers, among them Finn, Tristram, Conder, Oliphant, and Merrill, were led through the Balga by Goblan and his closest Nimr kin. In 1877, Shaykh Filah al-Nimr dictated the following note to Selah Merrill (1881, 417–18), inviting Roswell D. Hitchcock, head of the American Palestine Exploration Society, to visit the Balga under the shaykh's safe wing.

Camp of the American Exploring Party, opposite Jericho Ford, April 4, 1877.

Rev. Roswell D. Hitchcock, D.D.

Dear Sir: I have had considerable experience with the members of your exploring parties, and have tried to serve them faithfully while they have been in our country. I have enabled them to labor in peace and security without being interfered with or molested by any of my own people or by any of the neighboring tribes. I have often heard of you, and wish you could visit our country yourself. Every road would be open to you and every tent would offer you a welcome. I am sorry that Dr. Merrill and Mr. Van Dyck cannot now go to Kerak and places south of the Arnon. If they ever return, as I hope, and as they expect to do, I shall in future guard and protect them, and try to serve them in every way.

Yours respectfully,

Sheikh Fellah el Fadil en Nimr.

[His seal.]

When I met Hajj Khalaf al-Nimr for the first time, with 'Ali Barakat as my escort, the old man struck similar notes. He stressed the importance of spending time with the Nimr, especially if I wanted to record history and study the ways of the tribes. He likened me positively to "Kondor." I smiled, but I was not sure whom he meant. Faris would later explain to me that "Kondor" was Lt. Claude Reignier Conder, an English surveyor and explorer-antiquarian who had written flattering accounts of Goblan in the 1880s, several of which had been translated into Arabic by Suleiman Musa in *Kitab al-Rahhala* (n.d.). Conder was clearly impressed by this "bold and wily" shaykh, whom he portrayed to his Victorian readership as

> a tall, gaunt man, with a grey bronzed face, half-hidden by his shawl, one eye red and sightless from the sword-cut which has furrowed all one cheek . . . [a detailed catalog of Goblan's black, gold-embroidered headscarf, long striped *kumbaz*, shirtsleeves that hung down to his ankles, and red leather boots follows] . . . Over all he wore a beautiful *abba*, or cope-like mantle of broad white and amber-coloured stripe. This most picturesque costume was strangely at variance with the . . . red eye, the muffled voice, the thick obstinate nose . . . ; but the hand, so apt to wield the lance, was as soft and delicate to the touch as a woman's, with white nails carefully trimmed. (1883, 113–14)

"There is a touch of romance about his history and character," Conder tells us, adding that Goblan is known to be "sordidly covetous and of an evil temper" (1883, 114). About seventy years old at the time, Goblan was involved in a long-standing feud with the Bani Sakhr, one of whom he had murdered while stealing the man's horse. He was also busy contracting his latest marriage, despite having "sons and grandsons enough of all ages" (111). Goblan needed Conder's hard currency to pay bridewealth, and Conder, who was mapping the Balga without the permission of Ottoman authorities, was similarly dependent on the shaykh's antigovernment stance.

> There were two names Goblan could not bear to hear uttered, namely, that of the Sakhur Arabs and that of the Turks. The Arabs of Moab regard this venerable outlaw as their natural chief in case of any outbreak against the Turkish Government. . . . He is the most wily of the politicians beyond Jordan, and when, many years ago, his cousins of the Diab branch (the elder division of the tribe) were induced by promise of rewards and honours to go up to Nablus, Goblan counselled them not to do so, and refused to go himself. No sooner were they in the town than the treacherous governor seized them, and the old chief Diab got his leg broken by the brutal soldiery who took him to prison. Only by heavy bribery did they escape, and Diab was obliged to abdicate in favour of his son 'Aly Diab, who is now a Turkish favourite. (Conder 1883, 117–18)

This way of talking about 'Adwani politics is still common among Nimris today, who like to depict their Salih cousins as eager collaborators in state power—Ottoman and now Hashemite—and themselves as the savvy holdouts who maintain their independence, and their dignity, in the face of outside powers. "Such, then, was our Arab ally, and although an acquaintance with the Belka Arabs has not raised my estimate of Bedawin character, it is but fair to acknowledge that our success, such as it was, was greatly due to Goblan. Our treaty obliged him to furnish as guards and guides four mounted men, and he remained with us as a guest, and acted as my guide whenever I was out of camp" (Conder 1883, 118).

For Faris, Hajj Khalaf, and 'Ali Barakat, the déjà vu of hosting me and assisting in my research, just as their ancestors had led Conder and Merrill through the Balga countryside, was palpable. I had finally arrived at a dialogue of three. The conversation was scattered across time, it was redundant in parts, and it was held together by an odd assemblage of local stories and poems, excerpts from old English travel literature, and a particular set of genealogical ties. It was activated, now as then, by relations of escort and a special, competitive relationship between the Salih and Nimr clans. I was Conder, the 'Adwan were "the society studied," and my fellow scholars were no longer the anthropologists of today but all those Victorian travelers—consuls, Orientalists, clergymen, explorers, and mapmakers—who, like me, entered the Balga in search of knowledge and in need of protection.

Shared Itineraries

I had re-created in a few months the trajectory of travel in the Balga as it unfolded over the course of the nineteenth century. I began, as did the first travelers, in 'Abbadi territory, which was an anti-'Adwani space. When Burckhardt and Buckingham visited the region in the 1810s, the 'Adwan had been driven out of the Balga by neighboring tribes. To the north, the Salih lurked in the forests of 'Ajlun. To the southeast, the Nimr were living under the protection of the Bani Sakhr, enemies of their Salih cousins. The 'Abbadis were not reliable escorts or good hosts. They stole Buckingham's rifle and abandoned him, and Burkhardt found them so destitute—they had just been raided by the Bani Sakhr themselves—that "they could not afford to give us a little sour milk which we begged of them" (1822, 349). Both men retreated to the small town of Salt, where they quickly tired of the immobility and close scrutiny they experienced in Salti guesthouses. Buckingham, unable to find a guide to Karak, complained of bad food, vermin, smoke-filled rooms, and stifling sociability.

> Had I been granted the enjoyment of a single day alone, I should not have regretted my detention so much; but during the daytime the house was filled with visitors and enquirers; and in the night, the crowded state of the room, in which we were all shut up together, rendered it difficult to enjoy even one hour's quiet and unbroken repose. It was only in the intervals between sleep that I could find time at night to commit any facts, or remarks on them, to paper, by the light of a dull lamp, which burnt while all but myself lay asleep on the ground. (1825, 48–49)

The 'Adwan fought their way back into the Balga during the reign of Shaykh Hamud Salih (in the 1810s–40s), but the region was highly unstable and the travel literature sparse until the 1850s, when James Finn, British Consul in Jerusalem, negotiated a standing contract with the 'Adwan for the escort of British subjects (and other Europeans) to regions east of the Jordan River. Shaykh Dhiyab Hamud oversaw this agreement, and he gave the escort concession to the Nimr. The protocol, which was acted out during Finn's inaugural tour of the Balga in 1855, was to visit the region's antiquities accompanied by a party of Nimr shaykhs, who would receive an agreed-upon sum. Before leaving the Balga, the travelers would visit Shaykh Dhiyab's tent for a presentation of gifts and a shared meal. During his 1855 visit, Finn brought eleven English travelers (plus a dozen servants, cooks, and dragomans, and about one hundred horses and mules) to Dhiyab's encampment, where they shared pipes and coffee with the shaykh and his entourage: "The presentation of offerings was a grave and solemn affair. Each donor produced his tribute with an apology for the insignificance of the gift, which was then exhibited in silence by an attendant to the populace of the tribe crowding outside. The ceremony was concluded by shouts of welcome, and a huge meal of pilaff (rice and mutton upon a great tray of tinned copper) and leban, (curdled milk,) with more smoking. Here we took leave of the chief, who sent on a detachment of his tribe to escort us for the rest of our expedition" (1868, 24).

Soon enough, the Nimr were funneling a steady line of dignitaries through Dhiyab's camp, and the extraction of tips and special gifts—preferably firearms—became a source of tension between travelers and their 'Adwani guides. European nobility were notoriously liberal in their gift giving, unsettling the escort trade for years at a time. In 1863, Tristram complained of the Duc de Luynes and M. de Saulcy, who had paid the Nimr "like princes, and poured forth gifts with princely hands" (1865, 517). It took two days of hard negotiation to bring their protection fees down to a realistic commoner rate. By 1881, Conder was accusing Tristram of overpayment: "I fear Tristram has been spoiling our market by paying any amount of blackmail to the Arabs" (Conder 1881, PEF/ES/CON/3a). The Nimr were good at pushing rates upward over time, and they were likewise under pressure to give, or coax their clients into giving, more and better gifts to the Salih shaykhs.

Tristram saw firsthand the domestic side of the 'Adwani protection trade when, traveling with Goblan, his camp was attacked at night by a posse led by 'Ali Dhiyab, son of Shaykh Dhiyab Hamud, "who, ill-pleased to hear of the presents Goblan had got from the Duc de Luynes, had sent them to claim his share in the black-mail of the new visitors" (1865, 526). Goblan offered 'Ali Dhiyab a rifle, but he "contemptuously rejected it as not of first quality; and at length the youth was appeased by a present of ten napoleons, with which he departed" (ibid.) I sat up straight when I first read this passage. It reminded me of a moment when a bullish Salih shaykh—old, not young, but a lineal descendant of 'Ali Dhiyab—yanked from my hands the copies of old historical photos of 'Adwani shaykhs I had just made for a friend from the Nimr section, a lineal descendant of Goblan.

At times, I felt that I was the valuable object being confiscated and reconfiscated from temporary owners. Each recording session with a Nimr elder was followed by a long session with Muhammad Hamdan, my Salih host, who would correct, editorialize, provide alternative versions, and then introduce me to a "better" storyteller or poet. The Kayid, my initial hosts among the 'Adwan, fell away from the historical accounts I was collecting, just as they are virtually absent from the travel literature, even though the Turks entered Salt in 1867, establishing Ottoman rule over the Balga, with the helpful guidance of Ahmad Abu 'Arabi, a Kayid shaykh, and two allies from the 'Abbad and Saltiyya tribes. When I moved from the jurisdiction of Kayid narrators to that of the Nimr and Salih, I was reproducing, in the medium of historical speech, a relationship between outsiders and Balgawi protectors that, by the 1860s, was a requirement for safe travel through 'Adwani-controlled space.

The fact that I spent little time in Salt, the Balga's pre-Hashemite capital and market town, was also a replication of earlier trajectories. For much of the nineteenth century, the 'Adwan were reluctant to enter Salt, and they were forbidden to do so armed. The oral traditions I recorded from 'Adwani narrators routinely mentioned wars with the Salti tribes, a topical fixation that was already firmly in place when Finn visited the Balga in 1855. "But even now," he writes, "the 'Adwan cannot come near the town; neither can they quite forget that the Saltiyeh people, during a former war, killed both the father and grandfather of De'ab, and sent the head of the former to the tribe in a dish, with a pilaff of rice" (Finn 1868, 35). In 1862, the Nimr were still unwilling to linger in Salt. As the town's inhabitants vied to host Tristram, pulling him toward their guesthouses, Tristram's escort, Shaykh 'Abd al-'Aziz al-Nimr, was unnerved: "Leopard though he be in the forest, he was a very lamb in the city, and became very uneasy, and almost terrified, in his manner, knowing, doubtless, how many a grudge was owed him in the town. He implored, urged, and even threatened us, to accompany him outside; but we refused to leave without our companions; and, at length, the old Sheikh and his spearman slunk on ahead alone" (Tristram 1865, 553–54).

The 'Adwan Country

Although I understood why 'Adwanis likened me to Conder, I did not recognize the uncanny extent to which patterns of European movement through the Balga established over a century ago had outlasted the age of tribal escort to surface again in my work. My research was being conducted largely in the medium of stories, poems, and genealogy, not with steady reference to the travel literature, which I thought of, originally, as a kind of parallel check on spoken history. It was in the year after my ethnographic research, as I studied the travel literature more closely, that the strange likenesses and replications began to accumulate. Time in the archives of the Palestine Exploration Fund in London revealed to me the backstory of Conder's famous survey of eastern Palestine, in which the possibility of safe conduct in the Balga was a central concern. His reports to London were filled with strategic deliberations on escort, who could give it, and how to work around it. He needed an Ottoman permit but could not secure it; he wanted to pay nothing to his tribal protectors but had to; and he constantly feared betrayal. "The trap that I expect to have laid for us was this that a hint might be given to the Arabs that we were not under Government protection The hint would be taken at once A heavy bakshish or ransom would be demanded as soon as we got well inland & the Turks would wash their hands of us & say—get out of the mess as best you can" (1881, PEF/ES/CON/8a).

Conder produced a popular account of his activities, *Heth and Moab*, in 1883, and the official results of the topographical survey, the first of its kind, were published in *The Survey of Eastern Palestine* (1889), a huge compendium of Balga place-names, drawings of hundreds of antiquarian sites, and an appendix of information on the Balga tribes, most of it taken down during nightly conversations with Goblan, who accompanied Conder's party, very much against the wishes of the Ottoman authorities in Salt. Conder and his team could go only where Goblan could safely take them. This meant they could not take measurements in or near Salt. They avoided the upland territories of the Kayid, supporters of Shaykh Ahmad Abu 'Arabi, who were still working closely with Ottoman authorities. Neither could they enter Bani Sakhr territory (a long-standing constraint on 'Adwani escort and a personal risk to Goblan, who had Skhuri blood on his hands).

> Goblan pointed one day to the black tents of the Sakhur a mile away, surrounded with feeding camels, and as we slowly took our angles with a great theodolite, he remarked quietly, "If they knew I was here they would come and kill me." On another day . . . [Goblan] and I were alone near the same border, when his quick eye perceived a train of men on camels. He pointed them out, and begged me to finish my mapping as soon as might be. Yet he would not leave me till I was ready, and as we retired three horsemen appeared in the distance and followed us. We put a precipitous gorge between us and them, and they called across, as did David to Saul at the "Cliff of Division." It was one of the relatives of his victim with two followers, and although, while slaying him, they would no doubt have left me quite unhurt, an Englishman could not have stood by to see his venerable guide murdered in cold blood on account of a deed done many years ago. (1883, 114–15)

The Bani Sakhr had their revenge soon enough. When Muhammad Sa'id Basha, leader of the Hajj caravan, made his annual passage through the district, Conder notes that "the Sheikhs came as usual to greet him & he noticed the absence of Goblan and enquired where he was. The Chief of the Beni Sakhr replied 'with the English party who are measuring the land' I don't think such an answer was <u>inadvertent</u> it was due to the present feud with the Adwan and the desire of the Sakhur to get Goblan in trouble" (1881, PEF/ES/CON/22b). The Basha, infuriated, informed the governor in Nablus, who commanded that the survey be stopped. Through a variety of stalling tactics, and evasive maneuvers facilitated by Goblan, the work continued for another three weeks. "We surveyed in all nearly 500 square miles," Conder writes, "discovered 700 rude stone monuments, and obtained a volume of notes, plans, and drawings, while Lieutenant Mantell took forty photographs" (1883, 122).

Conder's topographical map, which is tucked in a flap on the inside back cover of *The Survey of Eastern Palestine*, startles me every time I look at it (see map 1.1). It covers most of the area in which I moved, visited, and recorded oral histories. The 'Abbadi tribes I lived with are located on the map, largely because the Nimr and Salih clans dominated the areas in which these particular 'Abbadi sections camped and farmed in 1881. The town of Salt is not on the map at all. The Kayid areas, which I eventually left in search of additional historical accounts, are not on the map. It seemed that all my attempts to get at the best sources of oral history, in 1989–90, would draw me into the space Conder represented on his map, in 1889.

But what is this space? If Conder and I somehow meet, or overlap, or replicate each other's movements, do we do so in physical space? Not exactly, because I was moving through time, through historical accounts told by men who occupied space, and their stories routinely addressed periods of banishment, when no 'Adwanis lived in the places on Conder's map. Cartographic literalism was never helpful. I failed in my attempts to generate my own tribal maps, since no one could agree on a single point in time at which 'Abbadi, 'Adwani, and other tribal boundaries should be fixed. Conder was not producing a tribal map per se, but he did create the map that best represented his safe movement through tribal territory. The terrain Conder and I share, across time and in very different spheres of knowledge production, is a name/space, the very form Dresch finds everywhere in Arab tribal societies. As if to prove this claim, Conder subtitled his survey, "Volume 1—the 'Adwan Country," giving it a tribal name and providing, in Appendix C, "The Arab Tribes East of Jordan," a (seriously botched) version of Goblan's pedigree and that of the Salih shaykhs, and a very long list of tribal groups aligned with and against the 'Adwan. The name/space is a container that, in its explicitly genealogical constitution, folds

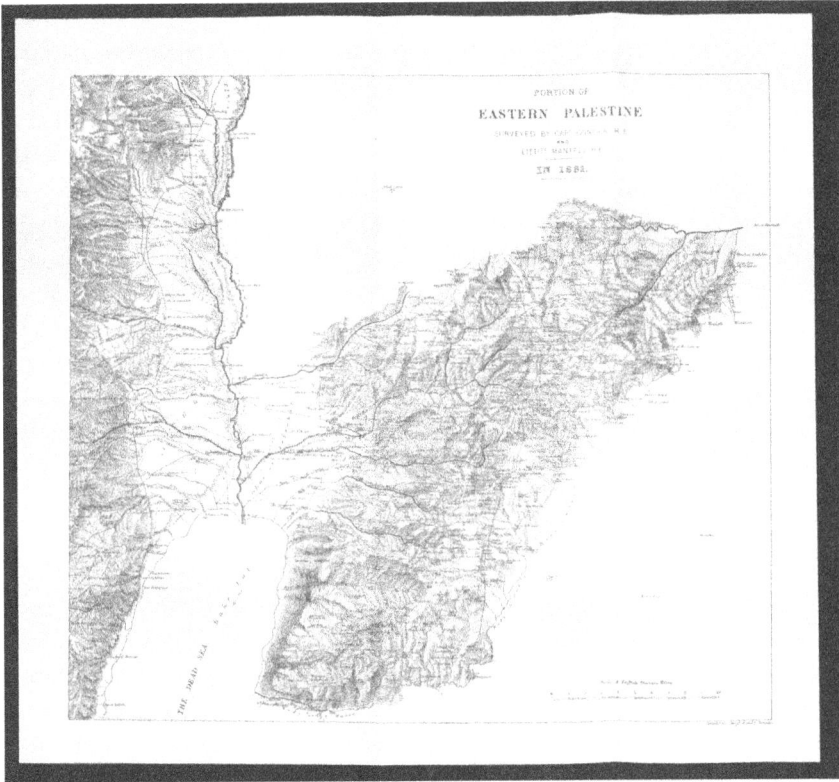

Map 1.1. Conder's topographical map. To see this map transposed on contemporary maps of Jordan, go to https://www.arcgis.com/home/webmap/viewer.html?webmap=3955f5cf36a34fb b9de1885429427af8.

space and time together. This is why, as a generator of historical evidence, and as context for knowledge production, it not only outlasts events but can distribute evidence of events in what appear to be multiple and irregular ways. As Dresch notes, it might be words here or texts there. It might be a map then and oral histories now. The moments of recognition are strong, as is the sense that a real connection must have produced the resemblance. The links between these sources, even when the links are absent, are genealogical. They are *felt* to be genealogical. It is our best way to imagine them and eventually to locate them.

So Productively Scandalous

The Balga of Jordan is no longer "the 'Adwan country," and many Jordanians resisted my movement toward that space. 'Adwanis themselves are the most sensitive to their loss of power over the last century, and many of them resent the way the Salih shaykhs have entered, and excluded others from, the patronage networks that define the Hashemite elite. In *Nationalism and the Genealogical Imagination* (1997), I explored several ways in which Balgawis are experimenting with their own past, remaking and rediscovering it in print media. Yet even in the most radical attempts to rewrite received traditions, the name/space is central. Dr. Ahmad Oweidi al-ʿAbbadi, who has unearthed his true identity as a *sharif* and relative of the Hashemite king, has done so by filling in massive holes in his lineage with new genealogical content. He has made a new name/space for himself, and he is trying to convince thousands of ʿAbbadis to share it with him. The creativity of this act, and its truthfulness, are subject to constant, withering critique by Jordanians, and the terms of assessment fixate on the authenticity of the descent lines Dr. Ahmad claims. As for Muhammad Hamdan, the ʿAdwani scribe, it is the traditional silence at the center of ʿAdwani power that motivates him to write history. Traditionally, the Salih shaykhs have been praised by others; they do not specialize in telling stories about their own past. Like Muhammad, I found nothing but refracted glory at the modern-day heart of the ʿAdwani shaykhdom. In my only audience with the family of Majid al-ʿAdwan, the last paramount shaykh of the Balga tribes (d. 1946), I was shown wonderful pictures of Majid by his sons, but they had little to say about the history of their lineage. Instead, they invited poets from the ʿAjarma, an ʿAdwani client tribe, to recite heroic verses and tell stories for the evening. These were the very stories and poems I had been studying for nearly a decade. In a bizarre ethnographic moment, the ʿAjrami poets and I traded rhymes as the shaykhs, amused, nodded approvingly.[11] When I told Muhammad Hamdan about the visit, he was not surprised. "This is why I must write the history," he said. "They are not interested. They want other people to flatter them. What will they do when the last ʿAjrami poet dies? No one has to flatter us now. If we want others to know and respect our history, we must write it ourselves."

But the silence of the great shaykhs is itself a durable historical pattern in the Balga. The plan for my evening with the sons of Majid was a reenactment based on generations of visits like mine. Indeed, the ritual seems to have stabilized during the late nineteenth-century visits of foreigners to the camp of ʿAli Dhiyab, during which the ʿAdwani shaykh of shaykhs would preside (without much comment) over a visit that included coffee preparation, a feast of rice and lamb, a poetry performance, and the giving of gifts to the shaykhs. My gift, during the 1998 visit, was a signed copy of my recently published book, and I varied the protocol by doubling in the role of praise poet. Yet again, I was traveling in a spatiotemporal loop, this one held together by multiple encounters with Salih hospitality.

It occurs to me now, as I consider these instances of precedent and connection, that they function more as affordances than as constraints. They facilitate movement, intellectual and physical, but they do not determine the direction one travels or the temporal plane in which one travels, hence the uncanny experience of looping. You arrive at a moment, or a place, or a realization, only to find that others have been there before, and they arrived by different routes. Not only have I encountered local Bedouin historians who share my interests, my sources, even my methods; I have met foreign scholars caught up in genealogical networks that overlap with my own. We immediately recognize each other as fellow travelers. One such colleague, Yoav Alon, studies the shaykhs of the Bani Sakhr,[12] traditional enemies and in-laws of the Salih, Nimr, and Kayid clans. Every ʿAdwani family that hosted me is married into the Bani Sakhr families that Alon was researching. When Alon interviewed a prominent ʿAdwani about an episode in which the Bani Sakhr gave sanctuary to Majid al-ʿAdwan, who was accused of murder, his interviewee was gravely offended by the implications—a powerful Salih shaykh would not need such protection, he thought (incorrectly)—and he threatened to sue Alon. I have only warm feelings for Alon myself, but I do read his accounts from a distinctly ʿAdwani perspective, and sometimes I raise my eyebrows! I also note that our crisscrossing movements in Jordan often reflect the delicate choreography of tribal escort, with ʿAbbadi go-betweens helping us shuttle between ʿAdwani and Bani Sakhr space, even though these spaces are filled with dense networks of blood relatives and affines. To do history productively in these name/spaces, certain people must be kept apart, precisely because they are close.

I also marvel at the gravitational pull of the name/space across different types of fieldwork theory and practice. In Yemen, Dresch privileges law and rarely gives much attention to local tribal histories as tribesmen tell them. In Jordan, I do nearly the opposite. Yet we end up contending with a few basic notions of house, host, guest, hospitality, and protection. These concepts have immense explanatory power, and it takes great patience to confine them to strictly tribal contexts. Perhaps we should not. They account for much in the political life of Yemeni sayyids, and it is possible, and in keeping with Jordan's own constitutional documents, to treat the Hashemite kingdom as a domain of "house politics" (Shryock and Howell 2001). It is also possible, as I have done for years, to use the name/space as a history-making, history-gathering device. More than any other factor, it is the scalar elasticity of the name/space, an attribute it manifests both spatially and temporally, that makes it so productively scandalous. As Benedict Anderson put it, "the disadvantage of evolutionary/progressive thought is in an almost Heraclitean hostility to any idea of continuity" (1983, 11). Simplicity, too, of the mathematical sort, arouses suspicion. That such basic architecture can support, even outlast, elaborate sociopolitical and religious worlds; that it can be modern, historical, and primitive at once, runs counter to much of contemporary thought, which assumes that these old, reductive things are surely doomed. Dresch, at the end of his first book, appears to agree. The tribes, he writes, "which have some of them been where they are for ten centuries, threaten constantly to slip out of time and thus out of the national history" (1989, 396). I doubt he really believed it. More likely, the tribes will bend time and national history into a different reality, thereby making new names and new spaces for themselves. It is a landscape Dresch has shown us how to cross.

ANDREW SHRYOCK is Arthur F. Thurnau Professor of Anthropology at the University of Michigan. He studies political culture in the Middle East, Arab and Muslim immigrants in North America, and new approaches to history writing. His recent books include *Deep History: The Architecture of Past and Present, Islamophobia/Islamophilia: Beyond the Politics of Enemy and Friend,* and *From Hospitality to Grace: A Julian Pitt-Rivers Omnibus.*

Notes

Many people have read and helped this paper. I should thank Geoff Hughes, Naor Ben-Yehoyada, Yoav Alon, Dale Eickelmann, Sally Howell, Greg Starrett, Jatin Dua, Susan MacDougall, and Hoda Bandeh-Ahmadi for good response. To Gillian Feeley-Harnik and Tom Trautmann at Michigan, I send special thanks for the attention you and your students in the Kinship Seminar lavished on the essay. And deepest thanks go to Paul Dresch and the entire crew who came together in Oxford in 2015, at the generous invitation of Judith Scheele, Morgan Clarke, and Walter Armbrust, to take stock of the peculiar anthropology we do.

1. A representative sample would include "The Position of Shaykhs among the Northern Tribes of Yemen" (1984), "The Significance of the Course Events Take in Segmentary Systems" (1986), "Imams and Tribes" (1990), and "Aspects of Non-State Law" (2012b).

2. A vivid example from the academy would be Martha Mundy's *Domestic Government: Kinship, Community and Polity in North Yemen* (1995), in which the word tribe is used with great reluctance. Instead, "arms-bearing farmers" belong to "rural political alliances." Dresch is taken to task for tribalizing his Yemeni subjects and for his close association with powerful shaykhs, whose point of view, Mundy believes, distorted his analysis.

3. For a fuller account, see Shryock (1997).

4. For a postcolonial critique of tribal formations in Jordan, one that emphasizes the constructed and co-opted nature of Bedouin identity in relation to the Hashemite state, see Massad (2001). For an analysis that covers similar ground but gives Jordanian tribal populations more historical complexity and political agency, see Alon (2007).

5. Not ironically, it is in Israel that one finds scholars and activists who treat Arab tribal populations, usually Bedouin, as "Indigenous people." The trope is cemented by poverty and dispossession by a European settler population; it also facilitates political activity that emphasizes, or disputes, the closeness of Bedouin to nature and the land. For a fresh look at these dynamics in the Negev, see McKee (2016).

6. Quoted from an early draft of "Wilderness of Mirrors," in the author's possession. Dresch's essays circulate in multiple prepublication drafts and bootleg versions. His readers often latch on to attractive phrases and formulations that, to our amazement, do not survive in print. To compare my version above with the official one, see Dresch (2000a, 111).

7. I allude here to urtexts of the genre, *The Invention of Tradition* (Hobsbawm and Ranger 1983) and *Imagined Communities* (Anderson 1983). To say that something is socially constructed (and therefore not as old as it seems) is one thing; to say that it has been socially constructed in roughly the same way for a thousand years is a new kind of problem!

8. Dresch (1986) argues that, among Yemeni tribes, events unfold (and are significant) within conceptual structures of opposition that change little over time. One must go to the written Zaydi tradition for a historical record of substantial depth. The model is reminiscent of Lévi-Strauss's distinction between "cold" societies, which are oriented toward stasis, and "hot" societies, which register and are alert to change (1983b, 28–30). In Jordan, tribal oral traditions run hot and cold at once. It is genealogy in a literal sense—not segmentation in a conceptual sense—that allows for this flexibility.

9. The term was used by Lila Abu-Lughod (1989) to describe areas, topics, and theoretical approaches that were influential among Arab world anthropologists. Her sense that Yemen was a "prestige zone" was clearly shaped by Dresch's early work; she criticized it at length, building her case almost entirely on a single journal article. How times have changed! In Deeb and Winegar's 2012 update of Abu-Lughod's essay, Yemen has fallen off the map. Egypt, Lebanon, and Israel/Palestine are the new "prestige zones." Dresch has fallen off the map, too. His name does not appear in the extensive bibliography, though his work addresses several trends Deeb and Winegar consider influential today: modernity, Islam, nationalism and the state, violence, and memory/history.

10. For the full cast of scholarly characters, named and assessed, see Shryock (1997, 11–37).

11. For a full account of this visit, which includes interviews with prominent 'Adwani women, see Shryock and Howell (2001).

12. Alon's latest work can be sampled in *The Shaykh of Shaykhs: Mithqal al-Fayiz and Tribal Leadership in Modern Jordan* (2016).

2

TOTALITY AND INFINITY

Sharia Ethnography in Lebanon

Morgan Clarke

I HAVE A KEEN INTEREST IN WHAT BRINKLEY Messick (2008) has called "sharia ethnography," the anthropological description and analysis of the varying ways in which Islamic legal discourse is produced, transmitted, and consumed. Sharia is in some ways an unusual topic for anthropologists given its forbiddingly technical and textual nature. In this chapter, I hope nevertheless to demonstrate the distinctive contribution to its study that the anthropological imagination—or a certain version of it—can offer. This is also an opportunity to develop further an argument that I have broached elsewhere (Clarke 2018).

My research into the sharia has largely taken place to date in Lebanon. As in many jurisdictions in the Middle East, family law in Lebanon follows religious precepts, albeit in distinctive ways. Under Lebanon's confessional legal and political system, jurisdiction over personal status matters is delegated to religious tribunals. Each of Lebanon's eighteen official religious communities is entitled to autonomy in this, among other respects, although only around fifteen have their own court systems. My focus has been on the "sharia courts" (*mahakim shar'iyya*), made up of two largely separate systems, for Lebanon's Sunni and Shi'i Muslims. Here, religious law is to be applied, and Islamic religious professionals preside as judges.

The substantive law to be adopted is defined in clause 242 of the fundamental, but largely procedural, 1962 Law of Sharia Courts. At the time of my major fieldwork on this topic in 2007–8, when I spent many months in the courts, it read as follows: "The Sunni judge issues his ruling according to the preponderant statements of the school of Abu Hanifa, except in those cases where the [Ottoman] Law of Family Rights of 8 Muharram 1336/25 October 1917 speaks, whereupon the Sunni judge applies the rulings of that law; and the Ja'fari [i.e., Twelver Shi'i] judge issues his ruling according to the Ja'fari *madhhab* and, where it is in harmony with this school, from among the rulings of the Law of the Family" (Zayn 2003, 75). Given the incomplete coverage of the 1917 Ottoman Law of Family Rights, much of the law applied in the Sunni courts was effectively long uncodified, until a major reform in 2011 instigated by pressure from women's rights activists (Ghamroun 2013). That reform privileged instead the rulings of the Sunni community's Supreme Sharia Council and introduced a new and reformed, if still far from comprehensive, code. The Shi'i, or "Ja'fari," courts resisted the calls for reform. The Ja'fari madhhab, which is to say the Twelver Shi'i school of Islamic law,[1] arguably differs from the Ottoman Law at almost every point and thus remains the uncodified source of substantive law, as it has been since the official institutionalization of the Ja'fari courts in 1926 under the French Mandate.

But how is one to know what the position of the Ja'fari madhhab is on any given point? That is not so simple. For reasons I will explain, it is also not wholly clear on what rests the authority of any given individual Ja'fari judge to determine this position. From the perspective of many of the Islamic religious professionals involved in the courts, the lack of codification and consequent freedom of judges to determine the law themselves is entirely proper and authentic to religious tradition. From another perspective, that of the civil law and of secular nationalist and women's rights activism, the consequent lack of transparency makes the religious courts seem arbitrary and constitutes an egregious instance of the problematic nature of Lebanon's confessional legal system. From my own point of view, as an ethnographer of the sharia, what remained unsaid presented a challenge. How, if at all, can or should we make this system of religious-legal authority add up?

I begin with a necessarily concise sketch of the issues at hand: I have described the institutions and ideas at work, as well as my fieldwork, in more detail elsewhere for those who wish it (Clarke 2018). I then think through how one might approach these issues theoretically. I start from the perspective of Islamic legal studies before turning to the ostensibly opposed "praxiological" approach of Baudouin Dupret. Both afford responses to my question, albeit, in my reading, dismissive ones: either my case cannot really be considered as authentically of the sharia, which explains my puzzlement, or the mistake is worrying about its Islamicity in the first place, rendering my puzzlement redundant. I then consider what I see as a more anthropological approach, here inspired by the work of Paul Dresch, which turns on situating my case in a wider comparative frame—in this instance, that of regional anthropology. By orienting the analysis to more general patterns, I gain access to different sorts of theoretical purchase. We can see Islamic legal discourse as a "structure of disagreement," a structure that finds parallels in other contexts. That provides a way to account for its privacy in this case, which speaks to themes of self-esteem and thus vulnerability, as well as the pitfalls for the anthropologist who seeks to reveal them. It also allows one to capture the ambivalence of religious authority. Things can remain unsaid for both deep and shallow reasons—they might be ineffable as much as unspeakable. That leads finally to a qualification of one of Messick's most quotable aphorisms of sharia ethnography, namely that the sharia is a form of "total discourse," addressing as it does the whole of life. To this notion of totality, I suggest—in terms borrowed from Emmanuel Levinas (1969)—we might add another: that of infinity. Sharia discourse can indeed form the basis of a joined-up religious-legal system that saturates the landscape of authority. But it can also constitute an ideal that transcends such limits—or at least that might provide an excuse for glossing over them.

A Sketch of the Issue

Let us start with the idea of the Ja'fari madhhab itself. This is in some senses an ecumenical notion, granting the Twelver Shi'i legal tradition an equivalence to, but also distinctiveness from, the major Sunni schools of Islamic law (Hanafi, Hanbali, Maliki, and Shafi'i). Like the other madhhabs, then, it is a tradition of interpretation and debate as to the sharia, God's law. If it is to be taken to encompass the whole range of Shi'i legal discourse, this is a potentially vast field, extending over centuries, with much difference of opinion, but also common standards and much agreement. Simply naming it as the source of the law is not enough to determine what the law to be applied will be—that is a matter of reasoned, expert opinion.

Outside of the courts, in the world of everyday religious practice (which is where I began my researches in Lebanon), knowing what the sharia is is important too, for knowing how to pray correctly, what is and is not acceptable to eat, the proper modes of interaction with non-Muslims—potentially the whole range of the human experience. In this context, one turns to authoritative guidance. In practice, that might mean the nearest religious professional, or shaykh, to hand. But, as the layperson knows, there is a hierarchy of religious authority. The local shaykh may well know more than you, but he does not know as much as others.[2] The dominant model within contemporary Twelver Shi'i Islam envisages a ladder of expertise culminating in those scholars truly qualified to determine the sharia for themselves, the *mujtahids*—those capable of properly exercising *ijtihad*, the derivation of sharia legal precepts from their sources. Some of these scholars become favored "sources" (*maraji'*, singular *marja'*) of authoritative opinion. By adopting, or "emulation" (*taqlid*) of, a marja's position, nonexperts absolve themselves of responsibility before God for their choice of actions. The marjaʿ is also the sanctioned recipient of one's religious tithes and charitable donations. Given that the most famous might have millions of "emulators," one can imagine the potential stature of the role. The example of Khomeini (d. 1989) would be indicative in this respect, albeit particular.

To quote the opening words of the three-volume guide to the sharia, *The Way of the Righteous (Minhaj al-salihin)*, issued by perhaps the most widely recognized marjaʿ in the world, Najaf's Ayatollah Sayyid ʿAli al-Sistani, "It is obligatory for every person religiously liable [*mukallaf*, i.e., before God] who has not reached the level of ijtihad to be, in all his devotions and transactions, and the rest of his deeds and his omissions, an emulator [*muqallid*, i.e., of a mujtahid]" (Sistani 2002, 1:9, sec. 1). That is, either one is a mujtahid, or one should act under the aegis of someone who is.

This is, then, in the model of the mujtahid class, a rather shallow hierarchy of religious authority. Now, it should be said that, as viewed from Lebanon at least, to be a mujtahid, and still more a marjaʿ, is a rare thing—tens of great scholars rather than thousands, let us say. Most will be found in the great seminary cities of the Shiʿi world, especially Najaf in Iraq and Qom in Iran. Lebanon had one claimant to the role, Sayyid Muhammad Husayn Fadlallah (d. 2010), who was a focus of my studies. Fadlallah had many supporters. But he also had many enemies who denied his claims, often in the most vituperative terms. In the scholarly centers, however, and not least in Iran, there really are hundreds of aspirants, more or less high on what is a more extended ladder of religious authority, and a range of titles—subject to inflation—has arisen to reflect that. The mujtahids are ayatollahs, or "signs of God" ("grand ayatollahs" now, in the case of the marjaʿs at least); beneath them are the "proofs of Islam" (*hujjat al-islam*). These honorific terms have not, however, entered the marjaʿs' handbooks.

The opinion of a mujtahid is definitive. And yet they disagree. If they did not, they would hardly need to exist. In one sense, such a diversity of opinion might be (and is) seen as a blessing. But in another, it might seem confusing. The majority opinion thus holds that all save the mujtahids should emulate the most learned (*al-aʿlam*) scholar of all. In this spirit, the 1967 law that belatedly defined the official institutions of Lebanon's Twelver Shiʿa beyond their courts speaks of "conforming to the rules of the noble sharia and the jurisprudence [*fiqh*] of the Jaʿfari school," here qualified as "within the limits of the fatwas emanating from the common authority [*marjaʿ ʿamm*] of the community in the world" (Zayn 2003, 216). That looks significant (not least because that authority would most likely not reside in Lebanon). However, the hope for a common authority does not necessarily entail consensus as to who that is. There are many who claim the title of "most learned" too. Lebanon's Shi'i community does not have an official marja'-mujtahid by whose opinion it is bound. The great divide of the age is between those who acknowledge the leadership of the Islamic Republic of Iran, now in the form of Supreme Leader Ayatollah (to his supporters) 'Ali al-Khamenei, and those who do not, for whom Sistani's more "traditional" (i.e., less politically presumptuous) aegis might very often be preferred. Fadlallah constituted a local alternative, controversial in his own way—as a political activist, but still more for his strikingly progressive legal opinions (in relative terms). For those in positions of official responsibility in Lebanon, discretion in declaring one's allegiances may be the better part of valor. More generally, whom one chooses to emulate is a private concern—not secret, but not necessarily a matter for advertisement (to ethnographers at least).

That is the world of observance and scholarship outside the courts. But what about within them? The preponderant scholarly view—according to eminently well-qualified academic commentators (e.g., Gleave 2003), is that not only is the mujtahid class qualified to judge by right, but also the judge himself should ideally be a mujtahid. Given the rarity of such big beasts, however, that would prove problematic as a model for recruitment in the Lebanese Ja'fari court system. But even if this is the best known position, it is not the only one. What do the judges themselves think? One explained, "In every court the judge applies either his own opinion—if he is a mujtahid—or he applies that of the mujtahid he sees as the most learned." So far, so textbook. I wondered whether, in that case, many of the judges in the courts were mujtahids. "Look," he told me, "you don't see someone who is forty who is a mujtahid. It takes years and years and years. And people have to judge you a mujtahid—they look to his writings but also to his works." Or, as another judge suggested, we would know them from their pupils, who should themselves be great scholars. Hence, "There aren't very many." That would imply that there are few if any judges in Lebanon who are mujtahids. One might also fairly assume that neither of these two sees himself as such, given that both are in their fifties at the most, rather than the seventies that might be the norm. While both are certainly scholarly, neither, as far as I know, is at this point the author of publications on Islamic law or the teacher of any noted students. The judge must have a license (*wikala*) from the marja', the first noted—that is, an authorization to judge. "This is important: I have to know if God is content for me to judge," said the first judge. But when I asked him whether he was himself a mujtahid and, if not, which one he emulated, he preferred not to answer. Another time, I tried a different approach, asking him how many mujtahids there were in all Lebanon. He told me that he did have a position on this, but he was not going to tell me what it was.

There are further possibilities, let it be said. In an interview, the president of the Ja'fari courts, Shaykh Hasan 'Awwad, also noted the broad opposition we have just encountered between the opinion that the judge does have to be a mujtahid and the opinion that he could be given the deputed authority (*wikala*) to act as such by a mujtahid. But further, he added, there are those who argue that a judge could judge without such license, inasmuch as he knows the relevant rulings and applies them. Or as the second of the two judges I cited above put it, while it might be true that Ayatollah Sistani, for example, holds that the judge has to be a mujtahid, in Lebanon they thought "it is enough that he knows what he is doing." Put otherwise (as two other highly placed figures in the court system did), most of the issues encountered in the courts are uncontroversial. Where there are differences of opinion, the judge can apply the best-known opinion (*al-mashhur*) within the school. It is in this spirit, and in response to demand from lawyers for a guide as to the courts' thinking, that a previous court president, Shaykh 'Abdallah Ni'ma, published a family legal digest with numbered clauses (Ni'ma 1996). But that remains an unofficial primer rather than legally definitive.

Differences of Opinion

While this might indicate a comforting uniformity and predictability, in practice judges do differ. I was sitting once with my first judge when a lawyer asked about an especially controversial point, the ages at which boys and girls are normally considered to have left the custody of their mother and to be transferred to that of their father. The preponderant opinion (*al-mashhur*) within the school is that this is at two years for a boy and seven for a girl. This is the position generally quoted as that the Ja'fari courts take, and in itself it has been the target of extensive criticism from women's rights activists. It was their activism on precisely this point that won reform in the Sunni courts, extending presumed maternal custody to twelve years for both sexes, although the Ja'fari courts resisted. A still more conservative opinion, presuming paternal rights to custody at two years for both boys and girls, is that favored by such distinguished figures as Sistani and, perhaps more important still, his great teacher and predecessor as leading scholar of the seminaries of Najaf, Ayatollah Abu-l-Qasim al-Khu'i (d. 1992). It is Khu'i's long preeminence rather than any "official" status that explains why passages from his legal handbooks are reproduced at length in a useful compilation of legislation relevant to Lebanon's sharia courts (Zayn 2003).

It was this more conservative position that the judge in question favored, as he told the lawyer. It depends on the judge, he explained. "Which marja' they follow?" she wondered. "No, how they read the texts." This seemed contrary to his previously stated position that, unless the judge was himself a mujtahid (which I doubted he would claim of himself), he would follow the opinion of the scholar he thought the most learned. Another time, I tried to pick up the same point in a different way, by commenting that I had noted that Khu'i and Sistani ruled with two years for both sexes but the courts generally did not, favoring instead the preponderant view of two years for boys and seven for girls. No, he corrected me. Rather, each judge rules according to his opinion. And if it goes to appeal, then the appeals court panel will rule with theirs.

My second judge also preferred the more conservative position. In this case, I asked him directly if this was because he was practicing taqlid of Khu'i or Sistani. He did not answer directly. Instead, he began by discussing the notion of "the most learned" (*al-a'lam*) and noting that Khu'i definitely was such. So, regarding custody, many scholars choose to follow his opinion. Or they go with the preponderant opinion (*al-mashhur*), or they follow their own ijtihad, within strict guidelines. Was ruling with two years for both girls and boys an instance of him following Khu'i or his own ijtihad? "A bit of both perhaps." The question seemed an awkward one and did not result in a definitive answer.

Another possible approach would be through the judges' written judgments, where they have to justify their decision. But here the main emphasis seems to fall more on the procedural aspects of judging, specified in the Law of Sharia Courts and various parts of Lebanon's civil law. "According to sections 17, 91 and 242 of the Law of Sharia Courts the ruling is decided considering the respondent so-and-so disobedient [*nashiza*] toward her husband" (Barakat 2005, 36). Sharia discourse, by contrast—which is where the notion of a wife's "disobedience" comes from in the first place—is referred to in only the vaguest terms: "the sharia" (*al-shar'*, 40); "Ja'fari law" (*al-shar' al-Ja'fari*; 74); "as is written in Islamic jurisprudence" (*ka-ma huwa muharrar fi-l-fiqh al-islami*; 204).[3] What is written in Islamic jurisprudence, and what the judge's stance is toward the various arguments that might be made in that regard, let alone where they situate themselves in the hierarchy of scholarly authority in play outside the courts, is not specified.

That goes, it is worth saying, for hard cases as much as easy ones. Take, for example, a complex divorce case where both parties worked for the United Nations. One spouse was resident in Croatia and the other in Georgia, where the wife was suing for divorce based on ill-treatment and a long-standing lack of maintenance. The two teams of lawyers mobilized a range of arguments drawing on Islamic legal references ranging from sayings of the Prophet and Imam 'Ali, to the works of distinguished authorities such as Lebanon's Shaykh Muhammad Jawad Mughniyya (d. 1979) and Ayatollah Khu'i, as well as Shaykh Ni'ma's compendium of Ja'fari personal status law mentioned above. But after pages reporting these arguments, the judge's final ruling swiftly dismissed the case without discussing them (Barakat 2005, 165–72). In another case where a divorced wife demanded that the dower (*mahr*) she was due be recalculated to compensate for the savage inflation Lebanon had endured since her marriage, her ex-husband countered that such recalculation is not (sharia) legal, citing in support a fatwa from Ayatollah Sistani. The ruling was in his favor but cited the less specific support of "the opinions of jurists" (*ara' al-fuqaha'*) in the discussion and did not mention any Islamic legal considerations in the final summary. However, the Ja'fari appeals court is in favor of such recalculation, according to a ruling on another similar (appeals) case. But their support is stated in the baldest of terms, noting merely that this is "the reasoning of this court" (*ijtihad hadhihi al-mahkama*) (206, 207). That reasoning, however, takes place offstage.

It is an analytical move on my part to bring together this relative dearth of sharia-legal justification in the judges' rulings with their reticence as to their scholarly status in my conversations with them. But there is one important exception to the general lack of formal discussion of the judge's place in the scholarly hierarchy, which rather looks like the exception that proves the rule. Notoriously, Islamic precepts give different powers of divorce to husbands and wives. While a husband can divorce his wife almost at will, a wife has to obtain her husband's consent to divorce. If she cannot, she needs to obtain a judicially imposed divorce. Historically, this has been no easy thing. As a result of the reforms of the Ottoman Law of Family Rights, however, in the Sunni courts a case for a judicial divorce on the grounds of irreconcilable differences (*tafriq li-l-shiqaq wa-l-niza'*) is relatively straightforward to make. The equivalent in the Ja'fari courts on the other hand, "divorce by the judge" (*talaq al-hakim*), is exceptionally arduous. That is in part because of the difficulty of establishing the necessary legal grounds, but mostly because in this case alone the judge in question has to be a mujtahid. As my Shi'i interlocutors put it, for the Sunnis "any judge in a court" can perform such a divorce, whereas for the Shi'a only the *hakim shar'i*, the "religiously legitimate judge," here taken to mean the mujtahid, can do so. In the discourse of the judges, this is because of the gravity of the matter, given that the Islamic tradition has made divorce a core right of the husband: it thus requires especial exactness. In the less official terms of one lawyer, this strengthening of the requirements is "because the regular judge [*al-qadi al-'adi*] is nearer to the regular man [*rajul 'adi*]," whereas "you don't get to be *al-hakim al-shar'i* unless you do not share the characteristics of a normal person." And a regular man might impose a judicial divorce for the wrong, possibly corrupt, reasons: "Maybe the woman says to the judge, 'Divorce me now and I'll sleep with you tomorrow.'" And this was a common, if, I assume, fantastic, trope in my discussions of the topic, the fallible (non-mujtahid) judge divorcing a woman if she will sleep with him.

Given the more restrictive conditions for bringing them, such cases are correspondingly rare. I never saw one in the courts and have only a handful of pertinent documents. Again, judges in the Lebanese courts are unlikely to put themselves forward as mujtahids. Ayatollah Fadlallah, on the other hand, given his claims to that status, felt entitled to take on such cases in an unofficial capacity. His rulings were not, however, accepted by the courts—indeed, they were actively spurned. One lawyer thought, "The courts don't like him, because he knows more than them." He mentioned one judge who, he thought, if he was presented with a ruling from Fadlallah, would "throw it in the bin." Rulings in the less controversial Sistani's name reportedly meet with a less predictable and ultimately unreliable reception.[4] The successful rulings that I have had access to, however, all date from a period when Shaykh Muhammad Mahdi Shams al-Din (d. 2001)—a noted scholar and intellectual, contemporary and keen rival of Fadlallah but without anything like the popular following—led Lebanon's official Shi'i community institutions. Not a judge himself, he nevertheless authorized a limited number of such divorces, which the courts ratified. So, for example, an appeals court ruling of 2000 upheld an initial court judgment nullifying a woman's marriage on the basis of a ruling of *talaq al-hakim*, issued by "the *marja' shar'i* [not a title claimed by or for him very widely] His Excellency Imam [a strikingly grand term] Shaykh Muhammad Mahdi Shams al-Din" (Barakat 2005, 113–21). The appellant was thus placed in the difficult position of having to challenge what was being presented as the very highest form of religious authority. He argued that Shams al-Din's decision should not be viewed as legally binding the courts even if issued by an acknowledged scholar (*faqih*), while simultaneously professing that "he respects and honours and bows before the *talaq al-hakim* arising from Imam Shaykh Muhammad Mahdi Shams al-Din" (116). One senses the awkwardness that the invocation of the scholarly hierarchy entails.[5] A lawyer's submission that I had access to in another such case gives a further sense of the problem: "The ruling of the *hakim* is not allowed to be contradicted, even by another mujtahid,[6] . . . [H]e who rejects the ruling of the faqih is rejecting the ruling of the Imam [here referring to the divinely inspired Hidden Imam, I assume] and the one rejecting the ruling of the Imam is rejecting the ruling of God, and any polytheism is mightier than that." Naming mujtahids turns legal arguments into religious politics of the hottest temperature.

Some Possible Responses

What are we to make, then, of what I am portraying as the more general reticence as to the Ja'fari judge's sharia legal credentials? For me, as an ethnographer, it piqued my curiosity—I wanted to understand how things worked and seemed to have prematurely reached the limits of what I might find out. But a number of the colleagues to whom I have presented this material find my puzzlement wrongheaded. What makes me think there really is a "problem" here that needs solving? Perhaps, they hinted, this perceived problem is largely a function of the expectations with which I was approaching the material.

For the sake of comparison, take another, very different project of describing and analyzing the courts—that of Human Rights Watch's 2015 report, *Unequal and Unprotected: Women's Rights under Lebanon's Religious Personal Status Laws*. Human Rights Watch is also struck by the lack of clarity as to legal authority in the Ja'fari courts (and indeed in the other religious court systems), and they certainly find it a problem. With reference to the issues of custody introduced above, they comment, "This lack of clarity and certainty leaves mothers dependent on the whims of judges or their estranged husbands" (HRW 2015, 71). With reference to judicial divorce, "There is no consensus about who is a Shia authority whose order is binding on the religious court. . . . The absence of [such] criteria . . . deters women from pursuing such cases and results in inconsistent judgements" (50). They work from the assumption that effective law requires transparency, coherence, and hence predictability, and they therefore recommend, among other things, that the religious law applied must be codified and that "state institutions must exercise oversight over religious courts and texts" (9).

The last remark gives a sense of why and how such suggestions might be resisted. Wittingly or unwittingly, Human Rights Watch here repeats a call that has been made since the French Mandate period. But one has only to think through the implications of subjecting the divine sharia and its sources, not least the Quran, to the approval of the Lebanese Parliament to see how unpalatable this might appear, or could be made to appear, from the perspective of the religiously committed. Given the evidence that Human Rights Watch assembles as to some of the egregious failings of the religious court system, one can hardly fail to be sympathetic to their calls for reform in general, as indeed are a great many of the religious professionals employed in the courts. But the Shi'i establishment continues to resist those calls. Significantly for the present discussion, a key theme of that resistance is the unacceptability of corroding the judge's right to exercise ijtihad.[7]

But it was not through the assumptions and expectations from which the civil legal activist sets out that my own puzzlement arose. I sought to understand the courts "in their own terms" (although one certainly hopes that such understanding might ultimately help rather than hinder the process of progressive reform). Perhaps fatefully, the terms that I took up were in the first instance those of the scholar-authors, the mujtahid class. This orientation toward the textualists is not a necessary one for the anthropologist of Islam generally (Zein 1977) but is clearly a natural move for the sharia ethnographer. And the impetus for my researches in Lebanon's sharia courts did indeed spring from the sorts of academic interests and conversations that could be broadly characterized as sharia studies (rather than those of gender or the anthropology of the state, say).

Thinking from within Islamic legal studies, one might nevertheless remark (as one discussant of this chapter did) that in hoping for explicit justification of the judge's sharia legal reasoning, I was approaching the material with the wrong sort of expectations, those of someone whose idea of the law is that of the common law perhaps. Unlike the latter, the Islamic legal tradition gives the judge's ruling little significance, in that it does not create binding precedent. Viewed historically, such rulings have very commonly been brief and relatively "textually silent." Their intended audience was their nonexpert recipients, the plaintiffs and respondents rather than the scholarly community (lawyers being a comparatively recent phenomenon). As far as the scholars were concerned, the judges' pronouncements were of no importance, for the role of the judge—as opposed to that of the mufti, or "jurisconsult"—was not as a law finder. Their proper province was that of due procedure rather than jurisprudence (*fiqh*; see, e.g., Messick 2014).

Here I should stress immediately, however, that my colleagues in sharia studies would in any case most likely see including my own Lebanese cases in this historical frame of reference as anachronistic. The mainline of recent work has argued against an alleged previous "Orientalist" consensus that Islamic law, as a form of "sacred law" in Weber's terms, or a mere "deontology" in those of Snouck Hurgronje, was always more ideal than practical—in some sense out of time (see, e.g., Johansen 1999). Rather, the sharia historically constituted the basis of effective legal systems, even if organized differently from, for example, the common law, as in the ways that I have just mentioned. However, that was before the rupture of colonial and postcolonial modernization, which, by changing the entire structure of education and legal reasoning and practice, rent the fabric of sharia-oriented society into tatters. A return to the rule of the authentic sharia in the context of the contemporary world of nation-states and codified law is impossible. Present-day sharia discourse must again be seen as out of time, albeit for different reasons (Hallaq 2009, 429, 500, 549–50; 2013). The modern republic of Lebanon represents a case in point. Its contemporary "sharia courts" would—on this line of argument—have to be regarded as not authentically of the sharia, at best a mélange of disparate elements, at worst sharia in name only.

Both the alleged "Orientalist" and post-Orientalist positions, if I can characterize them so broadly, thus provide a response of sorts to my puzzle. Either sharia discourse has never been practical enough to be instituted as such a coherent system as I am assuming, and so I am wasting my time worrying about why I cannot quite make things add up; or sharia discourse does allow such systematicity, of which there are historical examples, but, subsequent to the rupture of colonial modernity, it can do so no longer. And so I should be equally unsurprised that some things are not or cannot be fully spelled out.

There is an obvious sense in which such a response might—even if right—seem unsatisfying, especially to ethnographers, closely involved with their subjects. One hardly wants to write things up in such a way that those one works with end up as "dupes," as Garfinkel (1984) once put it. How much more Orientalist could one get? What complicates this still further, however, is that a good many of my interlocutors in the sharia courts (and outside them) say much the same sorts of things. These courts are not really sharia courts: "maybe only ten percent" sharia at best, if at all. Here they are thinking of the prominence of painful bureaucratic procedure, which they blame on the larger civil legal system within which the sharia courts are embedded—more a matter of human state law (*qanun*) than God's law, as they put it. If I wanted to know about the sharia, I was sometimes told, I would be better off looking for it in the books of the scholars or, better still, going straight to the source, the Quran. Of course, they added, things were different in times gone by. Some of those working in the Ja'fari courts had still more disturbingly Orientalist-sounding thoughts. Actually, they ventured, maybe the Shi'i legal tradition is indeed rather unworldly, at least in comparison with the Sunnis, with their long acquaintance with the practicalities of running states. "Here, it was too bad even to say you were Shi'i, let alone have 'Ja'fari court' written outside" as one judge put it. "There weren't any Shi'i judges. So this is all new." No wonder then it sometimes seems difficult to fit these contemporary courts into venerable religious models. This sounds a little odd in a world where the Shi'i Islamic Republic of Iran is the most obvious example of a contemporary Islamic state. But it is true that some branches of the Sunni tradition—and especially the Hanafi school—did develop more nuanced hierarchies of legal authority in response to the practical demands of administration (see, e.g., Al-Azem 2017).

Even if people find grounds for criticism from all sorts of different angles, including "religious" ones, the courts function nevertheless. Perhaps one needs to forget about such paralyzing issues of authenticity, then, and concentrate on that actual day-to-day functioning instead. This is the approach that Baudouin Dupret advocates, inspired by Garfinkel's (1984) ethnomethodology mentioned above. His work is on Egyptian courts, including personal status cases. In Egypt, like in Lebanon, family law is supposed to be "Islamic," albeit constructed as such in very different ways. Egypt has not had "sharia courts" since their abolition in 1955, but, since a constitutional amendment in 1980, the sharia is formally taken as the fundamental source of all Egyptian law. Family law in particular has in any case long been subject to codified but explicitly sharia-inspired law. Where those laws do not speak, as in Lebanon, jurists should turn to the Hanafi school of Islamic law. And yet here too, Dupret says, "At the very place where it is supposed to be massive and overwhelming, that is, in personal status law, references to Islamic law are conspicuous for their paucity" (2007, 97). One might be tempted to recall the longer-standing "textual silence" of the Islamic judge discussed above. But, for Dupret, it is precisely approaching such topics from the outset as framed in terms of "sharia" or "Islamic law" that is the problem. This is, to his mind, to fall straight away into the trap of essentialism. Rather than asking what, if anything, is essentially Islamic about such practices, Dupret says that instead we should ask, "What do people do when referring to Islamic law?" (81).

Otherwise put, the researcher oriented toward "pragmatic" and "realistic" description asks not why, but how. In this perspective, the terms and concepts usually deployed by researchers of Islamic law "lose their theoretical and scholarly weight and 'thickness': they tend then to correspond to what 'lies open to view' [a reference to Wittgenstein's *Philosophical Investigations*], not to the depths of a mysterious world that needs to be overseen by scholars for its interpretation" (Dupret and Voorhoeve 2016, 2–3). My focus on the question of the judge's right to exercise ijtihad, in its highly valorized Islamic legal sense, might be a case in point. In the context of court practice, civil as well as sharia, ijtihad has a less rarefied usage as simply a judge's deliberation. This, for Dupret, is the problem of much anthropology (he has Geertz most squarely in mind), its "ironic" stance, its insistence that anthropologists know better than those they study, because they can discern some deeper pattern that is somehow inaccessible to the local.[8]

In his Egyptian rulings—and, interestingly to my mind, this matches my Lebanese ones—one sees that what the judge chiefly does is take great care to ensure a correct account of procedure. In producing such a "procedurally impeccable ruling," the judge evinces his command of the demands of his essentially bureaucratic role. In so doing, he has in mind an audience looking over his shoulder, attentive to these points of procedure as potential avenues for argument, perhaps even in order to overturn the ruling. That audience would include his colleagues in the appeals court, but also the lawyers who work in the courts, trained in the civil legal tradition, and who take cases to appeal in the first place. In this respect, as in most others, Dupret (2016) suspects, Egyptian courts and courts everywhere else end up looking pretty much the same.

Following this line of thought, in his rulings the Lebanese Ja'fari court judge performs his role effectively not by placing himself in the framework of religious authority that applies in the scholarly world, but by explicitly following the procedural constraints that the Law of the Sharia Courts and parts of the civil legal apparatus place on him. Writing rulings is, however, only one part of the judge's work and craft, perhaps not even the most prominent or valorized one (see Clarke 2012). Handling sessions in court and managing the disputing parties toward a resolution of some sort—in many cases one that stops short of a final ruling—constitutes an equal if not larger part. The sharia is indeed invoked in those contexts, though generally in a nonspecific and idealized manner, as a mode of moral exhortation rather than legal argument, and often in order to draw a contrast with the unsatisfying strictures of the civil legal bureaucracy within which the courts operate. That these are supposed to be "sharia courts" is thus certainly material to the rhetorical strategies of the judges—and some plaintiffs, respondents, and lawyers too. And let us not forget that in Lebanon's sharia courts, the judges are shaykhs, Islamic religious professionals, and dress accordingly. Their work of mediation and pedagogy in court is part and parcel of what is expected of shaykhs more generally. Notwithstanding the pessimism of those shaykhs as to its authenticity, a show of the sharia is put on, even if somewhat wearily on occasion. This is no doubt different from the Egyptian case. But Dupret's larger point stands: the role the sharia has within court practice is not necessarily what the Islamicist might expect. If I focus on what the judge actually does, then, rather than on what I might expect him to do, perhaps my nagging questions would melt away.

With all this the anthropologist can be in sympathy, although Dupret's intellectual asceticism—ask not why; rest content with the thin rather than the thick; eschew irony—might seem less appealing. Anthropologists are indeed addicted to making connections and tracing out patterns. Again, in the present case, the source of my difficulty perhaps lies in the connection that I wanted to make between the discourse of the mujtahids and the world of the courts. But this was not even an imaginative, let alone counterintuitive or ironic, move. Rather, as I set out above, it was one invited by the laws that govern the courts, as well as the seeming solidarity of the Shi'i religious class.[9] Nevertheless, many might think the anthropologist's job is precisely not to fall into the trap of taking the schematic hegemonic discourse—the "official" account, in Bourdieu's (1977) terms—as definitive. Their task is rather to give voice to the unspoken "unofficial" assumptions that guide actual practice (see Jenkins 1994). But this is a law court—one might expect the official account itself not to be so elusive.

From within the courts themselves, it is true that the question of the formal grounds of the judge's religious-legal authority hardly seems to be asked. The judge simply has the authority to rule as he sees fit, and that is that. In the court sessions, the largely non-legal specialist petitioners and respondents do not, so far as I could see, presume to concern themselves with the details of

Islamic discourse and understandably take the legal and religious authority of the sharia court judge—bearded, middle-aged, dressed in his robe and turban, and sitting behind his desk—largely as a given. The forms of authority in play, one might say, should not be reduced to that formally granted by the religio-legal model. That is not to say that "lay people" do not criticize either the courts or the religious class. They do. But such criticism does not turn on how transparently the judges are situated in a hierarchy of religious authority or what the details are of their Islamic legal arguments. More surprisingly to my mind, the lawyers working in the courts also do not seem to dig very far into these questions—not in court at any rate.[10] The opacity of the system does not, generally speaking, seem a barrier to its formal functioning. One can certainly hear carping comments from the lawyers outside of the courts though. Of one judge presuming too much (power to impose a judicial divorce): "Who does he think he is?" Of one very high-ranking figure: "If there weren't any sharia courts, who knows? Maybe he would just be an [relatively low status] imam in a mosque."

It would seem odd to think of judges as a subaltern class. Being a judge in Lebanon is a privileged and well-paid position. The Islamic tradition does admittedly see the judgeship as in many ways problematic (Messick 2014). Working for the state in particular has long been viewed as potentially compromising, still more so in the Shiʻi tradition (Madelung 1980). Historically, the independent scholarly class and those working in state-recognized roles could be said to have formed "two parallel systems" or a "double religious hierarchy," in Sabrina Mervin's (2000, 93, 405) characterization, with the weight of prestige on the side of the independent mujtahids. Certainly none of the judges I worked with could really be said to be "in the game" for mujtahid status. But it still is surely not an empty question to ask how the two systems, if such they are (or "fields," etc.), are to be related—or at least not an empty gesture to point to the lack of transparency in this regard. Does the judges' reticence on this point—if I am right in diagnosing things in this way—speak to the silence of the subaltern, then? Or is it rather the mystifying mask of power? Or something else completely?

Dupret's position—look to the surface—seems more to preclude asking the question than to provide an answer to it. If one needed an answer, however, then despite the anti-positivist intent of Dupret's ultimate inspiration (Garfinkel's ethnomethodology), thin description surely holds out the unwelcome prospect of a slide back into what Paul Dresch (2012a, 11) refers to as "empiricism." "The idea that the world is given to direct experience" (11) looks attractively down-to-earth but ends up taking too much for granted. There are no "plain facts" simply lying in plain view. Action and understanding are constituted via assumptions, and it is the anthropologist's job to work out what those in play are. Otherwise, our own assumptions will come flooding in, and everywhere ends up looking the same. All the ideological elaboration, so richly varied between different contexts, becomes so much mere window dressing—pantomime sharia in our case—draped over a set of "falsely obvious" (2), "trivial" (5), and "dimly similar" (5) themes: the exercise of power, or its resistance, or the pursuit of self-interest. If we are to do otherwise, then we have to work out what it is we are missing. And so, "wherever fieldwork is done . . . one is listening for the unsaid" (Dresch 2000a, 122). Here, I suspect that I have heard it.

The Ineffable and the Unsaid

Dresch makes the last comment in an article thinking about the distinctiveness of the Middle East as a site of anthropological fieldwork. In some parts of the world, classic domains of anthropological research in sub-Saharan Africa or New Guinea, say, one is faced with "models of society wherein the moral world is largely a local world and in a sense pretends to self-sufficiency," and where the outsider can thus be readily spliced in. But the Middle East, by contrast (although not alone in this respect), is a domain of "'strong models' of people's worth in a larger universe," where outsiders remain such (Dresch 2000a, 115). This certainty about who is who comes bound up with a concern for the privacy of those who fall within a given model. Gaining access to the private domain becomes a challenge—writing it up still more so: "You've scandalised us," complains an informant of one famous anthropologist of the region. But "what empiricist anthropology sees as obstacles [i.e., ethnographic lacunae] are social facts" (Dresch 2000a, 112). There are patterns to what remains unsaid, patterns that vary from place to place, and they are significant in and of themselves. In the Middle East then, broadly speaking, we are in "a world in which privacy is highly structured and integral to the definition of social groups" (111). Therefore, and more generally, "conflicting orders of privacy, *and thus of self-esteem*, are a large part of what we study" (117; emphasis added).

Dresch takes as a paradigmatic illustration Andrew Shryock's (1997) ethnography of historical discourse among Jordanian tribesmen.[11] Members of different tribal sections are happy to boast among themselves of their own group's achievements, but repeating such boasts in the public sphere—especially in print—is eschewed as dangerously political. Finding the proper authority prepared to stand by an authoritative statement of each community's history becomes ethnographically fraught. The claims of others are denigrated as "lies." The truth of the matter can only lie outside the discourses of this set of opposed groups—in the archives of the British colonial authorities or the collections of Saudi genealogists perhaps. And thus, "what used to be described as social structure [one of "segmentary lineages" perhaps]—a rather public phenomenon—is *a structure of disagreement*, among other things of selective privacy" (Dresch 2000a, 118; emphasis added; paraphrasing Shryock's [1997, 57–61] "community of disagreement").

I see resonances with my own case—in structural terms at least. The comparison might seem scandalous in itself, in different ways for different audiences no doubt (see also Shryock 1997, 313–15). The tribesmen have historically been seen by the learned religious elite as their antithesis, illiterate and godless. And the topics of tribes and Islam have both been picked out as the most "Orientalist" of the preoccupations of anthropologists of the region. But, stripped back, Islamic law is in itself "a structure of disagreement" as to what the sharia is. Claims to authority and its proper transmission here too are imagined in genealogical terms (Messick 1993, 1–36). And the truth of the matter must again ultimately remain outside of the reach of the system, because only "God knows best," as the conventional conclusion to a fatwa, or Islamic legal opinion, has it.[12] Sacred law's transcendental object makes it inevitably "contingent" as a human project (Johansen 1999).

This seems a helpful shift in perspective. Rather than seeing a madhhab in concrete, solidary terms, as a "school of law" (or reified "system," "field," etc.), we can see it as a nested set of disagreements. And it then makes sense, to push Dresch's point further, that such a structure of disagreement manifests itself in some (if not all) important contexts not so much as a public phenomenon as a private one. Certainly, the notions of intimacy, privacy, and vulnerability—self-esteem indeed—would fit some of the ethnographic patterns I have described. Sharia legal arguments are not revealed to the audience looking over the judge's shoulder. Rather, they are conducted "offstage." Notwithstanding the differences in legal opinion that are the hallmark of the world of the marja's, in the courts "all the opinions are the same," as one judge put it to a worried litigant. Even if the competitive world of the marja's is, on the other hand, one of public rather than private difference, a mujtahid is not expected to put himself forward so brazenly. Rather, their followers make their claims for them. (And again, taqlid—which marja' one chooses to adopt—is generally seen as a private matter.) One thinks of another related category much evoked in the region, that of modesty—here not of the female body, endlessly discussed, but of claims to religious knowledge and authority, eminently contestable and vulnerable (Clarke 2014). One senior judge's (exceptional) comment that he did think himself a mujtahid was scoffed at when discussed with others. Even Ayatollah Fadlallah's claims could be "thrown in the bin."[13] But conversely, in terms of self-esteem, openly terming yourself a *muqallid*, an emulator of someone more senior, might sound a little feeble. At least, I never heard anyone in the courts do so.

Some of the potentially scandalizing consequences of the regimes of intimacy that Dresch (2000a, 111) identifies also resonate. Hard-won insights can seem tinged with a flavor of gossip, a sense of being let into secrets, ones that then become hard to use. Remember that in cases of judicial divorce in the Ja'fari courts, a genuine mujtahid is required, because "the normal judge" might succumb to temptation and "divorce women to sleep with them." Judge so-and-so was rumored to do exactly that. Another judge had allegedly given a favorable ruling in return for a particularly fine carpet. Another had proposed making a flawed ruling to allow a lawyer to bring an appeals case in return for splitting the ensuing fees. Allegations of corruption and politics (*siyasa*) in the courts are rife. To repeat such gossip is not intended as any reflection on the judges I encountered. Such rumors were patently false. It is rather to observe that, while the sharia court judge is nominally owed (and generally receives) respect as the face of the divine sharia, his particular status and even his motives can all too readily be questioned (offstage) in a mundane hermeneutics of suspicion. Thin description might actually end up looking similar in different contexts: the judge, like everyone else, has "interests" (*maslaha*). He can be both an authority and a fraud.

Structures of privacy thus create the possibility of reading what lies within them in radically different ways.[14] The public surface might promise something deeper within. Or it might turn out to be shallow after all. The play between surface and depth is what generates such ironies. These are, however, pace Dupret, the stuff of local life rather than anthropological arrogance.[15] The ironies multiply. Dupret's distinction between "what lies open to view" and "the depths of a mysterious world that needs to be overseen by scholars for its interpretation" simply reproduces what we might modishly term the ontology in question. And it was reproducing the world as seen from within the scholarly model that arguably led to the classicism and essentialism of the Orientalists that Dupret wants to kick against. As Dresch notes, strong models have a tendency to capture those studying them.

Not every category promises such depth or resists empiricism, however. Counting mujtahids is indeed hard—no one can agree as to who counts as a "real" one. Ayatollah Fadlallah's claims, supported by hundreds of thousands, might be rubbished. Even the then-seventy-eight-year-old Sistani could be dismissed by one venerable lawyer as "new" (in preference for Sistani's long-since deceased teacher Khu'i).[16] But one can certainly count judges. As state-appointed officials, their number is specified in law. Thin description will suffice here. A colleague who works on contemporary Iran—metropolitan in Shi'i terms— cannot quite see my mujtahid problem, but for different reasons from those I discussed above. In marginal and less confident Lebanon, mujtahids remain rare beasts, a deep category rather than a shallow one. But in Iran, under an Islamic Republican regime where much law is sharia inflected and a reformed seminary education provides degree-like programs in ijtihad, you really can count mujtahids, and judges really can be mujtahids. Rationalization begets empiricism. No doubt some sort of distinction between "real" mujtahids and paper ones still applies (just as while one may be able to count professors in the Western academies, true scholars are harder to come by).

At the beginnings of the Islamic Republic, however, while Article 162 of its constitution stated that judges had to be mujtahids, Khomeini allowed non-mujtahid judges to serve because of the lack of suitably qualified candidates. Where a judge did not himself exercise ijtihad, he was to follow a recognized authority (Article 167), in practice most often Khomeini (Schirazi 1997, 65–68, 82n27). That is to say, here the "system" really could be made to add up, all the while Khomeini's authority was preeminent (if not unchallenged). The same move could in theory work elsewhere. In practice, in Lebanon at least, making such hierarchies of dependency explicit—and thus flattening out the structure of disagreement—seems less compelling.[17]

Conclusion: Totality and Infinity

I started with my impression that the structure of religious-legal authority in play in Lebanon's Ja'fari courts was not wholly clear and that it seemed a somewhat awkward topic. In the terms of the formal discourse of "Ja'fari *fiqh*," things could in theory be worked out readily enough. But the actors involved seemed happier not to make explicit a concrete structure of authority, autonomy, and dependency. I thought through the issue in the terms of two opposing approaches to the study of Islamic law. Both had useful points to make, but on the issue at hand neither ultimately satisfied. I thus turned to Paul Dresch's remarks on the anthropology of the unsaid, which led me to the notion of a "structure of disagreement" and the themes of privacy, vulnerability, and ambivalence. In the light of the last in particular, I noted that sharia discourse could be the basis of an explicit hierarchy of authority, but also a bulwark for autonomy.

I want to end by suggesting a vocabulary with which to capture this ambivalence. Brinkley Messick, thinking of the potentially misleading nature of the familiar gloss of the sharia as "Islamic law," remarks, "The shari'a is better characterized . . . as a type of 'total' discourse, wherein 'all kinds of institutions find simultaneous expression religious, legal, moral and economic,'" quoting from Mauss's famous essay on *The Gift* (Messick 1993, 3; Mauss 1990, 3). Otherwise put, sharia discourse does not divide up the normative landscape in the same way as "bourgeois legality." Messick goes on to show, as he does still further in his most recent book (2017), how sharia discourse might thereby underpin a set of moral and legal institutions ranging systematically and coherently right across the life of a polity (see also Hallaq 2009, 1–3, 543–50).

Paul Dresch, for unrelated reasons, also takes up Mauss's ideas on totality in the context of a wide-ranging paper considering how Middle Eastern contexts might or might not fit into anthropological debates over the classic theme of exchange. For Dresch, the Middle East is not the domain of "total" societies, in the sense that he takes Mauss as intending. Admittedly, as he says (1998, 120), "What Mauss means by total is not transparent." But Dresch picks out what he sees as two key senses in play. The first (the one that Messick is alluding to) is that in total contexts, as Mauss has it, "everything intermingles" (1990, 3), or, in Dresch's gloss, "such typologies of social fact as economic, religious, juridical do not apply" (1998, 120). And the second is that parties to transactions are not individuals but groups, or "collectivities" (Mauss 1990, 5). Mauss, it would seem, finds some societies more "total" than others, in both these senses.[18] For Dresch, the Middle East lacks such total societies. Society and culture are not woven together here so coherently and completely at the local level, in contrast with some of the contexts that anthropology has made its own. The latter might be characterized by, again, "models of society wherein the moral world is largely a local world and in a sense pretends to self-sufficiency" (Dresch 2000a, 115). Rather, the Middle East is a region characterized by large-scale economic and political differentiation since the beginning of history (which indeed starts here). These are "parts of the world characterised by coins, empire, writing, religion beyond local domains and of complexities no bounded cosmology exhausts" (Dresch 1998, 128). Here, truth does indeed ever lie elsewhere.

The point is not to establish which of the two is the more faithful interpreter of Mauss. Both seem right. Sharia discourse is clearly totalizing, in that it has ambitions to comprehend and cohere a whole way of life (although it does differentiate it, even if in ways other than those of bourgeois legality). But no given actual sharia-centered society—cognizant of the legal individual, socially differentiated, necessarily cosmopolitan rather than parochial—could be said to be "total" in Mauss's terms. Further, while the model is total, it stands apart from society. Sharia-mindedness is almost paradigmatically "legalistic" in this sense, in Dresch's (2012a) terms. Real life will always somehow fail to measure up. Some things, and people, will fall beyond the pale (classically, the "ignorant" tribesmen). But also, and this is Dresch's (1998) point about notions of exchange in the region, the calculating systematicity of legalism can never comprehend the whole of God's ethical demand, nor indeed the incalculable excess of his generosity.[19] So too, as Messick (1993) shows, the sharia's divine source means that it is always open to further interpretation, ever spiraling outward. It can form the basis of a coherent legal system. But it can also always offer something more, spilling out over the boundaries of the state (Clarke 2010).

What I want to argue is that this ambivalence cannot be made simply to sit astride the dividing line of modernity, whereby openness belongs to premodern, authentic sharia, but was permanently foreclosed by the undoubted rupture of colonialism and modernization, such that its contemporary invocation would be merely anachronistic. Notwithstanding the undoubted flattening effect of codified, nation-state law, in some present-day contexts mujtahids still remain "deep." And, conversely, there were premodern attempts to limit sharia interpretation or harden its hierarchies. The dialectic between systematicity and the possibility of its transcendence predates modernity and endures after it. To quote Emmanuel Levinas, "It is a relationship with a surplus always exterior to the totality, as though the objective totality did not fill out the true measure of being, as though another concept, the concept of infinity, were needed to express this transcendence with regard to totality, non-encompassable within a totality, and as primordial as totality" (Levinas 1969, 22–23; emphasis removed). Levinas has his own particular concerns, of course. But with sharia ethnography in mind, the concept of infinity, set alongside that of totality, would indeed help express tensions that I would see as intrinsic to a transcendental legalistic tradition. The sharia might also be characterized as a type of "infinite" discourse, as well as a totalizing one.

We have traveled a long way, from a niggling ethnographic worry all the way to infinity. Dupret, for one, would no doubt disapprove. For all that, I should stress, this is an attempt not at a total explanation but rather at adding an alternative perspective when the obvious lines of conversation might seem unnecessarily truncated. At root, this is simply a matter of finding a way of describing basic patterns—here, categories that are open to interpretation versus those that are closed. Reimagining "sacred law" as a structure of disagreement allows us to retain the salience of its difference, while also de-exoticizing it for moderns. In the end, as Dresch says (1998, 128), anthropology's method remains that of Mauss: "Take the case on its own terms, find simpler terms in which to move to the next, show the cases as alternative workings out of principle."

MORGAN CLARKE is Associate Professor in Social Anthropology at the University of Oxford and a fellow of Keble College. He is author of *Islam and New Kinship: Reproductive Technology and the Shariah in Lebanon* and *Islam and Law in Lebanon: Sharia within and without the State.*

Notes

Many thanks are due to all those who helped me with my researches in Lebanon, as well as those who have helped me with this paper. The latter include the editors of this volume, the participants at the conference at All Souls at which the paper was first presented, and those at other meetings at New York University and the Oxford Centre for Islamic Studies.

1. Named after the Twelvers' sixth imam, Ja'far al-Sadiq, a noted jurist.

2. The scholarly world and that of the court authorities is, I should say, an almost exclusively male one.

3. Here I refer to a published lawyer's guide to the courts, which includes a rich selection of reproduced rulings.

4. See HRW (2015, 49–52) for a discussion of what they call "sovereign divorce" and some interestingly unpredictable examples of what does and does not seem to stick in the courts.

5. The case clearly posed problems for the judges too. Three members of the (three-judge) appeals panel recused themselves in turn and had to be replaced; and the final decision was by majority rather than unanimous.

6. The lawyer's point is sound in Islamic legal terms.

7. I draw here on a presentation by senior consultant Ja'fari judge Shaykh Muhammad Kana'an at the conference "The Legal and Religious Protection of the Family," College of Law, Political Science and Administration, Lebanese University, Sidon, March 29, 2008.

8. Some anthropologists might agree with Dupret's verdict on Geertz, but not so much due to his enthusiasm for thick description as for his failing to follow through on it, in some of his most famous later papers at least.

9. One small point seems worth noting here. In contrast with their Sunni equivalents, all Shi'i religious professionals, "official" or otherwise, wear the same turban and robes.

10. But see Barakat (2005, 130) for a rare example, where a lawyer appeals a ruling on the grounds that, although it supplied a legal justification, it did not provide a sharia legal one. As we saw above, however, it is not that the lawyers eschew sharia discourse completely in their submissions. But, again, in the judges' final decisions, such arguments are largely effaced.

11. Lest this be seen as exoticizing, one of course encounters similar themes of privacy in many other sorts of contexts, in the Middle East and beyond. The domestic level is obvious; but, to zoom out in the other direction, in today's global public sphere the eminently strong model of a world of nation-states seems to work likewise. National culture becomes potentially private (Dresch 2000a, 120; Herzfeld 2005; Shryock 2004b).

12. The phrase can be used to round off a debate about tribal history too (Shryock 1997, 257).

13. Bhalloo (2015) describes how, in nineteenth-century Iran, judges' claims to mujtahid status were rubbished as a way to overturn their verdicts.

14. Such ambivalence runs through ethnography of the region, as Dresch points out elsewhere. Cousin marriage is a neat example, "the preserve of the destitute and the mighty—either no one will marry with your family, or you will not marry with other people's" (1998, 122).

15. See Gilsenan (1976; 1982, 116–41) for some classic Lebanese examples. More formally speaking, the distinction between surface (*zahir*) and interior (*batin*) is fundamental to Islamic legal notions of evidence and procedure as much as mystical theology (Johansen 1999).

16. "There are no shaykhs today," as one of Shryock's (1997, 13) interlocutors has it, with reference to the great men of the tribal world.

17. To maintain the comparison, see Shryock (1997, 304–7, 311–12) on Jordan, where the genealogical difference of the tribes can be flattened out under Hashemite dynastic nationalism.

18. Some of his famous remarks later in the essay on "total social facts," on the other hand, are more ambiguous: are they ontologically distinct, social facts of a specific kind like "the gift" in "archaic societies"? Or is this a more general point on anthropological method? Both readings seem possible (Gofman 1998).

19. See Schaeublin (2016) for a rich ethnographic exploration of this theme.

3

A MIRROR FOR FIELDWORKERS

Christa Salamandra

IF THE MIDDLE EAST CONSISTS OF LOOSELY RELATED "part-worlds," as this
volume's introduction proposes, then the partial world of elite Damascus appears distinctly remote from Paul Dresch's rural Yemen. The "experiment in
self-historicizing" (Clifford 2012) I adopt here to explore his intellectual influence may therefore seem misplaced. However, a closer look reveals two uncanny and interrelated points of convergence: our ethnography rubs against
Middle East anthropology's prevailing grain, and our respective part-worlds
have suffered catastrophic and ongoing civil and proxy wars. In "Wilderness of
Mirrors: Truth and Vulnerability in Middle Eastern Fieldwork," Dresch evokes
a looking glass of professional disputes to elucidate contradictory assumptions
operating in field site, ethnography, and academia (2000a). He argues that truth
is partial, contingent, and ultimately elusive, and he does so in language so el-
liptical it leaves the reader not merely "listening for the unsaid" (122) but reading for the unwritten.[1] I take this seminal essay as a springboard to explore my
own production of scandal, one that involves competing truths, multiple vul-
nerabilities, and unexpected continuities. Focusing on the ethnographic self
to reflect on Dresch's legacy appears antithetical; he often advised me to write
myself out of my work, except where fieldwork interactions conveyed something significant about social relations. But my intention here is an archaeology of career that reveals the paradoxical orthodoxy that has governed, indeed
disciplined, anthropological theory and practice in the Middle East over the
past three decades, and to show how I was able to produce work that resisted—
or sidestepped—prevailing paradigms. Reflexivity reveals Dresch's subversive
mentorship.

I began my Oxford DPhil in 1990, at the height of the anthropological
self-critique galvanized by James Clifford and George Marcus's 1986 edited

volume *Writing Culture*. This work set an upending agenda; the excitement of its deconstruction animated new fieldwork methodologies and experimental ethnographies. It was a heady moment. We budding anthropologists sought to uproot lingering vestiges of colonial knowledge production and deal a final blow to Enlightenment scientism. By asserting our positionality and uncovering our assumptions, we would render explicit and reset the power imbalances inherent in the anthropological endeavor, surrendering authority to our subaltern interlocutors.

The *Writing Culture* debate held particular relevance for those of us interested in the Middle East. It dovetailed handily with a growing anti-Orientalist impulse that singled out research on contemporary Arab societies as a particularly pernicious form of postcolonialism.[2] Edward Said's critique of classic scholarship, whatever its faults and merits, was interpreted to proscribe any depictions that might be read as even vaguely negative. The prevailing climate made it difficult to open one's eyes in the field, let alone write ethnography about those now cast as "other," a concept and category the critique itself created. Accusations of othering befell anyone brave or foolhardy enough to suggest difference or, as I would soon do, explore similarities that were less than noble. When difference was allowed back in, it avoided the shared struggles of class and gender and replaced them with concepts of historical contingency.

Although the self-flagellation that nearly drove ethnography to extinction eventually ran its course, the *Writing Culture* counter-Orientalist ethos profoundly transformed the expectations and demands of institutions that mold, employ, and fund anthropologists.[3] It problematized intensive fieldwork and intimate knowledge and denounced ethnographic realism as outmoded empiricism. Linguistic competence and deep engagement wore the stain of unfashionable, undertheorized area studies. Research was pared to the minimum necessary to demonstrate deftness with continental theory. Ethnographic refusal gave way to grounded ethnography, no longer an oxymoron, but one way among many of doing anthropology, and not the most career advancing. In a methodological reversal, the field became a laboratory to test prepacked concepts and approaches rather than a place of difference in which to find or formulate them. Difference became equated with essence, and young ethnographers were invited to move beyond cultural particulars and toward human commonalities, tacitly understood as those that make informants—and ourselves—look good.

I did not suit this intellectual orthodoxy; neither did the field site that enticed me. But this was where the discipline was heading; I dared not diverge. Then Dresch dismissed the zeitgeist in summary fashion. He proudly called himself an Orientalist, noting the profound body of European scholarship that Edward Said had elided with American journalism. British anthropology, he noted, had never relied on concepts of culture in the first place. Dresch (1995) himself would soon write against the notion in a sophisticated analysis of multiculturalism on American university campuses. Documenting the ad absurdum fragmenting of identity, he demonstrates the derailing and supplanting of class-based collective identification and action with naturalized "cultures" that are public yet uncontestable, both celebrated and suspect, and whose formal or normative equality "ignores the inequalities both within sets and between them" (71). Dresch sidesteps the now-standard American social scientific strategy for relating cultural and economic categories: the discourse of intersectionality. He need not have. Here groups may not be formally separated in opposition or apposition, but they remain enmeshed in a "rhetoric of pure difference" (78). Treating socially constructed and material differences as equivalent variables further reifies the social and leaves imbalances of wealth and power unchallenged. In the anthropology of the Middle East, free-floating culture emerges, couched in other terms, in discussions of affect, embodiment, and piety. In both cases, identity replaces politics.[4]

New to Britain and its academic conventions, I reacted to Dresch's apostasy with what can only be described as *culture* shock (to use that verboten term). It was itself, as we say, an ethnographic experience that shook my firm grounding in academia's self-assured deconstructive uncertainty. I recovered and found myself freed to recognize, validate, and instrumentalize my discomfort with the key assumption of the new ethos: the ethnographer as privileged white male working with—and taking advantage of—vulnerable marginals. I was a homegrown subaltern, a white ethnic woman from a working-class background, postindustrial rather than postcolonial, raised in the cultural and economic backwater of rust-belt Trenton, New Jersey. I felt like an alien among the "we" who needed to reform—or abandon—the supposedly neocolonial ethnographic endeavor.[5]

Vulnerabilities and Truths in the Field(s)

Contemporary ethnography presupposes the relatively powerful anthropologist. The now-established anthropology of elites never fully problematized this tenet; those "studying up" (Nader 1969) and "studying sideways" (Hannerz 2010) rarely concede vulnerability, and they treat problems of access as obstacles rather than signs.[6] The shift in ethnographic ethos from "rapport" to "complicity" and, more recently, "collaboration" merely aims to equalize colonial anthropology's power imbalance (Marcus 1997, 2012; Samuel Collins et al. 2017). Activist anthropology aside, one wonders how often the assumption of reciprocity underlying the new language masks a debt that can rarely be repaid. For some fields, vulnerability demands attention; anthropologists who write about the aftermaths of conflict speak poignantly of secondary trauma (Sanford 2008). Those who share firsthand experience of violence, as Swedenburg (1995, 25) notes, risk deflecting attention away from their relative privilege and toward their own victimhood, rather than that of their interlocutors. Beyond realms of war and genocide, vulnerability emerges not as a fieldworker's subject position but as an ethnographic strategy. Authors opt to share, writing in sentiments of grief (Behar 1996) or embracing solidarity (Davids 2014). They are exposed not to their interlocutors but to their readers, two audiences that are generally assumed to be separate.

Published ethnographies attuned to affect and reflexivity deal with psychological, rather than structural, vulnerability. The latter typically appears outside peer review venues, in confessional blog posts and newsletter entries that recount young women ethnographers' experience of sexual harassment and violence and the denial they face upon reporting it to university administration and academic advisors, and call for institutionalized—rather than ethnographic—coping strategies (Evans 2017; Huang 2016; B. Williams 2017; Watt 2018). Here anthropologists attribute vulnerability to gender, age, or racial position, or to the activist dimensions of their projects (Berry et al. 2017). They call for approaches to writing about gendered violence that do not merely reinforce negative tropes. By invoking gender, generational, and racial hierarchies, they challenge the assumption of vulnerability as voluntary (A. Johnson 2017) but obscure its ubiquity.

Fieldwork's more general structural imbalance is rarely acknowledged beyond the gratitude of preface acknowledgments, let alone analyzed as a central problematic. Yet none other than that quintessential aristocratic white male colonial ethnographer, Bronislaw Malinowski, experienced a frustrating disempowerment, shockingly revealed in his posthumously published field journal, *A Diary in the Strict Sense of the Term* (1989). The diary's appearance prompted a flurry of anthropological commentary, with some censuring the unauthorized access it provided to their professional back stage (Forge 1967; Powdermaker 1967; Hogbin 1968; Richards 1968) and others indicting (Geertz 1967; Harris 1967; Hsu 1979) or exonerating (Powdermaker 1970; Mair 1980; Leach 1980) Malinowski for alleged churlishness, elitism, and racism.

Most discussions turn on Malinowski's subjective state: his isolation, alienation, personal grief, sexual yearnings, and romantic anxieties. Some justify the diary as a psychic safety valve enabling ethnographic empathy (Powdermaker 1967; Stocking 1968) or the discovery of the savage within (Powdermaker 1970, 347; Pitt-Rivers 1971, xxiii). More recent treatments rehabilitate the work as a disciplinary history, a groundbreaking literary innovation, an exercise in self-fashioning, and—with some irony—a precursor to reflexive anthropology (Clifford 1986; Kracke 1987; Geertz 1988; Rapport 1997; Behar 1999; Landsdown 2014). None address, except in passing, issues of access.

The diary's mix of imperious observation and self-castigation certainly makes for uncomfortable reading. The father of intensive fieldwork referred to his informants (for surely that is the appropriate term here) in disdainful, de-rogatory terms that belie his humanist ethnographic writing, sometimes criticized for rendering the Trobriand villagers virtual Europeans. A great deal of speculation attempts to reconcile this contradiction. Commentators invariably project their image of Malinowski as an inescapably elite European male, with all the attendant privileges, onto Trobriand context: "He was an outsider, even a *Sahib*. He lived in the middle of the village, but in a tent. He had servants, had means to pay his informants, was titled and treated as someone possessing a certain social rank" (Symmons-Symonolewicz 1982, 98; emphasis in original). Anthropologists appear tone-deaf to the Trobriand context, despite Malinowski's frank admissions. The diary's most cringe-inducing passages follow confessions of interpersonal impotence; Malinowski reacts with the petulance of a man unaccustomed to social irrelevance. That gifts of tobacco did not always yield the information he sought in return is evident in a startling and widely cited reference to Conrad: "At moments I was furious at them, particularly because after I gave them their portions of tobacco they all went away. On the whole my feelings toward the natives are decidedly tending to '*Exterminate the Brutes*'" (1989, 69; emphasis in original). The diary's natives frequently elude or lie to the ethnographer, engendering a "characteristic helplessness" that he identifies as "one of the main difficulties of my work" (176). Elsewhere, Malinowski envies fellow European expatriates—missionaries and colonial officials—for squandering their leverage: "These fellow have such fabulous *opportunities*—the sea, ships, the *jungle*, power over the natives—and don't do a thing!" (167; emphasis in original).

Many decades and ethnographic approaches later, I was off to conduct fieldwork among "natives" who had no need or desire for commodity gifts and whose social and economic capital often exceeded my own. I repressed an Oxford don's pointed question, "What makes you think they'll talk to you?" and got on with departure preparations, but I knew that choice of affect was illusory. I would experience a helplessness of context rather than character. I had one psychosocial advantage over Malinowski: I was used to low relative status. Beyond positionality, Dresch prepared me for a Middle East where vulnerability is a structural given, one where proficiency in the native language is deemed suspicious, private worlds of cultural difference are more closeted than political machinations, and degrees of access do not merely block or deliver data but reveal power relations. Despite the *Writing Culture* construct of anthropologist as neocolonial agent, I anticipated my relative weakness, given that, as Dresch puts it, I was working with people who "retained autonomy" (2000a, 124). Given my choice to examine processes of distinction among the urban elites of Damascus, it was certainly true that not only degrees of access but the very contours of experience would be "largely set by one's hosts, the forms of interaction are under their control, and where this is not so, little comes of it" (124).

Ethnography, Dresch maintained, is not about the data. Extending his insight, I argued that "a closed door can be as telling as an open one, a snub as significant as a kiss" (2004, 65). Despite the diagnostic richness of exclusion, the specter of denied access has haunted all my fieldwork in Syria. Dresch, too, seems unconvinced that "information" itself is less important; he dubs the more forthcoming society of Ghana, with less irony than I might hope for, a "fieldworker's paradise" (2000a, 112). Preparing for dissertation fieldwork, I wondered where I would find the requisite "protected space" amid the social flux of urban life. Clearly, there would be sites (or nodes) that I would have to carefully balance. Angst over giving offense or failing to amuse filled my notebooks. My first project, a study of heritage politics in Damascus, required a wide range of contacts across professions and networks, but it also relied on social circles for inclusion in private, semiprivate, and even public events. My current work on the television drama industry sparked fears of being thrown off film locations as a nuisance. An interlocutor turned close friend once quipped, "She never says no," given my ready acceptance of invitations. I felt compelled to grasp every hand, and I feared that existing relationships would turn sour, as they often did among Syrians themselves, strained under myriad pressures. My "go with the flow" fear of disappointing led me to participate, as a reluctant contestant, in a humiliating—but also sociologically revealing—beauty contest on the eve of my thirtieth birthday. More recently, it compelled a visit to a war zone, facilitated though security networks, for preproduction meetings on a drama serial to be shot in Damascus.

A city of mirrors deflecting blame and complicity, the part-world of Damascus 1992 offered me subject positions different from those I might have inhabited in Dresch's Yemen. In Syria, an authoritarian polity, the private knowledge Dresch found most protected merged with the political. Every utterance had implications, and everyone was potentially dangerous. My foreignness, what Dresch recognizes as the Middle East anthropologist's default position, endured. But I shifted from dangerous interloper to innocuous sympathetic ear as I moved, by "patiently listening in sometimes difficult settings" (2000a, 122), into realms of cultural intimacy, managing to evoke, through oblique reference, what was rarely discussed but keenly experienced.

Fascinated by linkages between social identities and urban spaces and imaginaries, I hoped to trace a shift, occurring globally in different ways and to varying degrees, from identities based on kin or production to those based on aesthetics and consumption. What I found was not so much a replacement but a reworking of the former in terms of the latter. New patterns of consumption emerged as the Syrian state rolled back constraints on foreign imports and local industry and as the nation shifted orientation after the collapse of the Soviet Union. I sought to understand how the waning Ba'thist ideology, and its stated goal of a classless citizenry, was giving way to new modes of social distinction. Class, regional, and religious differences were still taboo, even as they ascended. Early in my fieldwork, I discovered that the city, its past, and its people featured prominently in new and old forms of public culture—in restaurants, cafés, art exhibits, written memoirs, and television dramas. These celebratory, seemingly innocuous—high-brow, folkloric, or kitschy—representations of the local were hotly contested. Mere mention of projects to preserve or attempts to represent the Old City of Damascus unleashed a torrent of dangerous discourse, a bitter rhetoric of distinction that moved far beyond a discussion of architectural restoration and seemed an overreaction to a fictional TV serial.

This vitriol rarely targeted the leadership, and not merely because it was dangerous to do so; the regime was tacitly understood as ultimately culpable. This was the great unsaid, as Dresch might put it, a silence some analysts read as support for dictatorship. Instead, a "language of competitive disadvantage" (Dresch 1995, 67) comprised political critique. Syrians' "poetics of accusation" most often implicated those believed to benefit from the status quo, the complicit other, whose identity shifted from speaker to speaker (Salamandra 2004, 19–24). Truth was here, the property of one interlocutor, but it was turned upside down by another.

Perceptions of sectarian privilege grew over four decades of al-Asad kleptocracy, under a cloak of socialist secularism. For a small segment of Syria's heterodox Shi'i 'Alawi community—an estimated ten to fifteen percent of the prewar population—a stunning reversal of fortunes occurred within living memory. Before the 1960s, elite urban families—primarily from Damascus and Aleppo—dominated political and economic life in Syria. They had little in common with the majority population, beyond a Sunni Muslim affiliation. With the Ba'th Party takeover in 1963, political power shifted to a largely rural military elite, among whom 'Alawis dominated. Sunni Damascenes and Aleppines were systematically displaced from key positions. The urban bourgeoisie was forced to do business with their erstwhile social inferiors: 'Alawis from coastal villages whose daughters had only recently served in Damascene households. A cold peace ensued, anchored by shared interests but laced with mutual resentment. Each group assumed the other's advantage: 'Alawis pointed to the enduring prosperity of Damascus's "merchant princes," Damascenes to well-placed 'Alawis' control of licensing and smuggling. The majority of 'Alawis suffered an inaccurate association with privilege. Urban Sunnis sometimes acknowledged that many 'Alawis had remained impoverished. Nevertheless, the claim that "all 'Alawis are connected to power" had become a frequent refrain. More than a reference to religious belief, the term "'Alawi" connoted class and region; avowed atheists hurled sectarian accusations against each other (Salamandra 2013).

Contentious sectarian discourse emerged as interlocutors assimilated my seemingly innocuous presence: a diminutive young woman who listened intently and asked few questions. Their desire to be heard, at a time when few outsiders cared to listen, overrode their reluctance to air dirty laundry. It also neutralized the fear that much academic literature on Syria depicts as that society's most salient feature.[7] I had entered a realm of cultural intimacy, a space in which unpleasant yet commonly held images of self and other are shared (Herzfeld 2005). I bore, I believed, a responsibility to convey rather than conceal this multiplicity of positions. If our aim is to depict culture as self-consciously constructed, as negotiated and contested, then we must give voice to conflict and disagreement. What better way to combat stereotypes of essentialized culture than to reveal, for instance, secular Muslims debating the link between Islam and violence, as my interlocutors often do?

In translating this contestation and its logics to an academic audience, I faced an unnerving exposure. "The field is a myth," Dresch used to quip. One writes for a handful of experts. Yet our digital age provides no rarified scholarly cubbyholes; dissemination is academic survival. Ethnography garners reputation without having been read. Like the Damascus elites I worked among, colleagues may not know one's work, but they know of it. My research entered a fraught field of representational politics; US-based academics who teach and write about the Middle East work against a backdrop of negative imagery and sensationalism. We balance the treatment of very real difference with a knowledge that research may feed long-held and newly reinvigorated prejudices that have far-reaching and disastrous policy implications. Representations can be weaponized, and anthropologists who deal in "culture" operate at the front lines of a relentless war of images. Arab cultural producers—who critique their societies in writing, film, or song—clash with Arab Americans, activists, and academics battling bigotry (Abu-Lughod 2002; Shryock 1998, 2004a).[8] Anthropologists regularly witness—and are drawn into—heated debates after screenings or performances; the dilemma is continual and laden with real-world repercussions. The strategy we most often adopt is to avoid the very headline-grabbing topics undergraduate students often ask us to explain, and leave underexplored vast arenas where we might make helpful interventions. Historically inflected, accessible ethnographies of so-called honor killings, or the debates surrounding the patriarchal underpinnings of personal status laws, would go a long way toward countering the simplistic stereotypes of Muslim misogyny that our current pedagogical tools are ill-equipped to challenge.[9] We bear a responsibility to respect even those interlocutors who appear most like ourselves. We should treat, say, educated upper-middle-class intellectuals as authentic voices, no matter how "unrepresentative," and however jarring their elitism. Can we justly dismiss indigenous social critique as postcolonial auto-Orientalism? As we avoid essentialisms, we risk denying our interlocutors' rights to their own.

I assumed I would avoid accusations of essentialism, as my focus on social distinction through discourses and processes of consumption in Damascus was "modern," indeed contemporary. Sensitive to accusations of timelessness, I eschewed continuities that might have enriched my analysis and enhanced my reputation among Syrian readers for whom, Dresch would counsel, history lives. For example, I invoked a nostalgic text simulating a walk through Damascus but neglected its contribution to an "uninterrupted tradition of intertextual cityscapes" that dates to the twelfth century (Sajdi 2018, 6). There seemed little risk of primitivizing urban cosmopolitans merely by describing them (Dresch 2000a, 119). I depicted contestation as decidedly contemporary and offered an understanding—I hesitate to call it a theory—of sectarianism as an intersection of class, region, and religious affiliation, positing the latter as its least significant component. I attributed the sectarian-inflected poetics of accusation to the contradiction between the Ba'th Party's stated project to rid Syria of subnational distinctions and the al-Asad regime's policies that exacerbated them. A veneer of plurality in official government thinly concealed a security apparatus dominated by 'Alawis, its upper level functionaries controlling access to resources and, with liberalization, business licensing. This profound irony was not lost on the Syrians I came to know. Noting a deliberate divide-and-rule policy, they nevertheless fell under its sway. My writing pointed to the implications of both perceptual and real cleavages and warned against confusing a strong state with a sentiment of nationhood. The alienation expressed in and through popular culture in Damascus evinced the failure of Syria's national project (Salamandra 1998, 2004).

"Wilderness of Mirrors" argues that fieldwork in and ethnography on the Middle East are typically regarded as suspect (Dresch 2000a, 110–11, 120–21).

My Oxford examiners certainly found my dissertation implausible; they "referred" it for rewriting. One argued that it overstated sectarianism; the other wondered why it omitted "Islam" as an explanatory system. The degree of discord in everyday life appeared inconceivable; had I successfully penetrated Syrian society, I would have recognized a "social agreement" undergirding superficial contention. Like Oxford student banter, invidious discourse could not have been as vicious as a newcomer hears it. My account, they argued, read as if drawn from a brief visit to the field; structures of belonging—not those of disagreement (Dresch 2000a, 118)—would have become apparent with intense engagement. By depicting social life as deeply contentious, I had failed in my "anthropological duty of empathy."

My revision filled in literature gaps but retained contention. It appeared in 2004 as *A New Old Damascus: Authenticity and Distinction in Urban Syria*, the first English-language ethnography of a Syrian city and one of the earliest on elite consumption practices and mass-mediated culture.[10] Dresch enabled this career experiment; a more conventional or cautious advisor might have warned me against a site and subject that had attracted so little scholarly interest. Looking back, my naivety, even if ultimately serendipitous, astounds me. I thought I was carving a niche; instead I entered an academic isolate where contemporary anthropological concerns fit uneasily. How, for example, could I reconcile postcolonial theory with a city that remembers colonialism as four hundred years of Ottoman oppression? Indeed, early readers' skepticism suggested that a more strategically chosen place and project might have been warranted. The quotidian experience of sectarianism dissatisfied Syrian specialists preoccupied with authoritarianism and its persistence. My non-regime focus was deemed insufficiently attentive to "politics." Nor did my book jibe with then-fashionable accounts of domination and resistance; no easily identifiable oppressors appeared among my vying groups. In addition to complicating academic understandings of sectarianism, I examined the vagaries of what was soon to become ubiquitous: neoliberalism. A chapter on competitive consumption among elite women, in which I analyzed new leisure sites and practices, challenged depictions of female solidarity, and it faced pointed hostility as a result. I noted the refashioning of patriarchal structures in hotel resorts and health clubs, and how enduring forms of family status and prestige were reworked in the marriage market. More than one critic told me, "It seems you just hated them." Pushback came from Western academics; Syrian readers (even those featured) and colleagues at Lebanese American University found it unobjectionable. A Lebanese sociologist published two versions of my gender material in his edited volumes (Salamandra 2006, 2010). Was this auto-exoticism? I depicted not the urban poor, whom they might see as backward, but their neighbors and relatives.[11]

In hindsight, the antipathy that greeted my Damascus research seems unsurprising. The anthropology of elites, despite pioneering efforts decades earlier, had yet to consolidate. The journal *Public Culture* launched in 1989, but the movement it fostered had not penetrated work on Arab societies. Extant ethnographies of Arab cities focused on poor urban quarters, and most resembled transplanted village studies, their field sites confined to a few dozen homes. As a female ethnographer, I had no business ignoring the kitchen; a senior colleague suggested more fieldwork, as I had provided little sense of family life. Assumptions of public and private dichotomies still reigned, and the mass culture that blurs them was not yet considered an appropriate area for anthropological investigation. At a more visceral level, invidiousness is difficult to stomach, no matter how sensitively portrayed.

As more work appeared on Middle Eastern cultures of consumption, *A New Old Damascus* appeared more harbinger than outlier. Mass-mediated and popular culture ethnographies now abound. Fieldworkers turn attention toward consumption practices in the neoliberal urban experience of far-flung part-worlds of Amman (Tobin 2016), Beirut (Deeb and Harb 2013), Cairo (Abu-Lughod 2005; Peterson 2011; Singerman and Amar 2006; Van Nieuwkerk 2013), Dubai (Kanna 2011), Fez (Spadola 2013), Riyadh (Le Renard 2014), and Tehran (Mahdavi 2008; Varzi 2006). The politics of heritage and gentrification surface in Beirut (Sawalha 2010), Samarra (Panjwani 2012), and Istanbul (Mills 2010); they persist in Damascus (Totah 2014). Syria itself is no longer an ethnographic backwater; a growing number of ethnographers explore social life in prewar Syrian cities (Gabiam 2016; Rabo 2005; Shannon 2006; Gallagher 2012). Through working with elite cultural producers, I have undertaken forms of collaboration that are now widely advocated (Ginsburg 2005; Marcus 2012; Samuel Collins et al. 2017). This involves more than my interlocutors reading what I write, a practice facilitated by a new Syrian-operated online Arabic platform translating scholarship and journalism.[12] I also contribute to the Syrian drama industry's nascent critical journalism (Salamandra 2017).

Contention, too, is no longer controversial. It seems no coincidence that ethnographies of internecine, sectarian discord in Lebanon and Syria appeared during the Syrian War (Kastrinou 2016; Monroe 2016; Nucho 2016). It has become tragically apparent that regime-instigated social and religious contestation was not born of the current conflict; a battle of narratives about past, present, and future long predated the resort to arms. Indeed, fieldwork's Rashomon effect has haunted me throughout Syria's uprising turned civil-and-proxy war. Contradictory visions and competing truths have turned tragically violent; the death toll exceeds half a million, and much of the nation lies in ruins. Conflict is perhaps the most scandalous of continuities, but it can no longer be written out of our accounts of social worlds. Class, regional, and sectarian discord also inform the works of Syria's leading cultural producers, television drama creators, who are the subject of my current research. This work traces a more hopeful legacy and an enduring one: that of critique.

Continuities of Critique

The authoritarian structures that channel grievances into heritage politics also reroute sociopolitical critique into fiction television. Since the early 2000s, neoliberalism and authoritarianism inadvertently conspired to produce what has become known as Syria's "drama outpouring" (*al-fawra al-dramiyya*). While retaining its censorship apparatus, the Ba'thist state instituted privatization, spurring the growth of drama production companies. Pan-Arab satellite entertainment networks such as the Saudi-owned MBC and Dubai TV fill their long broadcast hours with Syrian serials. A distinctly Syrian form has emerged, shaped through competition with an established Egyptian industry and newer Gulf and Turkish ones. Syrian drama production endures today, holding steady at roughly twenty-five serials a year, half its prewar production level.[13] Like leisure sites and consumption practices, fictional television, in Syria—and across the Arab world's satellite television footprint—is where politics happens.

Syrian TV drama harnesses critical impulses that, in a less draconian polity, might have animated party politics, journalism, or academia. Restrictions on freedom of expression exercised over half a century have curtailed the development of an independent press. Privatization during the 2000s broke the government's monopoly of ownership but not its control; news media entrepreneurs often enjoy close regime links. Critical research in the social sciences and humanities has been similarly constrained, with academics not merely censored but also overworked, underfunded, and pressured to join the Ba'th Party. Neither accessible nor robust, "higher" art produces few public intellectuals. The country has meager cinema, theater, and book industries; television serials are the largest employer of and platform for artists and intellectuals. Prominent novelists and poets whose books are banned write most TV screenplays. The result is a sophisticated product imbued with philosophical musings and political positions.

In this differentiated industry, blockbusters like the multiseason historical *Neighborhood Gate* (*Bab al-hara*) generate enough revenue to fund the equivalent of American "quality drama," a genre Arab audiences know as "contemporary social drama" (*al-drama al-ijtima'iya al-mu'assira*) and one in which Syrian producers excel. Social realist serials set in informal settlements—the very regions that have experienced most wartime ferment and ferocious repression—form the core concern of my ethnography in progress. A (conservatively) estimated forty percent of prewar Damascus dwellers lived in "haphazard neighborhoods" (*al-harat al-'ashwa'iya*), as they are referred to in Arabic (UNEP 2006, 32). Also called *mukhalafat*—literally "violations"—these squalid, often illegal neighborhoods share the afflictions of (sub)urban poverty in much of the Global South: deficient infrastructure, crowding, hazardous construction, inadequate services, unemployment, and crime. Like informal districts elsewhere, they house recent migrants from the countryside, represented in drama through rural dialects, clothing, and the drinking of maté, a practice brought by emigrants returning from late Ottoman-era sojourns in Latin America. For many, these settlements become not a first stop to urban integration but barriers to upward, or inward, mobility. Drama creators depict haphazard neighborhoods as sites of crime and social dissolution, in contrast to traditional or popular neighborhoods (*harat sha'abiyya*), which they associate with high moral values and contiguous social relations. The informal settlements are shown not as examples of enduring tradition but as products of state corruption and neglect.

My core case study, Allaith Hajjo's *Waiting* (*Al-Intizar*), which originally aired in 2006, is now hailed as a classic, even by drama's harshest local critics (figs. 3.1–3.3). Set in the dilapidated suburb of Dweila'a, it gave birth to what became known as the haphazard subgenre. Works in this vein include numerous evocations of urban blight, including Marwan Barakat's *Summer Cloud* (*Sahabat saif*, 2009), which dealt with the plight of Iraqi and Palestinian refugees, child sexual abuse, and cybercrime; Samir Hussain's *City Dregs* (*Qa' al-madina*, 2009), which begins and ends with floods devastating already desperate lives; Samer Barqawi's *After the Fall* (*Ba'd al-suqut*, 2010), which depicts efforts to rescue tenants caught in the rubble of a collapsed building; Muthanna Subah's *Medium Sugar* (*Sukkur wasat*), set in 2010 but produced in 2012, which posits the haphazard neighborhood and its pathologies as precursors to the uprising; and Rami Hanna's *Tomorrow We'll Meet* (*Ghadan naltaqi*, 2015), in which the settlement becomes a refugee neighborhood in Beirut.

Screenwriter Najeeb Nusair recently told me his *Waiting* was an alarm that went unheeded.[14] Some Syrians would dismiss this as hindsight self-justification. Critics, themselves often Syrian intellectuals, see censorship as a smoke screen obscuring relations of near total complicity. Drama, they argue, acts as a safety valve; its trivializing critique promotes acquiescence. The anti-regime uprising of 2011 seemingly broke the "wall of fear" guarding the regime's control and deployment of mediated culture. Youthful satirists who

Figure 3.1. Setting a scene in the informal settlement of Dweila'a (2006, courtesy of Wael Sweidani).

Figure 3.2. *Waiting*'s Allaith Hajjo directs veteran Syrian actors Doha al-Dibs and Omar Hajjo (2006, courtesy of Wael Sweidani).

Figure 3.3. Allaith Hajjo with actors Qamar Khalif and Nasrine Tafish (2006, courtesy of Wael Sweidani).

flooded the Internet with caustic caricatures were said to have moved beyond the complicity of safety valve drama. This notion of rupture, articulated in the international media and echoed in scholarly discussions, attributed no role to Syria's established drama creators. Celebrations of this new dissident culture assumed the "traditional opposition," which includes many television makers, had been marginal to the protest movement. My work complicates this neat separation and counters the assumption that state-controlled drama does the regime's bidding. I argue instead that despite their limited autonomy, Syria's TV creators developed a distinctly dark aesthetic that equipped Syrian audiences, including anti-regime activists, with a potent visual language of critique. Attentive to continuity, I demonstrate how professional drama makers had in previous decades nudged along a moving barrier to freedom of expression (Salamandra 2012, 2015).

Satire pushed the moving wall of fear the furthest. This is where the clearest linkages appear between officially permitted and dissident culture. Director Allaith Hajjo's sketch program, *Spotlight* (*Buq'at Daw'*), provides a case in point. Commissioned in 2001 by a production company with strong links to the regime, the program often found itself chastised or censored for stinging lampoons of sectarianism, Islamic revivalism, and state corruption. Its formal connection to power was obvious, but this association never blunted the show's popularity. "Just like on *Spotlight*" became a catchphrase for the everyday absurd. One sketch enjoys an enduring wartime afterlife. "Spray Can Man" (*al-Rajul al-Bakhakh*) of 2008 opens with a ticking bomb graphic. The frustrated hero, a washed-up athlete living in a hovel, vents his frustrations on walls around Damascus, twisting regime slogans into acts of resistance; "patience is the key to remedy" he renders as "patience is the key to poverty." When he plasters "get off our backs" (*hillu 'anna*) on what appears to be an intelligence service (*mukhabarat*) building, agents invite Spray Can Man to a "civilized, democratic dialogue." The hero turns himself in but finds a whitewashed prison cell equipped with dozens of spray paint cans in place of a platform to address the nation. Numerous protestors from the early days of the 2011 uprising took inspiration from this fictional character. The Dubai-based oppositional channel Orient aired a news story interspersing scenes from the sketch with real-life graffiti artists. Actor and writer 'Adnan Zira'i, Spray Can Man's creator, was arrested in 2012, and he remains in detention. Officials purportedly charged that his *Spotlight* sketch incited rebellion. If the safety valve theory accurately accounted for the flourishing of drama in Syria, the regime's strategy has clearly backfired.

"Spray Can Man" evokes official manipulation of reformist language to expose its hollowness. I argue that television creators of all dramatic genres routinely do this. Largely progressive, secular, and urban, they see themselves as upholding tenets of a modernizing project the Ba'thist regime abandoned, first in practice, more recently in rhetoric. In 2000, many welcomed Bashar al-Asad as a potential modernizer, and they worked through state strictures and institutions in hopes of reforming the regime. Even those who benefited from the drama outpouring grew disillusioned. The war has fractured the drama field, or the field of art (*majal al-fann*, as Syrians call it), much as it has all of Syria. As the nation's public intellectuals, television creators are avidly followed and pressured to take public stances. The first years of the conflict witnessed a barrage of statements, petitions, interviews, and campaigns. Those who supported the protests, even faintly, were harassed by al-Asad loyalists. Those demanding the regime's demise faced assault and incarceration. Many fled into exile. Those who backed the regime or failed to show support for the opposition found themselves plastered on an internet "Wall of Shame." A few prominent actors—and one director and screenwriting team—have maintained support for al-Asad throughout the war. Yet most screenwriters— the industry's "brains"—have emerged in opposition, though few joined the organized groups that they found either too "Ba'thist" or "Islamist" for their comfort.

If I was once castigated for "hating" my elite Damascene interlocutors, I now face accusations of complicity with drama makers alleged to be doing the regime's bidding. Despite years of documenting the al-Asad dictatorship's deleterious effects on Syrian society, my criticism of the regime is now dismissed as "lip service" given that I attempt to understand rather than condemn anti-revolutionary perspectives. Nuances of voice give way to wartime polarization. To evoke a perception, I have learned, is to be associated with it. Merely acknowledging minority fears of post-Asad Islamization or sectarian retaliation signifies a reactionary positioning. One must pretend these voices do not exist or label them as internal enemies of the Syrian people. Academics linked to contemporary Syria through research and sentiment are deeply implicated; our positions, like those of our subjects, span the spectrum from its black-and-white extremes to its ambivalent middle ground. Our perspectives are colored, I believe, by our points of access. I have noticed, in published analyses as in more frequent social media posts and private conversations, that colleagues who work among Sunni Muslim clerics and Islamic institutions are less concerned by the Islamization of the opposition and, potentially, the post-Asad polity. Those whose research deals with minorities are uncomfortable with the possibility of Sunni dominance. Those exploring the work of young, secular, media-savvy activists see them as the core of a conflict that is primarily a revolt against tyranny. Questioning the opposition's vision of Syria's future has become tantamount to support for the Ba'thist regime. Alternatively, unreserved support for the opposition invites accusations of naivety, of denying the opposition's atrocities and anti-democratic and Islamic extremist elements.

Interior states are notoriously difficult to account for, and behavior—particularly in a police state—is complex and ambiguous. I disagree with those artists who advocate repressing the opposition, but I do not dismiss their fears as rationalizing weapons of the strong. I understand their various perspectives intimately and am unable to condemn them; I have mourned the death of friends who publicly backed the regime's repression as I have those who fought against it valiantly. I continue to view most of the drama makers I worked with as honest critics of dictatorship, given the degree of dissatisfaction they often expressed over my years of intense listening, the hallmark of Dresch's training. Yet many were wary of protest, fearing post-Asad Islamization or sectarian retaliation. Representing their positions without condemning them—exhibiting the anthropological empathy I earlier was advised was my duty—now appears a problematic analytical stance. What, then, are the ethics of continued engagement or of abandonment? I am not alone in these musings. My published essay (Salamandra 2014) on the politics of position taking in the Syrian conflict has received little public citation but much private gratitude.

The Continuity of Vulnerability

In relation to a quite different context, Dresch wrote that much field experience, if accurately conveyed, appears simply wrong in print (2000a, 121). Likewise, whatever one does in the field may appear off. I move through the space of fieldwork carefully, and I hope that the stories I am able to tell convey something real about the Syrians who open their lives to me. That this is both a privilege and a burden is even more true amid devastation. After I hosted Allaith Hajjo in New York in August 2016, he invited me to Damascus during the break between semesters. I hoped this was a polite but insincere "Damascene invitation." I should have known better; Allaith is from Aleppo, a city renowned for blunt "heavy bloodedness." I sent him my passport scan and photos, taken aback by his speedy follow-up. Soon the visa I thought would never be granted awaited me in Lebanon. My attempts to wiggle out of the trip—"I might not be able to make it for the New Year"—sparked indignation. The choice was clear, if not simple: I could vacation in a war zone, or risk losing a key interlocutor. I flew to Beirut in late December, still suspecting—secretly hoping—that flaws in the paperwork would stop me at the border. I worried how Syrians would receive me after their world had changed so drastically. I feared my mere presence might compromise them. I braced myself for potential hostility. Physical safety never worried me. During the filming of *Waiting*, Allaith had forbidden me from coming to the shantytown location on my own in a taxi, forcing me to rise at the crack of dawn each day to catch the crew van, so I knew he would have canceled my visit if security had been at issue. As for the mukhabarat, they called to ask if I had arrived safely.

A pall of weariness covered the city; it seemed colder and grayer than I had ever seen it. I wondered if my impression had been colored by *Regret (Al-Nadm)*, Allaith's latest serial, where in a reversal of filmic convention, Damascus of 2016 appears in black and white, and flashbacks to 2003 in color. Allaith told me the stark gray palate signifies not merely the grimness of war but the polarizing of opinion and position and the rending of social relations. I stuck mostly to private and cosseted spaces, but a shopping trip to the Takiyya Sulaymaniyya, a sixteenth-century mosque complex transformed into a craft market, revealed the absurd denial of what, despite the faint din of bombing in the suburbs, was still the "Damascus bubble." The shops were all open with no sign of customers. Those lining one side of the main passageway had recently been renovated; they were well lit and heated, their displays carefully staged. Each storefront featured a young artisan at work on eye-catching handicrafts. The cold, dark shops opposite them sold dusty silver jewelry indifferently piled. My companion, running late, sighed with relief when she saw me empty handed:

"I'm so glad I arrived before you bought anything from those new shops; they're all part of the First Lady's pet project."

Syrians sometimes assume that drama creators who left the country sympathize with the opposition and that those who remain are pro-regime. Even before returning to Damascus, I questioned this neatness of position. I arrived to find private utterances unsurprisingly ambiguous. The debates I heard in still-vibrant restaurants and cafés, and in the homes of old interlocutors, suggested anything but consensus. Positions fall along a finely grained and unstable continuum. Industry figures some dismiss as *shabbiha*—regime thugs— accuse others of being the same. Allegations swirled during a weekend dinner at a new, well-appointed restaurant. TV industry figures and their friends criticized a star actor, former regime intimate, now exiled dissident, who had just given an interview on a pan-Arab satellite entertainment network.

—He talked about his harsh ['Alawi] father and affectionate [Damascene Sunni] mother!

—He and X [TV director in exile] are pandering to the Islamists.

—Not true! X hates Islam personally but knows it's necessary to give voice to the majority.

—On the contrary, we elites need to raise the people up to our level, not sink to theirs.

—He left the country and is now talking against it.

—But his son, a little boy, was threatened! If it were my son, I'd be saying all that [denouncing the regime] and more.

—Before he left, he was even at the meeting with the president, the one where *I* told the president that opposition actors X and Y ought to be here in the country.

—But now you're calling him a traitor [*khayan*]!

—We never used that word!

—But that's what you meant.

—Look, we reached the stage when ideas [of Islamists] are more dangerous than guns.

—How can you say that, with five hundred thousand people dead?

Heated argument does not always preclude cordiality or cooperation. My dinner companions stressed, at the end of the evening, that I had seen for myself how they can air conflicting views and maintain civility. Allaith himself maintains relationships across the civil war divide, and this deft diplomacy appears in his work. For the serial *We'll Return Shortly* (*Sa na'ud ba'd qalil*), filmed in Lebanon in 2015, he brought together prominent, vocal actors, the pro-regime

Durayd Lahham and oppositional Kinda Alloush, as characters exchanging their players' own viewpoints.

Plans were in place for a serial the press heralded as a sequel to *Waiting*. It was not quite that but rather, as drama critic Maher Mansour put it, a response.[15] This was exciting. I had thought of this as a courtesy visit, but here was an update of my key case study. *Waiting*'s coauthors, and many of its cast and crew members, would join Allaith on *Fawda* (*Chaos*), a serial depicting the shantification of middle-class Damascus as a result of wartime displacement. But the production company was not *Waiting*'s small, congenial outfit. The sizable, well-connected Syria International (SAPI), the company that had produced *Spotlight*, owned this project. SAPI's resources promised high production values and salaries commensurate with Syria's acute inflation. During my brief visit, I attended preproduction meetings, as well as casting and location scouting, and the dour atmosphere was in obvious contrast to the lighthearted teasing and laughter I remembered from the filming of *Waiting*. Budget delays and quibbles over actors provoked general anxiety. This was SAPI, after all, whose notorious director would be loath to conciliate. Allaith dismissed this obstinance as characteristic posturing, certain that appropriate funds and his own casting choices would come through in the end. I chalked up the team's vexation to the burdens of war and the crisis mode that very often pervades media production (Powdermaker 1950).

In the months following my visit, *Chaos* reached a stalemate. Allaith refused to continue with SAPI. The company held rights to the screenplay and gave it to a lesser-known director for the Ramadan 2018 broadcast season. Social media postings lamented the ruination of a greatly anticipated project; my job is to parse out the unsaids among them. Full details have yet to emerge; ethnography in a police state is also about waiting for the unasked. Allaith—who had justified biannual filming in Damascus as employment for many facing economic hardship—vowed hyperbolically never to film in Syria again; but he is shooting a 2019 serial there. I had hoped to bookend *Waiting* with *Chaos* in my ethnography, but as screenwriter Najeeb Nusair noted, the project's failure is a more appropriate end to this story. Architectural symmetry will be sacrificed for something messier and uglier, but ultimately truer.

Enduring Connections, Unending Stories

Across twenty-five years of intermittent fieldwork, a discomforting dependency tinges the deep affection I feel for many Syrians. It produced an ethnographic account of their lives that resonated with them then and foreshadowed the civil war, but feels to me inadequate, then and now. Part of my role as an anthropologist with a long-term relationship to her field has been to endure continual imbalance. Efforts to mitigate vulnerability through "giving back" never undo it. I remind myself that the storytelling at the heart of ethnography relies on this asymmetry. Sadly, it may also preclude any palpable sense of completion, of a final and fitting parity between analyst and subject. When Nabil Maleh, the activist and "Father of Syrian Cinema," passed away in March 2016, I mourned the loss of a friend. I also grieved a book project's preclusion. My social history of Syrian cultural production was to be told through his life and work; it relied utterly on his personal reminiscence. To call my interlocutors "collaborators" feels aggrandizing. Despite the modicum of social capital I may confer, I still need them far more than they need me. They are central to my professional endeavor; I remain at most tangential to theirs. The imbalance is appropriate, however personally distressing.

In Syria, and perhaps also in Yemen, openness to what endures, after so much violent rupture, seems more difficult than ever. Engagement is heartbreaking, abandonment is more so. Syrian television's "field of art" lives on, even as the nation crumbles. Their task, like mine, becomes more difficult; we operate in separate but parallel arenas of representation (Fassin 2014b). The drama of everyday life, they say, exceeds anything they can script. They struggle to depict an ugly reality. If they meet that challenge and still pass through the censors, what is their contribution? As an actor put it over morning coffee before *Fawda* location scouting, "either you prettify, or you show things how they are." The regime's pyrrhic, temporary victory placates no one: every complaint—no water, no electricity, no batteries, no fuel—they punctuate bitterly with "But we've won!" (*Bas intisarna!*). Reconciliation lies ahead, and the role of both drama and ethnography remains to be worked out. Whatever opportunities emerge must be grasped. Social drama creators like to evoke an artistic truism: the universal is reached through fidelity to the local. For my ethnographic account of their work, also a construct of the real, Dresch's counsel to listen patiently in difficult settings, and to proceed through quiet implication, will be crucial. The result may not look good, but it must be loyal to our shared labor of representation.

CHRISTA SALAMANDRA is Professor of Anthropology at Lehman College and the Graduate Center, the City University of New York. Her work explores visual, mediated, and urban culture in the Arab world. She is author of *A New Old Damascus: Authenticity and Distinction in Urban Syria* and editor (with Leif Stenberg) of *Syria from Reform to Revolt, Vol. 2: Culture, Society and Religion*.

Notes

1. Anthropologists frequently pay lip service to the necessarily partial and contingent character of ethnography; they routinely belie it in professional book, manuscript, and grant reviews.

2. The Orientalist critique's geographic exceptionalism unwittingly replicates a classic "Orientalist" trope: the modern Middle East as uniquely backward and lacking in contribution to world civilization. Oft-repeated assumptions that other area studies, first South Asian, more recently African, are "further ahead" (in an ironically teleological notion of knowledge production), or are more theoretically sophisticated, persist. Middle East and North Africa anthropologists are acutely susceptible to self-perceptions of irrelevance. See Slyomovics (2013) for a genealogy of the field's self-reproach.

3. In an early intervention, Sherry Ortner (1995) argued that the attack on "culture" led to the sanitized politics and ethnographic thinness of celebratory resistance studies. Lila Abu-Lughod powerfully critiques *Writing Culture*'s exclusions and contradictions but retains its assumption of asymmetry, advocating a "tactical humanism, made both politically necessary and limited in its effects by anthropology's location on the side of domination in the context of a world organized by global inequality along the lines of 'cultural' difference" (1991, 159).

4. With few exceptions, ethnography of recent decades prefigures neither the economic basis of the Arab uprisings nor the election of Donald Trump to the US presidency.

5. A few colleagues who share my class background feature in Deeb and Winegar's (2016) recent work on the politics of Middle East anthropology, although none of the interviews reported convey my sense of alienation or critique assumptions of privilege.

6. See, for instance, Abbink and Salverda (2013), Dornfeld (1998), Gusterson (1997), Hannerz (2010), K. Ho (2009), Ortner (2010, 2013), and Shore and Nugent (2002).

7. Political science literature focuses largely on the regime and its machinations; here negativity presents no representational dilemma.

8. The debate over the Palestinian hip-hop group DAM's music video depicting an "honor crime" provides a telling case study. Notably, it appeared in *Jadaliyya*, an online English/Arabic publication that combines academic, journalistic, and literary writing and attracts a similarly varied audience (Abu-Lughod and Mikdashi 2012a, 2012b; Nafar, Nafar, and Jrery 2012).

9. Scholars do write about these topics. Studies of personal status law, for instance, range from early work by Mir-Hosseini (1993) and Joseph (1996), to more recent studies by Mahmood (2016) and Van Eijk (2016). Yet precisely because this research is nuanced and complex, it is ill-suited to the kinds of representational contests that unfold before a general, or even an educated, public. The key challenge is to create alternative publics in which delicate topics can be discussed apart from interests and agendas that are more appropriate to public relations.

10. Walter Armbrust's *Mass Culture and Modernism in Egypt* broke this ground in 1996, but it would take over a decade for popular culture to join the mainstream of Middle East anthropology.

11. Imad Mustapha, the Syrian ambassador to Washington, who posted a scathing review on his blog, proved the exception.

12. http://alaalam.org/ar/translations-ar/item/521-623080517; http://alaalam.org/ar/translations-ar/item/447-الطائفيّة-في-سوريا-تأمُّلات-أنثروبولوجيّة; http://alaalam.org/ar/translations-ar/item/476-635110217; http://www.jadaliyya.com/pages/index/26111/فهد-سوريا-الجزء-الأول; http://www.jadaliyya.com/pages/index/26112/فهد-سوريا-الجزء-الثاني

13. Some serials are still filmed in Damascus, others in Lebanon, Dubai, or beyond by creators in exile.

14. Personal correspondence, January 2017.

15. Personal correspondence, February 2017.

4

WHO ARE THE TALIBAN?

The Deflection of Truth among Tribal Pashtuns in Pakistan

Ammara Maqsood

IN 2013, I WAS SITTING IN THE GARDEN of a college hostel in Lahore with Fazal, an architecture student, when he began what at first seemed a rant against the Taliban. Fazal belonged to the Mahsud, one of the biggest Pashtun tribes that inhabit the Federally Administered Tribal Areas (FATA), situated along the Pakistan-Afghan border. Like many other Mahsud tribesmen, Fazal blamed both the Pakistani army and the Taliban for violence in his village and claimed that they were in league with each other. A week earlier, when we first met, he had regaled me with a gory tale of how, at the market of Miranshah in North Waziristan, the Taliban had beaten an alleged informant to death while soldiers from the nearby army checkpoint looked on. This time, however, our conversation took a different turn. Referring to his time in Lahore, Fazal said, "In the city, people think of the Taliban as resistance against American imperialism, but they never answer why we should live under this torture for everyone else's sake. Anyway," he continued in a casual manner, "what do *they* know about who the Taliban are? Ask *me* . . . after all, I was one of them." Sensing my discomfort at this revelation, Fazal reassured me: "Don't worry, I told you this because now we are friends, I can trust you with this information." Having only recently met him, I was not sure if I deserved such generosity, but it was obvious that I had no choice in the matter. "In any case," he said, "this was four years ago. My uncle kept going on [at me] to do something with my life, so I left them [the Taliban] and then tried to join the air force. I failed the eye test, so that was that, and here I am [in art school]."

At the time of these exchanges, I was part of a research initiative that aimed to collect life histories of tribal Pashtuns who had been displaced from FATA.[1] In the last decade and a half since the US-led invasion of Afghanistan, the tribal areas have been a site of major unrest and violence. Most significantly, the area has been the location for US drone attacks and ground operations by the Pakistan army targeting the Taliban. Precise figures remain disputed, but, according to the Bureau of Investigative Journalism, between 2,500 and 4,000 people have been killed by drone strikes since 2004, and Pakistan military operations have left hundreds dead.[2] Apart from these deaths, many more have been killed in suicide bombings and attacks by the Taliban. The majority of these attacks have been in Khyber Pakhtunkhwa (formerly the North-West Frontier Province) and the tribal areas. Specific figures for these areas are not available, but, in total, more than 59,000 people have died since 2005 in terrorist attacks across Pakistan. In 2014, the official number of people displaced from the tribal areas had reached one million, and recent reports suggest that more than another million have been displaced since.[3] Given the levels of violence, fieldwork for this project was classified by the research grant body as work in a "fragile context," and as a result, the research team was asked to complete a number of forms covering safety and ethics. In addition, we were asked to submit details on how, in an environment mired with violence and suspicion, we would gain the trust of our informants. In order to protect informants (and ourselves), it was suggested that we should avoid talking about politics and limit discussions solely to personal life histories.

The situation in the field, however, was far different from what one might expect from a "fragile context." Although most tribesmen repeatedly complained that it was dangerous to discuss politics with a stranger, it rarely stopped them from opening up to such topics.[4] As in the case of Fazal, it took only a couple of meetings before one was deemed a "trustworthy friend" and subsequently presented with, for instance, evidence on how the army supports the Taliban or how the latter is funded by the United States. The ease with which one encountered the sensational brings to mind Paul Dresch's classic comment on fieldwork as "a trade in secrets, though in a curious way. The more thriller-like the material, the less difficult to gather, to the point that one [is] constantly being told things unfit to print" (2000a, 109–10). At the same time, one confronted a contradictory array of positions. In one instance, the Taliban were presented, often in mystified terms, as an enemy responsible for countless brutalities and killings. In other remarks, they were depicted as a local and known group that one conducted business with or, as with Fazal, a group one joined out of career indecisiveness (a gap year of sorts). I suggest that these different, at times contradictory, positions were held together not through lies and deception—as assumed in statist discourse—but through a deflection of the truth, a sense that nobody could know for certain who the Taliban were.

In thinking about this in terms of truth claims, or the absence thereof, I draw on a larger epistemology, noted in tribal Middle Eastern contexts, that the truth lies elsewhere. This is visible, for instance, in oral histories of tribes that are formed and augmented through contestation and opposition and rest on a sense of deflected truth (Shryock 1997; Scheele 2009). Unlike the modern state, which often garners legitimacy through claims of transparency, accountability, and empiricism, tribal landscapes are not expected to be transparent. In order to maintain physical and moral boundaries, tribes rely not on conformity to rule-bound action but rather on structures of layered privacy, control, and vulnerability—what Paul Dresch has called "a peace." Knowledge and information do not float freely in such a context; instead, what one knows and what one does not depend on one's assigned place and position in a broader moral universe. This kind of selective privacy often generates a terrain of half knowledge, rumor, and accusation—a sense of which is available in Fazal's story. However, this world of layered privacy and half knowledge is not the domain of the "tribal" world alone but scales up to domestic and international politics.

Within this larger context, this chapter shows how, inflected with uncertainty, the category of the Taliban opens up space for transgression of moral norms and obligations. Much of this uncertainty stems from the conspiracy theories, rumors, and discussions of the Taliban in Pakistan, alongside the murky history of US involvement in the region. Thus, as much as the category resonates in particular ways among tribal Pashtuns, its position within the rhetoric of the modern state is equally uncertain. Not only is the authority to define this category continually contested and recast, it is often constructed through mystification. The deflection of truth, here, then depends on the rhetoric of the modern state and contemporary geopolitics in the region as much as it does on structures of privacy and secrecy that are usually associated with the "tribal world."

Suspicion, Secrecy, and Mistrust

Officially, Pakistan has been a strategic ally of the United States in the "war on terror" since the invasion of Afghanistan in 2001.[5] The relationship between the two countries, however, is mired in mutual suspicion and mistrust, and, away from joint statements made by their governments, officials on each side openly acknowledge their reluctance to cooperate with the other government. The need for the present alliance, as well as the roots of mistrust, stems from association with Afghanistan in the late Cold War. The Durand Line—the Pakistan-Afghan border, inherited from the days of British imperialism—cuts through tribal Pashtun lands and tribes, dividing them between two countries. Historically, the border has been porous. In the late 1970s, during the Soviet occupation of Afghanistan, this leaky border and tribal connections on either side were used to aid the anti-Soviet resistance. With funding from the CIA, Pakistani intelligence organizations (in particular the Inter-Services Intelligence agency, or ISI) set up border seminaries to recruit and train mujahidin.

After the Cold War ended, the United States lost interest in the region, leaving the country engulfed in a civil war with different mujahidin factions and warlords vying for control. The ISI, however, continued to maintain connections with these different groups. According to the accounts considered authoritative in academic and Western policy circles, in the mid-1990s, the ISI began to lend its support to a group composed of young poor men, often from impoverished families with little "tribal pedigree," who had fought against the Soviets and then returned to seminaries in Pakistan or their villages in Afghanistan (Rashid 2008, 80–81). Frustrated by the civil war and the politics of the warlords, these young men named themselves *talib*, meaning students, and set out to achieve a mission around restoring peace, disarming the population, enforcing Islamic law, and generally defending Islam in Afghanistan (Rashid 2001, 2008). At its conception, the movement was popular with locals and villagers who viewed it as way to end warlordism and disorder, yet, at the same time, it lacked funds. With support from ISI, however, it emerged as a strong military power and by 1996 had gained control of major cities, such as Kandahar, Herat, and Kabul, as well as much of the land in between in the north and west (Rashid 2008, 80–82). Not only did Pakistan offer its own support to the Taliban—the name the movement was given by this time—but it also persuaded Saudi Arabia and the United Arab Emirates to provide financial backing (channeled through the ISI) and recognition (ibid.). Osama bin Laden arrived in Afghanistan in 1998, on the invitation of the leader of the Taliban, Mullah Omar.

After al-Qa'ida's attack on New York in 2001 and faced with the choice of being either "with us or against us," as President George Bush proposed, Pakistan joined the "war on terror" and was expected to assist American-led forces in defeating the Taliban, who, in turn, were seen as allies of al-Qa'ida. The United States claims, with good reason, that the ISI continues to support some Taliban groups within Afghanistan, and indeed within Pakistani territory, including hiding fighters who flee across the border from Afghanistan to the tribal areas or to safe houses in Pakistani towns (Rashid 2008; Jalal 2008; Haqqani 2005). Meanwhile, Pakistani officials complain that the United States does not share information with them and runs operations—some of them through private contractors such as Blackwater (now known as Academi)—in

Pakistani territory without permission. (Such fears were strengthened in 2011, when it was discovered that Raymond Davis, an American "consulate worker" who shot two Pakistani men at a busy intersection in Lahore, was employed by a private security firm contracted by the CIA.) Although there has been some attempt to claim military operations against the Taliban as Pakistan's "own war" against extremism, there remains a strong sense in military and government circles that participation in the "war on terror" has had a high cost. Indeed, they lament that military operations against the Afghan Taliban in the tribal areas, ordered by the Americans, are what led to the formation of a Pakistani Taliban, the umbrella term used for a host of organizations that retaliate against the state by launching suicide attacks across Pakistan. In some circumstances, however, the mistrust surrounding the US-Pakistan alliance has its domestic use and is highlighted for a home audience. For instance, private communications between officials suggest that the Pakistani state tacitly supports drone attacks but officially condemns them to save face at home.

Mixed in with general wariness of the state and of the motives of "the West," the not-so-secret "secret" arrangements and discord between the two countries make for a flourishing environment of paranoia and suspicion. Fieldwork felt like being thrown into the plot of a Graham Greene novel.[6] Lahore was awash with rumor and speculation on the Taliban. No one knew the Taliban, apparently, but everyone knew something about them, similar in a sense to how people talk about "criminal castes" in India (Piliavsky 2011) or, indeed, the Mafia in Italy (Gambetta 1996). The postcolonial middle class, however, have a tendency to define themselves in terms of modernity, and it is often the case that the accounts suitable to this sensibility become authoritative history, in the process finding an international audience of academics and policy makers.

As I have written elsewhere, attachment to and nostalgia for the modernism of the 1960s is integral to the politics of distinction and class contestations in Lahore (Maqsood 2014, 2017). Old middle-class status and the liberal political values associated with it are established through linkages to the history of modernism in South Asia. For instance, this can be seen by displaying genealogical ties to the officers in the colonial government and the modernist aspirations of the early postcolonial state (particularly the military government of General Ayub Khan). Meanwhile, newer urban groups and their conservatism are often portrayed as a legacy of the Islamization program instituted by General Zia-ul-Haq, whose martial law is considered as the end of the "modern" trajectory of Pakistan. If "the Taliban" as experienced in everyday practice and rumor seem likely to be almost anyone, "the Taliban" as a public phenomenon are an offense against the modernist ideals that the old middle class associates with itself. In liberal newspapers, they are condemned as "fundamentalists."

For instance, an editorial in the *Friday Times* cautions readers that "Tehrik-e-Taliban [the official name for the Pakistani Taliban] is waging a ferocious war on the country . . . it rejects everything Pakistani and wants to impose a violent, reactionary Emirate upon us that will throw us back centuries" (N. Sethi 2013).

Viewing this as the lasting influence of General Zia's Islamization program in the 1980s and ISI's misadventures in Afghanistan, modernist intellectuals (usually from old middle-class backgrounds) argue that, instead of confronting Islamic radicalism for what it is, the ordinary public blames the violence on foreign groups. In 2013 there certainly existed a widespread belief in Lahore that foreign spies—thought to be lurking at every corner—were behind the suicide attacks that plagued the country. It was often claimed that CIA and Blackwater agents (in connivance with India and Israel) were destabilizing Pakistan by funding groups that posed as the Taliban and engaged in bombing. Such views, as we shall see, were hardly confined to the "ordinary public," and the public was not as blind to the murky politics of the army and the Taliban as middle-class commentators claimed it was.

In the neighborhood where I live in Lahore, everyone has known for years of a "secret" ISI safe house. Its location is so well known that it is often used as a point of reference when people give directions to their own houses. At times of relative calm, it is not the subject of much discussion. Lahore was the site of a wave of suicide attacks in 2009 and 2010, which had waned considerably by 2013. Still, there was an edginess in the city in 2013; news of suicide attacks elsewhere and ongoing military operations in the tribal areas served as a reminder that Lahore could soon be a target again. Amid this anxiety, the ISI safe house became a topic of conversation. At a local corner store, for instance, I was warned by the shopkeeper to avoid going down the road where the house was located. His assistant noted that they had heard from the tandoor next door that there was strange activity going on. It turned out the caretaker of the safe house would come every evening to the tandoor to collect roti for the evening meal. The caretaker claimed that the house was empty these days, yet he regularly ordered at least a dozen rotis each evening. "How can one man eat so many rotis?" the shopkeeper asked me. "It is clear that the ISI is up to its usual tricks . . . hiding the very men it is claiming to America that it's fighting against."

Rumors of shady dealings by the ISI were common in different circles in Lahore. Nor could it be said that the conspiracy theories postulating that foreigners were behind all this violence were limited to "ordinary people." On other occasions, the same shopkeeper who warned me about the safe house told me that there was no doubt, in his view, that America and Israel had their eyes on Afghanistan's untapped oil reserves (as far as I know, there are hardly any) and wanted to destabilize the region so that they could control it. However, I often heard similar stories in establishment circles. The wife of a prominent civil servant—very much part of the liberal milieu described above—once shared some disturbing news when, through "sources in the government," she learned that every time the police had recovered the body of a suicide bomber after a blast, it was found uncircumcised. In other words, the bombers were not Muslim. Opinions shifted, conspiracy theories flourished, and almost everyone claimed to "know things" that others had no idea of. Nevertheless, certain older patterns remained in place, not least a rhetorical contrast between the city and countryside, the modern and the backward.

Whoever the Taliban actually were, most people were convinced that they were hiding among, or were deliberately harbored by, tribal Pashtuns, who, as I explain in the next section, have migrated in large numbers to Pakistani cities from the tribal areas. Throughout my fieldwork in 2013, local spies must have shared this opinion, because my movements were conspicuously monitored, and mail delivered at my home always arrived opened. On one occasion, when returning from an interview, I was told that a man, who did not give his name, had left me a parcel. Inside it was a book on the history of a military unit known locally to work closely with the intelligence services. The book also contained a note that listed a phone number and the following message: "Include all perspectives [in your research?]." When I shared this incident with colleagues at a local university, they congratulated me and said that I must be successfully pursuing the Taliban if I had attracted such interest. As in *Our Man in Havana* (Greene 1958), it appeared that if everything was suspect, then, conversely, anything could also be true.

Neither the image of the Taliban as fundamentalist nor that of the Taliban as foreign-funded imposters captures the complexity of their appeal and the support those referred to as Taliban can garner. Throughout Pakistan, groups identifying themselves as "Taliban" control extortion and rent-seeking networks, make money by "protection" of trade, carry out kidnappings, and mediate disputes in unregulated markets. In the tribal areas, much like in Afghanistan, the Pakistani Taliban were initially supported because they were involved in settling conflicts, eradicating petty crime, and looking after the poor.[7] To align this with state and party politics would be difficult. Nor does an "ethnic" lens offer clarity. In Karachi, the Taliban side with the Pashtun nationalist party, ANP, but in Pashtun-dominated areas of the north, ANP party members are routinely killed by the Taliban. Such occurrences are regularly reported on television, and most—whether old middle-class intellectuals or the "ordinary" public—are aware of these contradictions. Yet they stop neither group from talking of and constructing the Taliban as a discrete entity.

Conspiracy theories and rumors are, of course, not restricted to Pakistan. Recent literature on conspiracy theories has emphasized their role in providing, not least in the United States, an avenue for expressing "scepticism towards centralized power" (Fenster 2008, 9) and a means for individuals to participate in the political process (see, e.g., Tanner 2008; Olmstead 2009). While most of these works have focused on what conspiracy theories do, Iqtidar (2014) suggests that their precise content needs more attention. Conspiracy theories about Blackwater in Pakistan, she argues, acknowledge the sedimented history of US involvement and intrigue in the region. This is certainly the case with rumors about the Taliban, who grew out of a resistance movement funded by the United States. The rumors in Lahore acknowledge the history of foreign involvement and, as the shopkeeper's story about the ISI suggests, of the powerful grip of the military and intelligence services on local and national politics.

What I want to highlight, however, is that as much as such stories criticize the state and, in particular, the army, they also mystify it. Cynicism and skepticism, as Yael Navaro-Yashin (2002) has argued, further entrench the fantasy of the state. At the same time, just as the state exists as a fantasy, so does the category of the Taliban. The rumors mystify by constructing the Taliban as a discrete and homogenous group with a specific purpose and intent, one that is separated from everyday society (Piliavsky 2011, this volume). But while the rumors mystify the Taliban, the secrecy and uncertainty—the sense that all is not known—allow for an ambiguity that enables connections and overlaps to exist despite opposition to discrete categories.

The remainder of this chapter focuses on how this uncertainty provides germane ground for deflection among tribal Pashtuns both in cities and in the tribal areas, and, moreover, on the roads and trade routes that connect them. To do this, I offer first a description of the tribal areas and contemporary patterns of migration in these areas. We find that, alongside the uncertainty about who the Taliban are and the exact nature of their relationship with the military, it is also hard to determine who the "real" tribal Pashtuns are.

The "Remote" Tribal Areas

The tribal belt is a classic example of a "remote area" (Ardener 1989), in terms of both its historical representation and the current discourses that surround it. Like other "remote areas" that figure centrally in the "war on terror" (see Scheele 2012, 12), the tribal areas of Pakistan are imagined simultaneously as a backward, wild, and static place and as the site from which technologically sophisticated terrorist attacks are launched across the world. The region, colloquially referred to as '*alaqa ghair* or, simply, tribal areas, is composed of seven administrative units (agencies).[8] As its official name, the Federally Administered Tribal Areas (FATA), suggests, the region is designated as a federal area, directly ruled by the Pakistani president through his appointed representatives. As an agent of the president, the governor of the Khyber Pakhtunkhwa province (formerly the North-West Frontier Province) appoints bureaucrats, called political agents, to each agency. The inhabitants of FATA are not governed by the Pakistani constitution and penal code. Instead, the region is governed through the Frontier Crimes Regulation (FCR), a law first promulgated by British colonial authorities in 1901 and enforced by the political agents in consultation with tribal chiefs *maliks*.[9]

The current administrative structure of the region largely follows on from colonial policy, which, in turn, was a result of practicalities of governance and geopolitical concerns with buffering British India from the neighboring Afghan and Russian empires (see, e.g., Ahmed 2013; Marsden and Hopkins 2011, 23–49; Nichols 1995). To provide a brief context, under the Treaty of Gandamak (1879), signed by the Afghan monarch Amir Yaqub Khan at the end of the Second Afghan War, parts of western Baluchistan and much of present-day FATA were ceded to the British. In 1893, with the view of creating a stable buffer to tsarist Russia, a boundary was demarcated between British India and Afghanistan. The Durand Line—which remains the border between present-day Pakistan and Afghanistan—divided the Pashtun tribes into two parts along a border that began at the foothills of the Himalayas and ran south to Baluchistan and the Arabian Sea. Alongside the long-term geopolitical interest of developing a buffer state against Russian imperialism, the short-term and immediate concerns of the British were related to governance (Nichols 1995, 2001). In dealing with the Pashtun tribes occupying the treacherous highlands, the colonial government was concerned with keeping mountain passes open and accessible for trade and minimizing armed raids in the settled, revenue-producing districts in the south, but without expending significant manpower (Nichols 1995, 2001). While these concerns remained constant, the policies and arrangements devised to address them varied. The British annexed Punjab in 1849, and its policy toward Pashtun tribes after that time was rarely stable, changing with differing understandings of the region and its people. At the end of the nineteenth century, however, colonial policy toward Pashtun tribes started to crystallize into an administrative structure of agencies and political agents that continues to be used today. In the late 1890s, the British created five special administrative units, called agencies, which together constituted the tribal areas (Ahmed 2013; Rashid 2008). In 1901, a new province, the North-West Frontier Province, divided into settled areas and the tribal areas, was formed out of the northern part of Punjab. The Frontier

Crimes Regulation (FCR), passed in the same year, gave administrators of this new province unlimited powers.

In present-day Pakistan, this administrative structure remains in place, although with a few minor changes.[10] There are now seven agencies instead of the original five. Additionally, in 1996, after decades of tribal elders selecting representatives for the national parliament, FATA residents were granted universal adult suffrage. In national elections in 2013, political parties, previously prohibited from entering the tribal areas, were allowed to nominate candidates and campaign in the region. However, there has been little investment in infrastructure in the region. Road and transport networks, aside from main towns, remain undeveloped; electric supply and telecommunication coverage are patchy; and hospitals and clinics are rare. Schools and colleges are primarily limited to main towns, such as Miranshah and Razmak in Waziristan. In villages, buildings built for primary schooling remain empty due to lack of teachers, and those that do function are of poor quality.

This history of legislative separation, along with lack of development, is drawn upon in discussions on the isolation of the tribal areas, both locally and in the wider academic literature. Such explanations direct attention toward the continuing marginalization of the tribal areas but, inadvertently perhaps, obscure a focus on long-standing patterns of movement of people and goods from and through the area. As Ardener (1989) puts it, "remoteness" stems not from isolation but from the type of relationship such places have to the outside world. The remoteness of the tribal areas endures not despite but because of the connections—always unequally and never fully contained from a local point of view—that its inhabitants have with different "centers," such as imperial powers or the nation-state: "The feature of a 'remote area' . . . is that those so defined are intermittently conscious of the defining processes of others that might absorb them" (Ardener 1989, 223).

Unlike the Pashtun tribes of Swat who rely on the fertile soil of the valley, an area made known in academic circles through the work of Fredrik Barth (1959, 1981) and, later, Charles Lindholm (1982), the borderland tribes have been unable to use their hilly and arid lands for large-scale farming.[11] For many of the tribes, payment for safe passage of caravans and goods by independent traders, kingly states, and imperial governments has been a historic source of income (see, e.g., Ahmed 2013; Rashid 2008; Nichols 1995). There has simultaneously been a continuing pattern of migration out of the region. For instance, in British India, there was steady movement of people from the tribal areas to colonial towns and cities and, in some cases, out of India (see, e.g., Nichols 2008).

Since independence in 1947, two distinct patterns of migration have emerged, both of which involve continuous movement to and from the tribal

areas. Most maliks have moved out of the tribal areas and maintain permanent residences in Peshawar or Islamabad, where their families have access to
good schools, health care, and city life, but travel back frequently to attend to
political matters. Among the younger generation of these families, some have
continued to retain the role of malik while others have branched out into other
professions, including bureaucracy and the civil service. In addition, particularly with the increase of foreign aid and US interest in the region, a significant
number of people from such backgrounds have entered the development sector and work for local and international NGOs, along with other civil society
groups.

The second kind of migration, the norm among my Pashtun interlocutors
like Fazal, involves families from more impoverished backgrounds. In the last
four decades, there has been a steady flow of young men from the tribal areas to
larger cities in Pakistan and the Gulf, a movement encouraged by the search for
income and livelihood. In Lahore, many such migrants are involved in seasonal
labor, such as working as fruit and vegetable sellers or in construction. In addition, others are employed, again as wage laborers, in steel and iron factories, or
work in the transport sector as rickshaw and truck drivers. Life in these occupations is not easy—periods of unemployment are common, and a dependable
stream of money is invariably difficult to obtain. Some, however, have been
more successful, beginning as rickshaw drivers and mechanics before pro-
gressing to own transport and trucking businesses. Others, particularly from
Waziristan, have migrated to the Gulf to work as construction laborers or as
security guards. The money that they have earned there has been predominantly invested in their children's education or used to start small businesses
(mostly in the transport industry). Finally, some have straddled the blurred line
between legality and illegality, using money earned from drug peddling, often
marijuana but also opium from across the border, to start small transport businesses or migrate to the Gulf to work in the security sector.

In all of these groups, it is commonplace for part of the family to reside in
the city while the others remain in the tribal areas to attend to the land. Such
arrangements are flexible and organized informally; adult males, along with
their immediate family, take turns (*bari*) living in the tribal areas while the extended family lives in the city. Irrespective of whose turn it is, school-attending
children remain in Lahore, while many of the family elders prefer to live in the
tribal areas, traveling to the city only when they need medical attention. Fazal,
mentioned at the beginning of this chapter, is an example of this type of migration. His father, Abdul Qari, from an impoverished Mahsud clan, migrated
from Waziristan to Qatar in the late 1970s, where he worked as a security guard
for the royal family. The money he earned was sent back home to support his

parents and siblings, as well as his own young family. Fazal was born in the family village in Waziristan, where he lived with his mother, paternal grand-parents, and uncles. For some years, he attended a local school in a village a few kilometers from his own, but when he was ten, he was sent with his broth-ers and male cousins to live in Peshawar with one of their uncles so that they could be educated there. Meanwhile, after two decades of working as a guard, Abdul Qari had saved enough money to invest in a small business. He returned to Pakistan to set up a trucking business in Hyderabad, in Sindh, where some tribesmen from his village had established a similar enterprise, which he could rely on for help. Fazal and his immediate family then moved to Hyderabad but traveled back frequently during school holidays and in the summer.

Depending on their resources, most have used money earned abroad to build homes in the tribal areas that demonstrate their success. For instance, Mohammad Jaan Alam's family from Mohmand Agency used money earned through a lucrative auto-rickshaw dealership to build an expansive house in their village that can accommodate up to seventy people in the main living room. One of the sons told me proudly, "Even the malik does not have such a big house. When people from other villages come, they are confused who is the real malik." Indeed, on my visit to their house a few months later, I found that not only was it the largest in the village, but also they had been able to install a landline in their house by paying the national telecommunication depart-ment. Although this landline was hardly ever used—due to unreliability, it was easier to walk to a high cliff where one could receive a mobile signal—it was a source of much pride, as it was the only house other than the malik's to have such coveted technology. Not everyone is able to invest in the tribal areas to this extent; nonetheless, it is common to find people making substantial efforts to build back home. As the saying goes in these circles, "*Pathan sheher mein kamata hai, aur watan mein khata hai*" (A Pathan earns in the city and eats in his homeland).

These patterns of migration and movement show that the tribal areas and their people are not entirely isolated from the rest of the country. However, the image of remoteness (as separation) persists, with Pashtun tribes often viewed as having no interest in or connections with the modern state. Such representa-tions are propagated by various groups within the country and with varying motives. In official and public statements, Pakistani state and military officials use this representation to justify their treatment of the region. The continuing use of the Frontier Crimes Regulation (FCR), the denial of constitutional rights to FATA residents, military operations, and a broader lack of investment in the area are often explained by asserting that this is a special and "contained" case, one that is different from the rest of the country. Meanwhile, the broader representation of the tribal areas as isolated and difficult to govern legitimizes the role of maliks as intermediaries who can help the establishment communicate with tribes and vice versa. (In practice, it is often the maliks' connections and accessibility to the center rather than to the tribal areas that allow them to become intermediaries.) Tribal Pashtuns who work in the development sector are often critical of maliks, viewing them as an example of the oppressive "tradition" that holds the tribal areas back from progress. However, in their commitment to develop and modernize the region, they too echo the discourse of isolation. "Remoteness," here, is produced from these connections between the tribal areas and the center.

If, in the world of nation-states, claims of ethnic marginality are a way to access state resources, such claims have become, in the realm of transnational activism, means for attracting the attention of development and civil society organizations. Both groups tend to inhabit "tribalness" but, at the same time, distinguish themselves through their education and "progressiveness" from the tribal population on behalf of whom they speak and politick. A well-known development activist, the son of a malik from the Afridi tribe, who now works for a UN agency, said to me, "I told my colleagues this from day one. If you want to have a relationship with us tribal Pashtuns, you need to understand our pride . . . our language of honor. If you respect it, you are our friends." While in this instance, he spoke of himself as one with the people he represented and worked for, in other engagements he would distance himself: "There is a lot of development work that needs to be done . . . the people of my village, they have a different sensibility. Unless there is education and schools, there can be no development in FATA."

Meanwhile, the tribal Pashtuns who are the targets of these development agendas—boys like Fazal and their families—cast doubt on the authenticity of maliks and others from affluent families. They claim that maliks may be from the tribal areas but no longer speak on behalf of their people or Pashtuns more broadly. In contrast, these upwardly mobile families speak of themselves as the "real" tribal Pashtuns and highlight their connections to home and tradition while downplaying their outside connections. Even though he had lived outside the tribal areas for a significant period, Fazal, like all other tribal Pashtuns I encountered, spoke of his village in Waziristan as his "real" home. Similarly, most contended that it was only through the support of family and tribe that they had been able to thrive in the city. Indeed, there was no doubt that assistance from kin was crucial for moving in and out of the tribal areas and in forming businesses (see Maqsood 2015). At the same time, however, these Pashtuns often built linkages with other groups and associations. Abdul Qari, for instance, relied on his kin for setting up his business. But over time in Hyderabad, he also become part of a faith renewal movement, the Tablighi Jamaat. In this context, he built relationships and alliances with several non-Pashtuns—many of which served his business well. Yet when discussing life in Hyderabad, these connections were rarely discussed, although not denied, and his emphasis was always on his extended family and tribal connections.

Other families and groups that I became acquainted with had built similar relationships with outsiders. Some, like Abdul Qari, had joined religious organizations, while others were part of local wings of political parties that brought them in contact with ethnic groups different from their own. Moreover, despite their constant complaints and antagonistic relationship with the military, many of them had links and relationships with lower-level military officers, crucial for the successful running of their business. Fazal had opted to continue studying in university after failing his eyesight test for the air force, but many young men his age have used their college degrees to get entry into the lower cadres of the army. Similarly, some have managed to enter junior positions in the national bureaucracy, usually through the "quota system" in which a percentage of seats are reserved for candidates from each province. Those who run businesses involving trade and transport have developed relations with soldiers and officers deployed at checkpoints on the roads that they frequent. The overarching image of tribal solidarity and the opposition of tribes to state and military remains intact despite these connections. Rumors about the Taliban and the murky dealings of the army, and the uncertainty that results from such notions, become a way not only to obscure these connections but also to keep tensions and inequalities within families and clans out of plain view.

Deflecting the Truth

Just as Lahore was alive with rumors, the tribal Pashtun community in Lahore was also buzzing with their own theories and ideas on the Taliban and the army. As mentioned, the launch of ground operations by the Pakistani army against the Taliban has caused widespread displacement in the tribal areas. Adding, perhaps, to the perception of tribal Pashtuns as a remote population, various human rights groups and NGOs have raised concerns about the number of people living in the camps set up for Internally Displaced People (IDPs) and have criticized the inadequate arrangements made to cater for such populations. Our life-histories project, however, indicated that a significant portion of people affected were those who belonged to families that lived between cities and the tribal areas, or were related to such families. Instead of moving to IDP camps, they had traveled to stay with their family members in the city, bringing with them news and stories about the army and the Taliban. Meanwhile, tribal Pashtuns who had been residing in Lahore were unable to go back to their villages and were often stopped and questioned for hours at checkpoints by the army. The frustration and anger at this treatment, not to mention the burden of hosting and providing for arriving relatives, offered flourishing ground for fresh conspiracy theories.

At one level, perceptions of the Taliban among tribal Pashtuns were not very different from those circulating in other networks in Lahore. In discussions about the complicity of the Taliban and the army, a story about the encounter of an old man with a soldier at a checkpoint was often narrated. A rickshaw driver, who hailed from Mohmand Agency, told me how, outside their village, an old Pashtun man was stopped at the checkpoint at night. The soldier asked him, "Baba, tell me, are you on the side of the Taliban or on our side"? The old man replied, "How can I answer whose side I am on? You are the Prophet, and they are your *sahaba*."[12] In other versions of this story, recounted by different families, the order was reversed, with the Taliban referred to as the Prophet, or, as the old man replied, "It depends on what you are pretending to be tonight."

This story, with its emphasis on a blurring between the army and the Taliban, mirrored the experience of many of my informants at checkpoints, both in the cities and on returning to their villages in the tribal areas. Here, they were the ones deemed suspect until proved otherwise. In Lahore, a young man from the Toori tribe complained that every morning, as he made his way to a local college on a motorbike, he was stopped at the army checkpoint and asked to prove his identity. He protested that the soldiers knew who he was but nonetheless enjoyed constructing humiliating encounters for him. "They say to me things like, 'We never know about you Pashtuns; you can turn anytime' . . . and this morning one of them pointed to my hotpot [his lunch was inside] and said, 'Is this a bomb?'" At the checkpoints in the tribal areas and on the way to their villages, most young Pashtuns are stopped for hours and questioned about why they have returned and whom they will meet. On these occasions, they are often asked to roll up their shirt sleeves and trousers to check that their arms and legs are not grazed or bruised, evidence that may imply training at Taliban camps. The irony of the army considering marks of physical exertion on male bodies as suspect was not lost on my informants. One of them recounted how, when he was waiting at a checkpoint, he saw that a young *jawan* was harassed by the soldiers for the marks on his legs. "I yelled at them, 'It's from your official training this time.'"[13]

As much as the story of the old man hints toward the sedimented history of linkages between the army and Taliban, it also reflects how, in many instances, the two are experienced in similar ways in the tribal areas. This was even more visible in another account told by several members of a family from Mohmand Agency. Khalil Khan, the eldest son of this family, had arrived in Lahore two decades ago, working his way up from an auto mechanic to a scrap metal dealer. As his business prospered in Lahore, his brothers and extended family joined him. But, as is the norm in these families, they continued to move back and forth, with the parents residing permanently in the tribal areas in a house built with the money earned in the city. I had become acquainted with Khalil Khan when he, on hearing from other kin in the area that I was "taking interviews," had approached me. "You have to come and listen to my mother. They were held hostage by the Taliban and then attacked by the army," he said. When I visited them the following week, I was told of how their family home in Mohmand Agency had been attacked in 2012.

The family present at the time included Khalil Khan's mother and father (now deceased), his brother and three sisters-in-law, and their children. The account that I heard was largely told by the mother with interjections from Khalil Khan, who had not been present at the time. One night, in the summer of 2012, a group of men, with long beards and guns on their shoulders, appeared at their door and demanded to be let in. On entering the house, they announced that they would be staying in the courtyard and that arrangements should be made to feed them. "They had come to our house uninvited, but they were polite men. We did not know them, but their accent was not foreign either," recalled the mother. "They stayed for a week; we gave them food, but they kept the courtyard clean." When they were leaving, they warned the brother that the family should be careful: this day, next week, they would be attacked by the army. The family did not pay much attention to this, but to their horror, their house was attacked as predicted. "I was standing outside in the open field with the children, and the girls [daughters-in-law] were cleaning inside," said the mother. Suddenly, there was a rain of bullets that came from nowhere. The mother started running with the children toward the house, but there was a huge bang, and, for a while, everyone was blinded by dust and smoke. When it cleared, they saw that a huge "rocket had fallen on the house."[14] The people inside had managed to run out just in time, and no one was injured, although two women and a small girl had reduced hearing after the incident. The house, however, was completely destroyed.

When the mother narrated this event, unlike Khalil Khan, she mentioned neither the Taliban when referring to the men who had come to the house, nor the army in relation to the attack. Instead she had used an abstract *wŏh* (them) throughout the narration. A member of my research team probed her on this ambiguity, asking if it was the Taliban who had come to attack them. The mother looked confused at the question and was silent for a while. In the meantime, Khalil Khan, familiar with the kind of urban rhetoric described earlier, said that it was clear that the army had known that the Taliban had been staying there and had chosen to attack when they left. "It was their usual drama," he said. The mother, listening to this explanation, then said, "Yes, he is right; that's what they were up to. Besides," she continued, "there is no difference between them; they come with their guns and do what they want. We are left with nothing." Later, when asked again by my colleague whether it was a rocket or a drone that had landed, she remarked, "When you are running away from a rain of bullets, you do not look to see what they are and who is firing . . . the Taliban, the army, it is all the same."

At the same time as such stories demonstrated how, at an abstract level, the Taliban and the army were experienced in similar ways, the uncertainty they produced obscured other connections and small kinds of "peace" that continue to exist. Among Mohmand tribesmen, for instance, many of whom were involved in the transport and trading of fruits, I often heard about an incident that had proved to them that the Taliban and the Pakistan army were mutually supporting. One evening, in the village of Sarrakhwa in Mohmand Agency, one of the *khassadar* (local patrol force) guards was told by an army officer from a nearby village that a convoy of trucks and jeeps would pass through their village late at night and should not be stopped. As the tail of the convoy passed through a makeshift checkpoint, some men from the last truck rose and fired, killing the khassadars on duty. Other khassadars were furious and vowed they would take revenge. Two days later, they got their chance: the same convoy was heading back through their village, this time occupied with clean-shaven "army-cut men."[15] The khassadars fired regardless, killing all of them. Afterward, so the story goes, they searched the vehicles and found briefcases filled with fake beards and wigs. "This is what is actually going on," explained Gul Khan. "It is a game of big powers, a new great game, and we are stuck in the middle. The army funds the Taliban because they keep wanting weapons from NATO. The US knows this, but they keep quiet because it wants to stay in Afghanistan." After this incident, Gul Khan said that his village no longer allowed safe passage to either the army or the Taliban, and no Taliban could seek refuge there.

Gul Khan and his family owned a truck business that transported apples grown in orchards close to South Waziristan "down to Pakistan" for sale in the wholesale produce market (*mandi*) in Rawalpindi. Oranges grown in the region are taken to Central Asia, which is much closer, but imported apples are not allowed there, so they must be transported to Rawalpindi. The roads in the direction of Rawalpindi are poorly maintained, and different sections of them are controlled by different extortion rackets, each demanding payment for safe passage. Meanwhile, the truck drivers need to reach the market within a day; otherwise, the apples become overripe and unfit for wholesale. Complaining about this situation, Gul Khan said that the only way to avoid paying each racket was to come under the patronage of the strongest racket and to let them deal with the lower-order rackets. "These days," he went on, "we pay the Taliban when going down. They ask for five rupees per crate, which is a lot, but at least we do not need to worry about the smaller rackets."[16] When I asked how they could do business with the Taliban here when they had refused them refuge in their village, he replied, "All kinds of people call themselves the Taliban these days; who knows who anyone is? These people we deal with, we have been dealing with them for years . . . now they call themselves the Taliban. If they were American funded, like the ones who came to our village, they would not be standing on the road with broken rubber slippers. They would be in a SUV."

While uncertainty about the identity of the Taliban offered room to navigate between collective obligations and business pressures, such depictions were also of use in concealing conflicts within clans and families. I became well acquainted with an influential family, also from Mohmand Agency, who had been settled in Lahore for several decades. Mohammad Jaan Alam and his relatives had a rags-to-riches story. When he and his brothers were teenagers, they cleaned cars at a petrol station to supplement their father's modest income as a wood seller. From this social position, the brothers had progressed to own a string of businesses, including three petrol stations and an auto-rickshaw dealership. Whenever I asked the brothers or their close relatives about how the business took off, they said only, "Allah has been kind." Their neighbors, however, suggested that drug smuggling across the Durand Line had been even kinder. Based on their commercial success, one of the brothers had also entered local politics, first as a member of the religious political party Jamaat-e-Islami and later as a member of the Pakistan Peoples Party.

Despite their established presence in Lahore, the family maintained connections in the tribal areas. They had built a big house in their village (as mentioned earlier, the only residence other than the malik's that had a telephone connection), where the elder and young family members would stay for extended periods. In Lahore, the family provided help to incoming migrants from their tribe, often accommodating close relatives in the family business or providing financial assistance. With their wide-reaching and diverse networks of patronage and authority, the family was very powerful, and it was rare to find anyone—no matter how distant a relation—speaking against them. It was as if Jaan Alam and his brothers had brought together *The Sopranos* with tribal etiquette; they operated like the mafia but with the kind of segmentation, deference to family solidarity, and layered privacy that is characteristic of the tribal world (see, e.g., Dresch 1989, 75–83).

Early in my fieldwork, Jaan Alam had mentioned how the Taliban had placed "a hit" on one of the brothers, demanding that they be paid Rs 40 million (approximately $330,000), or they would kill him. Jaan Alam and his younger brother Khadim Jaan, on whom the hit had been placed, had traveled to a small town near their village to negotiate with the Taliban leaders there. They told me that when they reached the checkpoint close to the town, they found that the soldiers on duty already knew why they had come. The soldiers told them that their "hosts" had gone to the village a few miles away and that they should meet them there. At the time, Jaan Alam used this as another example of how the army knew exactly where the Taliban were but refused to do anything about it. A few months later, I mentioned the story to Rahim Khan, a distant relative who had settled in Lahore as a rickshaw driver, and I was surprised to see him begin laughing. Usually, anything relating to the brothers was treated with deference and caution, and I was perplexed at his amusement. Rahim Khan asked me, "Do you know who these Taliban were? . . . They were his *chacha*'s [father's brother's] sons who had been demanding this ransom. Once they were part of the business, but last year they broke away and, for a while, demanded that the money they had invested in the business should be returned." He changed the topic after this exchange, and nothing more was mentioned about Jaan Alam and his brothers. But as I was leaving, Rahim Khan brought up the Taliban again: "We live in troubled times; no one knows what is going on . . . for all that is happening, one's own family could just become the Taliban."

One cannot be certain whether Jaan Alam's cousins had joined the Taliban—whoever they are—or if presenting them in such a manner helped maintain the appearance of family solidarity during an internal conflict. There is, of course, another possibility. Rahim Khan, who usually deferred to Jaan Alam's authority, was now insinuating something more sinister about him; that is, one's own family could indeed be the Taliban. All of these possibilities exist because one can never be sure who the Taliban are. Whatever one account proclaims can be countered by another. In the current context, with rumors and contested histories on all sides, the category opens up a number of positions without closing any. This gives it a kind of trickster quality, an invitation for transgressing established boundaries and hierarchies. Yet it sometimes promises more than it delivers, as Fazal, the erstwhile Taliban member that I started with, discovered for himself. When he joined the movement, tired of parental nagging about studying and choosing the right career, he envisaged himself as doing something grand. For a while, this desire was accomplished. At the time of joining, he was sixteen years old, and, reflecting back, he told me that he could never fully explain "the glamour" of walking around the village with an AK-47 on his shoulders. Yet after a time the effect wore off: "All we were made to do is to patrol the village and to make sure that everyone came out to pray, everyone donated money for jihad, things like that. It got tiring. Before I had joined, I had all these visions of going across the border in the middle of the night in a hidden convoy while being chased by CIA spies . . . things like that. None of that ever happened."

AMMARA MAQSOOD is Lecturer in Social Anthropology at University College London. She is the author of *The New Pakistani Middle Class.*

Notes

1. The fieldwork discussed in this chapter was funded by the European Research Council Grant "Tolerance in Contemporary Muslim Practice" (TICMP 313652).

2. The estimate for military operations casualties has been taken from news reports in the Pakistani newspaper the *Dawn* (http://www.dawn.com/news/1119392). It should be noted that *Tanqeed* has pointed out that most estimates of casualties are provided either by the military themselves or by embedded media outlets, such as the ISPR. It is also unclear how the military distinguishes between civilian and "terrorist" deaths. See, e.g., http://www.tanqeed.org/2014/07/media-watch-pak-press-covers-civilian-govt-unlike-foreign-press/.

3. There are no verified figures on the total number of people displaced. The numbers reported by Al Jazeera in 2014 (https://www.aljazeera.com/humanrights/2014/08/pakistan-idps-reach-record-one-million-201482712311342575.html) were based on the number of people reporting into camps set up for Internally Displaced People. Our fieldwork suggested that the majority of displaced people had not gone to camps but had instead gone to relatives who were already settled in the city. This led us to think that the actual number was far higher. More recent reports by Voice of America (https://www.voanews.com/a/tribesmen-displaced-pakistan-anti-militant-operations-demand-repatriation/3850777.html) suggest that over a million have been displaced since 2014 but make no mention of those displaced before. Discussing the violence since 2014, the United Nations (cited in Voice of America) has estimated that at least 95,000 families have been displaced.

4. A few people refused to talk to us, fearing that we would report them to the police or local intelligence agents. However, this was rare and occurred only with families who had very recently fled the war zone.

5. The "global war on terror" (GWOT in military and diplomatic parlance) was an expression coined in the administration of President George W. Bush. The phrase lost official status under President Barack Obama. However, as a number of authors have pointed out (e.g., Dresch 2014, 122), drone warfare against presumed terrorists actually intensified after the change of US administrations, with no attempt to explain precisely who these "terrorists" were or why they were being killed.

6. Both *Our Man in Havana* (1958) and *The Quiet American* (1955) come to mind. Sadly, no attempt was made to recruit me. Nor do I think, though it is hard to be sure, that I was ever locally attributed with foreign influence of the kind reported elsewhere (Shryock, this volume; Dresch 2000a).

7. The broader role of Islamist groups in charity work in Pakistan has been noted by others (Siddiqi 2014; Iqtidar 2012; Jalal 2008).

8. The term *ghair* literally means remote (*'alaqa* refers to area) and, as the term is used today, implies distant and unreachable. However, in John Platts's *Dictionary of Urdu, Classical Hindi, and English* (1884), the term has a legal meaning and is defined as "territory beyond the limits of (one's) jurisdiction." The seven agencies are as follows: North Waziristan, South Waziristan, Bajaur Agency, Orakzai Agency, Kurram Agency, and Mohmand Agency.

9. Several further changes have taken place since this chapter was first written. In May 2018, amid large-scale protests by young Pashtuns against extra-judicial killings, the Frontier Crimes Regulation was repealed. It was replaced by FATA Interim Governance Regulation (FIGR 2018), which merged FATA with Khyber Pakhtunkhwa province but outlined a separate legal framework to conduct proceedings in civil and criminal cases. In January 2019, the Supreme Court of Pakistan declared FIGR as unconstitutional and ordered all pending cases from FATA to be transferred to courts within Khyber Pakhtunkhwa province (https://nation .com.pk/17-Jan-2019/sc-declares-fata-interim-regulation-unconstitutional). There is an ongoing national debate on whether FATA should remain merged with Khyber Pakhtunkhwa or be given independent provincial status. I have not included these changes in the main text since fieldwork used in this chapter is from 2013. Moreover, despite these changes, the overall sentiment of marginalisation and oppression amongst tribal Pashtuns remain unchanged. The protests against extrajudicial killings have coalesced into the Pashtun Tahafuz Movement (PTM), led by Manzoor Pashteen, a civil rights movement demanding just and equal treatment of tribal Pashtuns and disclosure of enforced disappearances in the "war on terror" (https://www.aljazeera.com/indepth/features/pakistan-disappeared-cost-war -taliban-180418080944584.html). PTM's activities are heavily surveilled by the armed forces and intelligence, their rallies are often disrupted by the police, and there is heavy censorship in the Pakistani press on discussions about the movement. PTM's supporters (Pashtun or otherwise) are frequently harassed and threatened by state security agencies.

10. See note 9.

11. For a discussion on how such work was largely focused on landowning groups and overlooked the landless majority, see Asad (1972). Like the Pashtuns of the tribal areas, many of the men from these groups have migrated to cities in the south.

12. The literal meaning of *sahaba* is comrade or associate, but it is usually used for the companions of the Prophet.

13. In South Asia, *jawan* (lit. young, manly) is used for junior soldiers and as a general term for noncommissioned members of the armed forces.

14. The English word *rocket* is used in Urdu to denote any kind of propelling weapon, ranging from tank shells to drone missiles.

15. "Army-cut" refers here to short hair and clean-shaven faces, a standard associated with the army's grooming regulations.

16. In 2013, the wholesale price of a crate was Rs 300 ($2.50).

5

SECRECY AND CONTINUITY
IN RAJASTHAN

Anastasia Piliavsky

COMMON SENSE COMMODIFIES THE SECRET, ALIENATING THE VALUE of its content from its social context. But a secret perfectly kept dies in its circle of initiates. Few secrets, however, are dead on arrival, as their seduction lies precisely in their revelation. Most things said to be hidden are in fact nurtured through calculated concealment and revelation; secrets propagate themselves through circles of conspiracy, rumor, and gossip. As Tim Jenkins observed, "What is concealed, and the reasons for its concealment, serve to distract attention from the dynamic of the secret: what at first sight appears to be static and indeed dead, possessed by and known to only a few, kept in some dark place, in fact has a life and movement of its own; the secret propagates itself through a structure of secret and betrayal" (1999, 225–26). Open secrets may be kept, while their substance remains known to everyone, for a brief moment or centuries.

This studied movement of disguise and disclosure is intrinsic to power (Canetti 1962) and, as Simmel (1906) and Goffman (1959) taught, is a primary process of social life. Secrets incite suspicion and intimacy, jealousy, schism, and trust. Their power lies not in their content, which often proves a disappointment upon revelation, but in the rhetoric of their mystification. Mystified knowledge—the secret—can be owned, flaunted before or withheld from others, exchanged for allegiance, or sold (through treason or blackmail). Gossip, then, is not merely witness to the weakness of chinwags who cannot keep a secret. To dismiss it as the flotsam of boredom and fantasy is to ignore an entire domain of social production.

This chapter is about the life of one secret in the circles of its relentless reve-lation. More specifically, it is about the rhetoric of secrecy that surrounds a caste of professional thieves known as Kanjars in a rural part of the western Indian state of Rajasthan. Much of my material consists of what I initially dismissed as "mere gossip," but which eventually came to the fore of my understanding not only of the social location of the Kanjar community but also of some basic as-pects of local society, which, as it turned out, are very old. In popular discourse, official accounts, and their own presentations of self, Kanjars are a secret people possessed of secret knowledge, a secret tongue, and magical powers. Secrecy that surrounds Kanjars is a matter known and circulated in the open. Unlike "public secrets" that are "generally known but cannot be articulated" (Taussig 1999, 5; also Herzfeld 1987, 95–122; 2005) and are protected by the silence of their keepers, Kanjar secrets are enthusiastically proliferated by bazaar gossips, policemen, and Kanjars alike. Much like "the *active milling, polishing, and pro-motion of the reputation of secrets*" described by Paul Johnson as "secretism" in a Brazilian context (2002, 3; emphasis in original; following Simmel 1906, 486), the secrecy that surrounds Kanjars generates mystified knowledge that acts as a screen for the absent, the well-known, and the banal. Whereas public secrecy described by Taussig protects content that ought to remain hidden, mystifica-tion that surround Kanjars creates secret content where there is none; it is not what is concealed but the fact of concealment that is significant. The process of talking about Kanjar secrets creates a hidden and, as I shall show, essential social domain. Secret spaces, relations, activities, and people like Kanjars play a crucial part in the maintenance of polite and proper life on display, making the generation of secrets a central aspect of public life. While excluded from proper society in rhetoric, in practice Kanjars occupy some of its innermost domains.

Secrets Revealed

A few years back, I was in Jaipur, Rajasthan's capital, drinking midday whis-keys with some aristocratic Rajput families, people I like to visit periodically to keep abreast of current gossip. Our conversation drifted leisurely from polo ground drama to the new zinc factory inauguration party, the matrimonial matches to be made with the Jodhpur Rathores (a high-ranking Rajput clan), and the recent kills by man-eating panthers on the border with the neighboring state of Madhya Pradesh. I brought up Kanjars, an "ex-criminal" caste con-nected in the minds of many with illicit liquor production, prostitution, and petty theft.[1] At the time, I had come to frequent some Kanjars in a local slum. I mentioned to my Rajput acquaintances, rather cautiously, that I had heard that Rajput families employed "criminal castes," wondering if the present company could help me learn more about Kanjars and other such groups. Expecting tacit suspicion at best, I held my breath, prepared to blame the midday heat and the spirits for the implied accusation of criminal involvement.

Instead of suspicion, my question was met with enthusiasm and brought forth a host of stories about the Kanjars' bizarre habits and beliefs. My Rajput friends, eager to see me fill my notebooks with Kanjar "ethnography," overwhelmed me with "secrets" of Kanjar life. With a raised brow and in a lowered voice one of them said that Kanjars have many secret practices, the details of which he proceeded to describe; from the training of wall-climbing lizards (used in house burglary) to bizarre wedding arrangements, humans offered in sacrifice to bloodthirsty goddesses, and ritual rooftop defecation, my company claimed to know it all. In the heat of the moment, someone even suggested that there was little need for me to spend time among Kanjars because I could learn most of their secrets from the present party and other similarly "knowledgeable people," of whom, as I came to realize, there was never a shortage.

Common accounts describe Kanjars as an external people—socially, morally, and categorically. Their indecency is not simply common knowledge; it is proverbial. Across northern India parents often say to their ill-behaved children, "*Kanjarō kī taraf mat karo!*" ("Don't act the Kanjar way!" or "Don't do it like a Kanjar!"). *Kanjar* is also used as a term of abuse akin to the English bastard or whore. People describe Kanjars as *gandhe* (dirty), meaning vulgar, uncivil, and generally unsuitable for decent folk; the fact of a young "English girl" living in their midst provoked much disbelief and consternation.[2] The exclusion of Kanjars from mainstream society is reified in the observable sphere of everyday life. Kanjars almost invariably live in settlements (*bastī*)—never villages (*gāoṅ*) proper—that are separate from ordinary multicaste villages, or in slums on the outskirts of cities and towns, where they are engaged (both in repute and in deed) in all sorts of illicit and illegal activities: distilling, drinking, and selling country liquor (*dāṛū*); stealing, selling, and eating goats and sheep; and prostitution.

The concept of a secret community—which links notions of power, secrecy, magic, and vice—has a long history in South Asian narratives. Indian literature, ranging from ancient legal and statecraft treatises to epics and medieval folk stories, describes communities of peripatetic and jungle-dwelling peoples not only as socially, ritually, and morally set apart or hidden from ordinary society, but also as necessarily involved in thievery, understood as the art of disguises and the business of hidden possessors of secret knowledge and power.[3] Respect for and fear of thief communities in Indian writings have always revolved around their hidden nature, which has been cause for much fascinated elaboration in subcontinental literatures. Much like my Rajput acquaintances in Jaipur, authors of texts about the secret thieving communities describe their hidden worlds in substantial detail, imagining them as hereditary trade guilds that are "banded, cartelized and organized groups, that live together" (Bloomfield 1926, 205). In various texts thieving communities are said to possess highly formalized sets of professional skills, wear distinctive clothing, and work under the auspices of their own deities.[4] In short, the thieving communities of Brahmanic narrative have been imagined as castes like any other. Thieving, nevertheless, is a special business unlike pottery or the weaving of baskets. Contra Chris Bayly (1996) and Sandria Freitag (1998), who have argued that before the arrival of the British on the subcontinent, theft was a perfectly legitimate part of South Asian politics, neither in ancient narratives nor in precolonial politics has thieving been treated as a plainly legitimate trade. In Brahmanic narratives the robbers' hidden lairs harbor not only magical powers but also various bloodthirsty and barbarous vices. The colonial rubric of "criminal caste" shifted emphasis to the moral depravity and social danger of such groups. But, contrary to the prevailing narrative of current historiography, the idea of a "robber caste"—a hidden community of professional, hereditary, and deviant thieves—long predates British presence on the subcontinent (on this, see Piliavsky 2015; also Gordon 1985).

Describing Thuggee in the first half of the nineteenth century in terms reminiscent of older Indian writings, William Sleeman, the British officer who "discovered" Thuggee, defined this "cult of murderous stranglers" as a secret society. His voluminous catalogue of the Thugs' "underworld" included descriptions of their secret argot, ritual practices, omens, modi operandi, and bloodthirsty deities (1836, 1839).[5] As Radhika Singha observed, it is precisely through claims to "mystery unveiled and mastered that a group of [British] officers of the Political Department had lobbied for operations against this 'murderous fraternity'" (1993, 83). By the late 1840s, Sleeman shifted his attention from Thugs to the newly discovered "fraternities of hereditary robbers" (1849), which in later colonial legislation came to be defined as "criminal tribes." The criminal tribes, among whom Kanjars figured prominently, continued to be defined as hereditary professional guilds engaged in a secretive trade. Although their criminalization in colonial law and the attendant policing and penal measures removed such groups still further from mainstream society,[6] the terms in which criminal tribesmen were identified were not a figment of the colonial imagination. They drew substantially in old local ways of imagining robber communities, mixed with eugenics and Victorian angst about secret societies and collective crime (Piliavsky 2015, 341–2).

The mystification of thieving communities took a new lease on life after India's independence. Retaining their criminal identity in official practice, if no longer in statute, Kanjars and other such groups continue to be understood as a people hidden from moral society and the gaze of the law.[7] In 1998 the chief minister of the Indian state of Madhya Pradesh lamented that the state's educational programs had little effect on "the criminal instincts" of Pardhis (another "ex–criminal tribe") because, he explained, these instincts were nourished by the "hidden nature of their society, which is resilient to the ideas of modern education" (*Telegraph* 1998). A recent newspaper article about Kanjars accused of poaching peacocks described them as descendants of "famed highway plunderers . . . said to be habitual criminals who always carry country-made pistols and crude bombs with them." The police cannot track them down, the article claimed, because the Kanjars "disappear on the spot into their secret lairs" (Srivastava 2005). While local monographs on "denotified" (ex-criminal) castes call for their "upliftment" (Bhargava 1949; Garg 1965; P. Shah 1967; Gandhi 2008), official descriptions propagate old notions of their secrecy.

Such allegations fill the records, for instance, of local police stations. In areas that house Kanjar settlements, "Village Crime Note Books" (VCNBs), which are meant to record crime in all villages within a given police jurisdiction, record only crime committed by Kanjars and emphasize the inherent secrecy of the Kanjar caste. A characteristic account opens one such document:

> This area belonged to the chief [*jagīrdār*] of the Fararpur estate [*ṭhikānā*]. The chief used to live here. He used to collect land revenue [*lagān*]. But after the *jagīrdāri* system was abolished, the revenue was collected by the tax collector [*tahasīldār*]. This area is 300 years old. People of the following castes reside in this area: Rājput, Brāhmaṇ, Bālāī, Regar, Rebārī, Dhākaṛ, Sutār [Goldsmith], Nāī, and Kanjar. Kanjars live in the southern and western corners of the village. These people are involved in burglary and cattle theft. They kill and steal goats. In the village there is a primary school, the village council [*panchāyat*] headquarters, an accountant [*paṭwārī*] office, and other government offices. Agriculture is the local people's main occupation. Kanjars are involved in crime. . . . They have their secret [*gupt*] methods [of stealing] and a language of their own [*pārsī*]. It is very difficult for the police to catch them.[8]

Another document, the "Compendium Concerning Kanjar Gangs," an ethnography of local Kanjars compiled by police officers and kept on file in the district police headquarters, opens with the following statement: "The Kanjar caste is a criminal caste. From ancient times these people have roamed about committing group crime [including] theft, roadside burglary, looting, and dacoity [gang robbery]. They are a caste that is addicted to crime. They are very difficult to find because they can run very fast and when they commit a robbery, they disappear into the jungle or cross over the [state] border".[9]

The Kanjars' secret nature comes as an afterthought and an apology in both documents, each of which makes a point of noting the inability of the police to round them up. As we shall see, there are practical reasons for such disclaimers, and the rhetoric of mystification that they deploy masks relations that are meant to be hidden from the official gaze. The same terms and images—lizards, addiction to crime, magical healing techniques, secret tongues, and supernatural endowment—are as much a part of the official story as they are a part of rumor in the bazaar. VCNBs are curious places where popular images fill official documents and are cast as expertise and official knowledge. A section of regular entries in one VCNB reads as follows:

> August 9, 1995
> Today I came to the village of "Lakshmipura" to investigate case #264, 265/95 and I inspected the area. The village people believe that "Suresh" associates himself with Kanjars and takes their stolen goods. This will be investigated. The entries are complete and correct.
> Signed, SHO [Senior House Officer] of the "Fararpur" police station . . .

> December 17, 1996
> The SHO checked the area during his patrolling session and blocked off all passable roads for the inspection. No Kanjars were found. The entries are complete and correct.
> Signed, SHO of Fararpur station

> September 12, 1997
> Today the Kanjar settlement was raided for the arrest of "Raj". He was not found. Most Kanjars run away upon the approach of the police. They cannot be caught. The entries are complete and correct.
> Signed, SHO of Fararpur station

> December 16, 1998
> SHO came together with the police force in search of the criminal "Suresh" in relation to case #273/98 with accusation under IPC section 379 [theft]. He raided the settlement and made the arrest. He checked for the presence of the criminal "Gopal", who was not found to be present in the village. But we heard that he visited "Fararpur" town. His accomplices cannot be found. The entries are complete and correct.
> Signed, SHO of Fararpur station

> May 11, 2000
> Today we made a patrolling round of the village, talked to the village people and collected information from reliable sources. The entries are complete and correct.
> Signed, SHO of Fararpur station.[10]

The primary sources for such chronicles are the stories villagers tell about their Kanjar neighbors. The constables inevitably hear that "so-and-so visited the town," "the village people believe that so-and-so associates with the Kanjars," and so forth. The information is always gathered from "reliable sources," and the entries are invariably "complete and correct." This particular VCNB, which documents thirty-four years of patrolling one village, records but one instance of direct communication between police staff and the Kanjars: a particularly earnest officer noted that he conveyed to the residents of one Kanjar settlement the evils of meat eating, drinking, and theft. Otherwise, the record is filled with reports of Kanjar disappearing acts. While one may expect official accounts to be free of rumor and fantasy, in fact police and bazaar knowledge share a great deal. Most police officers are locals, and their accounts are full of folkloric stereotypes, which not only inform but also legitimize police records. While statements regarding Kanjar magical disappearances may raise an anthropologist's knowing smile, for villagers they are matters of obvious fact. When I relayed the content of some police descriptions of Kanjars to local farmers, they nodded with approval. "Of course," said one, "everyone knows that Kanjars can disappear—they have magic [*jādū*]—nobody knows how they speak and how they steal and where they go and where they come from."

In actual fact, the police make it their business to understand Kanjar lives in great detail. But such understanding is not meant for official chronicles. The record contained in police stations is what officers call a "formality" (using the English word), necessary as evidence of their work. "Real information" (*pakkī sūchanā*), as one sub-inspector explained, does not make it to paper. "True Kanjar knowledge" (*sachchī Kanjar jānkarī*) is almost never recorded because what is written is no longer hidden. Instead, records of contact with and information about Kanjars are passed down orally from one officer to the next within police stations and district police circles. In each police station where there are Kanjars or other robber castes under their jurisdiction, field officers (normally, a constable and an assistant sub-inspector) are designated for communicating with and gathering information about them. These officers often remain in post for many years (well beyond the formal limit of two years), during which they cultivate close relations with local Kanjars.[11] These officers are usually assigned to the circle of regular inspection in Kanjar villages and can often be found in civilian clothes, chatting with Kanjars in their settlement or the bazaar.

Some of them become "Kanjar experts," or district-level officers (no lower than sub-inspector in rank) responsible for collecting intelligence from and about Kanjar life. It is under their supervision that the Kanjar "ethnographies" kept on file in the district headquarters are compiled. Most Kanjar experts have extensive experience and knowledge of the life and work of the local Kanjars, and most have long-standing relationships with Kanjar communities and heads of gangs. Claims to Kanjar magic and secrecy written into police ethnographies leave the reader mystified, as they are meant to, for they are framed as privileged knowledge. Transmitted orally from one expert to the next and masked on paper by allusions to magic and secrecy, what the police do actually know about the Kanjars is preserved within and through the rhetoric of secrecy. The relations and activities screened by this rhetoric are of interest, and I will return to them shortly, but first let me turn to what Kanjars themselves make of such claims.

Nurturing Secrets

When I first arrived at my field research site, my Kanjar informants insisted that nobody outside of their community knew their language.[12] Much like their neighbors, Kanjars explained that this secret tongue (*āpas kī bolī* or "insider language") did not lend itself to learning but propagated itself as instinctual knowledge, acquired through being born and raised within the Kanjar community. As I slowly picked up the Kanjari dialect (which turned out to be a slightly modified form of the regional Mewari language), consternation spread—either I too had magical powers, like Kanjars, or I had been sent in by *sarkār*, the government, itself subject to much mystification. As I picked up more words, Kanjars themselves began to insist that there was yet another level of secrecy to their language, a secret tongue (*pārsī*) beneath their everyday speech. This tongue turned out to be a professional argot consisting of just a few dozen words. But, as my friends in the settlement taught me more of it, others insisted on the existence of two, four, or even a dozen secret tongues aside from that which I was learning, so that no matter how much I tried I would never have the "total information" (*total jānakarī*) about their secret language. It was secrets all the way down.

A senior gang leader, Kalpesh, who was my host and chief interlocutor, nonetheless persisted in teaching me the tongues, which turned out to be a kind of "pig Latin," formed by standard substitutions of phonemes and additions of prefixes. Our lessons were a transgression, since while others are to know *about* Kanjar secrets, they are not to be privy *to* them. Such deviousness, however, thrilled Kalpesh—the argot was our little-big secret.[13] Each time I blurted out a secret word, my Kanjar neighbors and hosts assumed that I had not "learned" it as one learns Hindi in school but had acquired it by a natural, if strange, predisposition. As it grew increasingly apparent that I was able to grasp the content of most "secret" conversations, my Kanjar hosts reached a consensus: I must have been a Kanjar in a former life.[14]

Another sphere of secret knowledge are the "eighty-four wisdoms" (*chaurāsī buddhiyāṅ*) the Kanjars are said to possess.[15] At the end of my stay, Kalpesh and I drove my motorcycle beyond the boundary of the settlement and settled under a banyan tree for my long-promised lesson on the wisdoms. He tried to remember as many of them as he could. What he revealed turned out to be a varied collection of thieving modi operandi, ancestral practices, and regulations of matters like bride-price and incest. Kalpesh also claimed that each adult (male) Kanjar has a treasure that he keeps hidden in the jungle. The long-awaited revelations of secret practices and ancient mores, from wall-climbing lizards to human sacrifice and hidden treasures, reiterated what I had heard in the bazaar and what I assumed to be the tall tales of ignorant outsiders. When I asked Kalpesh why I had not in fact seen any lizards or human sacrifice among Kanjars, he explained that these were very old practices and that, although neither humans were sacrificed nor lizards were reared, it was important that all Kanjars knew these "secret signs of Kanjar distinction" (*gupt pahachān*). Their divulgence, he warned me, would "ruin" (*barbād karnā*) their community.

Such revelations echoed an observation made by Paul Dresch, that "The experience [of fieldwork] was not well described as simply 'dialogue.' Nor was it 'data collection.' It was more like a trade in secrets, though in a curious way. The more thriller-like the material, the less difficult to gather, to the point where one [is] constantly being told things unfit for print: the more mundane and empirical the published facts, by contrast, the more collecting them resembled clandestine intrigue" (2000a, 109–10). While anthropologists are spoon-fed sensational material, the plain stuff of ethnographic interest—kin relations, household economics, religious affinities—may long remain obscure to, and deliberately obscured from, them. The basic "data" of ethnographic writing is often composed of others' secrets, which are rarely mentioned in everyday conversation and are often revealed only uncomfortably and in hushed tones. The very process of asking questions about such matters can raise alarm, making otherwise innocuous information suddenly unfit for discussion, leaving the interview not only a less than desirable but a potentially detrimental ethnographic tool. The "secrets" you ask for are then replaced with the secrets informants are happy to tell. Would you like some secrets? Here are some! Such readily divulged secrets, although often unpublishable, have serious ethnographic gravitas. Not only do they forge a sense of intimacy among their keepers, as Dresch observes, but they also define a sphere of their keeping as special. By relaying secrets, informants make anthropologists feel "in" on matters of exceptional value and interest, often without actually allowing them inside.

While little of the contents to which I was thus made privy came as a revelation, the presentation of some knowledge as hidden proved instructive. As it turned out, secrecy was just as central to Kanjars' presentation of themselves as it was to their mystification by others. The trick lay in revealing *that* secrets existed while concealing *what* they in fact were (as in P. Johnson 2002, 3). Unease surrounding the revelation of wisdoms and tongues had nothing to do with a fear of policemen learning things that they either already knew (such as Kanjars' modi operandi) or did not care to know about (such as bridewealth regulations). Instead, by disclosing things meant to be hidden, the divulgence of secrets threatened the mystery and the invisibility that are central to the role Kanjars play in local life. As one of my Kanjar interlocutors put it, "Our secrets [*gupt*] are our watering well [*kūṇṛā*]," the source of livelihood.

Secrets Concealed

Contrary to what they themselves and their neighbors claim, Kanjars are centrally involved in the proceedings of local life. They are connected to various "patrons" (*jajmān*), employers, and "friends" (*dost*) for whom they perform a number of crucial services. Village communities hire Kanjars as watchmen, and Rajput landlords (*zamīndār*) frequently employ them as watchmen, thieves, and intelligence agents.[16] One Rajput of my acquaintance told me that his Kanjar "servant" (*kamīn*) had been in his family's service for three generations, helping them to "push down others who stuck their heads up too high." Let me explain what this means.

Thieving groups have long been central to local dispute resolution, and continue to be so through their involvement in rural systems of watch and ward, intelligence, and conflict management. Such groups have been employed on all levels—from farmers to kings.[17] This practice carries on in the countryside. A clandestine nocturnal "raid" (*gemī* in Kanjari) of a house is the standard method of "pushing down" (infin. *dabānā*) others. The main aim of such raids is not resource extraction, and the commissioning party often gains little or no material profit. Instead, the raid is employed to intimidate opponents by penetrating their homes "to expose their weakness" (infin. *unakī kamajorī dikhānā*). The victim, who knows very well whose work this is, then has to plead with the commissioner of the raid to have the goods returned and is thus forced to resolve the dispute on more favorable terms. If successful, raiding contests are normally resolved through the reestablishment of rapport between the opponents and the restitution of stolen property.

Almost a year ago, a Rajput of my acquaintance awoke to find the contents of his living room neatly arranged in his garden.[18] The burglars took nothing, but the message was clear; the terms of sharing a field, on which he had been unable to agree with his cousin, were soon negotiated, and courteous rapport between the two was restored.[19] Such raiding tactics are not restricted to conflict negotiation within the Rajput elite; they are a common means of communication in local society.[20] In the decades since independence, however, many bonds between Kanjars and their hereditary Rajput employers have been severed, and today only two Rajput families in Fararpur continue to employ their families' hereditary Kanjar clients.[21]

Kanjars also find employment as "watchmen" (*chaukīdār*) in villages, orchards, fields, and family homes. For them, watchmanship (*chaukīdārī*) is one of the most reliable sources of income, and almost two-thirds of adult men in the settlement of my research are currently so employed. In fact, it is the only legal source of income in the community aside from small-scale cash crop agriculture. Yet this legal and fully legitimate business depends on illegal activity. Watchmen's duties lie both in policing their assigned domains (preventing theft, tracing culprits, and retrieving stolen property) and in negotiating conflicts within communities under their watch. Much of it is, in effect, a racketeering business: Kanjars protect villages from the threat they themselves pose (for more on this historically, see Piliavsky 2013b). They also engage in negotiations of disputes among their patrons. When family conflicts arise, it is the watchman who is called on to facilitate communication and, should that fail, to "put pressure" on the unruly party through the thieving tactics already described.

Secret Agents

The involvement of Kanjars in local politics and social control is not confined to the "shadow economy" of informal relations but is also central to the formal arena of state governance. Many Kanjars work for the police, providing them with crucial intelligence, means of control, and a source of income.[22] In return for their services, a blind eye is turned to their activities, a practice known as "adoption" (infin. *god lenā*). This practice is common across northern India, where police patronize various people involved in illegal activities (like theft, liquor distilling, or prostituting).[23] Such relations are typically initiated by heads of police stations (Station House Officers or SHOs) who establish connections with village leaders, usually gang leaders, who become informers (*mukhbīr*, or *mukhbar* in Kanjari) and mediators between the police and their own village. In exchange for information and a share of their spoils, heads of stations direct their staff to turn a blind eye to the activities of their informers' gangs, stop or minimize the filing of false cases, "write off" arrest warrants at little or no cost to their informers, and make the filing of court cases redeemable with moderate payments.[24] The best Kanjar clients are those who are most heavily involved in thieving, ideally gang leaders.[25] That is why most active Kanjar gangs remain protected on the territories of local police stations and why "history sheeters" (recidivists with a criminal "history sheet" on file in the police) remain so elusive in official records. It is also why Kanjars rarely raid areas outside the jurisdiction of their patron stations, targeting neighboring villages with increasing frequency (for more, see Piliavsky 2013a).

The local concentration of their activity has provoked a rise of violence both within and against their community, something I describe in greater detail elsewhere (Piliavsky forthcoming). While standing beyond the pale of formal legitimacy, such relationships with the police constitute the habitual and often socially sanctioned realities of local political life. As raiders, watchmen, informers, and mediators, Kanjars are employed when communication between different parties falters. Why this is necessary requires a pause for explanation.

Observers of Indian political communication—whether in caste and village councils (*panchāyat*) or in the Parliament of India—have remarked on the lack of dialogue. Discussions in village councils have been described, for example, as a trade in monologues—complaints, accusations, apologies, or conciliatory speeches meant neither as responses nor as prompts to rejoinders (D. Gupta 1997, 48–51). The same communicative asymmetry marks proceedings in Parliament, where havoc often ensues as parliamentarians rise out of order to shout out speeches that have little to do with the discussion, the particular questions raised, or the authority of the Speaker (Spary 2010).[26] This monologic communicative style defines interaction not only in the parliament or the village council but also in contexts ranging from the household to the courtroom.[27] Respect due to superiors prevents rejoinders from inferiors. In interactions between rank non-equals dialogue amounts to speech out of turn, which by violating the rules of hierarchical precedence, disrupts the community, inside and out, causing "anxiety" (*gabar*) within it and potentially incurring shame. To avoid such structural violence, people employ go-betweens such as Kanjars to negotiate.

Such monologic communication bespeaks a key aspect of local social life. The order of ranked relations in local society, its hierarchy, requires an asymmetry of exchange, communication, and rapport. The order of communicative precedence is set in accordance with the social structures of super- and subordination: fathers have precedence of speech over sons, husbands over wives, elders over youth, patrons over clients, and so on. When the order of rank is unclear (outside of the particular locality or among unranked cousins or friends), communicative problems arise.[28] Conflicts of interest and the need to speak out of turn do transpire, and they call for a medium of communication.

Not everyone can take on this role. Since dialogue is thwarted by an order of precedence that defines relations within and between communities (such as castes, villages, or households), conflicts require mediation from beyond the ranked social order. It requires external agency.

Mystified and rhetorically hidden, Kanjars are precisely that—people external to ordinary, ranked society—whose externality places them in some of the innermost domains of life. This is best illustrated with an example: a lengthy dispute between a man from the Gujar (herder) caste and his younger brother's wife, which was mediated by Kalpesh, my Kanjar host and the family's watchman. The woman stole five goats from the Gujar man and sold them in a village some twenty kilometers away. This left the victim, her brother-in-law, at a loss as to how to resolve the matter. Over the following two months, Kalpesh made a series of visits to both parties, relaying the concerns, and finally threats, of one to the other. The conflict was ultimately resolved with the woman paying for the goats and Kalpesh receiving one-fifth of the sum. To my query as to why they could not just talk to each other, Kalpesh, exasperated with my imbecile question, explained: "She is his younger brother's wife! How could he speak to her?" The victim of theft could not himself discuss the matter with her; as in most North India castes, face-to-face interaction between Gujar men and the wives of their younger brothers is strictly prohibited, a prohibition marked by veiling and the physical distance that men keep from the junior sisters-in-law (e.g., Freed and Freed 1964, 153; Mandelbaum 1970, 1:64–65). Verbal communication between them does not happen—a woman cannot address her husband's elder brother directly, but nor is she obliged to respond to him. Any persistence to provoke dialogue on his part would be interpreted as a violation of hers, his, and the family's honor. It is precisely on this prohibition that the younger brother attempted to capitalize, deputing his wife to steal the goats and thus depriving the plaintiff, his elder brother, of recourse. Besides, as Kalpesh explained, it was shameful for an elder to "beg" (infin. *māṅgnā*) for the return of the goats. In the hierarchical order of gift-service relations, elders cannot ask for things; they can only give them. The family needed an outside man to counsel the woman.[29] "I am," he added proudly, "just such a man!"

Discreet resolution of conflict within families (or clans or castes) preserves their public integrity and thus their "honor" (*ijjat*). While being rhetorically excluded from mainstream society, Kanjars are given access to some of the innermost dealings of families, whose public "face" they help save. Excluded from public life, Kanjars have access to family secrets without exposing their keepers to people who matter, on whose judgment family honor rests. It is precisely the Kanjars' discursive exclusion from ordinary, public life that gives them access to some of its most intimate proceedings. This poses a paradox: life on display relies on relations and persons that must be kept hidden, making the hidden an intrinsic part of public life. The Kanjar secrets, which hide them from public view, is precisely what sustains the public face of local society.

The involvement of Kanjars in local relations does not always take the deferent form of "explaining"; much of it also involves raiding and penetration. Such raiding is meant to be hidden, from state law as much as from public view. And this clandestine ethic of raiding negotiations is maintained by both perpetrators and victims of raids. Kanjars think of thieving as an art of disguises: they pride themselves on entering, robbing, and leaving homes unobserved, and they look down on "new players," unprofessional thieves who steal in broad daylight, leave behind traces, or struggle instead of fleeing if caught. The victims of raids, which they know to have been commissioned, are no keener to have them exposed. A raid is a communicative act, which leaves its victim penetrated and so humiliated, rather like rape. In the course of my fieldwork, not a single raid-for-negotiation was reported to the police or otherwise made public by victims. I learned about each one from my Kanjar hosts, who bragged about their successes. Rumors of them did seep into the bazaar, but even the biggest rumor mills treated them with care, describing them as the families' "internal matters" (*andar ke māmale*) not meant for discussion or judgment.

The growing involvement of Kanjars in state policing creates yet another domain of relations meant to remain unseen. With the post-independence decline of royal patrons, Kanjars have forged new patronal bonds with the police (Piliavsky 2013b). The involvement of Kanjars in state policing reveals something crucial about the workings of the Indian state. One sub-inspector described his relations with the Kanjar "secret agents," as he jokingly called his Kanjar informers (using the English term):

> According to [state] law, the government workers [*sarakārī naukar*] and the criminals [*aprādhī log*] should not have any connections [*sambandh*]. We [police officers] have to catch them, but how can we do that without knowing them or talking to them? The police stations have no funds for informers. But we need criminals to give us information [*sūchanā*] and to connect us to criminal networks. So, we build relationships [*ristā*] with them. I don't have money to give away, but I give food and clothes [to my informers]. We need to fill our quotas, so how can I not be friendly [*dostī rakhnā*] with Kanjars?

The rhetoric of separation between government servants and criminals, which the policeman invoked, creates a gap where crucial links actually lie. The contrasts between formal and informal, official and unofficial, legal and criminal, or indeed the government and the people, which are the stuff of modern state ideology, draw lines across relational spheres that are not, and cannot be, kept pure of one another (Abrams 1988; Mitchell 1991; Fuller and Harriss 2001). The Indian dictum that "it takes a thief to catch a thief" goes against the idea that those who steal and those who police are different people belonging to separate social and institutional spheres. As the sub-inspector points out, much policing is in fact conducted by criminals, making the formal logic of modern statehood fundamentally incompatible with the observable realities of local life. This disjuncture creates a sphere of social relations that must be kept secret, and this is where Kanjars can both thrive and perish. Relations within this sphere, which are habitually glossed over or written off as "criminal" or "corrupt," must be kept opaque not only to maintain the reputable standing of state servants but also to uphold the very idea of the state. The mystification of Kanjars, which propagates popular stereotypes in official paperwork—claims to their invisibility or magical escapes—is not only a mask of this hidden terrain; it reinforces the very logic of modern statehood that makes this sphere criminal and, in principle, hidden. Much as behind-the-scenes negotiations and thieving contests serve to uphold the public reputation of respectable families, relations that stand in the shade of officialdom in fact maintain the face of the state. This is not only a space where the enterprising thrive but also a domain of vulnerability that remains invisible to international watchdog organizations, Delhi officials, the press, and state law.

For the many Kanjars who do not have the good end of police patronage, this carries tangible consequences. Those without patrons in the police are subject to persistent predation, "erroneous" convictions, and protracted extra-legal imprisonment. Even for well-established informers, police patronage is often fickle, and they often find themselves as vulnerable as their unprotected caste-mates. Just after I left Lakshmipura, Kalpesh was thrown into jail without trial or evidence, where he languished for several months. The officer who patronized him was transferred to a new station, another one arrived, and Kalpesh quickly found himself without protection and in a lockup. When Kanjars disappear into jails for months at a time or are murdered by upper-caste neighbors, few are surprised—Kanjars are, after all, master illusionists, ever disappearing into "the jungle" or their secret lairs. This is how one jailer explained the absence of seven Kanjar inmates from his records: "Nobody ever knows where Kanjars are—they are always coming and going [*āte-jāte rahate*]; sometimes they are here and other times they are not. How can I keep track of them?"[30] While for some Kanjars the rhetoric of secrecy is a "watering well," for the community at large, it is a screen that conceals sites of vulnerability, violence, and abuse. The necessary outsider is also an expendable and often a necessary victim.

Conclusion

Kanjar secrets are hollow: their contents are either well-known or spurious. And yet ubiquitous talk of secrets defines persons, relations, and activities that are rhetorically excluded from, but are in practice central to, local life. The removal of Kanjars from public arenas places them into some of the deepest interstices of local life: household disputes, dealings between neighbors and cousins, and the delicate affairs that accumulate between state bureaucracy and everyday political life. This invisible domain is not just a mask of the illicit, the vicious, and the devious. Nor is it merely an abusive distortion of fact by local elites and state servants. The generation and preservation of secrecy here is a socially constitutive act that preserves the public proprieties indispensable to everyone, from police officers to farmers to landed elites. As Shryock remarks, "The production of identities meant to be public, that have publicity as part of their function, will create, of necessity, a special terrain of things, relations, and activities that cannot themselves be public but are essential aspects of whatever reality and value public things might possess" (2004c, 3). The state that blindly maintains law and order for all, or claims to do so, is the state that requires the criminal and endlessly reproduces it. This is the secret that Kanjars keep and reveal so well.

What presents a much more pressing intellectual puzzle than the capacity of the modern state to misrepresent and marginalize certain communities— every polity in human history has no doubt done that—is the remarkable endurance of the idea of a secret community of hereditary bandits. This motif has a history that stretches back many centuries on the subcontinent. British colonial authorities were certainly adept at propagating myths of secretive, criminal groups, as were their predecessors. But how and why has this basic idea persisted, despite so much change and as part of so many different governmental logics?

The rhetorical force of the stereotype of a secretive, hereditary bandit derives from it being just that—a simple, stable idea that can be repeated easily again and again. While setting in motion the mobile machinery of political life, stereotypes themselves are static, and they imbue momentary strategic decisions with the moral authority of fixed, eternal, or commonly recognized "truths" (Herzfeld 1990). Stereotypes are what Thomas Trautmann (2006) referred to as "locational technologies," or cognitive frameworks that remain exceptionally stable and that often come from the deep past. To be effective, stereotypes must be widely and readily recognized—they need to have cultural purchase. It was precisely because British rulers and their Indian subjects occupied shared cultural spaces that indigenous stereotypes were much more effective at classifying groups and justifying legal action than any foreign import or invention would or could ever have been. Simple ideas that can absorb shifts of emphasis and different shades of meaning, while still retaining a familiar shape, make for the most long-lived stereotypes. The idea of a secret, criminal caste is just like that. One can put greater stress on heredity or criminality, but the basic, recognizable out-line—a hidden community of hereditary, professional robbers with special skills, power, and an ethical code, operating under divine mandate—retains its shape. Those who turn these continuities into a scandal and see in such durable ideas only traces of imperial bewitchment or postcolonial fallacy do so necessarily at great heuristic cost.

ANASTASIA PILIAVSKY teaches social anthropology and politics at King's College London, where she is Senior Lecturer at the King's India Institute. She is editor of *Patronage as Politics in South Asia* and author of *Nobody's People: Hierarchy as Hope in a Society of Thieves*.

Notes

This chapter is based on field and archival research conducted between January 2005 and December 2008 and funded by the Rhodes Trust, the Wenner-Gren Foundation, and subsidiary grants from the Richard Ellis Katz Fund, the Ada Draper Fund, the Oxford Institute of Social and Cultural Anthropology, and Wolfson College (Oxford). I thank Filippo Osella, Crispin Bates, Jonathan Norton, Judith Scheele, Roeland de Wilde, and the participants of seminars at the Universities of Oxford, Edinburgh, Cambridge, Sussex, and the London School of Economics, where I presented drafts, for useful comments. Paul Dresch patiently read multiple drafts, and Andrew Shryock nursed the piece to life, now more than once. My biggest and ever-growing debt is to the Karmawat, Chhattrapal, Sisodiya, Nat, and Singh families, whose generosity, patience, and good humor made my research possible. I follow J. T. Platts's *Dictionary of Urdu, Classical Hindi, and English* (1884) in my transcriptions, replacing "c̆" with "ch" for readability, and use pseudonyms for people and places throughout.

An earlier version of this chapter appeared originally as Piliavsky, A. 2011. "A Secret in the Oxford Sense: Thieves and the Rhetoric of Mystification in Western India." *Comparative Studies in Society and History* 53 (2): 290–313. Reproduced with permission.

1. According to the 2011 *Census of India*, 206,467 people self-identified as Kanjars across northern India and 53,816 in Rajasthan, where they are classified as a Scheduled Caste. Historically, Kanjars have practiced a variety of trades, ranging from dancing and singing to genealogy, prostitution, mercenary thievery, and watchmanship. The majority of Kanjars in

southern Rajasthan, where I conducted most of my field research, work as watchmen-cum-professional thieves.

2. Such perceptions are not new. In the eighteenth century, Punjabi poet Waris Shah (1966, 79) wrote that "Kanjars know not what love is. God's curse on the casual light-o-loves. Touch them not."

3. The robbers of Brahmanical narratives dwell in the moonless night, the underground lair, and the jungle—the perennial periphery of civilized life in South Asia (Bloomfield 1923a, 195–96; Glucklich 1994, 192; Passi 2005, 514). Describing professional robbers as "invisible" (*aprakāśataskara*) people, Manu insists that theft itself is an art of deception and of disguise (Manu 1886, 9.258; Bhattacharya 1990).

4. For an overview of descriptions of thieving guilds in Sanskrit and vernacular Indian literature, see a series of articles by Maurice Bloomfield (1913, 1923a, 1923b, 1926). For descriptions of thieves' professional practices, see, for instance, *Jātaka Stories* (1895, 5:248), Śūdraka (1905, 47–49), Schiefner and Ralston (1906, 37ff), Parker (1910–14, 2:45–46, 2:326), H. Johnson (1920, 159ff), Bhāsa (1930–31, 39), and Daṇḍin (1966, 1.48). A number of Sanskrit "thievery manuals" (*steyā-śāstras, cora-śāstras,* or *steya-sūtras*) describing thieving societies and practices are now available in translation (*ṣaṇmukhakalpa* 1991; Aklujkar 1996; Passi 2001, 2005). These appear to be part of a larger genre of imaginative writing about thieving and thieves (Passi 2005). For the hereditary nature of the thieving profession, see *Jātaka Stories* (1895, 1:68), Hemavijaya (1920, 66–71), and Bloomfield (1923a, 100–101). For descriptions of thief-deities and peculiar ritual practices, see Śūdraka (1905, 47–48), Bhāsa (1907, 46–51), *Pariśiṣtas of the Atharvaveda* (1909, 1:128–133), Somadeva (1923, 141–42), and Bhāsa (1930–31, 11.2 et seq.). For descriptions of thieving "families," see H. Johnson (1920, 165–66) and Somadeva (1923, 141–42).

5. In the record of Sleeman's interviews with his Thug informers, it is precisely this old conception of a deviant yet professional caste of marauders to which the Thugs appeal in their attempts to prove themselves "proper" robbers deserving of Sleeman's highly desirable patronage (e.g., Sleeman 1836, 144–63).

6. On special policing and penal measures, including forced resettlement and confinement in reformatory colonies, administered under the Criminal Tribes legislation, see Nigam (1990), Tolen (1991), Radhakrishna (1992), and Major (1999).

7. In 1952, the Criminal Tribes Act was replaced with the Habitual Offenders Act, whose provisions, however, closely mimicked its predecessor's. Today the lists of "habitual offenders" are thickly populated with names of members of former "Criminal Tribes." In the police jurisdiction where I worked, for instance, twenty-four of the twenty-nine "habitual offenders" on file belong to "denotified" castes, and twenty-two are Kanjars.

8. Record office of the "Fararpur" police station. "Lakshmipura" VCNB 1977–present, p. 3.

9. Compendium Concerning Kanjar Gangs Resident in "Gopalpur" District. "Gopalpur" District Police Superintendent Files (access restricted). This "Compendium" is compiled and updated by the district police office staff by the order of the district superintendent of police. It combines information collected from Kanjar informers by officers designated as "Kanjar experts" (to be discussed) and "people's knowledge" (*logō kī jānkarī*) about Kanjars gathered by more junior officers. The "Compendium" proceeds to describe the deities worshipped, garb worn, and foods consumed by Kanjars, who, the document claims, are hopelessly "addicted to crime." It goes on to mention miraculous bone-setting practices, which involve the patient's overnight immersion in a barrel of cow manure, and describe a practice of rearing lizards used in wall-climbing burglary. A segment entitled

"Customs and Habits" states that Kanjar youths are considered unmarriageable until they partake in at least two burglaries.

10. Record office of the "Fararpur" police station. "Lakshmipura" VCNB 1977–present, p. 3

11. Since low-ranking police posts are often inherited, some bonds between Kanjars and officers span multiple generations.

12. Most of my field research was conducted in and around a Kanjar settlement in southeastern Rajasthan.

13. The use of "secret languages" is common among professional communities across South Asia: Charan genealogists use a specialist language called Dingal to make their records (A. Shah and Shroff 1958; Smith 1975; Ziegler 1976), merchants employ special terms to conceal matters from buyers, and each rank-grade in the police has its own argot used to keep things from outsiders and officers of other ranks. David Washbrook (1991) pointed out that Sanskrit too functioned as a Brahman argot. For a more general discussion of Indian secret languages, see Mehrotra (1977).

14. By the end of my field research, I realized that several other non-Kanjars who frequented Kanjar villages, whether to drink or make deals with them, also had a basic grasp of the Kanjar argot, although they did not tend to advertise the fact. Most "Kanjar experts" and other police officers were also privy to these tongues.

15. Eighty-four is the conventional number of parts in an ideal whole in South Asia. Rajasthani merchants, Gujarati Gujars, Brahmans, and Thugs alike have all been known to claim membership of eighty-four clans or tribes (Tod 1920, 1:120; Elliott 1859, 2:58-66; Wagner 2007, chap. 4).

16. Plunder is a long-standing element of statecraft on the subcontinent (Gordon 1969; Vidal 1997; Kasturi 2002, chaps. 5 and 6), recommended as early as the third century BCE in Kautilya's statecraft treatise (1967, 13.3, 7.4, 7.14) and still widely employed today. Indian rulers of various ranks (heads of states, gentry, and village landlords alike) have long employed professional marauding communities (many of them hillsmen or itinerant castes, some of whom rose to the status of Rajputs) for tax collection, intimidation, and intelligence gathering (Wink 1986; Kolff 1990; Guha 1999; Skaria 1999; Mayaram 2003; Wagner 2010). As early as 1774, Warren Hastings, the first Governor General of India, referred to the landholders of Bengal as the "nursing mothers" of criminal groups (O'Malley 1925, 305–6). Later Sleeman observed that "a Rajput chief, next to leading a gang of his own on great enterprise, delights in nothing so much as having a gang or two, under his patronage, for little ones. There is hardly a single chief, of the Hindoo military class, in the Bundelcund, or Gwalior territories, who does not keep a gang of robbers of some kind or other, and consider it as a very valuable and legitimate source of revenue" (1844, 1:188). For more on the landholders' patronage of thieving communities in Rajasthan, see Tod (1920, 2:493).

17. Others have noted the policing and spying functions of such groups (e.g., Bayly 1996, 163ff, 372–76), but little has been said about their role in disputes.

18. A similar episode was reported in 1923 in Calcutta. Upon arrival in his new posting in Calcutta, a British sub-inspector was approached by local Kanjar watchmen who suggested that he would not manage without their help. The officer refused them, and in a week found the contents of his office neatly laid out in front of his house and in his back yard. Nothing was missing, but the message was clear, and he soon employed the Kanjars as watchmen and approvers. See Samuel G. Pinhey, Letter (No. 35), May 28, 1925. West Bengal State Archives. Foreign (Internal-A), May 1925, proceedings 118–22.

19. Not all conflicts are so easily resolved, and some raiding contests may last for months or years. Some may employ a more desperate and dangerous "game" (*khel*, as Kanjars call it) and plant incriminating matter (such as opium poppy) in the opponent's home, which can then be used as blackmail. This tactic can carry serious consequences (the standard, non-bailable prison term for opium possession is a decade), violence, and permanent destruction of the relationship between the two parties.

20. Most services of the sort are commissioned on a one-off basis by men of different castes.

21. After joining the Union of India in 1949, the rulers of Rajput states and smaller chiefs lost their judiciary and fiscal rights and, after 1971, also their privy purses. Many could no longer afford to employ even a small fraction of the men previously in their service, leading to the dissolution of most of their patronal relations. Before independence, for instance, the Rajput lord of the local market-town supported twenty-seven temple priests alone. Today, he supports only one. Most bonds between Kanjars and their Rajput patrons have also dissolved.

22. Rural police in Rajasthan normally patronize a few gang leaders and their gangs, who provide information about the activities of other Kanjar gangs, and so help the police to keep smaller gangs from proliferating. See de Wilde (2009, 127-33) on the same technique used by police to control opium trafficking in Rajasthan.

23. Of the sixteen Kanjar settlements in the administrative block where I conducted most of my research, twelve are currently "adopted."

24. "Writing off" means reporting the absence of wanted offenders to court. Whereas unprotected thieves may have to pay 100–200 percent of the (often greatly inflated) value of property they are accused of stealing, protected thieves are expected to contribute 25–50 percent of their loot to their patron station in return for being cleared of the charge.

25. This system is patterned on the system of Thug approvers established by Sleeman in the early nineteenth century under the scheme of the Department for the Suppression of Thuggee and Dacoity, which "made use of informers who turned state's evidence" (Cohn 1996, 10; Wagner 2007).

26. While in the context of the *panchāyat* the order of super- and subordination is clearly set, in Parliament where the order of precedence is unclear, discussion frequently degrades into disorderly shouting with no regard for the general agenda or the Speaker's authority. In the Lower House in 2007 alone, disruptions cost 128 hours of parliamentary sitting time (Spary 2010, 338). Such parliamentary communicative disasters have been dubbed symptomatic of the decline of India's political institutions (Rubinoff 1998) and a "disease of democracy" (S. Chatterjee 2007).

27. Unilateral, top-down communication is the general rule in families and households, where superiors give directives and inferiors receive instructions. When dialogue does occur, it often provokes conflict that is frequently accompanied by shouting matches or even the use of violence. References to rules of communication on the subcontinent are scattered throughout ethnographic writing (e.g., Babb 1975, 51; Fuller 1992, 4). Caroline Osella and Filippo Osella (1998) offer a nuanced discussion of the physical and verbal form of hierarchical and subversively egalitarian communicative forms among South Indian youths. Nevertheless, a focused ethnography of the Indian communicative terrain, of the sort produced by William Beeman (1986) in Iran, is yet to be written.

28. See, for instance, David Pocock on the perils of decontextualized and unranked caste relations among East African Gujaratis (1957).

29. *Samajhānā* means literally "to explain," or appeal to reason that has been blurred by passion in dispute (Carstairs 1957, 47).

30. Policemen frequently incarcerate Kanjars without warrant or trial, often to extract a "bail" payment for their release. Such incarcerations are left unrecorded, provided the head jailer is willing to accept a small fee, usually a fraction of what the Kanjar families pay the police. There are virtually no inspections of prisons, and jailers and policemen have little fear of being caught.

6

THE PLACE OF STRANGERS IN MOROCCAN DOMESTICITY

Nostalgia, Secrets, and the Continuity of Scandal

Mary Montgomery

IN HIS ESSAY "FOREIGN MATTER: THE PLACE OF Strangers in Gulf Society" (2006a), Dresch explores how notions of privacy, status, and moral order play into public policy to "manage" a suspect population. He describes how Sharjah's citizens demanded that the state control public space to eliminate "disturbing gatherings" of Asian domestics who might otherwise disseminate "the secrets of citizens' houses" (212–13). Whereas the oil-rich political economy of the Gulf is (relatively) new and exceptional, the patterns of secrecy and public knowledge that render strangers problematic are not. These are evident in Dresch's work on Yemen (1989, 2012b) and reappear as an interest among his students. Strangeness, like privacy, of course is relative. We are reminded of Bourdieu's series of concentric circles, the domestic realm being the "first world of secrecy" (Bourdieu 1965, 223), which is to be protected from the "next concentric zone," whether the street, quarter, or village, and, moving out from there, the region and the wider world. Strangers appear then as a structural necessity not just for economic reasons, as with Simmel's stranger-trader (1999), but as implicated in a moral system of repute and vulnerability.

Domestic workers, as outsiders inside the house, "potential wanderers" (Simmel 1999, 185) whose belonging is conditional and therefore temporary, have everywhere been figures of scandal. A cursory review of literature on the subject—anthropological, historical, or fictional—suggests that Sharjah's

Asian domestics are simply new players on an old stage on which servants have for centuries moved forward plotlines while other characters took leading roles. "Telling Family Affairs," or rather, the importance of not doing so, is fifth among forty subjects covered in *A Present for a Servant-Maid*, an eighteenth-century manual for moral conduct in service (Haywood 1743). Eliza Haywood, also an actress and novelist, warns her "dear girls" against "blabbing small things" lest they be "suspected of not being more retentive in greater" (13). Bridget Hill argues, more generally, that restrictions on servant girls socializing in eighteenth-century England were to avoid the spread of family secrets as much as to prevent immoral behavior (Hill 1996, 55; see also Horn 2004).[1] While householders could control the social lives of those in their employ, when a servant left for good, the master and mistress were at their mercy, a logic that appears in England, the Gulf, and everywhere in between. For early twentieth-century Fès, Goichon (1929, 48) noted that relations would be severed if a domestic left to place herself with another family; she posed a threat to the privacy and honor of her initial patrons by her potential to tell stories about them to her new ones. In Spain, the collection of laws that regulated domestic service until the nineteenth century (*Nueva Recopilación de Leyes del Reino*) ruled that servants who left their masters without agreement must leave the region. Servants who were formally dismissed, on the other hand, could work at another house in the same locality (Casares 2004, 205).

In a structural sense, domestic workers are like guests, who must be treated with care. Out of the house, servants become witnesses or gossips, while departed guests are potential "poets" (Shryock 2004d, 36–37), a term that leaves the relative social status of guest and host ambiguous while acknowledging the guest's power to praise or defame the host in the outside world. In Morocco, "*fiha l-hadra*" (she talks), often said of domestics, has class connotations and never indexes panegyrics. If hospitality solves "the problem of how to deal with strangers" (Pitt-Rivers 1977, 94),[2] an answer to "the servant problem" is more complicated. Like guests in local "tournaments of value" (Shryock 2004d; following Appadurai 1986 and Meneley 1996), domestics belong to a set of moral claims that a house makes about itself and serve as a test of these claims. But, unlike guests, servants are required to cook and clean. They must therefore be "kept in their place," although spatially their place is that of their employers—they share a home. Both worker and house are therefore put to the test in specific ways. This testing, born of the tension between prestige and privacy, intimacy and inequality, is my concern in the present paper.

Studies of global domestic labor usually skip over several "concentric zones" to consider persons so distant from each other that differentials of value, both on the ground and in analysis, are lost. Here I shall explore instead the passing of strangers through *sha'bi* or ordinary households in Rabat, where local difference is magnified by Moroccans serving Moroccans. The account is based mainly on fieldwork conducted during 2012 and 2013 in Rabat's l'Océan quarter, where about one in ten households had a live-in Moroccan domestic and many more had casual help. Although human rights organizations and the press focus attention on *petites bonnes* (child domestics), most workers I encountered were adults. Known and therefore trustworthy domestics, who as adults potentially have lives of their own yet are nonetheless "like daughters," are valued but hard to come by, and as nostalgia would have it, increasingly so. New workers are thus presented as *ma'rufa* (known), although it often seems to matter little who precisely knows them. At crucial junctures the ambiguities produced become contradictions. Workers who are welcomed as daughters are thus often denounced as thieves or, at best, as ingrates when they leave. Oddly, they are not individually denounced as gossips. Nonetheless, the moralizing that facilitates the cyclical affiliation and disaffiliation of strangers parallels the patterns of historical knowledge production described by Shryock, which were shaped by the "possibility of getting into one space and out of another cleanly" (this volume). By paying particular attention to this movement into and out of Moroccan households, we are able to untangle continuities from discontinuities and find that all is not as it seems.

Nostalgia for Neighbors

In the early days of my fieldwork, I fretted about how I would gather coherent material on domestic life among people whose main concern seemed to be earning enough to live in the capital city.[3] Doors were closed; people did not sit outside in the evenings as they had done where I previously lived in Marrakech. I could not remember why I had chosen to work in Rabat—something to do with the university? In my desperate state, "door knocking" occurred to me as a likely way in, less from any training in ethnographic method than from my small-town upbringing where doorstep salesmen were part of everyday life. Starting on my own street, my plan was to knock, ask if the household employed a domestic worker, and, well, see what else I could find out. My reception was a mixture of pity, curiosity, and hostility. Two responses recurred, however, and neither was good news for my study: "People rarely knock on our door," I was told, "not even the neighbors"; and "There are no workers anymore!"

That residents were unaware of the presence of domestics in their own apartment buildings was related to a lack of interaction with neighbors. These issues, in fact, are closely linked. Neighbors and workers are ideally one and the same, and preferably double as kin too. Yet this kind of worker ("known," as it were, without having to ask) was little in evidence during my fieldwork except as a figure from the past. And I often heard people say, "We don't have neighbors," as when one woman, Hinde, came to old friends in l'Océan to borrow an electric whisk. Knowing that she lived a twenty-minute taxi ride away, I wondered why she had come so far to borrow such a ubiquitous appliance:

"Don't you have neighbors?"

"No, we don't have neighbors. If I had neighbors I would be all right."

Hinde did not mean that no one lived in the apartments next to hers but rather that she did not know them well enough to ask a favor. This conception of neighbors as existing only insofar as they behave like neighbors recalls statements about "real *komšiluk*" (real neighborhood) in the Muslim Bosnian village of Henig's (2012) study. The *komšiluk*, Henig argues, is a moral rather than physical way of living in proximity—"the space where people live *with* one another, rather than *next to* each other" (2012, 14–15; emphasis added). In l'Océan residents spoke nostalgically of an era when people sat outside in the evenings and greeted one another in the street. My host father, Hassan, now in his late fifties, thus described the l'Océan of his childhood, where neighbors as much as family made up community; indeed, kinship and propinquity were equivalent:

> We used to play outside and when it was time for *casse-croûte*[4] we would just pick any house in the block and have our food there. We weren't obliged to go to our own house. Everyone in the block was your family. Whoever you found was your mother. We had eight families in the block. Eight mothers, eight fathers. You went in, they gave you food and you sat and ate with your brothers and sisters. We respected everyone who was older than us like our own fathers. Someone in the street would say to you, "Go inside!" You'd go inside. Nowadays if someone said that to a boy, he'd laugh at them, or spit. There's no respect. No one knows who is who. Now everyone just goes into their apartment and shuts the door and the windows.

In l'Océan's imagined past the "moral proximity" (Henig 2012) described by my host father meant domestic work was performed by known women: neighbors, poor relations, or the informally fostered daughters of rural clients. A young girl could be taken in by a household, brought up by them, and married off. She would be referred to as "one of the family," a "daughter of the house." People often denied to me that servants even existed in those days: "We didn't need them. . . . There was always a cousin, an aunt, a widowed family member who came to live with us."[5] A widow or divorcée could subsist by staying with kin and doing housework. Similarly, neighbors and family would help on special occasions: "At weddings we never used to have servers. The people you knew, *awlad l-huma* [children of the neighborhood], would come and serve. Or your own people: cousins, aunts. And you'd talk together and mix and have fun. Now people have to get a company in and they wear a uniform and we don't even look at them and we don't know who they are. And they don't talk to us. They wear those plastic gloves, you know . . . so the food is not contaminated." In this model of an ideal world, where everyone knows everyone and neighbors are "like family," kinship disguises inequality in long-term relationships so that work is not always explicitly rewarded. We have met these poor relations before: they are the Fanny Prices, Jane Eyres, and Margaret Hales of Morocco. Indeed, where the rhetoric of kinship was most intense and plausible in l'Océan, I sometimes found myself thinking of Fanny Price in *Mansfield Park*, who, whatever her virtues, was "not a Miss Bertram" (Austen 2003, 12).[6] Moroccans, however, talk about cooperation of the kind that is colored in family terms as part of being sha'bi.

To be sha'bi parallels in some respects the Egyptian identity concept of *ibn al-balad* (lit. son of the place or country) described by Messiri (1978) and Early (1993). It is telling that people describe themselves or others as "still" (*baqi*) doing this or that that makes them sha'bi. They "still" sit outside in the evenings. They "still" go in and out of one another's houses. They "still" say "*s-salam 'alikum*" (peace be upon you) when they meet other people on the street. In Morocco as in Egypt, this ideal is defined through its association with the past, and the assumption is that all Moroccans, rural and urban, were once sha'bi, but today only rural Moroccans and particular urban Moroccans remain so.[7] In Armbrust's discussion of an Egyptian television serial, *ibn al-balad* is "a real Egyptian, a regular guy" (1996, 25). Similarly, sha'bi Moroccans consider themselves "real" Moroccans, ordinary people who (among other things) do not "make a difference" between their own children and their domestic worker—she will eat with the family and sleep in the children's bedroom. For sha'bi Moroccans, domestic service is embedded, woven into the fabric of common life so those in need receive care and give useful work through, in Gudeman's words, "relationships kept *for their own sake*" (2001, 10; emphasis in original).

At the time of my fieldwork, the mix of urbanites and country folk, serving and employing classes, made l'Océan a sha'bi neighborhood; but this was being threatened by unneighborly newcomers. Newer, taller apartment buildings meant there were simply too many people for everyone to know everyone else. L'Océan residents maintain that it has become more difficult to get people to help them on what I call a "cousin labor" basis; wage labor has become the norm for urban women, and a greater proportion of girls are now in school and so less available to help kin, neighbors, and patrons with housework. Several women on my street claimed to have employed a live-in domestic in the past but to have given up the practice because of the impossibility of letting a stranger into the house: "How can you know what she will be like? There's no trust anymore."[8]

In villages, meanwhile, Crawford found a preference "by ever more local patriarchs to send their children to the cities for wage labor rather than loan them to relatives who need help" (2008, 6). Whether people really cooperated in neighborly fashion in the past, and what the forms of inequality or exploitation may have been, is less important for the present purpose than that these memories influence thinking about contemporary domestic service.

A central mode of thought among employers (and indeed among many employees) is nostalgia. When things go wrong in Moroccan households, the problem is articulated as one of a stranger coming into the home, and people reminisce about a time when the concentric limits of the moral world fell, at most, in wider circles. In Morocco as in the Gulf, the presence of strangers is often seen to have supplanted a moral unity. Dresch notes, "Almost everywhere in the modern Gulf an image recurs of an older world where everyone knew everyone else" (2006a, 206). This ideal, together with guidelines for the proper treatment of outsiders and neighbors, is enshrined in Islamic law and ultimately expressed in the single community of believers or *umma wahida*, which has both historical and aspirational significance. Such imagined cohesion is of course not confined to the Muslim world.

While it matters that my field site is North African, twenty-first century, and lower middle class, many parallels exist with service in other times and places where "one just can't get the staff these days." The recurrence of nostalgia for an older kind of servant hints, indeed, that workers who were "known" unproblematically may never have been more than an ideal even in Morocco. On the surface it seems *no longer* possible to get housework done through relationships kept for their own sake. But if this could be considered new during fieldwork in 2012–13, it was not new for the first time. As long ago as the 1980s, Salahdine recorded the same wistful strains: "It used to be *dadas* [female slaves assigned to the care of the children of the house] respected us, they never dared to raise their eyes to us. We were everything for them, their parents, their family. Today everything has changed; not only are they no longer respectful and feel no attachment but at the slightest reproach, they leave you because they are sure they will end up finding another house and a higher salary" (1988, 112–13). Local criticism of flighty domestics often points to the monetization of domestic arrangements as the root of the problem. This, according to Mernissi, was novel more than thirty years ago: "The domestic who is paid a wage is a new phenomenon; traditionally domestics lived in and were supported, but received no actual wage" (Mernissi 1982, 31). Residents of l'Océan now complain about workers "following the money," an innovation on "following the bread," which expressed the humble pursuit of daily necessity rather than greed. A similar discourse surrounds changes in employer-domestic relations in Calcutta as loyal retainers who served the same family for generations are replaced by part-timers who "follow the money" (Ray and Qayum 2009). This accusation is notably absent from other economic sectors with their own histories of monetization.[9]

A parallel, albeit usually less regretful, narrative of change is present among workers, as this conversation with Ilham, a Moroccan worker in her thirties, shows. Ilham told me she was not afraid when she went into service at the age of fifteen or sixteen:

> "You went to people who were *ma'rufin* [known] . . . not from the family but . . . the person who took you there was from the family. And the [employers] were known to him. *Madmuna* [(you were) guaranteed]."[10]

> "Ah, so that was better than now?"

> "No, now is better. You can change if you don't like it. You can find a job with more money. . . . You phone the *samsar* [broker]. He says, 'Okay, leave.' He phones someone else and you have another job. . . . He makes it easy."

Although Ilham cites "more money" as a reason to move on here, she, like others, took into consideration the volume of work demanded and the quality of *mu'amila* (treatment) offered by employers. It goes without saying that the employers who matter in this regard are primarily women.

Note that Ilham's contact with an employment broker is facilitated by her mobile phone. In fact, Ilham had three mobiles, each with a different SIM card, so she could top up using whichever network provider was offering the best deal. Maroc Telecom's sales slogan, "*alam jadid yunadikum*" (a new world calls you), reinforces the idea that the phone connects you with those not previously part of your world, and in the advertisement a young man smiles alluringly as he holds out the new thirty-dirham top-up card promising two hours of call time. While the phone is relatively new, at least in its mobile form (which makes all the difference for migrant workers), connecting with strangers cannot be. The picture of nineteenth-century Morocco painted by Ennaji (1999) is not one in which neighborliness of the kind my host father was thinking of features prominently; fugitives, kidnappers, and negotiators mark the contours of a society peopled with strangers while "quasi-feudal powers, establishing themselves as clans, carved out large domains, acquiring slaves, henchmen, and large clienteles" (88). The boundary between "clansmen" and outsiders was presumably as shifting and contingent as moral boundaries are now.

If strangers per se are not a new problem, what does the constant emphasis on the novelty of dealing with them signify? Might novelty itself be a useful framework for the affiliation and disaffiliation of strange domestics, for their passing cleanly between households? Other researchers encountering nostalgia have worried that it reflected an overreliance on older informants, whose presumably hazy reminiscences obscured what the past was really like (Moore 1975, 282; Guillet 1980, 157–58). But if we see nostalgia not as an obstacle but as a social fact (Dresch 2000a, 112), the question of why it crops up whenever people talk about getting on or not getting on with others becomes interesting. Much as locating the truth elsewhere (Maqsood, this volume) produces a durable system from fragile relationships, so pointing to an ideal community that is always vanishing makes room for maneuver in the present.[11] Nostalgia allows an impossible moral system ("equality" in an unequal world) to hobble along imperfectly; it means people have to make do, to adapt and improvise given that things are not the way they used to be or, more importantly, should be. Moral reversals and intractable contradictions of a kind that exist in the long term are rationalized as people work out alternative systems for the temporary incorporation of a supposedly new kind of outsider.

Much of this local argument reads like a DIY manual for repairing claims of personhood, house, and class amid the long-standing contradiction of inequality in an intimate space, where "daughters" are paid and "guests" wash the dishes. Modes of domestic recruitment that present workers to employers in a variety of ways are a productive place to begin investigating our problem more generally. Just as a range of cleaning products labeled from toxic to mild might be considered to tackle a stain, a number of options, differentiated by the urgency of the "stranger-danger" labels attached, are available for sourcing elbow grease: physical marketplaces, brokers, and recommendations from friends. I will deal with these in turn.

A Stranger's Solution

Those people I knew in l'Océan who used to employ live-in help now did most of the housework by themselves. They might, though, bring in a woman from the *mawqif*, the day-labor market (lit. a stopping or standing place) to help with the *grand ménage* every two weeks. A worker recruited here may be a stranger, but at least she would come, do her work, and leave, thus minimizing fears brought on by lack of trust. These labor markets, allegedly instigated by the French to tidy the droves of *chômeurs* (the "unemployed") into places where Europeans could conveniently hire them, are found not in quarters of the city originally inhabited by Moroccans but only in newer quarters that were once all but wholly European. According to my host father, locals had no need of a marketplace to find workers; they could knock on the door of a likely candidate or, better still, send someone small to fetch her. I have found no historical record of the establishment of day-labor markets in Morocco, and elsewhere they seem much older, at least for agricultural laborers,[12] but since the mawqif exemplifies what domestic service in the sha'bi world should not be, it is important that in local discourse, the idea came from strangers.

Finding several day-labor markets across Rabat and the neighboring town of Salé, I naively chose the one closest to my house in l'Océan to frequent regularly, which was awkward when a neighbor saw me sitting with the women there. The next time I went round for coffee with her, she admonished me, "Be careful, Mary! . . . Don't trust everyone!" The mawqif women were not people of l'Océan, and as unvouched-for strangers with no personal ties, they usually worked under close supervision, a precaution practical only for short visits. I soon learned that no one wants to be seen at the mawqif by those they know personally. Workers who live in Salé thus pay for the thirty-minute bus ride to a mawqif in Rabat, while those who live in l'Océan or Rabat's medina do not go to the l'Océan mawqif or the nearby Jarda but to Agdal or Hassan. On Nabila's way to l'Océan from her home in Salé, her bus passes near the Hassan mawqif and terminates just beyond Jarda, where she gets off and walks another fifteen minutes to reach the l'Océan mawqif. Why not at least go to the mawqif in Hassan?

"My brother lives there."

"But what's the problem?" I asked.

"It's not nice to be seen in the mawqif. It is *hashuma* [shameful]."

"This is the lowest of jobs," another worker interjected.

"But they know you do it, don't they?"

"No," replied Nabila, "my brothers don't know I come to the mawqif. I tell them I work by the month [i.e., a semi-permanent position with one family]."

As a reversal of the sha'bi ideal of help among kin or neighbors, the public element of mawqif work, and its resulting shame, propels workers to a location as far from their homes as practicable. The same logic is explained by Ashraf, a day-laboring painter from Patna (Bihar, northeast India) and protagonist of *A Free Man: A True Story of Life and Death in Delhi* when the writer, Aman Sethi, suggests he go home:

"Patna . . . no chance. All my friends have become collectors and policemen and lawyers and judges. What face shall I show them? I can't be a mazdoor [laborer] in my own town, Aman bhai."

"So who builds the houses in Patna?"

"Runaways from Kanpur." (2012, 168)

That Patna is twelve hours by train from Delhi, eight from Kanpur, puts a half-hour bus ride across Rabat from neighboring Salé into perspective. Dislocation is layered, however. Nabila's family, like that of most other domestic workers, is not originally from Rabat anyway.

While face, or saving it, is a concern vis-à-vis people one knows well, external appearances matter in a different way when one is out of context. An opposition between moral in-depth acquaintance and humiliating superficial appraisal emerges in historical literature elsewhere. In England, for instance, an 1870 handbill warned parents about the dangers of Northamptonshire "mop-fairs" where employers could hire new domestics (often runaways from other jobs): workers were "stared at and picked out" by "masters about whom they know nothing and who know no more about them than the cart or horse which they judge by appearance" (Mullins and Griffiths 1986, 8–9).[13] At the Moroccan mawqif, employers judged on appearance a worker's ability to get heavy work done quickly. This was important since they would be agreeing a rate up front for the variable quantity of "a day's work." I once ventured that I could make up a second person for a job (only one worker was present), and the likely employer just looked me up and down: "You're small. You'd faint. It needs someone who has . . . " She patted her biceps.[14]

Appearance also distinguishes deserving from undeserving workers. While male day laborers in Morocco and elsewhere are often identified by their tools (a shovel or roller and brushes stand as metonyms of their expertise and proof they are not beggars), for women tools are redundant as signs of specialism (sitting in the street could only mean one of two professions), and the buckets, cloths, and chemicals required for cleaning are the responsibility of the householder. Dress, however, is vital. One worker told me she does not wear "nice clothes" to the mawqif: "They won't hire you. Or they won't pay you. They'll say, 'You're wearing a jellaba that's better than mine.'" Needy-looking workers were thought likely to accept lower wages. Moreover, hiring a needy worker amounted to a charitable act that could earn employers religious merit (*ajr*) and cast the wage-labor relation back to the sha'bi days when everyone looked out for everyone else (Montgomery 2019). Yet the moral responsibility toward a mawqif worker need last only a day.

The limits of household incorporation through the mawqif were illustrated by a worker who tried to perform day labor for the Sebbaris, a family she knew because her daughter Loubna had spent periods as a teenager living and working with them. During my fieldwork Loubna began to work for the Sebbaris again, but she barely stayed a month. After that time Loubna's mother, rarely finding work at the mawqif, would go to the Sebbaris without their calling her, but she complained that they only paid her fifty dirham—half the going rate for day labor. Loubna's mother saw the Sebbaris as patrons who should respond to her need: "My daughter stayed with them lots. . . . They should take care of me!" By paying her so little, the Sebbaris were letting her know they did not see her as their responsibility. Loubna's mother was not a dependent, in their view, yet nor was she a stranger, and therefore she did not fit the bill as a mawqif worker.

The same logic governs what has been heralded in Europe and North America as "the gig economy." Here new technologies facilitate "peer-to-peer" exchange, and promises of greater freedom disguise "a fresh chance for the rich to exploit the poor" (Sundararajan 2015). Sick days, for instance, are the worker's problem. An older example of limiting moral responsibility can meanwhile be found in the English Poor Law, which meant parishioners were shunted from one parish to another before a year's hiring could attach them as the ward of a particular one (Steedman 2009, chap. 4). From the Moroccan workers' point of view, in choosing mawqif work, they traded off the security of having patrons to care for them (this can be perfectly real, I should stress) with the freedom to work only when they wanted. Mawqif workers themselves thus felt no moral obligations toward their clients. They needn't go to the mawqif if they felt disinclined. But the modes of interaction must be kept distinct. In l'Océan, a local woman caused endless problems by trying to persuade workers to accept jobs from her elderly neighbors, who, too frail to do their own housework, tended to offer the lowest pay. By trying to have these neighbors seen as charity cases, she upset the otherwise impersonal approach of the mawqif workers, who, although they gathered each morning on her street, were by definition not neighbors.

A Known Worker?

It would be risky, so people say, to hire someone off the street for anything more than daywork. For householders considering bringing a stranger not only to work but to live in their home, modern "agencies" offer the convenience of a mawqif with the added dimension, supposedly, of a screening and matching service. Sha'bi people do not, however, trust agencies: "They don't *know* the workers." Because the sha'bi ideal privileges personalized connectedness, workers packaged as strangers are a last resort. Brokers, or *samasira* (sing. *samsar/a*), are often more approachable for sha'bi employers than are agencies, not only because they charge less[15] but also because a samsara can be approached as a "friend." But, like the mawqif, the very necessity of a samsara undermines the sha'bi ideal. Collectively or from a distance, they thus appear as outsiders—witchlike figures maligned by the press and consulted surreptitiously by those who have exhausted other options.[16] Face-to-face, they themselves are usually sha'bi people, and most Moroccans can recommend a samsara who, conveniently, is "not like other samasira."

One is always referred to a samsara by someone else, and the samsara, in accordance with the sha'bi ideal of people being "known," will usually want to know who it was. I was referred to a broker named Warda by a friend of a friend. Living in a cheaper suburb than l'Océan with a high proportion of recent migrants from the countryside, Warda also maintained a strong link with her village of origin to source workers. She explained how her business operated: "It's not an agency. . . . This is just something I do for people. . . . People tell their friends." She asserted that she placed only girls whose family she knew—for example, sisters or friends of someone she had placed before— and outlined to me an oddly formal process of obtaining permission, transfer of responsibility, and a guarantee of good behavior: "I always go to the family. Not if they are far away—in that case I go to an uncle or aunt who lives here. I say to them: 'Are you sending this girl to work?' They say, 'Yes.' I say to them: 'Will she create problems, steal?' They say, 'No.' So I don't have to worry about placing her? No. Do you guarantee her? Yes. They always say yes." The claim is moral, of course—sometimes in a very obvious sense. Warda, knowing I was studying domestic service, was keen to show me how she was different from other samasira, so she took me out to a busy transport hub and indicated a man there sitting on a bench: "It is *ma'ruf* [well known] that he is a samsar, and he also sends girls as prostitutes. He places anyone with anyone. He doesn't know the women, he doesn't know their families. They could steal. We had a woman from this samsar and she stole the whole house. He doesn't know the employers, or his clients. He treats the women like *bida'* [goods]. This is not what our Lord wants. I go and find out about the girl's family. I don't send workers to just any client. My clients are all *naqiyin* [clean]."

A placement in which I regrettably played a role showed me, however, that "knowing people" is a flexible concept. My friend Zineb asked me to ask Warda if she had work for her sister, Sharifa (twenty-three years old at the time), and, in retrospect, what I did was typical of the sha'bi world: I overstated my knowledge of Sharifa (I did know her sister, after all) in order to move things along and return favors.[17] Warda met us in l'Océan, took one look at Sharifa, and telephoned a potential employer, Nuzha. "My friend from England knows them. She does research about domestic workers and knows them well." I felt *very* uncomfortable. After a series of questions from the employer (how old was Sharifa; had she worked before?), Warda reassured her, saying, "The girl seems nice and straightforward to me, not one of those people who wear nail polish." Hearing this, Sharifa laughed, a little hurt, and looked at her chapped hands. Nail polish is often a point of contention between domestic workers and their employers. What Warda did not know was that just minutes before our meeting, Sharifa had, saying she felt cold, changed from her tight jeans and denim shirt into a long skirt and shapeless cardigan.

Once we were at the employer's house, Nuzha repeated her enquiry about whether Sharifa had worked previously. Warda said, "I look at their hands." She took one of Sharifa's hands and held it up. I have not seen a Moroccan domestic use gloves. Lethbridge (2013, 71) points out that, until rubber gloves were manufactured for household use in 1960s Britain, the condition of domestics' hands was a "painful badge of their profession," but it struck me that Sharifa's skin would be chapped anyway from washing clothes and dishes in cold water at home in the countryside. If work experience in the city was what Nuzha wanted, Sharifa's was limited to two weeks. No attempt was made to contact the former employer for a reference. Although Sharifa was presented as "known," her physical appearance stood in for knowledge of her character, just as it did for the day laborers. And here too, signs of social status (unpolished nails, shabby clothes) were as important as signs of experience of housework (chapped hands, muscular arms).

When we got up to leave, Sharifa looked overwhelmed; Nuzha, the new employer, looked panic-stricken: "You haven't told me anything!" "Well," said Warda, "there she is, there you are. She is ma'rufa [known]. *She* knows them." Warda nodded toward me. Warda even got Sharifa's name wrong. I was increasingly aware that the responsibility for "knowing" the worker fell on me, and I was the guarantor, the *dimana*. The emphasis placed on the worker being known while little was done to find out about her from this "knower" (which would quickly have disqualified me) showed acquaintance to be a kind of formulaic performance, in which broker, employer, worker, and guarantor were complicit. The situation was reminiscent of recruitment in the 1930s in Britain, as observed by Fremlin: "I remember answering an advertisement that seemed to require the very highest of high-class references; and when I approached the lady in question, she engaged me on the spot, without asking so much as my name. As for the 'references' that had figured so large—I might have been the trunk-murderer, a spy, a leper, a homicidal maniac; she did not raise a finger to find out" (Fremlin 1940, 21–22).[18]

Not only did Warda not know Sharifa; she did not know Nuzha either, had never been to her house before, and was not sure who had referred her. Sharifa worked just two weeks for Nuzha, complaining of long hours and finally leaving when she was falsely accused of hitting Nuzha's daughter. She asked Warda for a placement without children. Warda, hosting Sharifa for an interim period, decided she did not "have a way with work" and sent Nuzha a second domestic, who only stayed one night and exclaimed, "She's crazy! I will not work for a woman like that." I resolved not to give Warda's telephone number to anyone else. Hearing my sorry tale, a worker's mother commented, "Of course the samsara doesn't know people. She can't possibly know them. She only knows money." A broker is nonetheless part of the sha'bi world and will downplay the monetary side of the transaction, cashing in on contacts passed along by friends, who, like me, are "trying to help."

Many connections between workers and employers are made, of course, by friends and acquaintances without money changing hands. This is seen as *khayr* (doing good), sometimes even described as doing *ajr* (a deed earning religious merit) or *wajib* (duty). Nejlae, a resident on my street, never used an agency or samsara: "It's impossible for me to let someone I don't know into the house." Instead, she always asked her building's concierge to find her someone: "It's his job to know lots of people." The concierge asks current workers in the building to ask their sisters, other family members, and neighbors, or he brings someone from his own *blad*. Although Nejlae did not require a worker she herself knew, it was important that the worker was known by someone. The number of links in the chain did not seem to matter much. Nejlae's concierge might only "know" the worker to the extent that a samsara "knows" the worker (a friend of a friend of a friend), the difference being that he will not charge placement fees. Of course, there is still someone at whom to direct complaints when things go wrong. Sha'bi employers trust those performing the service free of charge because the transaction is then situated within a moral economy based on "doing good." By establishing a privileged connection with those they help and making themselves indispensable, such do-gooders are of course rewarded in the long term. The concierge and the samsara offer the same product but packaged differently, and by choosing one or the other, houses are able to make claims about who they are and, specifically, how sha'bi they are—claims that must be remade when the worker departs.

Passing Cleanly

By hiring "known" workers (even if links are tenuous), sha'bi Moroccans can infuse the relationship with moral value. If they knew the girl before handing her a dustpan and brush, then the relationship is primary, her work secondary, especially if they knew her to be needy. A question of moral range or "scale" arises that is not itself at all new. The term ma'ruf, Mattson (2003, 40) points out, figured in the jurist Shafi'i's (d. 819) rulings on entitlement for zakat, which prioritized giving to local people before strangers, not only to relieve social tension between rich and poor neighbors but also because of community knowledge of poverty. (This becomes a particular issue in contexts of migration.)[19] The incorporation of a known worker into the household as a "daughter" can then be defined charitably, as a kind of fosterage, which potentially earns the employer ajr (religious reward). Gifts of clothing and the provision of certain items such as shampoo are signs of the employers' care, for which workers are expected to be grateful.[20] In the past, arranging the girl's marriage was also testament to the family's care of her (Goichon 1929; Davis 1983). But workers I met in the field rarely stayed long enough for this, often leaving when they perceived that a honeymoon period of relatively good treatment from employers was coming to an end. The contradiction of a daughter who leaves must then somehow be worked out by those left behind. The worker likewise has contradictions of her own to deal with as she moves from house to house. The way in which Malika passed through the Sebbari household illustrates both sides.

Malika (then twenty-one) told me she was hired through a samsara in Fès. The Sebbaris, who owned the building where I rented on arrival in Rabat and who occupied, in "extended-family" style, several of the apartments themselves, introduced Malika to me as a friend of their daughter Zahra—"like a sister" to her. Other visitors were given similar introductions. The two young women, roughly the same age, shared a bedroom. Malika complained to me that she did not want to be treated as a daughter and would prefer her own space. She was keen to point out the ways in which she resisted being made one with the household, drawing boundaries through the minutiae of domestic life, between clean and dirty, proper and improper. As she slowly washed, peeled, and chopped vegetables one long Ramadan afternoon in the Sebbaris' kitchen, Malika explained how her method of doing things was better than that of the Sebbaris. When they peel vegetables, they leave the dirty peel next to the sink. Malika peels into a plastic bag, which she then places in the bin; she never puts things into the bin unbagged.[21] Malika detailed the correct components of a salad, of which her employers were evidently in ignorance. She also showed me coriander and parsley, which she had been told to chop up and freeze so it could be added to the spicy *harira* soup with which they broke the fast each day. "At home we do it all fresh, so the flavors are good, not like this," she told me.

Four years later, I found myself catching up with Malika in her own kitchen; she was now married with a young daughter and was expecting a second child. We chatted as she made an elaborate fish tagine to which she added some herbs from the freezer. "Coriander and parsley," Malika explained. "I chop them and put them in the freezer, so I always have some." Taking a shortcut with some everyday herbs is hardly the sort of household secret that would cause scandal if spread abroad, but it does illustrate the contradictions of a ranked outsider on the inside. If Malika needed to assert superiority over her employers as compensation for their constantly putting her down, it did not stop her from being able to take the things she learned away with her to other households, including, eventually, her own.[22]

Malika stayed six weeks with the Sebbaris. After she left, they continued to talk about her with visitors, including me, but stopped defining her as known or as kin and started to find other ways to make claims about the kind of household they are—differences between Malika and the Sebbaris were now exaggerated. These had little to do with the work she had done. Unlike her employers, she was *ikhwani* (a term referring to the Muslim Brotherhood but used loosely in Morocco to designate those who dress conservatively), yet she slept "naked," which, according to the Sebbaris, made her a hypocrite. That Malika went to bed on summer nights in a vest and leggings had been unremarkable during her stay. Malika was now also talked about as a thief, a recurring narrative among employers that, like the "charity" with which they initially welcome domestic workers, points to a denial of reciprocity and exchange between equals. Where workers were not accused of theft, they were considered ungrateful for all that was given to them (Montgomery 2019, chap. 3).

These narratives from both sides facilitate workers' passing, whether cleanly or not, between households. The daughter-shaped opening that is made for the worker must be patched up when she leaves, which employers can do most easily by redefining not themselves but the worker—she was most undaughterly. In turn, differences that were useful for workers to distance themselves while inside the house can be assimilated afterward. Since the two parties are so altered from their temporary employer-worker state, it is best if they do not meet, and least of all at the moment of inversion. In fact, to avoid complications at the point of departure, workers often leave without telling employers they will not be returning. A well-rehearsed exit strategy involves suddenly having to go home to visit a sick mother, another simply going out for their day off, or even on pretense of running an errand, and not returning. This is referred to among workers as "going light" since workers gradually move their belongings from employers' houses so that when they go out for the last time, they take only a handbag, and their move is thus a clean break.

The indefinite quality of domestic arrangements worked, of course, both ways. Rarely were trial periods agreed upon, so employers who wanted to get rid of workers they had initially welcomed as daughters felt they had to come up with excuses such as long vacations or house moves in which the worker would no longer be required. Others, sensing workers were going to quit, showed detachment: "If you want to leave, just leave. What are you waiting for? Do you think there'll be a firework display?" Not surprisingly, I sometimes heard contradictory versions of an exit story, the employer claiming she told the domestic to leave, the domestic insisting she told the employer she was quitting. It was reminiscent of people who, sensing a breakup is imminent in a love affair, rush to be the first to say, "You're dumped." In both contexts power, or at least avoidance of hurt, is on the side of the decision-maker. Hondagneu-Sotelo (2003) argues that looking at how domestic jobs end "exposes the degree to which domestic labor is viewed as something other than 'real work'" (2003, 56). Intimate relations, whether forced or elected, are distinctive. Apart from the recurrence of difficult departure scenes for female ethnographers in the Middle East (Dresch 2000a, 115), we might note, for instance, the "breakup" between the British celebrity chef Nigella Lawson and her personal assistants. Accounts of the resulting lawsuit point to a transition from "familial" to "contractual" language that was baffling as well as hurtful to both sides.[23]

Although workers frequently switched between Rabat, Tangier, and Casablanca—a vast pool of potential employers—in the relatively short time I spent with small groups of them on days off, we passed a remarkable number of their ex-employers out and about. So much for the anonymous city! Watching ex-employers from across the street, workers often divulged to me details of their personal lives that could be damaging if revealed to people who knew them. But given the way workers were recruited, they rarely had mutual friends who would take much interest. And what would be the point in divulging information anyway? Revenge is sweet only among people who matter. The upsets at moments of transition are diagnostic of moral structure but not of more general sentiment.

Writing about domestic workers in Britain, Selina Todd argues that in view of servants' readiness to leave their positions when other economic sectors were expanding in the first half of the twentieth century, servants' relationships with their employers were characterized by "detachment." This, she suggests, is a more useful concept for social historians than deciding between "deference" and "defiance," which had been a preoccupation of academic writers between the 1960s and 1980s (S. Todd 2009, 183). Without using the term detachment, Steedman argues for a similar attitude among servants in late eighteenth-century Yorkshire. Their "disaligned, disconnected stoicism" in the face of employers' idiosyncrasies showed that "they are not mothers, daughters, sisters, wives but domestic servants, hired hands" (2007, 213), who worked primarily to put aside some savings. Women's eagerness in Britain to escape domestic service when the chance arose is well known.[24] Beyond domestic space lies at least the pretense of autonomy, which the anonymity of public space allows.

A main concern for Moroccan domestics who saw former employers was thus to avoid recognition; meeting would only be embarrassing. When one worker, Miriam, spotted an ex-employer across the street, she suddenly linked arms with me and talked animatedly. Later she explained, "I wanted her to think, 'That can't possibly be Miriam, talking to a foreign girl. It must just be someone who looks like her.'" This embarrassment of domestics meeting former employers, akin to meeting an ex-boyfriend in the street, is related to the fact that a relationship that was private now features in a public space. Problems of equality that were kept under control by the reinforcement of a household hierarchy, making one woman superior to another, are flaunted. The two appear on an equal footing; both may be out for leisure; both may be wearing designer jeans.[25]

Problems of damaged hierarchy rather than damaged reputation seem then to define the servant problem in contemporary Morocco. While the literature is full of secrets, my fieldwork was not, at least not secrets of the scandalous kind. Admittedly, no promise of confidentiality would induce a Moroccan to tell someone like me that they fear the domestic might gossip about some specific family scandal, but people might easily tell me of such misfortune or misconduct among others. They did not. I heard all manner of stories of men going off with their maids, but I did not hear a single tale of a maid divulging a household secret. My sha'bi interlocutors were concerned that servants would take not secrets but valuables (watches, Italian blouses, husbands . . .) away with them when they left, and requesting a "known" worker was an attempt to guarantee someone who would not steal, a fact of which Warda, the samsara, was acutely aware. Have secrets then been misunderstood? By returning to the foreign workers with whom we started, we might find an answer.

Foreigners Welcome

As a foreigner myself, I had no one to vouch for me. But despite a professed fear of strangers, sha'bi Moroccans were welcoming, hence in large part my focus on their world. Perhaps they knew that I was likely to take away secrets only about coriander and parsley, although one worker suggested the reason her employer, perfectly affable the first time, was frosty on a second visit was because she feared I would steal her husband. She need not have worried; I was much more interested in talking with her wrinkly domestic, who came from the Sahara a long time ago. In contrast with the (relative) openness of two-bedroom apartments in l'Océan, however, I was invited into few gated villas. There, the family rhetoric is absent: "There's no 'my son,' 'my daughter' here," a security guard outside one villa told me. "They don't want you to be that to them." Because these employers envision neither an intimate sharing of space nor a maternalistic relationship, they do not place the same emphasis on the problem of having a stranger-domestic, and many hire Filipinas, a phenomenon that has become more common over the past decade, especially in Rabat and Casablanca (Mounib 2012).

The logic of employing a Filipina is the polar opposite of the sha'bi preference for locals. It is a bid for upper-middle-class status among social circles in which sha'bi means "backward" or "common." "There are three reasons why we employ Filipinas," a well-traveled Moroccan friend explained to me: "prestige, English, and they are hard workers." Maria, a Filipina worker, agreed and added a fourth: "And because they can't understand what is going on in the house, and they can't tell a Moroccan. You know, for example, when the man . . . [has an affair]." Fears over Moroccan staff spreading secrets outside the house reemerge (in the view of a foreign worker) as a reason to hire foreigners instead. But it is not the case that the very same Asians who are to be prevented from gossiping in Sharjah are marvelously discrete in Morocco. Since Filipinas are outside the moral, social, and linguistic community of Moroccans, privacy becomes a non-issue. Moroccan worries about secrets conceal a still more scandalous reason to replace local workers—that hiring foreigners leaves local hierarchies intact. In the Gulf intimate hierarchies seem less problematic since almost all workers are foreigners who, en masse, provide a ready contrast for citizen privilege.

The question of hierarchy is not especially new. In interwar Britain, Fremlin suggested that the solution to the "servant problem" was "to employ girls of alien culture, but competent and intelligent; treat them on an entirely business footing, and give up once and for all the vain attempt to work in a spirit of casual give-and-take which, except in very rare cases, is only possible between members of the same class" (1940, 161). Concerns about privacy, which highlight obvious spatial divisions, continue to be a way to worry over moral boundaries. But the question may well be a more fundamental one of difference (Fremlin's "alien culture") and equality (Fremlin's "class" for "casual give-and-take"), and here we find ourselves on familiar anthropological ground. The "type of event" likely or possible in a given society shifts more slowly than the "course of events" (Dresch 1986), which is where we find our questions about change and continuity. But certain features of event types may hardly vary at all, and an anthropology drawn to the glitter of rupture has largely overlooked the implications of this (see introduction, this volume). If the problem of strangers (Pitt-Rivers 1977) might thus recur at any place or period in any society, the salience of women in domestic affairs is almost as widespread and with it the dominance of women over other women. The diversity of references, from Jane Austen to Nigella Lawson, that serve as comment on the Moroccan situation makes this plain. But, in the course of contemporary events in Morocco, a certain class of not very wealthy employers who invoke the sha'bi ideal now feels under threat. So do "senior" women within that class who care for and control younger or poorer women whom they characterize as "like daughters." The Sebbaris, whom we have mentioned several times, would furnish material for a lengthy novel. A certain non-shaʿbi vision of the world would sweep all this away.

Neither Moroccan nor Filipina domestics are covered by the Moroccan labor code, but a "special law" for household workers appeared in draft form in 2006 and was adopted in July 2016. It is yet to come into force. The law includes provision for annual leave, a minimum wage, and state surveillance, something that employers, shaʿbi or otherwise, argue against.[26] But behind opinions on the draft law lies a conflict between two implied systems. On the one hand, the shaʿbi view, presupposing not only connectivity but inequality, balks at the impersonalized domesticity that state regulation would enforce. On the other hand, the "modern" state view, held by policy makers and NGO workers, sees the personal as oppressive, to be remedied by laws ensuring moral equality for atomized individuals. The two standpoints are inversions of each other, but neither is tenable. When the price of progress is transparency to the state, local forms of empowerment disappear; things that were dealt with locally are taken on by outsiders with "social worker" badges and clipboards. If we insist on legal entitlement at all costs, we walk away from a world where neighbors say *salam* in the street and lend each other electric whisks.

Conclusion

For Moroccans who do not value the shaʿbi world, an answer to puzzles of community and autonomy seems to have been to do away with locals altogether. This logic has been taken to an extreme in the Gulf and now recurs widely. By employing Filipinas, Moroccans free themselves from give-and-take with neighbors and pseudo-kin and from having to clutch at straws (nail polish, frozen herbs . . .) to maintain difference. Filipinas in Rabat do not need to wear a hand-me-down jellaba or go out in their pajamas to be evidently the worker and not the employer. But something of the moral order is lost along with the borrowing of electric whisks, and this must be reinvented. While new configurations of intimacy and inequality set new questions for the moral household, the responses provoked are old and familiar. It does not matter if Filipinas keep secrets or spill them; what matters is that households contain something worth protecting. The same logic applies to the disappearance of items that must have been worth stealing and turns servants, once convenient recipients of charity, into potential thieves. Prestige comes then from the *concern* for privacy and security as much as from the ability of the household to actually keep the inside in and the outside out. The latter is possible only if one does one's own cleaning—hence nostalgia for a time when everyone was an insider but rarely an equal, and when those in subordinate roles had often no alternative until age, if they were lucky, allowed them to subordinate others in turn. These days they may think instead to get "up and out." [27]

Local workers too are thus bypassing the complex domination of compatriots by seeking employment outside Morocco. When, three years after my main period of fieldwork, I went back to visit Warda, our catch-up was interrupted by a phone call from a local mother who had heard she now sent Moroccans to the Gulf: Could her daughter go? How much would she earn? Warda wanted to see the girl before pronouncing. "For the Gulf, they have to be old or ugly," she explained to me after hanging up the phone. In this particular new-old regime for the incorporation of strangers into households, Moroccan women workers no longer needed to be "known," but they continued to be implicated, as female domestics usually are, in potential scandal.

MARY MONTGOMERY gained her doctorate in social anthropology from the University of Oxford in 2015 and went on to hold a teaching fellowship at the London School of Economics (LSE). She is author of *Hired Daughters: Domestic Workers among Ordinary Moroccans*.

Notes

1. Concerns about indiscretion were not restricted to female servants, of course. E. Turner's (1962) title, *What the Butler Saw: Two Hundred and Fifty Years of the Servant Problem*, is a nice example of British understatement.

2. See Rivière on hospitality among Amerindians "extended more through the fear of strangers and as a form of self-protection rather than through any charitable motives" (1984, 81). The puzzle to which Pitt-Rivers points is general, although the fear can be of sorcery, spying, or contagion.

3. As the seat of government, Rabat is home not only to "important people" but also to large numbers of low-ranking civil servants or *petits fonctionnaires*. The high cost of housing meant it was not unusual to find double-income families with three or more children living in narrow two-bedroom apartments.

4. A light meal between lunch and supper, usually consisting of bread, pancakes, or pastries with tea or coffee.

5. Servants, known as *khaddamat* (workers), did exist but were rarely defined as such within a given household.

6. We are dealing with some distinctively female areas of inequality. Almost wherever we can speak of households, we find women dominating women, and the language of kinship, whether given or imposed, recurs widely.

7. See Rodary (2002, 118) on the sha'bi quarter of Sidi Youssef bin 'Ali in Marrakech, in which sha'bi is characterized as an attachment to tradition.

8. Studying the fishing industry in North America, Doeringer et al. similarly found that Italian captains who recruited from among kinsmen "often complain about the 'shortage' of crewmen. Their complaint meant, however, that they could not find enough men whose

families and friends they knew—not that there was a true shortage of qualified job candidates" (1986, 51).

9. Both male and female Moroccan domestics working for the French were paid in cash, often supplemented by employers' cast-offs and *"l'anse du panier"* ("the basket-handle": helping oneself to provisions or keeping back money from errands) (Etienne 1951, 24). For some servants, the job came with lodging (Montagne 1952, 115). But it would be a mistake to see monetization as a result of colonization; paid women's work, including spinning, carpet weaving, and catering, could be found well before the Protectorate (Rodary 2007).

10. The custom of requiring a guarantor has served in many societies to regulate both the treatment and the conduct of domestic workers. It recurs in seventeenth-century Japan (Nagata 2004, 214) and nineteenth-century Rio de Janeiro (Graham 1988, 19). The institution of *kafala*, whereby citizens as a matter of law personally guarantee foreign workers, is notorious in the Gulf but also exists in, for instance, Lebanon.

11. See Ivy (1995), Özyürek (2002), and Shryock (2004d), who deal with nostalgia in terms of commoditization, privatization, and modernity. What perhaps we can safely say is that where "modernity" is an issue (a rhetoric of change and progress), nostalgia is a likely counterpoint.

12. The biblical parable of the workers in the vineyard (Matthew 20:1–16) suggests first-century Judeans were familiar with the practice of hiring day laborers from the marketplace and is presumed to have reminded listeners of earlier instruction to pay needy workers daily, whether they be "a fellow Israelite or a foreigner residing in one of your towns" (Deuteronomy 24:14). Rabat almost certainly had its own needy outsiders before the arrival of Europeans tipped the balance of outsider status to the side of employers. Historical records, if they could be found, are unlikely, however, to capture the mawqif's "moral density" (Scheele 2012, 17) which, despite appearances, seems high.

13. This comparison with a livestock market is reminiscent of descriptions by appalled European travelers of Moroccan slave markets for the "ignoble public auction of human beings, like cattle" (1884 letter from British minister plenipotentiary to the Moroccan minister of foreign affairs, cited in Ennaji 1999, 117). It was not only the sale of people but the humiliating public assessment of their bodies that was ignoble.

14. Plainly there were other reasons not to hire me. I was not Moroccan, thus matter out of place. Still, my humiliation was made complete when, on the arrival of a second worker, the same householder told her there was no heavy work involved, just washing up and dusting.

15. Broker's fees varied from 200dh to 600dh. Formal agencies charged 500–700dh. The going rate for daywork, as mentioned, was about 100dh, whereas a live-in worker's monthly salary could be 1500dh or 50dh a day.

16. See, e.g., Abdderraḥman Mshat, "Tawwasiṭṭ al-'ishrin khadima muqabil 1000 dirham tdfa'ha al-'a'ilat al-mushaghila," *Sahara' al-maghribiyya*, "Milf: khaddimat al-biyut," May 27, 2013, p. 8.

17. I first met Zineb at the mawqif in l'Océan. She soon found permanent work with a family who asked her to ask me to tutor their children in English. By accepting, I could see Zineb at her workplace twice a week. I also visited Zineb's family in the countryside, where I met her other sisters, but Sharifa by then was already working for her first employer in Rabat. I met her the same day Warda did.

18. Celia Fremlin, an Oxford graduate better known for her suspense fiction, took jobs in British domestic service as a way to investigate class divisions in the 1930s. Few studies of

domestic service result from participant observation, but for something of a modern parallel, see Ehrenreich (2010).

19. In medieval Egypt, "Knowing the person, or at least obtaining the testimony of someone who knew him or her, was an important key in the verification 'system,' employed in both public and private charity" (M. Cohen 2003, 61). Strangers arriving in the Jewish community of Fustat thus carried letters with multiple signatures "vouching for their neediness in anticipation that communities or individuals might be reluctant to support unknown persons from distant locales" (55).

20. See Rollins (1985) on the significance of hand-me-downs and unwanted gifts in American domestic service.

21. Incidentally, at the time of my fieldwork, Morocco was the second-greatest consumer of plastic bags globally. Their production, sale, and use were banned in July 2016.

22. I intend a serious point here. The markers of women's lives, when domestic, tend to be ignored, and it is one of the virtues of Meneley's work that she makes plain how apparent trivia, such as competitiveness about clothes, matter. See, for instance, Meneley 1996, 109–15.

23. See, for example, Hayley Dixon, "Grillo Sisters Feel 'No Guilt' over Exposing Nigella Lawson's Drug Use," *The Telegraph*, January 7, 2014, accessed September 26, 2014, http://www.telegraph.co.uk/news/celebritynews/10555358/Grillo-sisters-feel-no-guilt-over-exposing-Nigella-Lawsons-drug-use.html.

24. See Laslett (1965) on how sudden and radical a change this was in twentieth-century England. In 1901 domestic service was a vast domain of female labor. It declined even through the economic hard times of the 1930s and by 1951 "had practically disappeared" (226–27).

25. English novels, not to mention memoirs, are full of alarm at not being able to distinguish between mistress and servant by their dress in public. In Morocco, Montagne's (1952, 240) sketch of "brazen" women wearing their employer's lipstick and mingling with the European crowd points to similar concerns. At home, of course, one can impose forms of dress that leave no doubt, and workers I knew complained of being made to run errands or accompany employers to a shopping mall in their "pajamas." Since no self-respecting woman would venture far from home in her loungewear, this was a humiliating sign of servile status.

26. Although some Moroccans seem content to have a stranger working in their house, they still use the concept of the sacrosanct home to argue against inspection by a government official.

27. A dream of escape from social constraints recurs widely. While government and elders may favor cousin marriage, for instance, men in the UAE who want to be masters of their own houses might prefer to marry outside the local system altogether (Dresch 2005, 137).

7

CLAIMING AN INDIVIDUAL NAME

Revisiting the Personhood Debate with
Afghan Poets in Iran

Zuzanna Olszewska

The deeply-held indigenous values [that motivate action and symbolic representation] among Middle Easterners . . . include egalitarianism, competitive individualism, and the quest for personal autonomy—values that are shared with the West, and especially with America, but that are not to be found in most cultures. (Lindholm 2008, 10–11)

I employ [the concept of] connectivity in a culture in which the family was valued over and above the person or society and in which "individuation," "autonomy," "separateness," and "boundedness" as understood in the American psychotherapeutic literature were less valued than bonding with and commitment to family. (Joseph 1994, 56; writing on Lebanon)

THIS CHAPTER IS AN ATTEMPT TO BUILD A stronger connection between the theoretical debates on personhood in anthropology, dating back at least to Mauss's 1938 lecture on the notion of the person, and ethnographic material on the subject gathered in the Middle East and Iran in particular. The latter, while rich and detailed, is not often analyzed in comparative perspective or related back to the vigorous theoretical debates that have focused on other regions. As the two contrasting quotes above demonstrate, we have not really had the last word on whether persons in the Middle East are "individual" or "dividual," something in between, or indeed whether these categories are useful at all, beyond baldly ideological assertions. Yet this region raises some particularly interesting questions for analysis in this vein, as I hope to make evident through an ethnographic analysis of contemporary Afghan poets, paired with a historical analysis of the recognition of individuality of Persian-language poets in the region.

Let us begin with Charles Lindholm's confident assertion cited above, which forms a running theme throughout his book *The Islamic Middle East: Tradition and Change* (2008). Lindholm argues that this "trait complex" of egalitarianism, competitive individualism, and the quest for personal auton-omy is shared among people from Morocco to Afghanistan, and it is this com-monality, in fact, that allows us to speak of this vast area as a cultural whole of sorts. It has developed partly due to the ecological particularities of the region[1] and was given a big boost by the notion of equality in the eyes of God pro-claimed by Islam. Yet Lindholm is then forced to temper this claim in the rest of the book when he considers the various forms of hierarchy and subordina-tion that have undeniably existed in the Middle East, including the dependent status of women in patriarchal families and a long history of slave ownership. He thus retreats somewhat and writes that this contradiction represents the key paradox that the region's people have had to negotiate.[2]

Gender, it would seem, is the key stumbling block here. Lindholm admits that up to about two-thirds of the way into his book, he has been talking only about men. He then underlines the importance that Islam and women them-selves place on their own moral autonomy and their ability to act as independ-ent agents, in many cases owning property and engaging in economic and pol-itical activity. This is certainly borne out by many classic ethnographies from a variety of settings: Abu-Lughod (1986) argues that Bedouin women (like men) master their potentially volatile emotions to voluntarily submit to tribal norms; Meneley (1996) describes the competitive and highly political visiting and hos-pitality practices of Yemeni women, through which they, too, contribute to the honor of their families; and Nancy Tapper ([Lindisfarne] 1991) describes the political importance of marriage arrangement among Afghan Pashtuns and the significant roles that women play in performing it.

An equally impressive array of ethnographies, on the other hand, focuses more on the relational qualities of persons in the Middle East. Suad Joseph, as we see in the second epigraph, emphasizes the "connectivity" between broth-ers and sisters as they grow up in working-class Beirut, which socializes each into their appropriate gender roles through a kind of interdependence based on both coercion and love. This is the affective glue, Joseph argues, that pro-vides much of the normative power that underwrites patriarchy. For Joseph's informants, "one's sense of self is intimately linked with the self of another such that the security, identity, integrity, dignity, and self-worth of one is tied to the actions of the other. Connective persons are not separate or autonomous" (1994, 55). Such relationality is generally seen as dysfunctional and a sign of immaturity in the West, she claims. She argues that this judgment stems from "evaluations of persons in Western, industrialized, market, and contract-based societies organized around the expectation of mobile and autonomous selves" (1994, 55–56).

Singerman (1995) similarly, though less polemically, discusses the ongoing importance of the family rather than the individual as the basic unit of study in the Middle East, underlining the need for the interdependence of all its members for economic survival in a popular quarter of Cairo. More recently, Wellman (2014) focused on the moral interdependence of family members in Iran by exploring the central role pious women play in warding off corruption and ensuring the spiritual and physical health of all their family members through practices of prayer, appropriate food preparation, and feeding. Indeed, the three examples of Abu-Lughod, Meneley, and Lindisfarne above could also quite easily be read as emphasizing the contribution of women, however much motivated by a spirit of competition with others, to the collective security of their families as the only ultimate guarantors of their own. Even in that classic account of competitive egalitarianism in the challenge-and-riposte routines of the Kabyle, Bourdieu shows that a man's *nif* or point of honor is intimately tied to all that he has to defend—land, women, dependents, agnates whose deaths must be avenged and who will take up arms to avenge their kin—"the point of honor has a meaning and a function only in a man for whom there exist things worthy of being defended" (1977, 61). In other words, individual honor, personal autonomy, and individual competitiveness are a nonsense without relationality.

What are we to make of these apparent contradictions? Are the epigraphs mutually exclusive, or might they be equally true on some level—and if so, what is the relationship between the individual and the relational modalities? Are they comparing apples and oranges, with Lindholm looking at ideology while Joseph seeks to understand experience? Has there, as Lindholm has argued, been an ideological preference for individualism in the Middle East that has not necessarily been borne out in reality (as is undoubtedly the case also for the West)? Before I can answer these questions, it will be necessary to delve deeper into recent developments in the anthropological debates on personhood.

The Anthropology of Personhood: From Dichotomy to Convergence

I take personhood to represent emic models of what it is to be a person, how to be a good one, and the nature of that person's relationship with others. But it is also an etic analytical category that allows us to view such models in comparative perspective. Conceptions of personhood are tightly bound up with ideas about the self, kinship, gender, the body, and politics, and they also constitute juridical categories. Mauss (1985) was the first to remark on the historical uniqueness of the individualized, self-contained, autonomous conception of the person in the modern West; Geertz later concurred, claiming that this was "a rather peculiar idea in the context of the world cultures" (1984, 126). Subsequent anthropologists of the non-West seemed to support this view by uncovering forms of personhood more accurately seen as "dividual" (Marriott 1976; Strathern 1988), with "permeable" or "partible" bodies (Busby 1997), or subsumed within holistic collectivities and hierarchies that prescribe their social roles and identities in their entirety, as Dumont famously argued of India (1970).

However, more recently anthropologists have found it more appropriate to critique this dichotomy and describe a productive interplay or tension between modalities of individualism and dividualism present in all societies, as LiPuma contends (1998, 56). There is simply too great a diversity of cultural conceptions of personhood worldwide for the representation of a "West versus the Rest" dichotomy to be adequate (Spiro 1993, 143–44). Ideologies of individualism often ignore the true interdependence of all persons, of which "mutuality of being," in Sahlins's (2013) terms, anthropologists of kinship everywhere are keenly aware, even as they continue to dispute the nature and basis of that mutuality (Shryock 2013).[3] Even some social psychologists have become comfortable with the idea of a "distributed self" no longer bounded by the human body (Wetherell and Maybin 1996). Bloch (2011) has taken a different tack, seeking to integrate social and cognitive anthropology approaches by arguing for a basic unity in the way human beings experience their bodies and selves, with culture variance being expressed largely at the level at which such selves are narrated.

Thus, individualism and relationality do not describe distinct types of societies but remain analytically useful if we recognize that they may be copresent, although the relationship between them manifests itself differently in different places, whether as a conflict, a productive tension, a paradox, or a seamless whole. For example, we can find a compelling account of how both a heightened sense of individualism and an intense collectivism coexist in ideology and practice alike in Walker's (2013) ethnography of an Amazonian community, the Urarina of Peru. For the Urarina, "the striking importance accorded to individual autonomy, enskillment, and personal liberty [was closely] wedded to equally salient notions of mutuality, dependency, and responsibility. Central to being an individual were the practices of living together with others; each was possible only with and through the other" (2013, 13). The Urarina do not see this as a paradox.

Elsewhere, LiPuma (2001) contends that even for the paradigmatically "dividual" Maring people of Papua New Guinea, individual action has long been recognized (and condemned) in the practice of sorcery. Meanwhile, the unequal global power relations at work in the modern era have meant that Western ideologies of individualism have been imposed on colonized people through a process he describes as "encompassment." Mines (1988, 1994) has taken the proponents of the Indian dividual and the Dumontian *Homo hierarchicus* to task by showing that individuality—which he defines as "the aggregate of traits that distinguish who a person is" (1994, 2)—*is* understood and valued in India, although it is a different kind of individuality from that associated with the West: it is context dependent, unequally distributed, and highly gendered, and it increases with a person's age. Further, the "big-men" and women of a South Indian Tamil community who are able to claim most distinction do so precisely by building a reputation through myriad relationships with patrons, clients, and dependents; in other words, public preeminence and individuality are always constructed through service to and against the backdrop of groups (1994, 13).

This latter point echoes Amit and Dyck's formulation in the introduction to their volume *Claiming Individuality* (2006), pointing to the oxymoronic nature of the dichotomy of individualism and relationality: "To proclaim forms of personal distinction rather than merely to think them or to prescribe them is to express, implicitly or explicitly, a dependence on others for their mutual recognition, acceptance or emulation of that endeavor. And that dependence intrinsically entails social risk. It is in the calculation and management of such risks that the cultural politics of distinction are manifested in contexts that range from the mundane to the extraordinary. . . . Individuality, as a form of social enactment, is *fundamentally and necessarily relational*" (9; emphasis added). This allows for a distinction between individuality as a personal project and individualism as an overarching ideology, showing that the latter is not a prerequisite for the former. Instead, Amit and Dyck's contributors consider how people engage reflexively in the cultural politics of distinction in diverse contexts, composing their lives against, with, or through institutions, conventions, expectations, and other people (2006, 11–12). This "cultural politics of distinction," more than a simple conflict or paradox, is a useful framing for the way the Afghan refugee poets with whom I worked in Iran, both men and women, sought to make a name and a life for themselves while for the most part remaining loyal members of large patriarchal families. It is to them that I will turn after clarifying one final definitional matter.

One of the difficulties with the translatability of the concepts of individualism and dividualism is that they have multiple facets, and there is a great deal of imprecision and variety in the ways notions like "self" and "person" are defined (Spiro 1993).[4] Anthropologists have used these terms to talk about matters as diverse as perceptions and experiences of the boundaries of the body, the attribution of agency in ideology and in practice, the appurtenances of persons such as names, reputations, and biographies, and prosocial or antisocial behavior. My intention here is to tease out two separate aspects of individualism, central to claiming individuality, that might commonsensically be conflated: the assertion of moral autonomy on the one hand, and the recognition of one's unique attributes, deeds, talents, or virtues, as a unique person with a unique biography, on the other. Mauss, in his discussion of the Pueblos and the Kwakiutl, among whom he claimed a limited pool of ancestral names circulated and people's social roles or *personnages* were prescribed for them by these names, certainly seems to conflate the two. In what follows, I make the case that these two aspects need not always work in tandem, and indeed the suppression of one may sometimes lead to the widening of the other.

Poetic Activity and Distinction among Afghan Refugee Poets

> I had just interviewed Elyas [a young poet] in the office [of the Afghan refugee cultural organisation with which I worked]. Everyone else had gone home and we stayed to chat informally. We were eating cashew nuts. I asked him what it was about being a poet that he liked. Maybe because he didn't have much faith in my Persian, he decided to demonstrate. He lined up a few cashews evenly on the table, then slid one of them out of the row with his finger. "Do you understand?" he said, cryptically. "These are the others, and this is me." (From my field notes, October 2005)

Poetry had certainly allowed Elyas to stand out from his peers. He had won numerous cash prizes in literary competitions and had been recognized by Afghan and Iranian juries for the pleas for social justice often contained in his poems. And he was not alone in this quest.

Among the million or so documented Afghan refugees in Iran, poetic and other literary groups are one of the most noticeable cultural activities.[5] My fieldwork was with an Afghan cultural organization in the eastern city of Mashhad, in whose literary activities young men and women are active in about equal numbers. Most of these young people had had at least a high school education in Iran. They often struggled with their families' wishes for their futures, going to great lengths to continue their education in the face of various legal restrictions imposed by the state. They also often wished to find their own spouses rather than submitting to the kind of arranged kin-group (often close kin) marriages that remain the norm in Afghanistan. So, at first glance, it seemed that a more "modern" ideal of personhood as an autonomous individual had spread even to this very economically and socially deprived population in Iran. The example of Afghan refugees in Iran, in fact, makes a strong case for the argument that following the Islamic Revolution the state has succeeded in creating subjectivities that are some combination of Islamic and "modern" even in the most marginal of its residents, through a heavy investment in education and public health care. For hundreds of thousands of Afghans and millions of poor Iranians who became newly literate in the decades since the revolution, these investments coincided with their aspirations for a better life, as the state-promoted ideologies and lifestyles were seen as a path to upward social mobility.

Among the refugee poets that I studied, the pursuit of fame and prestige were an important motivation in their craft—indeed, in a situation in which Afghan refugees could legally work only in menial occupations, it was one of the very few ways for them to improve their lives both socially and materially. A poet whose verses circulated and were admired (orally, in print, or online), who was active in a literary circle and knew many people, could attain a positive reputation among other educated Afghans. Such people were described in Persian as persons who were *nāmdār* (famous, lit. "having a name"), *barjasteh* (prominent), *nokhbeh* (elite), or even (more rarely) *nābegheh* (genius). If poets also put in the labor and leadership required to publish books, magazines, or blogs and to organize seminars, literary soirees, and other events, as well as taking the time to mentor others just starting out, they would eventually come to be known as *asātid* (singular *ostād*), master poets or maestros. I often heard from poets that poetry had been a way for them to discover themselves, to become an *ādam-e khodsākhteh*, a self-made person, with individual achievements and opinions and a way to express them, someone who took their life into their own hands and who was known for this quality.

It may be tempting to place such a push for individuality—as name and as autonomous action—in the context of social, legal, and political changes in postrevolutionary Iran, and I was initially inclined to do so. The coming of republicanism after the 1979 revolution had given mainstream legitimacy for the first time in Iranian history to the idea of individual rights (*hoquq*), including women's rights (Osanloo 2009). Even the religious ideologues of the revolution had emphasized the idea of individual subjectivity and agency, albeit mediated by God's will (Vahdat 2002, 134–81). This change in the normative ideology of personhood in Iran has been well documented by Adelkhah (1999) in her ethnography of Iranian ways of being modern, which stresses the continuities of the Islamic Republic with the modernizing processes of the twentieth century that have produced the kind of individualized, self-reflexive subjects that Giddens (1991) sees as the hallmark of the late modern age. Much as LiPuma argued for Melanesia (1998), the coming of modernity, the nation-state, and associated legal and economic structures to Iran has encouraged the foregrounding of ideologies that envision and celebrate more individualist conceptions of personhood.

But two complications must immediately be noted. On the one hand, as I will show in greater detail below, this push for greater individualism is happening in a context in which many of my interlocutors were still living as members of large, patriarchal families that continue to play an important role in defining and securing their interests, and whose honor and reputation are important to everyone. Thus, for many, the self and its fortunes remain to a great extent relational and dependent on these collectivities.[6]

On the other hand, the more I delved into Persian literary history, the more it became clear that there were deep historical continuities to the seeking of individual distinction of the kind described above. It is not simply an artifact of modernity; there have always been pathways to individual fame and esteem in Persianate societies, and literary stardom in some form has long been one of them. In the monarchic political systems that dominated the region for centuries, one such pathway was being an *adib*, or scholar-poet, often employed at a royal court, where the dual meaning of *adab* as both literature and proper moral conduct could be cultivated (Kia 2014). From the twentieth century onward, being a "court poet" under political patronage began to be much more controversial because poetic authenticity was now thought to derive from moral and political autonomy (similar to the transformation Bourdieu [1996] documented in modern Europe). Thus, in the circles I studied, "court poet" was actually an insult. But becoming a poet (now recast as a critical intellectual) was still a way for Afghan refugees in Iran to cultivate a unique self and win the esteem of others—both Afghans and, to some extent, Iranians.

How are we to understand this complex of seemingly contradictory norms and pressures? The simplest answer is that for the Afghans in Iran that I worked with, individuality was hierarchical and contextual, in the sense that more powerful people had more scope for individual action and their individuality was more pronounced and more widely known. This point is particularly important in relation to gender: traditionally, a woman's individuality was a matter for the privacy of the home and her closest family and was hidden from the public eye, and young Afghan women still remain subject to these constraints. This of course resonates remarkably closely with Dresch's vision of the Arab world, "a world in which privacy is highly structured and integral to the definition of social groups" (2000a, 111). Each such piece (or "peace") is imagined as a cone (1986, 311) with "an outside of repute and an inside of vulnerability . . . often coded as male and female" (2000a, 111).

In Persian culture, this inside/outside dichotomy that readily maps onto female/male is very explicit and frequently made a conscious subject of discourse. It is further transposed onto the paradigmatic cultural bifurcation of *zahir* and *batin* (in Arabic, or *birun* and *darun* in Persian). The zahir, the outer self or public facade that one wears, is a form of calculated, restricted expression and politeness in situations of uncertainty, between status unequals, or simply when confronting the "corrupting" everyday reality of the outside world. The batin, one's inner or "true" self, is the seat of one's deepest emotions and is typically concealed except in situations of free, unguarded expression, such as in the secluded realm of the family sphere or between status equals and intimate friends (Beeman 1986, 11; 2001, 38). God and saints may also be included in the range of intimates who have insight into one's true self (Betteridge 1985, 198). Beeman further argues (2001) that in some situations, such as the inhospitable *birun* ("outside") when one is among strangers or status unequals, one's batin must be deeply concealed and protected. Communication will thus be restrained and reveal little of it unless there is a need for a particularly strong emotion to be expressed or sincerity to be "performed." In this case various communicative strategies from the secluded realm of home and family are employed, including less formal diction or physical displays of grief or anger. Betteridge has argued, therefore, that this distinction lies at the core of the Iranian conception of the person: the zahir involves a kind of flattening out of individuality, while one is seen in one's fullest individuality by those few who have access to one's batin.

Perhaps this might help us see Lindholm's argument as less paradoxical. Historically, it is not that women in the Middle East were not individuals, but rather that the number of those who could know them in their full individuality was heavily circumscribed. And in Persianate society, at least, where public interactions often have a ritualized, aesthetic aspect, the fullest individuality of *both* men and women was realized in private—at its deepest level, it could be known only to God and the saints (the *emāmzādeh*s or descendants of the Twelve Shi'a Imams, whose shrines were often visited for the purpose of confiding one's deepest secrets). Thus, one may accrue a rather stereotyped public reputation and biography; but on the other hand, people have private ambitions, dreams, tastes, personalities, loves, and interests, and many are prepared to go to great lengths and even face conflict with their families to realize them, though reconciling the two is preferable if at all possible. Where there is a contradiction, these personal interests may remain secret, known to only a few confidantes; but in most other cases, as Mines (1994, 13) also found in South India, one's public and private lives are closely intertwined.

It should also be noted that over the past century or so, modernizing move-ments in Iran have gained for women the right to an education, to vote, and to work and participate in public life in almost all the same arenas as men. Many Afghans in Iran are also increasingly embracing these ideals.[7] Thus, both young men and women push for their individuality to be publicly known, but this transformation takes a good deal of tactical negotiation and may never be complete. In the next section of this chapter, I present the story of a young fe-male poet that illustrates the disjuncture of the two salient aspects of individu-ality that I have identified: moral autonomy and renown for unique individual attributes.

Fatemeh and Abbas: A Love Story

For the average Afghan family in Iran, marriages are still largely family negoti-ated for many reasons, including a desire to maintain group endogamy or to build strategic alliances, a need to ensure that the proper exchanges of money and goods take place, and (no less importantly) a genuine interest in the future well-being of their children. Yet the people I studied considered themselves intellectuals and cultural pioneers, and they instead were pushing for compan-ionate marriages based on love between individuals whom they perceived as uniquely suited to each other. But because of the reality of close emotional con-nectivity between family members, most young people chose to negotiate this change tactically and tactfully rather than rebelling openly. Even in the case of elopements, families would still have to come together after the fait accompli to negotiate the terms of the marriage and the amount of gifts and goods to be exchanged between them.

The courtship and marriage of Fatemeh and Abbas is a case in point. Fate-meh was a poet and a sayyida (descendant of the Prophet) who lived in Mash-had, while Abbas was a penniless student of the Hazara ethnicity[8] resident in a European country. They met online through an Afghan chat room as she searched for funding for an anthology of Afghan youth poetry that she was editing. I unwittingly played a role in their courtship when Fatemeh asked me to meet her secret internet suitor, whom she had never seen, while he was visit-ing friends in London. Each of them wanted to hear about the other through a neutral third party who had met each of them in the "real" world. I reported back: both were lovely people. A few months later, when I was back in Mashhad, Fatemeh came in to the cultural organization's office one day, very flustered. She confided in me and another friend that she had just met Abbas for the first time—he had come to Iran to ask her to marry him and to seek her family's ap-proval. "I set him a test in my mind," she told us. "I thought to myself that if he tried to shake my hand, I would call the whole thing off!" Fatemeh was a pious young woman who usually wore a black chador in public and wouldn't dream of shaking hands with an unrelated man, while Abbas was a self-declared agnostic socialist, but he had the sense to keep his hands by his side, thus earning her trust and gratitude. He had come to know her and her unique combination of beliefs and desires, and he respected them. It was not long before they were married and Fatemeh joined Abbas abroad.

Eventually, I learned from them the full story of their courtship and the many obstacles they had overcome.[9] Fatemeh had once very passionately insisted that she would never marry. She was full of patriotic ideas and wanted to serve Afghanistan in some way, especially through writing and education. Through many months of online chatting, they first became friends, then gradually and cautiously fell in love. Abbas eventually traveled to Iran to ask her parents for her hand in marriage. The courtship and marriage proposal to her parents were very secretive and had to be carefully negotiated, with no detail revealed too soon, to prevent distant relatives getting involved and hijacking the process, since the marriage would be a challenge to the norm of hypergamy (sayyid women do not marry "down"). "What we did was contrary to tradition in a traditional society: a breaking of the Hazara-sayyid [marriage] taboo, a struggle against ethnic prejudice. In addition, I wanted to be the decision-maker in my own life. Usually girls don't have the right to choose in Afghan traditional society. That's why I kept quiet. If I had said something, I, my family, and Abbas would have faced harassment." Fatemeh said that her father's time in Iran had led him to change his thinking on the subject, despite the threat of pressure and harassment from their extended family. The nuclear family's faith in and support of their headstrong young daughter could also be attributed to social changes experienced in Iran. The principles that replaced endogamy and kinship-based marriage were a deep knowledge of and respect for each other's personalities built up over time, and a perception of uniqueness (neither Fatemeh nor Abbas saw each other as being "like other Afghans") that led to a strong bond of emotional intimacy. A great emphasis was placed on virtues such as patience, perseverance, being a moral (*bā-akhlāq*) person, and above all honesty.

For idealistic young people of an intellectual bent like Fatemeh and Abbas, the will to support each other in making a contribution to their homeland and their people has become a highly desirable quality in a life partner. So doubtful was Fatemeh of her ability to find someone who would permit her more than a life of "slavery and servility" that she did not initially want to marry at all. In Abbas, however, she found a companion who admired her precisely for those qualities and encouraged her to study and continue her poetry and activities on behalf of Afghan refugees. For young Afghan intellectuals, then, the individualistic pursuit of companionate marriage has become a patriotic project in the name of progress, greater rights for women, and ultimately of a healthier society.

Romantic love itself is, of course, a highly individualistic sentiment and has therefore been dangerous for a social order in which it was for centuries an "extra-structural" phenomenon, as Gell has put it (2011). Indeed, the perils of love are made amply clear in the large body of classical Persian romance verse narratives, none of which end well for the lovers—many of them end up dead or mad, wandering the wilderness. Yet it has been celebrated and cherished in the Persianate poetic tradition, albeit often sublimated to a higher cause—the love of God or a ruler, or even the love of one man for another, seen as the purest kind compared to mere carnal relations between the sexes for the purpose of procreation.

This suggests that individualism of this selfish, destructive kind (rather than the world-building, competitive individualism described by Lindholm) was long recognized and managed in Persianate societies, much like the antisocial sorcery that LiPuma (2001) describes among the Melanesian Maring. Indeed, without referring to LiPuma, Gell himself makes the connection between "extra-structural love" as a destructive force and Melanesian ideas of sorcery. Thus, in the context of "encompassment" by more powerful global normative cultural models, existing native understandings are sometimes co-opted and reappraised for new purposes. Love is domesticated in the name of companionate marriage and gender equality, as is the idea of unruly individualism itself.

The process, however, often has to be tactfully and tactically managed in ways that tell us much about the way individuality is claimed in this community. In Fatemeh's case, her scope for autonomous action (in choosing her own spouse) widened precisely when she carefully concealed the details from public knowledge, at least temporarily. She had to be *less of an individual* in her public biography to achieve her aims. Further, the marriage was not so much an act of willful rebellion as an act of whose sound basis both she and Abbas knew they had to persuade her parents. Its success, as in many other cases of such marriages that I heard of, relied on the bride's parents standing by her in the face of the threat of ostracism or violence by extended family members. Thus, even the quest for personal autonomy is mediated by connectivity with others, and any individual biography is perhaps better described as a "poly-biography" (Mines 2006).

Despite this complexity at the level of practice, it must be recognized that the ultimate outcome of Fatemeh and Abbas's love marriage strengthens the ideological case heard ever more loudly in modern Iran and Afghanistan that women *do* have the right both to autonomous action and to be known for their unique traits outside their familial "cones of privacy."

Tazkirah and *Takhallos*: Writing Distinctiveness and Distinction

In 2010, I reinterviewed Gholamreza, a young Hazara poet I had gotten to know during the main period of my research several years earlier. When I asked him to reflect again on what role poetry had played in his life, he said, "I know Gholamreza only from when I began writing poetry. Before that, there was no milestone in my life to let me say that I'd achieved something, or had a life I was proud of—no. At least, this feeling that I exist and have existed, I've only felt it since I entered the world of literature and poetry. Before that, my life was, as one poet says, a kind of 'gradual death.'" Gholamreza had been through a difficult period and had been feeling particularly suffocated in Iran due to the many restrictions that the Iranian government places on refugees. So he traveled to Afghanistan to see if there might be better opportunities in the homeland he had never known. There, he was amazed to learn that many people he had never met before knew and loved his poetry. One ministry official he contacted to sort out some paperwork before he could return to Iran even knew many of his poems by heart, and helped him solve his bureaucratic problem. Gholamreza had become famous through the circulation of his poetry in literary magazines, and this gave him unexpected privileges and a new confidence to take his life into his own hands. After returning to Iran to finish his master's degree in sociology, he went on to marry a fellow poet for love and became a magazine editor and lecturer in Kabul. Poetry, then, helped Gholamreza claim his individuality, and the circulation of his verses helped increase his agency in a way that can be read as a very Gellian case of "distributed personhood" (Gell 1998, 21). But my growing familiarity with Persian literary history, particularly recent developments in its study, made it increasingly clear to me that this was nothing new.

   One of the ways in which men and, to a lesser extent, women living in the Persianate world have sought to claim distinction for centuries is by becoming known as poets. Verses circulated widely, whether orally, in manuscripts, or later in print. One of the markers of success was writing enough poetry to publish, in manuscript or print, one's own *divān* or poetry anthology. That people were able to make an individual name for themselves as poets and that these names became widely known is attested by the popularity of biographical compilations known as *tazkirahs*.[10] The word comes from the Arabic root *dh-k-r* "to mention, to remember," particularly with a view to praising someone (Dudney 2013, ix). The prototypical Persian tazkirah was the thirteenth-century *Tazkirat al-Awliyā'* (Biographies of the saints) by famed poet-mystic Farid al-Din 'Attār of Nishabur. From medieval times, poets—along with Sufi saints, hadith masters, and faqihs or religious-legal scholars—were among those deemed worthy of individual memorialization in such compilations, which contained their biographies and selections of their works. These usually comprised basic information such as the place and date of birth and death, if known, and the poet's teachers (*ostāds*) and profession, but they also often included anecdotes and comments on the poet's personality and character that likely circulated orally as gossip before being written down (Pellò 2015, 309–13).

Fortunately for historical comparison, a wealth of material has recently been explored in what one scholar has called a highly productive "tazkirah moment" in the cultural and literary history of the Persianate world and its immediate descendants, particularly in premodern and early modern South Asia.[11] For late Mughal Persian-speaking poets, for example, the tazkirah "can be thought of as an attempt to catalogue and archive, in a narrative-fictional way, specific individual personalities and the internal dynamics of the Persian-writing poetic community, and thus to describe (in terms that are also prescriptive) its protocols with regards to poetic education, poetic production, reception, and criticism. In other words, the genre of literary tazkirahs can be understood as a kind of autobiography or, even better, auto-hagiography of Persian literature by its own protagonists" (Pellò 2015, 303). While the tazkirah fulfilled numerous functions, including didactic and critical ones that are beyond the scope of this chapter, it is the biographical and ethical dimension that most concerns us here, particularly as it evolved over time. For, as numerous literary historians make clear, the tazkirah was itself a discursively shaped genre whose framing and content shifted over time (Pellò 2015, 305) and indeed could be highly idiosyncratic, with much of the framing at the compiler's discretion (Pritchett 1994, 66).[12] But individuality was an important preoccupation even when accounts of it proved to be changeable and stereotyped, as Bray has argued for analogous Arabic biographical compilations: "That all that remains of a person after death, even where firm facts can be, and are, gathered, is a literary tradition—of anecdote, of controversy—is tacitly and unanimously agreed. The great importance of this fragile and mutable legacy is also an agreed matter" (2010, 253). Tazkirahs as literary texts thus offer useful insights into the changing ways in which public narratives of distinction, or the distinctiveness of literary personalities, could be constructed and the types of people whose distinctiveness could be claimed. They are also valuable in showing how relationships among poets, often presented as a *majles* or convivial poetic gathering across space and time, were imagined in different contexts.

The public narration and circulation of distinctiveness and distinction is, therefore, discursively constructed for men as much as it is for women, but specific problems arise in the case of women due to a greater need for propriety (without, however, making it impossible). I will focus on tazkirahs of women poets in this section to illustrate what happens when the stakes of privacy are particularly high. Most tazkirahs commemorate male poets only, even though female poets have been active in the literate Persian poetic tradition throughout its thousand-year documented history. But there have been exceptions, either with female poets added in separate sections at the end of the work (as in the late nineteenth-century work *Hadiqat al-shu'ara'* [The garden of the poets]; Brookshaw 2014, 119), or tazkirahs devoted exclusively to women. Two notable examples of the latter include the mid-sixteenth-century work *Javāher al-'Ajāyeb* (Jewels of wonder) by Fakhri Heravi, a native of Herat who migrated to India, and *Noql-e Majles* (The confection of the assembly), an early nineteenth-century tazkirah written by Mahmoud Mirza, a son of the Qajar king Fath 'Ali Shah.[13]

The common features of these latter two works, written three centuries apart, reveal certain trends in the literary activity of women in late medieval and early modern Iran. Firstly, most of them already held privileged positions in society, and this seems to have been a prerequisite for being able to claim distinction through poetry. Mahmoud Mirza's volume is extraordinary in that most of the female poets it describes were also members of the Qajar royal family and thus closely related to Mirza himself. As a *mahram*, a male relative with whom a woman could freely interact without disturbing the cone of privacy, and an accomplished poet and scholar himself, it was he who tutored many of his sisters and nieces in poetry, and he who assigned many of their pen names (*takhallos*). Women's access to poetic knowledge, then, usually came via men; many other Persian female poets who gained fame and were memorialized were often the wives, daughters, or mothers of male literati.[14] The compilers of tazkirahs were also typically men. Fakhri's earlier tazkirah, meanwhile, deals mostly with women poets and scholars of Timurid Herat (1370–1507), a context in which noblewomen and those associated with the court were politically active to a rather extraordinary degree and were frequently patrons of architecture, the arts, and the sciences (Szuppe 1998).

Despite both their authors' connections to royal courts, there is evidence that these tazkirahs were meant to circulate beyond their walls to broader contemporaneous and future audiences; in the frequent cases where oral transmission was broken or manuscripts of divāns were lost, the tazkirahs became the sole repositories of memory about some individuals and fragments of their verses. How, then, was such public reputation building negotiated in the case of still-living poets, given that "women's poetry (especially that penned by royal women) was still considered to be private in some respects, and . . . there was a certain degree of anxiety over its dissemination" (Brookshaw 2014, 121)? First-ly, most Persian poets before the modernist period were known primarily by their takhallos or pen name, a mark of poetic individuality, and women were no exception. Many tazkirahs were actually arranged in alphabetical order by pen name. However, in the case of women, there was a striking pattern: names like 'Effat or 'Esmat (both meaning chastity), Mahjoubeh ("the veiled/modest one"), Mastoureh, Makhfi, or Nahani (all meaning "the hidden one") were used as pen names of women poets across the Persianate world, as if the takhallos could function as a symbolic veil, allowing their words to circulate while preserving their privacy. This changed in the early twentieth century onward, when women began to publish with their full names and simultaneously to unveil, as F. Milani (1992) has documented in great detail.

My interlocutor Fatemeh herself, with all her careful management of appearance and reputation, was one of the few contemporary poets I knew who had a takhallos, though she always published it alongside her name and surname and sometimes used only the latter. It was *Hesār*, meaning a fortress or enclosure. I have not come across a historical precedent for it, though its continuity with all the Mahjoubehs and 'Esmats is clear, albeit with a slightly more defiant tone. Now living in Europe and writing poetry less frequently, she no longer uses it, but she told me recently that she still loves it and that it has roots deep in her being. "Hesār to me means that I have preserved my values, such as decency, purity and modesty, which in the world of technology no longer exist. My thinking has changed: for example, hijab no longer has the same meaning as it did in Iran. It doesn't mean you necessarily have to cover your head."

Another modality of controlling public reputations was (and is) editing and censorship. Mahmoud Mirza confessed to having removed some of the more "indecent poems" from his initial selection by his contemporary royal female relatives (although he kept sexually suggestive poems by others, such as the long-dead twelfth-century poet Mahsati Ganjavi). Meanwhile, the twenty-first-century editors of the first critical edition of the work expunged further material found to be "in breach of chastity" under the rules of the Islamic Republic (Brookshaw 2014, 128).[15]

A handful of women were able to exert some control over their own memorialization. Mahmoud Mirza's work was in fact commissioned by his full sister Zia' al-Saltaneh, who was highly educated and very influential in the court as private secretary to their father, Fath 'Ali Shah (Brookshaw 2014, 122). She seems to have had some influence on the choice of poets (including herself), and poems by other women praising her are also included in the volume.[16] But it is important to note that she was able to exercise this agency only through her brother, the compiler. Thus, public recognition of her unique traits and talents did not necessarily expand her autonomy of action, except through the men of the royal household to whom she was related.

In these ways, certain female poets, often of already privileged backgrounds, could create, leave traces in the world, and hope for a wide dissemination and memorialization of their individual public personas and unique accomplishments, without violating the norms of seclusion. They also did so in a relational way—relying on males to, as Brookshaw puts it, gain "literary agency by proxy" (2014, 123). This situation changed radically in the twentieth century, when modernizing movements both in literature and in politics championed women's right to public individuality. Many of the older logics persist in tandem with modernizing trends, however.

The Afghan poets in Iran have taken upon themselves the mission to document and commemorate the individual protagonists of the literate poetic tradition of Afghanistan specifically. They do this in a variety of ways: obituaries and commemorations are published for the deceased; individual poets' publications are reviewed and subjected to critique (*naqd*), both in writing and in public seminars; elaborate farewells are held and written for those who migrate to other countries; and the most prominent poets and writers are celebrated with a *bozorgdāsht* (honoring of an esteemed—*bozorg*, or great—personality) as part of the annual Afghan literary festival held in Tehran.

Other practices can be seen, I believe, as a continuation and reformulation of the tazkirah tradition. Fatemeh's aforementioned anthology of youth poetry contains the year and place of birth of each poet. Visual identification now being central to one's unique individuality, small headshot photographs of poets, both male and female, are printed beside their full names and poems in literary periodicals (fig. 7.1). One glossy Afghan literary magazine produced in Mashhad, *Khatt-e Sevvom* (*The Third Script*), also regularly marks out certain individuals for special attention by printing larger color photographs of them—or stylized computer graphics based on these—on its inside front and back covers, along with fragments of their verses (fig. 7.2). These images are usually of living poets, male or female, while the back cover usually bears an image of a historical Afghan poet together with his or her dates of birth and death (fig. 7.3), more likely to be male.

A rather innovative tazkirah-like publication of the Dorr-e Dari (Pearl of Dari) Cultural Institute has appeared in recent years: an annual blank diary or journal, whose dated calendrical pages are interspersed with biographical sketches of poets and writers identified specifically with modern Afghanistan (i.e., from the late nineteenth century onward) and arranged in chronological order throughout the book. While by their nature these diaries might be considered ephemeral publications rather than definitive works, the chronotopes they

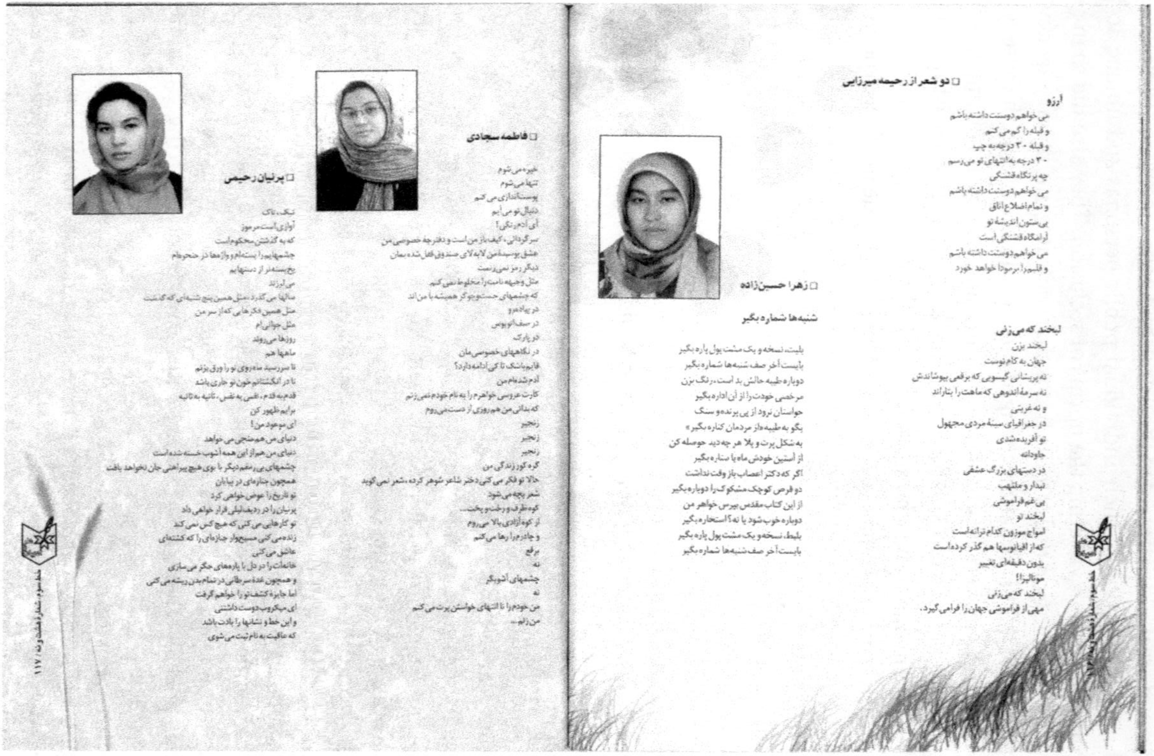

پرنیان رحیمی

فاطمه سجادی

زهرا حسین‌زاده

شنبه‌ها شماره بگیر

دو شعر از رحیمه میرزایی

آرزو

لبخند که می‌زنی

Figure 7.1. Headshots of female Dorr-e Dari poets accompany their poems in *Khatt-e Sevvom/The Third Script*, no. 8–9 (Spring–Summer 2006; 1385 Persian Solar Hijri calendar). Reproduced with permission from the Dorr-e Dari Cultural Institute.

صبح می‌شود و باز، کودکی بهانه‌گیر
خستگی، ملال، غم نان و چایی و پنیر
چشم را نمی‌شود روی صبح واکنی
صبح چادری به سر رفته پشت نان و شیر
صبح رخت‌های چرک، صبح کوه ظرف‌ها
در اتاق کوچکی، باز می‌شوی اسیر
در خودت فشرده‌ای ابرهای تیره را
صبح تازه‌ات بخیر... آسمان دور و دیر!

محبوبه ابراهیمی
(شاعر)

Figure 7.2. Photograph of "Mahboubah Ebrahimi (Poet)" and one of her ghazals on the inside front cover of *Khatt-e Sevvom/The Third Script*, no. 8–9 (Spring–Summer 2006; 1385 Persian Solar Hijri calendar). Reproduced with permission from the Dorr-e Dari Cultural Institute.

عبدالرحمان پژواک (۱۲۷۴ ـ ۱۲۹۷ ش)

Figure 7.3. Photograph of Abdul Rahman Pazhwak (1919–95), Afghan poet and diplomat of Pashtun background, on back cover of *Khatt-e Sevvom/The Third Script*, no. 8–9 (Spring–Summer 2006; 1385 Persian Solar Hijri calendar). Reproduced with permission from the Dorr-e Dari Cultural Institute.

invoke are telling: unlike other tazkirahs arranged according to the social status of the poets (like *Noql-e Majles*) or alphabetically, here the user moves through the days of the year, simultaneously encountering an array of poets processing in chronological *national* time. The poets metaphorically assembled in this majles belong to the territory of the nation-state Afghanistan, even if many of them have spent a good deal of time in exile. (The diaries are also peppered with edifying couplets from classical poets from across the Persianate world, serving as a contrapuntal reminder of a wider prenational literary sociality.) But again, this framing to serve the interests of a particular editor is in itself nothing new.

Conclusion

In this piece, I have endeavored to show how poetic activity in the Persianate world, whose documented traditions date back a millennium, offers a useful insight into the ways in which individuality as distinctiveness and distinction has been claimed and negotiated throughout history, by both male and female poets. To understand how such individuality functions in this context, however, requires us to disentangle the idea of individuality as moral autonomy from individuality as a unique and consistent package of a name, biography and set of attributes known by all. The love marriage of Fatemeh and Abbas in a contemporary Afghan society reveals how such an "individualistic" challenge to social norms could succeed only when publicly presented as a corporate decision by their immediate families rather than Fatemeh's exercise of her moral autonomy. Meanwhile, the commemoration practices of female poets in the past reveal that while many could and did make a name for themselves, winning public renown and admiration for their verses, the scope of their moral autonomy did not necessarily widen—at least in public accounts, which emphasized the agency of their male relatives. In addition to such social continuities, the literary genres and conventions of the tazkirah and the takhallos themselves, while undoubtedly malleable in response to the exigencies of diverse times and places, have also exhibited extraordinary levels of continuity—a continuity that has outlasted events and major political ruptures.

Is such historical continuity scandalous? If it is a question of finding premodern precedents for assumedly modern traits like individualism in Iran, it will not be an odd or unwelcome argument in the field of Iranian studies; scholars in Iran today delight in finding quranic attestation for phenomena described by modern science, and one secular Iranian political theorist has gone so far as to argue that Iran has had numerous "encounters with modernity" (A. Milani 2004, 9), including one that long predated the European Renaissance that is generally accepted as the dawn of the modern era. Less frequently undertaken, and perhaps less popular in the study of the supposedly distinctively Iranian trait of a bifurcated self (the flattened, stereotyped external zahir and the unique, deeply buried batin) is ethnographic comparison. Such comparison reveals striking spatial continuities with neighboring regions—whether Arabic-speaking populations with similarly structured "cones of privacy" to the west (Dresch 1989), or South Asian communities to the east whose possibilities for public individuality also vary according to status, gender, and power (Mines 1994).[17] One of Paul Dresch's lasting imprints on my work has been a constant, restless encouragement to seek out such comparisons in space and time and to subject to particular scrutiny any excessive claims of novelty. For this I remain enormously in his debt.

ZUZANNA OLSZEWSKA is Associate Professor in the Social Anthropology of the Middle East at the University of Oxford and a fellow of St. John's College, Oxford. She is author of *The Pearl of Dari: Poetry and Personhood among Young Afghans in Iran*, winner of the 2015 Houshang Pourshariati Iranian Studies Book Award from the Middle East Studies Association, and winner of the 2017 Middle East Section Book Award from the American Anthropological Association.

Notes

This chapter is based on ongoing ethnographic research, beginning in 2005, with a group of Afghan refugee poets and intellectuals initially based in Iran and now dispersed around the world. Earlier versions of this chapter were presented in the Anthropology Departmental Seminar Series at the School of Oriental and African Studies, at a conference on "Ethnography of Iran—Past and Present" at Princeton University, as well as at the workshop in honor of Paul Dresch at Oxford. I am very grateful to the participants in these events, particularly David Mosse for his remarks on India, and to the editors of this volume for their insightful comments and suggestions. I am also grateful to Julia Bray, Dominic Brookshaw, and Richard Williams for sharing their work on tazkirahs and for some very fruitful conversations on the subject.

1. "This fluid and unreliable setting has favored an entrepreneurial ethic of risk-taking, individual initiative, adaptiveness and mobility among opportunistic co-equals who struggle over ephemeral positions of power and respect, constrained only by participation in a framework of elastic patrilineages" (Lindholm 2008, 259).

2. Lindholm tackles this "dilemma of subordination" by arguing that slavery in fact helped perpetuate the ideology of equality among *free* men: "It is precisely in a society with an all-embracing egalitarian ethic that the pressure is greatest for a superior individual to differentiate himself by rendering his inferiors not only completely dependent, but also symbolically subhuman—an effort which finds its most extreme expression in the actual emasculation of slaves" (2008, 216).

3. I consider one of the most glaring and unfortunate gaps in anthropological literature to be the dearth of ethnographic studies of the experience, rather than the ideology, of personhood in Euro-American societies, which would surely reveal that we are far less bounded and autonomous than Mauss's interpretation of our moral and legal categories would allow, even though we often deny it. That this would be a fruitful area of inquiry is illustrated by a lighthearted blog post by Lindisfarne and Neale (2015) that explores, among other things, dividual personhood in American popular song lyrics. On the other hand, one might posit

that there are strong countervailing trends within Euro-American thought and political practice that are held by some proportion of the population: both historical materialist and poststructuralist theories of subjectivity might in fact be seen as deeply relational—even dividual—emic theories of personhood.

4. So frustrated is Bloch, for instance, by this "indistinct galaxy" of terms, as well as scholars' frequent unconscious elision of the *experience* of being a human person with *metarepresentations* of it, that he resorts to flippantly calling the resultant conglomerate "the Blob" (2011).

5. For further background on Afghan refugees in Iran, including their migration trajectories, ethnic composition, social transformations, management by the state, and cultural activities, see Olszewska (2015). Of particular relevance for us here are two facts: refugees have had access to good-quality public education in unprecedented numbers, raising literacy rates most strikingly among women; at the same time, Afghans continue to face legal discrimination and social prejudice. There are, for instance, heavy restrictions on their participation in the labor market (educated refugees cannot work legally in their professions) as well as costly requirements for continued legal residence, leading to the constant threat of deportation.

6. In fact there might be a great deal to say in the Persianate context about the very kind of dividualism emphasized by anthropologists of some cultures, notably Melanesia, in their focus on the way the boundaries between bodies can be blurred through various practices of substance sharing or gift giving. In my ethnographic context, such blurring was deeply embedded in everyday speech. For example, parents in Iran today typically address their children by the same kin term that their children use for them (*māmān* or *bābā*), emphasizing their identification with each other. Common terms of endearment in Iran and Afghanistan are *jānam, jigaram*—my life/soul, my liver—which emphasize profound spiritual and corporeal connectedness. There is also an abiding interest in classical mystical poetry that dwells on a union with the friend, the beloved, or the divine that obliterates the boundaries between self and other.

7. In Afghanistan, too, women's rights activists are striving for a greater public recognition of women's individuality. In the summer of 2017, for example, they launched a social media campaign with the very telling hashtag *Nām-am kojā-st* (#whereismyname) to encourage the use of women's given names in public, which is still considered shameful. (Instead, on tombstones, on wedding invitations, and in everyday conversation, they are known as the daughter, wife, or mother of so-and-so.)

8. Hazaras are a disadvantaged, largely Shi'a minority in Afghanistan who make up the majority of Afghan refugees in Iran.

9. Fatemeh's narrative is recounted in fuller detail in Olszewska (2015).

10. The same is true of the Arabic-speaking world, in whose enormous numbers of biographical compilations "questions of identification and identity were a major preoccupation" in the medieval and early modern periods, even if in both frame and content they often followed convention and archetype (Bray 2010, 253).

11. Richard Williams, personal communication. See, e.g., Pritchett (1994), Szuppe (1998), and particularly Dudney (2013), Kia (2014), Tabor (2014), Brookshaw (2014), and Pellò (2015).

12. See also Pritchett (1994, 63–64) on transformations in the form of nineteenth-century Urdu tazkirahs that developed from the Persian tradition, as well as scathing twentieth-century modernist critiques of the tradition that further reformulated it.

13. For a detailed analysis of *Javāher al-'Ajāyeb*, see Szuppe (1998); on *Noql-e Majles*, see Brookshaw (2014). Another notable text was *Kheirāt-e Hassān* ("Virtuous and Beautiful

Women"), a monumental three-volume biographical dictionary of prominent women in the Islamic world throughout history, written by Qajar statesman E'temad al-Saltaneh in 1886–89. This was itself a reworking and translation of an earlier compendium in Ottoman Turkish (Brookshaw 2014, 116).

14. For more on women poets writing in Persian before the modernist movements of the twentieth century, see F. Milani (1992), Brookshaw (2005, 2013), Sharma (2009), and Olszewska (2011).

15. For ethnographic explorations of editing as a modality for revelation, expression, and the preservation of knowledge rather than its constriction in contemporary Iran, see Manoukian (2012, 62–106) and Olszewska (2015, 185–209).

16. Richard Williams (2017) describes an entry in a nineteenth-century Urdu tazkirah of women in which an accomplished female poet who is *pardanishin* (living a strictly gender-segregated life in domestic seclusion) knows the compiler of the tazkirah and specifically asks *not to be named*—except by her takhallos, "Tahereh" (Chaste, Pure). The entry reads, "She is a highly respectable lady. She is a poet of the current time. But she has never produced a [longer] work. . . . Even I only have permission to print one or two verses. Although I know more than this, I am not at liberty to write it." Such teasing of the boundary between public and private speech, namelessness and claiming a name, protects her propriety while allowing her to gain renown for her skill.

17. Similarities may easily be noted further afield as well. See Lienhardt's discussion of a private self and a public persona among the Dinka of Sudan (1985).

8

SEGMENTATION VERSUS TYRANNY

Politics as Empirical Philosophy

Judith Scheele

Enfin . . . le structuralisme: c'est la bonne anthropologie.
(Lévi-Strauss, cited in Sahlins 2010, 373)

A T ITS INCEPTION, THE NOTION OF "STATELESS SOCIETIES" represented one
of the "problems" that anthropology was supposed to be good at solving.
Indeed, it has been (incorrectly) argued that other key interests of the discipline—most notably kinship—derived from attempts to understand political
structure in nonstate societies. More recently, much of this interest has been
decried as imperialist and overly functionalist, and the notion of stateless societies has fallen out of use. The anthropology of politics, where it has not been
absorbed into reflections on "power," has largely become the anthropology of
the state or, perhaps, of the margins or the breakdown of states. Although many
of these studies are inherently critical, they leave little room for alternative concepts of politics. In this respect, Paul Dresch's work is exceptional: the Yemeni
tribes of his description exemplify a world in which the modern state is not
taken for granted; they constitute an example that allows us to think through
the oddities of the contemporary world. Three main points emerge: first, we
need to beware of functionalism and the assumption of the identity of morality, humanity, and bounded political community (a.k.a. the state) that underpins not only much Western political philosophy but also contemporary common sense. Second, politics cannot be reduced to wrangling over power, with
power (like greed) assumed to be a universal category that requires no further

explanation. Rather, we need to analyze the principles that underpin political action. These principles, in turn, are rarely locally bounded but tend to inscribe themselves into broader movements that have their own geographical contours and historicity—that, in fact, produce their own kind of history and regional connectivity. This means that we need to find a conceptual vocabulary to deal with what Dresch calls, in his early work, "structure," and later on, "shared assumptions," that, like language and kinship, tend to go beyond the local without being imposed by a centralizing power or reducible to economic matters.

With these things in mind, this chapter revisits three ethnographic areas—Kabylia and the Touat in Algeria, and northern Chad—where state politics, although certainly important and familiar to all, cannot exhaust political interactions and imaginations on the ground. It argues that it is worthwhile and indeed important to hold on to an interest in stateless forms of social organization, without, however, assuming that a definition by lack results in any coherent content. This argument in turn raises several questions that are somewhat scandalous within contemporary anthropology: the continuity—spatial and temporal—of certain political forms, or at least their constituent features, in the absence of political centralization or even a literate tradition; and the need to find ways of expressing such overarching continuity, but also its limits, internal contradictions, and unspoken counterparts.

From Political Anthropology to the Anthropology of Politics

In a certain reading of the history of anthropology, political anthropology was at the heart of the discipline in the decades after the 1940s. After the publication of Fortes and Evans-Pritchard's *African Political Systems* in 1940 ("a work that, in a single blow, established modern political anthropology"; Lewellen 2003, 7), research on local political systems, typologies, and classifications flourished; it preoccupied a whole generation of what came to be the founding fathers (more rarely mothers) of British anthropology.[1] Their almost exclusive focus on the African continent, however, and their pronounced functionalism—the assumption that all elements present in a society had to serve an overarching purpose, which in the last instance was the society's coherence and survival—has meant that their works have since been mostly rejected, partly on the grounds of colonial complicity (Asad 1973a), partly as a broader disavowal of structural functionalism. Whereas the actual impact of social anthropology on colonial rule is difficult to assess, as is most anthropologists' and colonial officials' enthusiasm for collaboration (James 1973),[2] there is certainly much truth in Asad's observation that the bounded and static nature of societies thus analyzed had more to do with a militarily imposed Pax Britannica than with their internal structure or even harmony. "Political anthropology," Asad (1973b, 269) con-cluded, was thus mostly a description of "African political systems operating within the colonial systems of Indirect Rule."[3] This, of course, made it easy to reject not only the ethnographic but also the conceptual tools and aspirations employed by the authors of *African Political Systems*. Structure in itself became a rude word implying stasis and hence colonial complicity.[4] The other half of the equation—functionalism—was also condemned, but halfheartedly so, as its deconstruction would have required a thorough reflection on basic assump-tions that underpinned (and still underpin) much of the social sciences. Much of it has thus survived, implicit but unharmed, in contemporary social analysis.

This is due to two assumptions: one, a widespread elision of conceptual with political order and of political order with governance (pace Clastres 1977); the other, imaginations of "social wholes" within which calculations of "so-cial order" can be made, and that seem to be animated by a collective "will to survive" resulting in the possibility of ultimate causes. Candea (2007, 178) thus speaks of "the paradoxical reconfiguration of holism implicit [even] in the multi-sited imagery" that aims to "grasp whole systems" and thereby presumes the existence of a totality "out there"—boundaries might be in unexpected places, but boundaries there are. Durkheim's metaphors of machines or organ-isms thus easily creep in through the back door, suggesting functional wholes and a certain stability of purpose, although Durkheim himself was perhaps the first to emphasize the priority of potentially unbounded conceptual systems, linked to language or what he called "civilization" (Durkheim and Mauss 1903; also Durkheim 1991, 59, 721). One of the reasons why the idea of bounded to-talities is so commonsensical is that it overlaps in many ways with the modern state, or rather, with the image that the latter likes to project of itself. "The quest to find order or reason among the primitives makes use of a language of order that is inherited from—and indeed part of—the modern European state. In this sense, anthropology has always been, in many unacknowledged ways 'about' the state—even (and perhaps especially) when its subjects were consti-tuted as excluded from, or opposed to, the forms of administrative rationality, political order, and authority consigned to the state" (Das and Poole 2004, 5). This easy slippage between "community" and "the state" is shared by other disciplines and thus tacitly informs whole strands of legal philosophy and pol-itical science.[5]

This fundamental influence of state-based images, Das and Poole continue, can lead to two conclusions: we should be wary of our bias, or we should lucidly endorse it. They themselves opt for the latter. "An anthropology of the margins offers a unique perspective to the understanding of the state, not because it cap-tures exotic practices, but because it suggests that such margins are a necessary entailment of the state, much as the exception is a necessary component of the rule" (Das and Poole 2004, 4). Different conceptions of politics leading to "exotic practices" are thus discarded, as, in any case, "it is impossible to think of political systems in the contemporary world as inhabiting any form of stateless societies" (Das and Poole 2004, 6). And indeed, since the 1980s, the state itself has become the privileged subject matter of political anthropology. The *Comparative Political Systems* (R. Cohen and Middleton 1967) of the 1960s are thus replaced by the *Anthropology of the State* (A. Gupta and Sharma 2006; note the singular replacing the plural). Postcolonial embarrassment is thereby avoided by resolute modernism. Problems of "social structure" are similarly sidelined, as durable patterns and constraints are simply blamed on the state and its administrative apparatus, colonial or other. Where states are questioned, this is increasingly *par le haut*, through an analysis of the growing influence of supranational entities (see, e.g., Ferguson and Gupta 2002; Ong 2006; Rancière 2006; Abélès 2014) or a focus on migration and transnationalism.

Alternatively, or perhaps rather in parallel, politics dissolved into power, following a potted version of Foucault.[6] Even a cautious introduction to the topic concludes that "political anthropology . . . consists mainly in the study of the competition for power, and the way in which group goals are implemented by those possessing power" (Lewellen 2003, 85). Following Foucault, however, "power" can be found everywhere, thus potentially disabling any interest in political institutions qua institutions. This is an old debate (see, e.g., Balandier 1970, 195–96; Clastres 1977, 13), and one that easily turns on labels rather than content, but it seems true that, statistically speaking, to replace a focus on political thought with one on governmentality redirects inquiry to North Atlantic systems. Moreover, once power is seen to pervade anything, it becomes difficult or rather irrelevant to study conscious political action and imagination in their own terms as anything but false consciousness. Other people and places thus quickly start to look like an (imagined) "West." As Sahlins observes, "the current Foucauldian-Gramscian-Nitzschean obsession with power is the latest incarnation on Anthropology's incurable functionalism. Like its structural-functionalist predecessors, hegemonizing is homogenizing: the dissolution of specific cultural forms into generic instrumental effects. . . . Now . . . 'power' is the intellectual black hole into which all kinds of cultural content get sucked, if before it was 'social solidarity' or 'material advantage'. Again and again we make this lousy bargain with the ethnographic realities, giving up what we know about them in order to understand them" (Sahlins 2002, 20). More recently, the "ethical turn" in anthropology, also drawing on the later Foucault (see, e.g., Faubion 2001; Laidlaw 2013), arguably leads to an avoidance of larger political questions altogether, in favor of an emphasis on individual self-fashioning.

Two problems seem to be at issue here. The first one, very general, is that of the recognition of difference, which is acceptable in certain circumscribed areas of life (food and dress, for instance, unless it concerns deep-frying kittens, slaughtering animals in one's bathtub, or "the veil"; see Shryock 2004c). But it is unacceptable in others—forms of political organization that do not rest on an institutionalized monopoly of violence or its routinized avoidance, for instance. As Clastres put it, forty years ago, "the still robust adversary was recognized long ago, the obstacle constantly blocking anthropological research: the *ethnocentrism* that mediates all attention directed at differences in order to reduce them to *identity* and finally suppress them" (1977, 11). Or, in Dresch's terms, "the point of anthropology is judicious assessment of the sense people's worlds and actions make, and to make them the same so thoughtlessly is to deprive each one of us of moral autonomy. . . . False resemblance is as much a problem as exoticism ever was" (1992, 26, 28). The second problem is that of the ability to imagine "civilized" or even just politically complex life beyond a state. However much anthropologists might be keen to criticize actually existing states, this is done rarely in terms of a radically different political imagining but rather in the name of, say, human rights, individual agency, or resistance. States are thus taken to account for not living up to their own image of themselves (see Lea 2012) but rarely for their inherently coercive nature. As a result, "anthropology seems a discipline terrified of its own potential" (Graeber 2004, 97).

In Dresch's work, the state is present, but it never exhausts the range of conceptual possibilities. In his 1989 book, the Zaydi state plays an important role, if only as a foil to argue against, and there are no structural reasons why tribes might not turn into states apart from historical contingency (Dresch 1989, 360n). In his later work, modern statehood becomes a more threatening prospect, having absorbed most spaces, "physical and conceptual, that would provide alternatives" to its rule (2009, 199; see also Dresch 2006b, 308; 2014, 121-22). The three edited volumes on *Legalism* can be summarized as a reflection on different forms not just of law but of sovereignty—Yemeni legal codes are contrasted to the "municipal model" of Western legal philosophy. While in the latter legal status is granted (and thus potentially withheld) top-down by a central authority or a bounded community, the former "assume a set of minor, often personal, sovereignties that in a pressing sense precede the law" (Dresch 2012b, 152). Law works sideways, and "starts from an idea of mutual recognition" (Dresch 2012b, 146; see also 2006b, 280, for parallels with early Europe). "No matter how just the polity, the language of the jurisprudential state invites always the equation of one moral regime with humanity itself, and of moral action with the exercise of power. Other legal traditions . . . offer means at least to retain distinctions of understanding among justice, morality, and political order" (Dresch 2006b, 304, 308). By contrast, the Yemeni tribes act as a (conceptual) alternative or rather an Archimedean point whence better to observe the "deeply authoritarian law-bound world where we find ourselves" (Dresch 2012b, 150–51).

Kabylia

Working on North Africa, it is difficult to discard the notion of a "stateless society" altogether as it corresponds, partly at least, to a "native category." Montagne's (1930a) treatment of Moroccan history as an opposition between the *bilad al-makhzan* (the land of government) and the *bilad al-siba* has long been criticized as an oversimplification, and as an Orientalist one *de surcroît*. But if it is true that this opposition was never quite so clear-cut, and that leading institutions within the bilad al-siba acted as proxies for the makhzan (Hammoudi 1980), the notional opposition it expresses preceded Montagne by centuries. Hence, Touati (1993) analyzes the use of the term in a collection of seventeenth-century *nawazil* (legal responsa) from southern Morocco but also notes that it was current in North African jurisprudence from the eleventh century onward (Touati 1996, 110; see also Berque 1970 for a fifteenth-century example). In these texts, the bilad al-siba is characterized by three main features: people follow custom rather than Islamic law, they are ignorant of true religious prescriptions, and they do not recognize a central government (Touati 1993, 98). This in no way implies that life in the bilad al-siba was any more disorderly than its opposite—indeed, for the *'ulama'*, Maghrebi princes were quite as often responsible for disorder, violence, and misery (Berque 1970, 1332)—but that Islamic legal institutions there could not function properly. Any kind of transactions conducted with people from the bilad al-siba were thus potentially invalid, as their wealth was acquired perhaps in illegal but certainly in extralegal ways (Berque 1970, 1347; Voguet 2009). There can be no doubt that this describes an aspiration rather than a reality, as interactions were as common as they were necessary; but it is an image whose symbolic strength and longevity is arresting.

It might be useful here to look at the terms employed more closely. The bilad al-makhzan is in fact the "land of the money box"—that is to say, where taxes are (supposedly) paid, into one central coffer, in exchange for protection of some sort. The image used is less of governance than of tribute and of a particular skewed circulation of goods that takes into account the creation of a center—a center that, in the Maghrebi context, is often also imbued with baraka, or the spiritual potential to create, keep safe, and redistribute wealth. This is relevant inasmuch as throughout the bilad al-siba also, storehouses are much in evidence, and often at the heart of local councils and customary law (see, e.g., Montagne 1924, 316; 1930b), and as the institutions that in the bilad al-siba might most easily be identified with centers of political authority—*zawaya* or religious strongholds—are perhaps best described along similar lines.[7] Seen from the bilad al-siba, the opposition is thus one of scale rather than kind; of a plurality of centers (and protected spaces) as opposed to one. One is reminded of Dresch's description of Yemeni tribal law, where he opposes "states" that "of their nature are monist, so to speak" to "pluralist" tribalism (Dresch 2006b, 303). The distinction matters: if we follow Agamben (1997) in his definition of sovereignty as the power to exclude, such power is severely curtailed if sovereignty is multiple and fragmented. "Outlaws" in such a context routinely become in-laws elsewhere (see also Dresch 2014).

Kabylia, a Berber-speaking area northeast Algiers, used to be one of the stereotypical buldan al-siba. Nominally under Ottoman control since the sixteenth century, only the fringes of Kabylia ever seem to have paid taxes. According to Peysonnel, who traveled through the area in the eighteenth century, the Kabyles "have neither chiefs, nor nations, nor governors. Everybody is master and free to his will. They are, most of them, thieves, or rather, wild beasts living in these mountains. Neither the Turk, nor anybody else, has been able to subdue them; they live miserably as they please" (Peysonnel 1987 [1724–5], 213). Similarly, half a century later, al-Husayn al-Wartilani described the whole region as "*sa'ib*" (al-Wartilani 1908, quoted in Touati 1996, 116). It is important to note here that al-Wartilani was no stranger to the region but was himself born, bred, and educated in Kabylia. This was possible because, despite al-Wartilani's wholesale rejection of the region as a land of ignorance, Kabylia has long been a center of Islamic scholarship, attracting students from elsewhere and exporting religious scholars to adjacent regions. In the same way, relations with neighboring states have always been close, and neither the Hafsides in the fourteenth century nor the Ottomans from the sixteenth century onward could have asserted their domination of the coastal plains and managed their economies without the help of Kabyle soldiers and allies (Haëdo 1998 [1612], 56–58). More generally, the relationship between Kabylia and Ottoman Algiers "was an intense and intimate one and it produced identifiable effects on both parties" (Roberts 2014, 150). Kabylia's uncouth reputation seems to derive precisely from this close connection. Its "unheededness" in fact describes not the absence of a relation but, in Ferguson's (1999, 238) term, a relation in its own right, albeit a negative one. Like the Yemeni tribes analyzed by Dresch, Kabylia constitutes a "half-world" (Dresch 1989, 398) and needs to be understood as such; and its description as bilad al-siba is at the heart of this relation.

Beyond this, however, Kabylia looks very different from the Yemeni highlands. Although the region's Arabic name—*bilad al-qaba'il*—refers to tribes, legal and moral authority was mostly vested in villages. These were governed by an assembly, which met usually once a week, often after Friday prayer. It included nominally all male resident villagers who had come of age (who had publicly completed a month's fast at Ramadan), although Roberts's (2014, 110) description as "an assembly of land-owners who bear arms" is probably more accurate. Assemblies were assisted by the village imam, most often recruited from the resident *mrabtin* (hereditary religious specialists), in particular with family law and the drafting of legal documents. Village assemblies made their own law (*qanun*, plural *qawanin*), a list of finable offences that were mostly preoccupied with the maintenance of the village as a bounded community (Scheele 2014).[8] On the most basic level, this meant maintaining village peace and what was conceived of as necessary public order: regulating rubbish disposal and festivities and managing agricultural land, animal trespass, and water. Women's movements were monitored, children's quarrels fined, any kind of deviance discouraged. Villagers were urged to bring their conflicts before the village council, much as they were exhorted not to marry beyond the village and not to borrow money from or sell village land to strangers. The latter were generally depicted as fomenting disorder, sparking "civil war" in the village, corrupting villagers or village officials, conspiring to buy village land, spying, gossiping, and committing rape and theft. They therefore had to be managed collectively, mostly through compulsory hospitality and, that failing, the threat of hostility between villages.

We hence seem to have an example of the kind of bounded moral community whose historical exceptionalism is one of Dresch's recurrent themes. Dresch in fact routinely opposes European political thought based on ideas of a "body politic, that is, a bounded entity in which power and morality coincide," to a "pre-modern world," characterized by "a plethora of different spaces to which different rights attach" (Dresch 2006b, 283). Nineteenth-century French observers clearly described Kabyle (and other Berber) villages in the former terms: "politically speaking," Kabylia was "a kind of savage Switzerland," wrote Daumas (1864, 232); and "the Berber village" was more generally best thought about as *"Rome à l'état naissant"* ("Rome about to be born"; Masqueray 1886, 222). Were these descriptions correct, Kabylia would appear as an early example of the kind of "community" dear to contemporary communitarian philosophers: "The distinctiveness of cultures and groups depends upon closure and, without it, cannot be conceived as a stable feature of human life. . . . To tear down the walls of the state is not . . . to create a world without walls, but rather to create a thousand petty fortresses" (Walzer 1983, 39). But, as Dresch (2012a, 29) further notes, "the coincidence of law and bounded community is always a special case, and the seeming naturalness of their elision always requires examining." In Kabylia, such an examination yields a complex picture. Village qawanin in fact concentrated on a small aspect of life, assuming encompassment in a larger transactional and Islamic world and setting aside a space of legal exceptionalism within it.[9] The central concept of villagehood was not the exclusion of outsiders but rather the twin notions of protection and hospitality (or its reverse, war). The maintenance of the village as a village was a reflection of relations with neighboring settlements: a village's *hurma* (honor) was bound up with its collective ability to grant protection, *'anaya*. Individuals who violated the village's 'anaya were banned from the village, while external aggression necessarily resulted in war. Villages, then, were necessarily part of a larger moral world, within which the interplay between village hurma and 'anaya could acquire meaning: individual villages derived their worth from a larger system of values that presupposed the existence of similar moral spaces elsewhere, mediated through rights of refuge and hospitality.

This was so in a general environment where outside connections were not exceptional but the norm. In a system that recognized banishment, refuge, and vengeance, village membership was necessarily fluid. The possibility and at times even the legitimacy of changing village allegiance were recognized by the qawanin, and family histories generally speak of distant origins (see Scheele 2009, 102–3). The image of the Kabyle peddler is as widespread and stereotypical as that of the Kabyle soldier and migrant laborer, and Kabylia has long been part of wider market dynamics. The salience of cash values in the qawanin bears witness to this, as does some villages' long-standing reputation as expert money-forgers (Peysonnel 1987, 264). Landownership was at the heart of village membership; but despite continuous attempts by the *jama'a* (village assembly) to prevent this, land could be and frequently was sold to outsiders or mortgaged to outside moneylenders. "Kabyle society may well give the appearance of a certain rigidity. . . . But the rigidity in question is not that of kinship structures. All the evidence suggests that pre-colonial Kabylia was the theatre of unusually intense movements of population in all directions, at any rate from the early sixteenth century onwards. The rigidity which one may observe there is the rigidity of political arrangements which were evolved in the context of this turmoil and in response to it" (Roberts 2014, 59). Kabyle village law seems to have been developed in the face of and to counteract a much more fluid and centrifugal reality. The boundaries they established were neither impermeable nor exclusive but depended on participation in a larger system. Legal personality was not derived from community membership but prior to it, as people could and regularly did move through different moral and legal spaces.

Kabyle villages, then, were not bounded moral communities but rather nodes in a larger whole. The latter in turn formed a region of sorts that was held together by common assumptions of legitimate interaction and moral person-hood. Yet Kabylia has never been united or even ruled in any meaningful way. Its limits have been determined by what comes beyond them: the world of the state. How, then, can we conceive of such regions of mutual intelligibility, intelligibility that can be blamed neither on central rule nor even on a shared literate tradition? A similar question seems to lie at the heart of Dresch's work, both on segmentation ("formal relations that characterize the types of events possible"; Dresch 1986, 309) and on legalism ("conceptual order in what otherwise would be indeterminate"; Dresch 2012a, 32–33). Both concepts share a constant reference to a wider world without implying "globalization," old or new. Both are hence scandalously continuous, if only in spatial terms. Segmentation "is abstract. It cannot be derived from observation on the model of perceiving terrain, and it transcends the perception of any one informant or group of them: indeed, it orders within a scheme any number of groups who may seldom if ever lay eyes on each other. Yet it also claims to inform people's everyday lives and does not reduce at all easily to a map made by outsiders" (Dresch 1988, 52). "Through legalism," similarly, "people invoke a vision of the world whose historical conditions may be obscure to them but whose reach is indefinitely broad" (Dresch 2012a, 36).

We might take a hint here from Dresch's frequent (oral) reference to Lévi-Strauss's characterization of "Indian America" as "a kind of Middle Ages which lacked their Rome": "An undifferentiated mass, born of an old syncretism whose texture was certainly very loose and within which survived, here and there, for several centuries, centers of high civilization and barbarian peoples, centralizing tendencies and centrifugal forces" (Lévi-Strauss 1964, 16). The quote is famous—indeed, not so long ago Hugh-Jones (2008) claimed that the decentralized regional unity it posits is the one question that South Americanist anthropology has to address in the future.[10] If taken seriously, it implies two things. First, the need to shift investigation not just to an analysis of relations but indeed one level up from "observation on the model of perceiving terrain. A group . . . owes its character to the fact that it . . . crystallizes in a semantic field that is already there, and whose elements have already been combined in all possible ways: less for the sake of imitation than to allow many small societies to affirm their respective originality drawing on . . . a dialectic of opposition and correlation, framed by a shared conception of the world" (Lévi-Strauss 1964, 16). In Dresch's (1986, 312, 318) terms, structures do not "emerge" from actions, but rather actions presuppose structures: conceptual categories are prior to political relations, and they are what makes action possible in the first place.[11] Second, it implies the rejection of a certain type of history. "Structural analysis," as Lévi-Strauss (1964, 16) defines it, "poses a problem to history," rather than being "limited to the premises circumscribed by historical investigations." Structural similarities can be found beyond the units of historical research—most commonly, states and other political groupings. "Politics," in the conventional sense, emerges within such units bound together through a shared but endlessly transforming conceptual order, but it does not encompass them. This results in a focus on midlevel regions, different among themselves but wider than either "societies" or "communities"—"civilizations," as an older anthropology might have put it.

Saharan Assemblies

Returning from such heady heights, Kabylia might appear rather parochial—after all, today, most Kabyles seem content to act in the way of ordinary "ethnic groups," and reference to pan-Berberism is popular but easily wrecked on national prejudice. There is little that is scandalous in claiming Kabyle unity of some kind; and the parallels observed above can easily be explained, "*dans le goût moderne*" (Berque 2001, 162; see further Dresch 2009, 186), in terms of actual personal contacts and exchange. If we compare the Kabyle material to its Moroccan counterpart, however, which is much older and less homogeneous, something very much like "structural transformations" springs to mind. In southern Morocco, customary law was not the monopoly of villages but was established by all kinds of "superimposed groups" (Montagne and Ben Daoud 1927, 402): families, clans, villages, tribal segments, tribes, tribal federations, markets, collective storehouses, or even mosques. As in Kabylia, these codes were essentially lists of fines, but the institutions receiving these fines varied considerably, showing the flexibility and adaptability of the basic legal principles applied. Despite these differences, a similar logic of "community," or rather of community creation and protection in the face of a centrifugal world, runs through the Moroccan codes. Codes aim to create protected spaces, be they *qsur* (fortified oases), villages, tribes, storehouses, markets, or zawaya; and any of these protected spaces could, like individual houses or perhaps even more effectively so, act as sites of refuge. Interaction with the outside was mediated through hospitality and potential hostility; and there was an underlying assumption of particularism but also of mutual recognizability. Beyond these local protected spaces, Islamic law applied, and interactions with the makhzan could at times be successful because they were conducted in terms of sharia.

Parallels with the Kabyle case are thus many and obvious; but how can we explain this, short of reverting to colonial stereotypes of a Berber "atavism" that has, over the centuries, "resisted" Arab encroachment? This would not do, as Berque noted long ago. "The opposition between a local core and oriental

[Arabo-Islamic] additions is . . . suggestive. But it is largely a myth. It accounts for sentiments rather than facts. In this region, there is no reality so secret, so preserved, that it is not in some way derived from Islam, or at least interpreted according to its method. But neither is there any application of the law rigorous enough to truly elude local forces. So many exchanges have taken place that the elements involved can only be isolated in theory, beyond any claim to historical precision" (Berque 1953, 160). What seems to be at stake, rather, are simple underlying principles that can be recombined in different ways, that might be labeled "pagan" or "Islamic," "Arab" or "Berber" (cf. Berque 2001, 168), and that are capable of absorbing other elements—of framing history in a particular way. "With regard to the sets that we can observe today [among the Seksawa in southwestern Morocco] . . . their constituent features, when taken separately, are mostly unremarkable, and can be found in a geographical area that extends beyond the Atlas and Morocco" (Berque 1955, 62)—and even beyond North Africa. Hence, "originality resides not in facts, but in their combination" (Berque 1955, 63), which yields a "mosaic . . . infinitely fine-grained; its many colors always deriving from the same range" (Berque 2001, 163). In Berque's Maghreb, this dovetails with a fundamental tension between the "permanent tendency of fragmentation" and the appeal of universalism, "the ambition of the general" (Berque 2001, 169). "Everywhere, in this country of obstinate particularisms, we can observe the hegemony of extensive types" (Berque 1953, 150).

Berque is characteristically cryptic here, and Dresch might have put it more clearly when he writes (of Yemen),

> If the tribal system . . . is to be seen as a source of problems for modern politics, it has also been capable of absorbing and indeed containing an extraordinary range of conflicts imposed on it from elsewhere in the course of the last thousand years. Its resilience has, in its own way, been as great as that of, say, the great religions and philosophies whose combinations of a few clear principles with an indefinitely wide range of practice gives the illusion of unchanging permanence. It has reduced most interventions to the terms already known to tribesmen, and for the moment it continues doing so. (Dresch 1989, 355)

But neither Berque nor Dresch addresses the question of how and why this extraordinary resilience is produced (see also Shryock, this volume); nor does either account for noted differences between the Mashreq and the Maghreb. In fact, Berque (1955, 62) proposes Yemen as a possible point of comparison, rather glibly ignoring the fact that many of the recurrent features that he discerns in "Maghrebi social structure"—the jama'a, most obviously, although it is "the principal figure of the system" (Berque 1955, 63)—do not exist there, or at least do not seem to have the same conceptual centrality. Although this might seem to be a relatively minor point, it poses crucial questions of scale.

Anthropologists, says Lévi-Strauss (1964, 19), in opposition to philosophers, "prefer the observation of collective understandings" to "the hypothesis of universal understanding"; structuralism à la Lévi-Strauss is hence, as Ricœur said and Lévi-Strauss (1964, 19) himself quoted, "Kantism without the transcendental subject"—it is plural but not relativist. Where, then, do we draw the line between such different "understandings," and how can we substantiate it?

If we move further south into the Sahara, the "hegemony of extensive types" and the role played by local jama'at within them becomes even more complex. Even more so than Kabylia, the Sahara is the heartland of the bilad al-siba, abode of raiders and pagans, with whom even standard economic transactions are of dubious worth (Voguet 2009; Hall 2013). In the Algerian Touat, an oasis belt a thousand kilometers south of Algiers, state rule (by the Moroccan sultan) has in fact been sporadic (Martin 1908). And here also, although most people spoke Arabic rather than Berber, most day-to-day business seems to have been managed by assemblies of some kind. "In the districts of the Gourara and the Touat, every qsar is administered by a jama'a. . . . The jama'a is the meeting of the notables of the qsar. These notables or *kibar* are those who, by their age, their personal influence or their wealth, have influence over their fellow citizens. The number of kibar is not restricted. There is no special meeting place, the kibar meet at the house of one of them when this is necessary."[12] Touati jama'at, then, were not "institutionalized" to the same degree as their Kabyle counterparts. But we can nonetheless discern similar underlying principles: the jama'at are in no sense "total" institutions (cf. Dresch 1998, 111, 121), people might belong to several, and property is key. Many of the assemblies described by the French seem to have been in actual fact irrigation councils, whose membership depended on ownership of water rather than residence (Grandguillaume 1975; Scheele 2010, 358).

And here also, protection and hospitality are the main concerns of assemblies, although some claim that they have had legislative powers in the past.[13] "The jama'at suppress minor and criminal offences with disciplinary punishments, namely beating and fines. The fines are used to buy provisions for guests. As there is no public treasury, they are immediately converted into staples. These staples are kept in a communal house."[14] Or else: "In the Touat, everybody who owns anything contributes to the food of guests passing through his qsar. Specific days are ascribed to him over the course of the year in proportion to his wealth, generally assessed according to the share of water he owns. . . . In every qsar, a special place is assigned to guests and their mounts."[15] This emphasis on hospitality makes sense, in an environment where trade was an essential part of local economies and where hospitality was often the best way of dealing with potentially harmful strangers.[16] Yet, as seen above, it also translates a certain relationship with the outside and assumptions of mutual recognizability: it mediates between Berque's "obstinate particularisms" and the wider moral world that created them.

The jama'at were assisted by local Islamic scholars described variously as *tullab* (schoolteachers, notaries), *fuqaha'* (jurisconsults), 'ulama' (scholars), or *quda* (judges).[17] In 1896, Didier noted, probably with some exaggeration, that there was "a *qadi* in every qsar"; many of these were educated locally, in institutions funded and administered by local jama'at.[18] The status of these quda was problematic: on the one hand, the exercise of proper judicial authority requires at least nominal reference to a central authority (Johansen 1997, 336); in the Touat, scholars attempted to define the jama'a as such, but in terms so vague as to betray their own lack of conviction.[19] "The 'ulama' [were] horrified by the kind of local democracy that prevail[ed] in the bilad al-siba] and that turn[ed] the assembly into a kind of authority"—Touati's (1993, 98) statement, made with reference to seventeenth-century southern Morocco, was probably valid in the Touat also. On the other hand, property was key to membership in the assembly, and as property was defined in Islamic terms, it made such membership inherently fragile, porous, and beyond local control.[20] Yet explanations that assume an "outside imposition" of Islamic law on recalcitrant locals (see for instance Grandguillaume 1975, 320) are not supported by the evidence. Rather, here as in Kabylia and Morocco, the Touat seems to have imported Islamic law quite voluntarily, as adherence to the sharia was at the heart of local notions of full moral personhood. We can explain this, with Dresch, in terms of the broader appeal of universalism or even "legalism" that "suggests of its nature a larger world than one's immediate relatives or neighbours" (Dresch 2012a, 37), and that mattered more than strictly local concerns of administrative ease, profit, or indeed communal closure.

The real problem, then, is posed not by Berque's "hegemony of extensive types" but rather by his "obstinate particularisms" in an inherently centrifugal world. Most obvious would be here the persistence of the institution of the jama'a that seems to defy historical explanations but rather, to paraphrase Lévi-Strauss, poses a problem to history—if, that is, the latter is primarily conceived as a narrative of change. In North African material, jama'at are indeed everywhere, to the point where the Touati quda themselves sit as a council and accept the jama'a's testimony above all others, although they are clearly well aware of the legal difficulties this entails.[21] Stewart explains this persistence and the contrast it creates with the Mashreq as the result of "the influence of the customary laws of the people who were there before the Arabs, notably the Berbers" (2006, 245).[22] "Influence," with its suggestion of process and mutuality, is clearly a step up from "atavism," but Stewart's statement nonetheless remains deeply unfashionable in a general academic environment where distinctions between Berbers and Arabs are generally conceived of as oppositional categories with little content beyond the linguistic and folkloric. The introduction to a recent edited volume on the topic states this clearly. "Whereas colonial scholars searched for absolute truths about Berber culture, today's scholars see ethnicity as a constantly changing orientation, shaped and reshaped by forces both within and outside the group" (Hoffman and Miller 2010, 4). Berbers are thus primarily defined as one "ethnic group" among others (a definition that is probably more difficult to apply to their supposed opposite, "the Arabs") with all the global comparability, relative boundedness, and moral neutrality this implies (cf. Dresch 1995). This is perhaps justified in the contemporary context, but we need to keep in mind Ardener's (1989, 212) warning that "there is always the danger . . . that we may run the risk of so relativizing the distinction that we forget the original problem." Or, as McDougall (2010, 18) puts it, "on an everyday social level, local knowledge in North Africa has defined individuals and groups primarily by judgments of their moral worth." Barth's radical individualism, which the editors cite as their main reference for their transactional approach, makes such moral evaluation meaningless, as it does not allow for continuity and hence difference of content or worth (Asad 1972, 92; Dresch 2012a, 9–10).

It also means that the one institution that contemporary Berber movements invariably cite as their own, "village democracy," is generally left by the wayside, primarily due to fears of colonial associations (Mahé 2000, 179). Maghrebi political and legal traditions that have long posed a challenge not so much to existing states but to the conceptual apparatus that underpins them and that "tolerates at home no rivals" (Dresch 2006b, 284) are thus subsumed in "Berber culture," incidentally simplifying more complex historical realities and making them compatible with modern statehood. Roberts's (2014, 221) reminder that "the origin of the 'cultural originality' of [Kabylia] was its *political originality*" is thus exceptional. So is his insistence on continuity: "significant social development was occurring in Kabylia well before the colonial period. The kind of order which prevailed there by the mid-nineteenth century was not that of a society without a history. And central to the history of pre-colonial Kabylia was the establishment of political institutions and a system of self-government based upon these institutions, and the development thereby of political traditions which have survived the colonial impact and with which the independent state still has to reckon" (Roberts 2014, 26). And indeed, it can plausibly be argued that although contemporary Kabyle (and Moroccan) village associations and protest movements bear little resemblance to precolonial jamaʿat, some of the political principles they expressed (and that cannot simply be subsumed in "democracy") continue to inform local conceptions of legitimate political action (Mahé 2000)—much as Silverstein (2010, 84) notes that people in contemporary southern Morocco still refer to themselves as living in the bilad al-siba.

Roberts is particularist in his own way and scoffs at any attempts to compare Kabylia to other parts of the Maghreb, Berber-speaking or not (as if temporal and spatial continuity all at once were just too much to deal with). Nor does he propose a model for the persistence of certain key institutions over time. Berque (2001, 165), meanwhile, is moved at some point to explain the astonishing longevity of tribal names in North Africa—which similarly straddle the literate and the local—through "onomastic differentiation" or "the interplay of verbal mutations." Dresch (2009, 188) makes a similar argument with regard to "schemes of identity" in Arabia: "in many circumstances they are less an 'historical' product than the basis of a certain kind of history; in others they seem merely words." Again, this is a delicate backing away from content. It is hard to claim the same with regard to political institutions and to deprive them of all genealogy. For this, we might have to question our own assumptions. While the continuity of a literate or a state-based political tradition over centuries hardly raises eyebrows, and while it is thus permissible and indeed legitimate to speak of Islam as a "discursive tradition" (following Asad 2009, 20–24), unwritten institutional continuity seems so scandalous as to become unmentionable. Partly this is due to a misreading of history as a narrative of change, and of continuity as its antithesis. Partly it derives from a naive approach to the written word. Writing and literacy in and of themselves do not guarantee continuity; nor can it be taken for granted that things labeled "Islamic" are necessarily more permanent than others—although the labels themselves might last, in particular in a tradition biased toward emulation.[23] But there is no reason to think that categories of thought and action that are not explicitly defined as Islamic are less capable of traveling through time than others, in particular if, as throughout the history of North Africa, the "Islamic" and the "un-Islamic" tend to nest in the interstices of one another.

Northern Chad

Any analysis of regional and temporal continuity needs to take into account its limits, external as much as internal, as well as its unspoken counterparts. Indeed, these tend to create a dynamic tension that in turn might account for continuity as well as spatial reach. Lecocq (2015, 29) argues that the Sahara is held together by a "common culture of political organisation, which the inhabitants of the Sahara—both nomads and oasis dwellers—share with the inhabitants of North Africa and the Middle East." On the face of it, the Tubu, who today live in southern Libya and northeastern Niger and constitute the majority population in Borkou and Tibesti in northern Chad, indeed look like a reflection, at a distance and with some distortions, of the patterns and institutions discussed so far.[24] This is a society of pastoralists with a strong interest in date production, in an area that has rarely been governed by states but that has always been close to them, geographically and socially. Political authority is fleeting and decentralized, and matters of dispute are brought forward in popular assemblies. "There is no juridical authority. Victims themselves carry out the necessary investigations to find the perpetrator and to obtain reparation. . . . Matters are decided in assemblies, called *cofono*, that include everybody who lives nearby, i.e. most tent-holders and all the curious, even blacksmiths and old women. . . . After long, feverish, passionate debate, the perpetrator mostly accepts the general decision, or suggests a compromise" (Chapelle 1957, 320). Yet these assemblies seem to have been even less institutionalized than in the Touat. They had no existence beyond particular events, no institutional memory or what we might call a "public purpose." Indeed, the term cofono is "used for private reunions, around a shared meal, as much as for political meetings that aim to resolve conflicts between two men" (Le Cœur 1950, 83). Today, these "assemblies"—which mostly meet to decide on matters of *diya* (compensation) payments—tend to include a large number of outsiders, especially military personnel and other local strongmen. They issue recommendations that are frequently ignored. We have thus come a long way from the Kabyle jamaʿa with its exclusive legislative powers.

Tubu have mostly figured in the (scant) ethnographic record for their political "atavism" of a peculiar kind: one based not on the longevity but on the absence of local political institutions. Assemblies, as we have seen, are rudimentary; similarly, there are no tribes, exogamous "clans" (*yele*) barely matter (Le Cœur 1953; Baroin 1986), and there are no genealogical schemes that might link Tubu to a broader political imagination. This fluidity is more widely reflected in Tubu social organization. Tubu are resolutely bilaterally exogamous over up to seven generations. Tubu kinship is a matter of individual ties and personal bilateral genealogies rather than of definable and defining groups, and not much else intervenes to create groups or even sets of any kind. There are no "discrete units" (Baroin 1985, 15). "Each nuclear family is attached to far-reaching criss-crossing relations of mutual aid that involve kin and affines, in such a way that it is both autonomous and bound to the others. This leads to a fluid social mesh, without centre or periphery, in which each Tubu is placed at the centre of his own personal network" (Baroin 2009, 136). "Kinship," however, is not an independent cause of other patterns in society.[25] Here, it does not create but partakes in a more general fluidity of Tubu society, which in turn seems to point toward a conscious political strategy, or rather, a conceptual preference. From an internal point of view, actions and conduct make sense primarily with regard to personal values of excellence and honor, and aspiration to personal autonomy. From an external point of view, the Tubu are not only disorganized and unpredictable but also unknowable. This has made them resilient to incorporation into any kind of grander narrative, historical or political. Throughout the historical record, the "Tubu slot" endures as a gap, to be filled mostly with negative stereotypes.

Yet this is clearly not the result of a local "ignorance" of "civilization." On the contrary, the Tubu have always been intimately connected to their neighbors and dependent on regular exchange with them. As far as the historical record can take us back, northern Chad has been in the margins of and in close or even intimate relations with neighboring cultural and political formations: long-standing Sahelian states to the south, with early claims to Islamic legitimacy; the Ottoman Empire to the north; and probably the busiest and perhaps oldest trans-Saharan trade route skirting it to the West. There can be no doubt that Tubu regularly and successfully interacted with these formations, not as a group but individually. According to legend, the state of Kanem was founded by Tubu, and the ruling family had to marry Tubu wives (Chapelle 1957, 55). More prosaically, Tubu own property in Kanem, Fazzan, and Waddaï, where they are settled in large numbers. Relations with Kanem in particular are still so close that the fact that the Kanem is not generally counted as belonging to the Tubu world—an inclusion that would result in a configuration of a minority of pastoral nomads depending on but also ruling over a majority of settled peasants, as tends to be the case elsewhere in the southern Sahara (Retaillé 1998, 73)—is clearly the result of political rather than "ethnic" categorization. Similarly, Islamic conversion in the area probably dates back to the sixteenth century. The stereotype of Tubu as "pagan" seems to be of equal venerability (Hornemann 1802, 107); four hundred years later, Layish (2006, 68) can still affirm that "generally speaking, the Tibbu do not observe all of the precepts of Islam." If, then, the Tubu are "savages," or even "pagans," this is due not to their ignorance but, here as in Kabylia, to a structural relation of opposition. And in fact, throughout the historical record, the image of the Tubu appears to be an exact inversion of the most consensual markers of "civilization": living in ephemeral huts, dressed in animal skins, eating uncultivated food, religiously pagan or at least uncouth, devoid of political institutions and laws. "They have no idea, no notion of even the simplest things common in civilized countries" (al-Tunsi 1851, 537). This image was so strong that early twentieth-century sources can still speak of the Tubu as armed uniquely with spears, at a time when they were busy running a lucrative contraband in firearms.[26]

The Tubu, then, tend to be defined throughout the historical record by a lack—an absence of political institutions, social order, Islam. The durability of this stereotype is remarkable, especially in a context marked by high rates of both emigration and immigration, resulting in little demographic stability. The continuity in fact seems to be one of a particular relational (and occupational) niche, not of a "people." What seems to be a stake here, as for the intimate opposition between "Berber" and "Arab" elements discussed above, is a pattern of moral evaluation, whose "negative" side is already contained in the institutions it rejects—and vice versa. The rhetoric that underlines the Tubu's insufficient Islamization thus hides their long-standing integration into the Islamic world as a people to reform, over and over again, as an eternal and relatively stable object of missionary endeavor. This brings to mind Sahlin's historical antitypes: "differentiation by competition . . . with the result that the major institutions and values in each society appear as inverted forms of the other" (Sahlins 2004, 8; see also 69)—and that intimately depend on each other for their self-definition. This in a context where boundaries between different Tubu groups and between them and their neighbors are notoriously labile and uncertain, where Tubu regularly (and necessarily) marry out, and where Tubu speakers have long participated, often in leading roles, in the economic and political formations that surround their "homeland" and that follow radically different political traditions—and continue to do so today, at least in Chad (Buijtenhuijs 2001).

"The Tubu" thus appear as the inevitable counterpart of the various scandals of continuity discussed above. Intimately connected to "civilization," they are the kind of people who tend to be left out of orderly accounts—even if they are only orderly in the conceptual sense—of local assemblies, segmentation, or other forms of nonstate institutions. They occupy a structural niche, more visible in northern Chad than elsewhere, but one that also exists between the lines of Dresch's Yemen: those who accept "black shame" if the price is right, or for the sheer fun of it; those who have always refused to obey the rules of the game of honor; those who do not pay their debts or indeed acknowledge their existence. For most of history, in the Sahara and even North Africa, people like the Tubu have probably been in the majority—"who could doubt," as Berque (1970, 1347) quipped, "that most of the great of this world have become what they are through illicit means, that they have grown fat on illegally acquired goods?" Hence the great effort made by Kabyle and Touati village assemblies to keep them at bay, and hence also their unspoken centrality to North African political systems. Virtue, here as elsewhere, tends to thrive on vice.

Conclusion

Within contemporary anthropology, interest in stateless societies tends to be muted or (unless it occurs in the company of modern protest movements) deeply unfashionable. "While it may be true that anthropology offers a critical repertoire to those seeking alternative forms of sociality, an anthropology configured as a collection of case studies of social isolates, bounded communities, tribes and other theoretically archaic units of analysis is barely recognizable as an anthropology of the 21st century" (S. Nugent 2012, 214). This chapter has argued that Dresch's reading of "tribalism" and its deeper implications can provide a way out of this apparent conundrum. It sheds doubt on the overwhelming reach of the state and investigates political imaginations that go beyond it or are indeed antithetical to it. Rather than returning to "archaic units of analysis," this change of focus directs attention toward issues of scale and the articulation of political (or at least conceptual) regions that in many cases predate and often also extend beyond the limits of states. This in turn raises a series of questions that much contemporary anthropology is ill-equipped to answer: most obviously, how to think through and express the continuity, spatial and temporal, of certain political forms or at least their constituent features, in the absence of political centralization or even a literate tradition, and what the implications of this might be for social analysis more generally. Much of what an older anthropology called, rightly or not, "structure" is today in fact blamed on states, crediting them with at times extraordinary creative power but also reducing analysis to administrations and their entailment, disembedded individual agents.

This is of course an optical illusion, but one that might deserve some thought. As Dresch notes, "the analytical problem here is not the tribe but the state, which from a certain viewpoint is as much a work of the imagination as tribes are and yet seems to have far more power" (Dresch 2009, 196n). Although it is possible to attempt to understand Kabyle political structures uniquely in terms of their opposition to the Ottoman state, this exaggerates the latter's influence. It also fails to account for regional differences across the Ottoman Empire and parallels beyond it, most noticeably with Morocco and what is now the Algerian Sahara. Such parallels are striking, but they remain just that: parallels, not identity; a feeling of mutual recognition; variations on common themes that do not emanate from a center and cannot be explained through a narrative of domination. The phrasing here is reminiscent of structuralism, as is Dresch's insistence, quoted throughout, that conceptual order must be prior to social or political order, both logically and in our analysis. Yet structuralism cannot exhaust the questions these parallels pose: like tribalism, institutions such as the jamaʻa or even the carefully choreographed "anarchy" that reigns among Tubu speakers clearly have been transmitted vertically as well as horizontally; they might have provided a political grammar over time and across large distances, but they were always also historically inflected. In other words, they are firmly rooted in the particular terrain that creates and reproduces them over time, and they in turn produce their own historicity, by defining the kinds of events that are possible and recognized as such. To conclude with Dresch (1989, 37), "The distinction between structure and event is of the analyst's making, and one must not pretend otherwise."

JUDITH SCHEELE is Directrice d'études at the Écoles des hautes études en sciences sociales (EHESS) in Paris. She has carried out research in Algeria, northern Mali, and Chad. She is author of *Village Matters: Politics, Knowledge and Community in Kabylia* and *Smugglers and Saints of the Sahara: Regional Connectivity in the Twentieth Century*, and co-author of *The Value of Disorder: Autonomy, Prosperity and Plunder in the Chadian Sahara*.

Notes

1. Developments in the United States and in France were somewhat different. See Lewellen (2003, 10) for an outline.
2. Indeed, Wendy James's characterization of colonial anthropologists sounds uncannily familiar: "I see, therefore, the colonial anthropologist as a frustrated radical: and his claims to scientific status, the separation of his work from any apparent moral or political views, and the avowal of its practical usefulness, as largely determined by the need to make a convincing bid for the survival and expansion of his subject" (1973, 50).
3. This same argument would of course also hold for French anthropology, although it has not been made in the same terms (Abélès 2007, 71). This has contributed to different developments in the two countries and perhaps lent greater credibility there to Lévi-Strauss—rather than, say, to Foucault.
4. The exception here was Leach's (1970) *Political Systems of Highland Burma*, where structure became itself dynamic. Although he is still widely cited (and his book has recently [2004] been reedited), few people seem to have followed his lead concretely. On anthropology's current aversion to structure, see Sahlins (1999, 406).
5. This is particularly noticeable in discussions of criminal law. See Marshall and Duff (1998, 14) and Lamond (2007, 618).
6. Abélès (2007, 70) speaks of a "referential relation": "While reference to Derrida and Foucault becomes more and more frequent, anthropologists rarely try to define their relation with these philosophical texts."
7. For descriptions of zawaya in these terms, see Pascon (1984), Hammoudi (1980), Gutelius (2002), and Triaud (1995, 503–5).
8. The largest collection of published qawanin is Hanoteau and Letourneux (1872–73) and Masqueray (1886, 263–324). For a full list of published texts, see Scheele (2008, 900n).

Qawanin have long been neglected by scholars working on Kabylia, mostly due to a general mistrust with regard to this kind of colonial documentation (starting in Kabylia with Bernard and Milliot 1933 and Bousquet 1950). Recently, they have regained some scholarly credibility and interest. See Mahé (1993, 2000), Hanneman (2002, 2005), and Gahlouz (2011).

9. "Among the Beraber," as claims a comparable code from neighboring Morocco, "rules are only valid where they are made," and "if something happens and nobody knows what to do, sharia will automatically be applied" (Nehlil 1915–16).

10. Regional similarities that span lowland South America are today more commonly explained with reference to a precolonial time dominated by complex societies governed by states: contemporary Amazonian societies are "fragments of shipwrecked tribes, utterly forgetful of their former incarnation" (Descola 1988, 819).

11. Dresch is drawing here on Winch (1990 [1958], 52) and Collingwood (1961).

12. "Plan général d'occupation à adopter au Gourara et au Touat, après la prise de possession des oasis par nos colonnes, par le général commandant la division d'Alger," n. d. (early 1900s), Archives nationales d'outre-mer (ANOM), Aix-en-Provence, box 22H56. See also Général de la Roque, "Lettre au gouverneur général de l'Algérie," February 17, 1896, ANOM 22H56; and the "Rapport annuel, poste du Touat," 1909, ANOM 23H91.

13. Simon, "Notices sur le Tidikelt," June 20, 1900, ANOM 22H50.

14. "Plan général d'occupation."

15. Annexe du Touat, "Propositions du chef de l'annexe pour l'hébergement des hôtes arabes au chef-lieu," April 9, 1902, ANOM 22H48.

16. Such "guests" were thus at times potential raiders—see, e.g., *Nawazil al-ghuniya* (NG), p. 142. The *Ghuniya* is a collection of legal cases brought before the qadi Abu ʿAbd Allah Sidi al-Ḥajj Muḥammad b. ʿAbd al-Raḥman al-Balbali (born 1155 AH / AD 1742, died 1244 AH / AD 1828) and his son Sidi Muḥammad ʿAbd al-ʿAziz (born in 1199 AH / AD 1776). The copy referred to here is the one held in the library of Shaykh Bilkabir in Mtarfa (courtesy of the shaykh). On Touati *nawazil* and the context of their production, see Warscheid (2017).

17. "Rapport annuel, annexe du Touat," 1908, ANOM 23H91; "Lettre du général Risbourg, commandant la division d'Oran, au gouverneur général de l'Algérie," October 29, 1900, ANOM 22H50; and Lt. Ray Hardy, "Une terre qui meurt: Le Touat," April 30, 1933, ANOM 10H86.

18. Didier, "Projet d'organisation du Gourara et du Touat," May 5, 1896, ANOM 22H56; "Rapports annuels, poste du Touat," 1908, 1939, and 1951, ANOM 23H91; "Rapport annuel, poste du Gouara," 1908, ANOM 23H91.

19. NG, p. 616.

20. Contrary to many if not most Muslim rural societies where real estate is key, people in the Touat did not systematically disinherit women. Moreover, debt relations were rife, which means that crucial resources—water, especially—were held quite as often by outsiders as by local residents.

21. NG, p. 646.

22. "Judicial councils are apparently the result of Berber influence, and are not known among the Asiatic Bedouin" (Stewart 2006, 265), as are fines "payable to a body representing the community, which is prominent in Berber customary law" (266).

23. As Wink (2002, 432) notes with regard to internal historical traditions in the Indian Ocean, it is often difficult to locate change within them as "change meant lawlessness and the only terms in which it could be conceptualized were those of heresy, immorality, sedition and treason."

24. I use "Tubu" here to refer to speakers of Tedaga and Dazaga, two mutually comprehensible languages spoken in northern Chad, northeastern Niger, and southern Libya. "Tubu," a term derived from Kanembou, is used in Libyan and Chadian Arabic, the French sources, and academic writing to refer to some or all speakers of these languages, but there is no one local term that corresponds to it (see further below).

25. Cognatic systems in general do not allow groups to be defined unambiguously through descent (Caplan 1969; Noricks 1983), but many cognatic societies nonetheless define groups, for instance through coresidence.

26. "Rapport de Mission de M. le chef de bataillon Rottier," 1929, Archives Nationales du Tchad, N'Djamena, box W 18.

9

THE REPUBLIC OF PRECARITY

'Abd al-Fattah al-Sisi, Trickster Politician

Walter Armbrust

[A middle-aged man on a talk-show set faces the camera intently] Beware: thirteen, thirteen, 2013 [he smacks his hand on the desk]. . . . If you're alive . . . thirteen, thirteen, 2013 [said very slowly and clearly], the Freemasons . . . [he is suddenly distracted by a voice off camera] what do you want? . . . Say it, don't be afraid . . . what? [he recovers and addresses the camera again] I'm sorry, thirteen 2013, excuse me . . . thirteen 2013 . . . pay attention, there's no thirteenth month . . . good . . . the 13th day, on the 13th night, on the 13th party, in the year 2013. *This* is the greatest challenge—the greatest. The *greatest*. Before that there is, like 'Imad just told me in the earpiece, he said, there is a 12/12 2012, also there's some talk more or less, that they might make another attempt. But the date 12/12/12 for them, in the Masonic system, I mean, it doesn't make them deliver a forty dollar ticket [*mayikhallihumsh yiwassalu tazkara bi-arba'in dular*] . . . 13/13 2013, not the 13th month, not the 13th *month*, the 13th night. Hmm? The 13th *night*. In the year 2013, on the date of the 13th, that will begin from the *night* of Christmas. Hmm? From what night? Christmas. Do you get it? (Taufiq 'Ukasha on "Masr al-Yaum," November 15, 2011)[1]

[the actor] Adil Imam smokes some hashish and comes in saying "I've smoked hashish Su'ad'" . . . this Su'ad is the actress Yusra, and I've brought her with me. (An imaginary conversation between Egyptian President 'Abd al-Fattah al-Sisi and German Prime Minister Angela Merkel)[2]

PAUL DRESCH'S WORK FOCUSES ON QUESTIONS RAISED BY continuity in places and ways of life that were implicitly seen as incompatible with it, particularly Yemen in which tribes both predated and outlived a succession of more legibly state-like formations. Revolutionary Egypt presents a starkly different setting. The modern Egyptian state may be thought of as "deep" or "broad"—either a Leviathan reaching deep into the lives of Egyptian citizens or a more balkanized set of governing entities that are equally decisive in setting the terms of human affairs, but partially at odds with each other. Deep or broad, the state's importance in Egyptian lives is rarely questioned whether one focuses on its effects (through analyses of statecraft, governance, and the formation of subjectivities) or on understanding challenges or resistance to its effects. Similarly, if Dresch is fascinated with the phenomenon of continuity, then revolution seems to be a different problem altogether. But maybe it is not. The status of revolution as an event is predicated precisely on a sense of departing from "normality," and equally on a consensual transition to some sort of "new normal." It goes without saying that consensus can be fiercely contested for quite some time. Initially anyone who said "the revolution" in Egypt meant those mythical eighteen days culminating in the fall of the Mubarak regime on February 11. The fallacy of that assumption was obvious very quickly. Now most observers who count what happened in Egypt as a revolution (and I am one of them) would probably acknowledge that ʿAbd al-Fattah al-Sisi defeated it, or argue that it continues at some subterranean level, or else insist that it "failed," though to me failure has to be seen as something that was made to happen rather than an inevitability. To me it matters, however, that by January 26, 2011, if not earlier, Egyptians were calling their uprising a revolution, whether they were opposed, indifferent, or committed to it. To invoke the term poses questions of continuity but also of radical "structural" change, political and otherwise.

My aim in this chapter is to argue that the victory of what is sometimes called a "counterrevolution" in Egypt in 2013 was not so much a restoration of the old regime as the emergence of a kind of "trickster politics" that may to a degree be enabled by conditions of precarity and perhaps the "encysting" (or echo-chamber effect) of digital media, but which was also turbocharged by the January 25 Revolution. Tricksters are creatures of liminality, or in this case of a liminal crisis. Liminality as a concept has tended to fall into disuse to the extent that anthropologists and other scholars now interpret the world in nominalist terms, for example, by references to Deleuzian "assemblages." Nominalism is a form of empiricism—an "ontological position that rejects the existence of abstract objects, of universals, or of both of them altogether" (Bialecki 2012, 302). Dresch often warned against the shortcomings of such empiricism: "Empiricism is the idea that the world is given to direct experience and, as in schoolroom science, one has only to eliminate sources of confusion (to establish 'no parallax' conditions, as it might be), then observe and record. But human life is not like that" (Dresch 2012a, 32). In contemporary Egypt also, every time the word revolution is uttered or invoked as a description of what happened in 2011, we can grasp its significance only by reference to categories. "Equality, subordination, mystification, and discontent all depend upon how the world of human affairs is classified and how such classifications of the world are accepted, contested, or manipulated. (To distance action too far from categories, meanwhile, implies an analytic individualism that few of us could willingly accept)" (Dresch 2012a, 18). "Analytic individualism" is particularly deadly for understanding revolution as a liminal crisis, which sets a perfect stage for the performance of trickster politics.

The Warm-Up Act

For me the decisive point in the January 25 Revolution was a period of massacres and street battles that took place between October 2011 and February 2012: Maspero, Muhammad Mahmud (I and II), Port Said, and the Ministerial Council. In the beginning of that decisive period, the rank and file of most of the revolutionary political spectrum, furious at the callous violence employed by both the military under the command of the Supreme Council of the Armed Forces (SCAF) and the security forces controlled by the Ministry of Interior, was chanting "down with military rule" at demonstrations. Many politically less-engaged members of a broad middle class looked on, unsure whether or not to side with the nominally interim military rulers or the revolution. By the end of these four months, the wider public, and to some degree those who could be described as politically mobilized, had experienced a sea change. The "sectarian card" had been played with a vengeance by the government and exploited by Islamists. Whatever SCAF may have wanted at the beginning of its interim rule, by the end of 2011 it was left with little choice but to hand over power to a civilian government. Consequently, if a long-suspected political bargain between SCAF and the Muslim Brotherhood might have remained unconsummated at the beginning of October 2011, by early February 2012 there was no question that it was a fait accompli.

The most interesting event that I observed during that period was a sideshow to these momentous spasms of violence. It was an anti-revolution rally in 'Abbasiyya Square near the Ministry of Defence, on December 23, 2011, to be precise, not long after the violent breakup of a sit-in at the Ministerial Council (Maglis al-Wuzara') to protest the appointment of a Mubarak-era dinosaur, Kamal al-Ganzuri, as prime minister. This was implicit punishment for a massive six-day street battle the month before, on Muhammad Mahmud Street, after a government official announced a plan to get all the political forces to agree to "supra-constitutional principles" that would grant the military near-complete autonomy from civilian control. During the breakup of the Ministerial Council sit-in, a shocking video was made and widely circulated of a woman beaten to the ground by soldiers in army uniforms. Revolutionary forces called for a large demonstration in Tahrir, dubbed "the Friday of Regaining Honour" (*gum'at radd al-i'tbar*) on December 23. That demonstration was well attended, by quite a few thousands.

The parallel 'Abbasiyya counterdemonstration was called "the Friday of the Crossing" (*gum'at al-'ubur*) in honor of the crossing of the Bar Lev Line in the 1973 October War, a moment widely considered to have been the finest hour of the Egyptian armed forces. Only a few hundred people attended that event, most of them un-uniformed security or military forces. The atmosphere was menacing. Banners calling for the execution of pro-revolution media figures hung from a nearby traffic flyover. Tough-looking men held signs condemning the revolution or praising the army, police, and judiciary. Journalists from presumably unsympathetic organizations were reportedly roughed up. I edged out of the crowd and left when some of the attendees started asking if I was a journalist.

The Friday of the Crossing was promoted by and publicly attributed to a television talk show host, Taufiq 'Ukasha, who was mercilessly mocked by the pro-revolution camp. I have written about him elsewhere (Armbrust 2013) and will not dwell on him at length here. On air 'Ukasha spun wild conspiracy theories about plots against Egypt by immense collectives of enemies: Freemasons, the Revolutionary Socialists, Qatar, the United States, world Jewry, the April 6 movement, Hamas, the Kefaya movement, Google, the Muslim Brotherhood (but *not* their nominal allies at the time, the Salafis), NATO, Hizballah, Israel, and Iran. He pitched his rhetoric in a blatantly populist register. 'Ukasha was vulgar to the point of absurdity and apparently ignorant; at one point he famously warned of a Masonic conspiracy that would unfold on "13/13/13"—the thirteenth day of the thirteenth month of 2013.

'Ukasha was particularly adamant about the dangers posed to Egypt by the Muslim Brotherhood and was slavishly devoted to the military at a time when "*yasqut hukm al-'askar*" (down with military rule) seemed to be on everyone's lips. Many observers said he was flat-out an operative of military intelligence, at the time headed by 'Abd al-Fattah al-Sisi. Later, when Muhammad Morsy was elected, 'Ukasha played a prominent role in planting the notion that Sisi was a crypto–Muslim Brother. 'Ukasha appeared on the air in what many assumed would be his last appearance before the government banned him, warning the public to beware of the Muslim Brotherhood's "man in the armed forces," none other than Sisi: "I will hold the Muslim Brotherhood in particular responsible for my security, and responsible for closing the Fara'ayn

214 | *The Scandal of Continuity in Middle East Anthropology*

Channel. That's first. Second, I hold the Military Council responsible for my security, from Field Marshall Muhammad Husayn al-Tantawi down to the last member of the Military Council, who is General 'Abd al-Fattah al-Sisi, the Director of Military Intelligence, and the Muslim Brotherhood's man in the armed forces."[3] At the end of 2011, thousands across the country were demonstrating against the military, as opposed to the few hundreds at 'Ukasha's rally. Yet clearly, in hindsight, the small demonstration in 'Abbasiyya was a far better barometer of Egypt's political trajectory from that point on than the much larger one in Tahrir Square. How, then, should we assess the significance of 'Ukasha for Egyptian politics?

Liminal Crisis

Undoubtedly 'Ukasha was a mouthpiece for counter-revolution. But more than that, he was a harbinger of General 'Abd al-Fattah al-Sisi's accession to power—part of a pattern, not simply an operative of the counter-revolution detachable from the style of governance that would emerge a year and a half later. Moreover 'Abd al-Fattah al-Sisi, the eventual president of Egypt who came after 'Ukasha's initial revealing flicker in 2011, has ruled in ways that articulate with larger political currents that go further afield than Egypt. The moment of instability that made 'Ukasha audible to Egyptian publics was characteristic of political fluidity in a revolution, which we may characterize as a liminal crisis—a state of "anti-structure" from which there was no clear exit. But the substance of governance that followed, when Sisi took power, in effect echoed many of the themes 'Ukasha had articulated as a quasi-outsider: extreme nationalism, paranoia, and an obsession with security buttressed by conspiracy theorizing and mirrored by utter devotion to Egypt's security establishment. Sisi ended the revolution, but the new political normality in which his regime governed was structured by forms of precarity that were distinct from the revolution but that echoed its liminality more enduringly, thereby rendering the "paranoid style" that 'Ukasha pioneered so colorfully a long-term feature of the political sphere.

In what follows I want to first elaborate on the theme of revolution as liminal crisis, and second explore some of the implications arising from it. To speak of revolution as liminality may sound odd to those whose professional brief normally includes the study of revolutions, particularly historians, political scientists, and political sociologists—unlike anthropologists, who have given limited attention to revolutions, though much attention to phenomena associated with them.[4] But Taufiq 'Ukasha, my point of entry to this line of thinking, can productively be understood as a Trickster, and such figures flourish precisely in conditions of liminality, which is a political inflection of what anthropologist Victor Turner called "the ritual process" (V. Turner 1977).

In the ritual process initiands pass out of normative social relations into a state of liminality, followed by reintegration into a state of normality, which can be described by a variety of terms, but in a transformed social state. In the narrowest terms, rituals are rites of passage that require masters of ceremonies. But the important aspect of ritual in this context is not ritual qua ritual (and there are many other ways to understand ritual than through Turner's approach). It is rather that the ritual process carries greater social significance than a narrow focus on rites of passage marking birth, coming of age, marriage, or death, for example, might suggest. Rites of passage and rituals more generally have masters of ceremony not because there is an unwritten rule that a ritual has to have them, but precisely because liminality is *dangerous* and must therefore be managed when it can be. While techniques for managing liminality vary tremendously across cultures, liminal conditions are independent of ritual, and the function of a master of ceremonies is incidental to the fact that transitions involving liminality are inevitable. Indeed, it is precisely transitions that are most crucial to the ritual process. Sometimes transitions manifest as "critical events" (Das 1996, 6), which are then institutionalized in collective memory. But such institutionalization happens only by means of a passage across a threshold and through liminality. Victor Turner's writing on the ritual process amounted to a refocusing and expansion of insights about liminality made by Arnold van Gennep (2004) half a century earlier. "[Any] application of liminality must, as a minimum stay close to one aspect of its original meaning as defined by van Gennep: namely, that it has to do with the passing of a threshold and therefore with transition. If it is not about transition, it is not about liminality" (Thomassen 2014, 15).

Institutionalization is the end point of the process, the point at which initiands have been transformed, not the process of transformation. Critical events can include political cataclysms, but also natural disasters. Bjørn Thomassen suggests that the Lisbon earthquake of 1755, or to be more precise, the doubt and fear left in its wake, changed the course of European modernity by pushing Immanuel Kant to organize his philosophy of reason as "a heroic struggle against the chaos of the surrounding world" (Thomassen 2014, 99). The January 25 Revolution, a thoroughly unnatural event but certainly one that will be institutionalized in memory, is an instance of a passage through liminality lacking a master of ceremony. Such a lack is not a given in political revolutions, but it often exists, at least in their initial stages. Because revolutions happen in modern states, the perpetuation of a "liminal crisis" (Thomassen 2012, 687–90)—an uncloseable state of liminality—is intolerable. The questions of who seizes the master-of-ceremonies role and how they do so are key issues for understanding revolution. If we see the January 25 Revolution as a political passage comprehensible through the liminal phase of a transition unmediated by convention or ritual, then at the point the revolution's most crucial phase, October 2011, it was not clear where the country was headed. The feeling of transition was everywhere and inescapable. Questions of "who brings this to an end and how" were on everyone's mind.

Communitas and Liminality Revisited

The turmoil of October 2011 was thrown into higher relief by its stark contrast with a state of *communitas* that had characterized Tahrir Square during the early days of the January 25 Revolution. Communitas, a term coined by Victor Turner in the 1960s, refers to a "moment in and out of time" (V. Turner 1977, 96) in which a general utopic euphoria reigns, temporarily dissolving hierarchical distinctions. It is simply Latin for "community," but Turner was looking for a slightly displaced term to distinguish a characteristic social modality of the ritual process from the everyday sense of community as an "area of common living" (Thomassen 2012, 96). The idea was that communitas was precisely an *uncommon* experience, or more precisely, one connected to the ritual process. Thomassen describes the ritual process as more like the discovery of a pattern that is "both culture-dependent and universal" (Thomassen 2014, 5) than a theory (2–3, 37–38).

Anthropology makes few claims of universality, as the discipline is on the whole dedicated to exploring cultural variation. The ritual process is universal insofar as moments of transition are inevitable for all humans and must therefore be elaborated in all social systems. More expansively, liminality is an indispensable aspect of human life. The ritual process, with liminality at its core, is a highly flexible form that neatly sidesteps certain of the dilemmas that anthropology and other social sciences historically faced. It is not prone to fall into false distinctions between individuals and Durkheimian "collective representations." It potentially accommodates scales of social performance ranging from the intimately personal to the "civilizational." Nor were the intrinsically Eurocentric evolutionary assumptions characteristic of Durkheimian sociology or Marxism an element of the ritual process as van Gennep had envisioned it.

Aside from the potential (but historically unrealized) capacity of van Gennep's insights to avoid epistemological pitfalls, the emphasis in *Rites of Passage* on the spatial dimension of ritual was "fundamental for the cultural elaboration of ritual transitions and cultural transformation" (Thomassen 2014, 37) and articulates very well with attention given to place and space in contemporary anthropology (Low 2011). The immense symbolic importance accorded to Tahrir Square and struggles over control of it resonate clearly with the study of spatialization and also, in complex ways, with neoliberal securitization of space that structured the city and society in which the revolution occurred (Amar 2013). Liminality also goes very well with anthropological engagements with performance (see, e.g., V. Turner 1982). The January 25 Revolution was spectacularly performative. This aspect of the revolution articulates with processual approaches to politics in political science and sociology (Tilly 2008; Alexander et al. 2006), though with less positivist emphasis, and leaving a more central place for pure contingency (Thomassen 2012).

However, in thinking through revolution in terms of liminality, skepticism toward Turner's signature concepts must be addressed. While it is likely that many anthropologists thought of communitas as the January 25 Revolution unfolded in its early stages, few of them voiced that thought (but see Armbrust 2013; Peterson 2015a, 2015b; Thomassen 2012, 2014). This is because since the 1980s Turner has largely been written out of the disciplinary lineage, if not entirely out of its history. If one says "Victor Turner" to an anthropologist, the sound is likely to stimulate an almost Pavlovian response: "functionalist." In one of the most influential interpretations of Turner's legacy from my own days as a graduate anthropology student, Sherry Ortner painted Turner as a Marxist-inflected British structural-functionalist whose work carried "a deep continuity with British social anthropology concerns" (Ortner 1984, 131).[5] These "concerns" were manifested as an analytical preoccupation with "the maintenance of integration, and specifically on the maintenance of the integration of 'society'—actors, groups, the social whole—as opposed to 'culture'" (131–32). Subsequently, a generation of anthropologists learned to dismiss Turner's ritual process as nothing more than a mechanism for maintaining static social structures. Ortner's (and others') influential image of Turner as a warmed-over Durkheimian functionalist was highly misleading. His encounter with van Gennep's *Rites of Passage* in 1963 was the point at which he decisively *broke* with British social anthropology (Thomassen 2014, 78–79). This is not surprising given that van Gennep, particularly in *Rites of Passage*, had in his day fiercely opposed Durkheim, who retaliated for van Gennep's criticism of his work by preventing him from ever getting a job in French academia.

Turner's anti-structure (a synonym for liminality in the ritual process) was written off as "the dialectical complement to structure" (Kelly and Kaplan 1990, 139) at a time when the discipline was in the process of discarding structure conceived as a totalizing phenomenon (see also the introduction to the present volume). The most prevalent alternative concept at that time, and to a degree still today (Postill 2010), was "practice theory" and its complement, "habitus"—"structured structures pre-disposed to function as structuring structures" (Bourdieu 1977, 72). The systematic in human societies was conceived as patterned habits that emerge from the sum total of what individual people do rather than a transcendent matrix independent of human agency. Turner was undoubtedly aware of the debate over the nature and importance of structure. In one of his later writings, he offered an assessment of the discipline, mentioning that "anthropology is shifting from a stress on concepts such as structure, equilibrium, function, system to process, indeterminacy, reflexivity—from a 'being' to a 'becoming' vocabulary" (V. Turner 1985, 152). The rest of his text leaves no doubt that he regarded himself as one of the agents in bringing about this shift, and the gist of this passage was not out of step with "practice theory" as it was then conceived. In hindsight one might have thought he should be seen as a key figure in helping formulate that movement within the discipline rather than end up consigned to functionalist hell.[6]

In this context two observations are in order. One is that Turner wrote rather little about normative structures because he was in fact far more interested in exploring liminality as a form of passage or transition, not only as a means of social reproduction, but as a crucible for creativity, adaptation, and change. It seems to have been assumed that an outmoded Durkheimian notion of structure was implicit in his outlook simply because he came from a British social anthropology background. None of the participants in the "practice theory" debate of the 1980s, when Turner's star began to fade, recognized how much van Gennep was actually opposed to fundamental presuppositions of Durkheimian sociology, and consequently how profoundly Turner's revival of van Gennep in the early 1960s moved him away from his functionalist roots and toward an experience-oriented processual anthropology that articulates with contemporary suspicions about abstracted system or structure. Unfortunately, a thorough exploration of van Gennep, and in that connection Turner as well, did not take place until Thomassen started publishing in the mid-2000s.

Second, anthropological thinking about the nature of structure may have changed in the 1970s and 1980s, but this hardly meant that the discipline abandoned all interest in pattern or normativity. Bourdieu's habitus, for example, touted as a conceptually robust alternative to totalizing visions of structure or "system" (Ortner 1984, 148), was offered as an explanation of how normativity emerges, not as a denial of its existence. Indeed, contemporary anthropological attention to marginality, liminality, hybridity, ethnicity, or borders, for example, would be impossible in the absence of social constructs of normativity, whether we label them structure, habitus, culture, a constantly shifting Deleuzian assemblage, or some other term.[7]

Ritual exists to control the transitions we *know* will happen, whereas societies (and individuals) are often obliged to undergo transitions that are unexpected. When unexpected transitions happen, the *form* of the ritual process (not the "content," or more precisely, the social significance of the transition, which is inevitably contingent on many factors) can still tell us much about how individuals and societies adapt to them. One way to understand revolution is, in Thomassen's formulation, as a "liminal crisis," an entry into liminality in which there is no "master of ceremonies" to usher initiands back into a recognized social position. When the liminal phase of a social drama becomes protracted, crisis ensues, and consequently "sides are taken and power resources calculated" (V. Turner 1988, 91). This happens precisely in such circumstances as civil wars and revolutions, when "taking sides and calculating resources" obviously raises the question of who leads, in the sense of both familiar leaders operating on a shattered political terrain and new leaders emerging in the liminal void.

The Main Act: ʿAbd al-Fattah al-Sisi

In a liminal crisis, the Trickster becomes an especially dangerous type of leader. A Trickster is a being at home in liminality—the wanderer who appears in a village and captivates its inhabitants with alluring stories. The term designates both a character and a type of narrative found in various forms across all modern cultures and in antiquity. From Prometheus in Greek mythology to Wadjunkaga of the Native American Winebago people, the Trickster is the fulcrum of cautionary tales about the dangers of uncontained liminality.[8] On the political stage, the American politician Donald Trump plays the same role. The potentials of liminality, both creative and destructive, are at the heart of the Trickster, who is exquisitely ambivalent: potentially powerful, ridiculous, and dangerous.

In modern politics Tricksters acquire a following when the conventional signposts of social and political life are thrown into doubt. Normally Tricksters are objects of ridicule. But in liminality such outsiders can be seen as a solution to crisis. "Having no home, and therefore no real human and existential commitments, the trickster is not really interested in solving the liminal crisis: he simply pretends" (Thomassen 2014, 104). One way to perpetuate liminal crisis is to foment strife, which ʿUkasha did with gusto, as he worked assiduously to set the public against the revolution, revolutionaries against the Muslim Brotherhood, and Egypt ostensibly against the world, which was, in his narrative, rife with grand coalitions of plotters aiming to destroy the country. But if ʿUkasha may be entirely legible within the terms of Trickster politics, then what can we say about 'Abd al-Fattah al-Sisi? At first glance it might seem odd to speculate that an iron-handed populist dictator can be understood as a Trickster politician. But I think he should be, in full acknowledgment of the many nuances that characterize Egyptian politics at this historical juncture to be sure, but also in the context of universal forms of liminality, which can be a productive analytical framework for understanding contemporary politics globally.

It is important not to be misled by the form of a Trickster as literally a "demonic clown" (Forlenza and Thomassen 2016). Politicians such as Donald Trump or Boris Johnson fit the conventional Trickster form: "a figure of excess, especially of eating and drinking, and of sexual exploits, often depicted with an enormous phallus—the very grotesqueness of his figure denoting an inversion of order . . . a breaker of taboos, a joker and prankster, the best of companions, but also a thief, a liar and an impostor" (ibid.). Sisi is certainly not that Trickster. His internationally circulated image is of a dour ruler admired by realpolitik Western politicians, presiding over the harsh suppression of Islamist insurgency and revolution, commanding the country to get serious and get back to work—all no-nonsense, and don't you dare laugh.

But the *role* of a political Trickster, as opposed to the literal form, fits Sisi rather better: the pretend politician, a man with no existential commitments (one notes his halfway position between the head of a civilian government and head of a military that sees itself as distinct from and above the state that supports it), a purveyor of false charisma, and above all, a suddenly prominent person who presents himself as "a solution to the crisis" when he is in fact just a skillful mime adept at telling people what they want to hear. The fulcrum of a Trickster tale is that people are duped into feeling empowered for a while, but all too soon the feeling "dissolves into nothingness" (Forlenza and Thomassen 2016).

Sisi's status as a pretend politician became obvious rather more quickly than most Euro-American observers knew. The process of dissolving his false charisma into nothing was already well advanced when in June 2015 'Abd al-Fattah al-Sisi visited Germany as part of the steady process of Western governments normalizing his rule. The centerpiece of the meeting was economic; the engineering and technology giant Siemens had just signed an €8 billion deal to provide natural gas and wind power plants to Egypt. Back home the trip caused a minor stir for a different reason. Some twenty media personalities, a collection of movie stars past their primes and a few of the most vehemently pro-regime talk show hosts, had formed a "popular delegation" to accompany the president in order to oppose the Muslim Brotherhood crowds that would presumably dog Sisi's visit. Everywhere he went they appeared cheering for him and waving Egyptian flags. It is hard to know what the German press made of this gaggle of aging media personalities. They do seem to have been noticed, or at least one of my Facebook friends (a critic of Sisi) posted a picture of a pile of German tabloids with Egyptian actors' faces on them. The Egyptian press covered the story of the actors' initiative positively and politely, and only slightly over the top in a few instances, such as a *Shuruq* headline that described it as "the largest popular delegation" (Faruq 2015). The text of the article clarified that it was "the largest since Sisi took power."

Apparently some sort of confrontation between the delegation and Egyptians critical of Sisi did take place, though I could find no video of it. But I did locate a video of Ahmad Musa talking about this alleged fight. Musa was an 'Ukasha-clone talk show host on the Sada al-Balad channel owned by Muhammad Abu 'Aynayn, a former NDP stalwart and one of the suspects in organizing the Battle of the Camel. Musa was particularly noteworthy for his on-air emotional outbursts, which he typically delivered in a high-pitched whine:

> Terrorist elements today engaged with the artists and the delegation from Egypt and attacked them. At first they introduced themselves, and "how do you do," and then started talking to them. And after that they started saying stupid stuff, that silly talk of theirs. And then a fight started, with insults and, you know . . . they're "real polite." They said some really strange stuff that has no relation to religion or with . . . and by the way, those people are criminals, and every day they confirm it. It's not just us who say it. The Germans could see it. What do they see? They see that they have a terrorist group living amongst them. All along they haven't known that they're terrorists. All the time they're saying "what's happening in your country?" Here you are, they're doing it here in your country.[9]

Islamist and independent websites critical of Sisi mocked the delegation mercilessly. The news website *Wara' al-Ahdath* ran an article asking pointed questions about who paid the delegation's bills (it was said to have been an independent initiative with no official link to the president) and quoting a number of sour remarks about the "scandal" of the nation having been represented by "a bunch of dancers" (Muhammad 2015). But the cleverest commentary by far was the Facebook cartoon quoted in the epigraph of this chapter. How *would* Sisi have explained his retinue of devoted media personalities to Angela Merkel? The prankster who created the meme makes Sisi sound like an empty-headed gossip columnist reveling in glory reflected by the stars: "[The actor] Adil Imam smokes some hashish and comes in saying 'I've smoked hashish Su'ad' . . . this Su'ad is the actress Yusra, and I've brought her with me. And the slightly chubby one, that's Ilham Shahin. She once played the role of Lawahiz, the cousin of Sayyid, and this 'cousin Sayyid' was played by *ustaz* al-'Alayli [another actor]. . . . I've brought him with me too.[10]"

Of course in reality, Sisi's role in enabling the gaggle-of-aging-actors incident was probably no more than letting it happen. One can easily imagine a president being too busy to even care about such things. Nonetheless, from the beginning, spectacle was a substantial element of Sisi's rule, sometimes on a grand scale and at other times on a weirdly personal scale through long, contrived televised chats with journalists—a tactic one could never have imagined in the case of Mubarak. In the case of the much-hyped meeting with Merkel, Sisi comes across as possibly the person who was tricked rather than as the Trickster, depending on how much complicity one assumes in allowing this retinue to accompany his official diplomatic mission. The delegation may have gone over well with confirmed supporters of the president, but it was laughter fodder for anyone not already in his camp. Sisi was not 'Ukasha; surely he would have been better off not soiling the jealously accumulated "prestige of the state" (*haybat al-daula*) by inviting ridicule. But aside from the ambiguities of this particular episode, Sisi more often was the Trickster rather than the tricked.

In the run-up to the election that confirmed his grip on power in June 2014, he had famously said in an interview that he would not specify a political or economic program and that those who expected to see gains for "sectoral" (*fi'awi*) interests would be disappointed. "*Mish 'adir adik*"—"I cannot give you [anything]."[11] He said it again more loudly to be sure he had been heard. And he indeed did not give anything of practical value. The decades-long decrepitude of national institutions continues unabated; electricity generation is still in crisis; the tourism sector remains relatively moribund; the currency has been devalued, causing steep inflation; poverty and unemployment are very high. Given the long-term nature of all of these problems—not to mention longer-term structural problems such as a looming shortage in the water supply and environmental degradation—Sisi has effectively inoculated himself politically by promising nothing. On the other hand, at the same time that he promised nothing, he promised the sun, moon, and stars.

The public got its first inkling of Sisi's pretend politics long before his trip to Germany with his retinue of actors. In February 2014 a press conference was held, allegedly attended by both Prime Minister 'Adli Mansur and interim President 'Abd al-Fattah al-Sisi,[12] in which an Egyptian military doctor named "General" Ibrahim 'Abd al-'Ati announced that he had invented a cure for the stubborn Hepatitis C infection, which plagues Egypt more than any other country in the world. Moreover, the same device could cure AIDS! A caller on a talk show who was allegedly a doctor on 'Abd al-'Ati's "team" revealed that it could even cure cancer and diabetes. Famously, 'Abd al-'Ati claimed that his device takes AIDS from the patient and feeds the patient on AIDS: "I give it to him as a piece of *kufta* [roast lamb sausage cooked on a kebab skewer] to feed

Figure 9.1. Title frame from a YouTube "mashup" commenting on ʿAbd al-Fattah al-Sisi's apparent backing of the fraudulent "Kufta Doctor" Ibrahim ʿAbd al-ʿAti.
"You've seen the story of a piece of kufta, from the skewer to the trash can."

on." Thereafter ʿAbd al-ʿAti became known as the "*kufta* doctor." Another device called C-FAST, invented by the same doctor and unveiled at the same press conference, could supposedly detect the presence of any virus noninvasively, merely by pointing a kind of divining rod at the patient.

The inventions were quickly debunked. ʿAbd al-ʿAti turned out not to be a real general—his title of *Liwaʾ* was strictly honorary, bestowed by the director of the military's Engineering Directorate because "he liked ʿAbd al-ʿAti's ideas" (*Radio Sawa* 2014). ʿAbd al-ʿAti also turned out not to be a real doctor but rather an herbalist (ibid.). An attempt to patent his devices was ludicrously unsuccessful. The research backing the devices was published without a shred of peer review in a "predatory journal" that publishes anything for a fee.[13] The non-invasive C-FAST remote virus detection device that looked like a divining rod turned out to be less useful than a divining rod. It was identified as a fake bomb detector that had been sold in Iraq and very likely resulted in loss of life to people who believed it worked (Ohlheiser 2013; Spencer 2014). The "Complete Cure for AIDS" turned out to be a giant hoax, described in one article as "the greatest scam in Egyptian history" (fig. 9.1; *Radio Sawa* 2014).

It may seem a cheap shot to pin the Great Kufta Hoax on Sisi. He was not directly responsible; obviously the military's Engineering Directorate, which organized the press conference, had been taken in. Quite a few media personalities fell in line, both praising the invention and denouncing anyone who cast doubt on it,[14] but many heaped scorn on it, including Sisi's own science advisor ʿIsam Higgi (Hasan et al. 2014). In a world of old-fashioned politics, Sisi would have benefited immensely from just walking away from the spectacle and saying as little as possible. Instead, the military's Engineering Directorate upped the ante by announcing that treatment by the devices would begin for the public on June 30, 2014, the first anniversary of the Tamarrod demonstration that ultimately resulted in Sisi coming to power. June 30 2014 came and went with little fanfare. A few Facebook postings asked sarcastically when the treatments would begin. The military finally made the scandal go away by announcing that further tests would have to be done, and once that happened the device would begin treatments at some vague future date. But by the time that happened, new and bigger spectacles were in the works.

The Neoliberal Music Man

The Kufta Hoax was less an anomaly than a tone-setter for everything Sisi did outside the security sphere. Aside from the iron fist employed in a permanentized state of emergency justified by the alleged threat posed by the Muslim Brotherhood and the horrific regional situation beyond Egypt's borders, Sisi employed a consistent strategy of using high-profile spectacles to divert attention from his actual exercise of power. The spectacles consisted of megaprojects that were almost as pretend as 'Abd al-'Ati's Complete Cure for AIDS. Many of these were repackaged projects from the Mubarak era.

The most successfully packaged of these was a "new Suez Canal"—actually a fairly routine infrastructural upgrade but sold to the public for its supposed capacity to more than double the income of the canal within eight years. The project was announced in the summer of 2014 and inaugurated lavishly (and expensively) a year later.[15] The government predicted in no uncertain terms that the project would pay for itself rapidly.[16] The real trick in this drama was the financing through the sale of bonds to the public at 12 percent interest. The interest rate was roughly the same that Egyptian commercial banks gave for savings bonds in the local currency, but they were purchased far more enthusiastically. One of my pro-Mubarak interlocutors (who was even more pro-Sisi), a book dealer of quite modest means, was one of the purchasers of these bonds. I have never been able to get him to tell me how much he invested or whether the promised interest was paid on schedule. *Mish 'adir adik*—"I have nothing to give you"—was what Sisi told the public when he was not promising them easy money from the "new canal." Yet he always had plenty to give to his own political legitimization, and the genius of this particular trick was that he got the public to pay for it willingly and then to celebrate the project as a miraculous national achievement.

In the end the most important objective of the project was regime legitimation, and on that level it worked very well. Reservations about the quick economic payoff of the project were recognized from the beginning, and so too was its political nature. The canal expansion was an exercise in confidence and morale building—something worthwhile to Sisi's supporters even if the economic criticisms did turn out to have merit. Of course Sisi also linked the canal extravaganza to his omnipresent security rhetoric. Consider this passage from the speech he gave on the opening of an extension of the Suez Canal on August 6, 2015:

> I say to Egyptians that you . . . that Egyptian civilization . . . have presented, to-day . . . Egypt presents to humanity . . . a gift, maybe not a really big gift like in the days of the ancient Egyptians, but in one year they've exerted great efforts on behalf of the world and for Egypt . . . a gift for humanity, for development, for building, for restoration. I want to tell you something. Egypt didn't do this just within this past year, or the past two years to be precise, just this one project. No. History will record that Egypt has repelled and confronted the most dangerous terrorist extremist thought that, if it had been established in this land, would have burned it. It was the Egyptians who repelled this thought. They opposed it in order to say to humanity "no." They presented the true tolerance of Islam and Muslims. They presented building and restoration and development and progress, not the killing, ruination and destruction of humanity.[17]

Confidence is the essence of a con job. The situation was reminiscent of the American film *The Music Man*—a classic Trickster tale. A traveling salesman comes to the fictional town of River City, Iowa, intent on swindling them. He pretends to be a band director and cons the citizens of the town into paying him to create a boys' marching band. They have to pay for uniforms and instruments, but his intention is to collect their money and then leave town before the band can actually be created, and since he is not actually a band director, he has no hope of training the boys anyway. He seals the deal by inducing a moral panic over the effects of a newly opened pool hall, which he says will corrupt the youth: "Ya got trouble, trouble right here in River City" (one can hear Sisi in his inauguration speech: "Ya got terrorists, terrorists right here in Umm al-Dunya"). In the end he gets outed by a rival salesman (just as Sisi's canal inauguration extravaganza was outed by multiple experts), but has in the meantime fallen in love with the town librarian and decides he wants to stay. The uniforms and instruments arrive. The illusion of the "band" he was supposed to create and train seems on the verge of being revealed to all, and it will result in him being tarred and feathered. But miraculously, when the untrained ragtag River City youth band starts playing, the townspeople do not hear the actual out-of-tune notes. They hear what they want to hear: a magnificent precision band marching through town playing "76 Trombones" in perfect synchrony ("Egypt presents to humanity . . . a gift . . . a gift for humanity, for development, for building, for restoration").

The morale building was undeniable in both cases, but for Egypt the stakes were infinitely higher than for the citizens of River City. Sisi's *mish 'adir adik*—"I can't give you anything"—turned out to be frighteningly selective. It did not apply, for example, to the brand new French Rafale jets that zoomed overhead during the canal inauguration, wowing the crowds.[18] But in the regime's public rhetoric, the military was not the only sector exempt from the *mish 'adir adik* dictum. More civilian megaprojects were on the horizon, though they were slow to get off the ground. Every single one of them was a disastrous desert development scheme that sucked the state's resources away from the cities where people live, often in desperate need of adequate housing, education, and health care, and into speculative real estate ventures that make billions of pounds for politically connected businessmen (and, in the Sisi era, the military).[19] The explosion of suburban development and the accompanying state spending on phenomenally expensive infrastructure (roads, drainage and sewage, electricity, and most crucially water), mirrored by the much more densely populated *'ashwa'iyyat* (informal neighborhoods), were fundamentally the reasons the revolution happened. Unfortunately, "down with luxury housing" made a poor political slogan, even though it would in fact have been far more practical than "bread, freedom, and social justice." It was the flight of resources and investment to the suburbs that made all of them impossible.

The regime operated through violence, an ongoing state of emergency justified by threats from Islamists impossible to disentangle from the regime's own provocations, and harsh suppression of even the slightest criticism. On the other hand, Sisi promised everything to everyone—vast housing and commercial projects, a revival of the failed Tushka "second Nile" fed by waters of Lake Nasser pent up by the High Dam, and most spectacularly, a "new capital city" built in the desert between Cairo and the Red Sea, a metropolis to house seven million Egyptians and to be built in seven years. But Sisi had already reached the pinnacle of his grand gestures with the canal extravaganza in 2015. Even before the canal celebration, the public became increasingly skeptical and began to label Sisi's projects as *fanakish*—the plural of the word *fankush*, which comes from an old popular movie (Galal 1984). A fankush is a fake object sold by a slick salesman to a naive customer. Basically, a con job. The word first emerged in 2012 during the presidential campaign, when the Muslim Brotherhood's "Nahda Program," a political platform full of unrealistic developmental projects, was described as a fankush. "Morsy is selling the fankush," as an eloquent man put it in an interview that went viral. By 2016 the term fankush was owned exclusively by 'Abd al-Fattah al-Sisi.

Sisi was spectacularly bad at forging political alliances, as befits an outsider seemingly determined to remain an outsider. Many of the non-Islamist intelligentsia were at first desperate to justify what they argued, somewhat deli-cately, as a necessity for a coup on grounds that Morsy posed a mortal threat to the nation. A modicum of freedom of expression and a light security touch on non-Islamist political figures would have kept many of them on side. Instead, Sisi's undiscriminating scorched-earth approach to potential political oppon-ents has squandered support. Quite a few intellectuals, opinion makers, and artists continued to dissociate their support for removing Morsy from their current political stance. I was in Cairo on a visit in the summer of 2013, when Sisi was on the brink of massacring almost a thousand Morsy supporters. One of my neighbors, a university professor, justified his tolerance of Sisi through his disgust at the Muslim Brotherhood. He had never accepted Morsy's legit-imacy and bristled strongly at the suggestion that the country should have let him serve out his term in office rather than remove him even through a coup if necessary. As he put it, *"Khalluni akul khara. Wi dilwa'ti yi'ulu lazim akam-miluh?"* ("They made me eat shit [i.e., accept Morsy's victory in the presidential election of 2012]. And now they say I have to *finish* it?"). And yet his accept-ance of Sisi was at best conditional. He expected Sisi to evolve into an Egyptian Putin: undemocratic but still a limited improvement over Mubarak. It did not take long for him to be disabused of that notion. The next time I saw him, a few months later, he was as scornful of Sisi as he had been of Morsy.

Sisi the Trickster had told this particular public what it wanted to hear—that the Rab'a massacre had been a price that had to be paid. And the public briefly saw what it wanted to see: a strong, charismatic leader who would make Egypt flourish economically if not politically. "The sense of empowerment that tricksters manage to produce feels real enough for a while, but it evaporates as suddenly as the trickster entered the stage, and dissolves in nothingness" (Forlenza and Thomassen 2016). The canal ceremony by all accounts did feel real to the public in July 2015—it was by far the most successful political the-ater the regime has mounted since Sisi's accession to power. But by April 2016, the exuberance of the previous year was gone, as spontaneous demonstrations erupted against Sisi's gift (or "return" as the regime termed it) of the two Red Sea islands Tiran and Sanafir at the mouth of the Gulf of Aqaba to Saudi Ara-bia. An attempt to amplify the initial demonstration ten days later was brutally suppressed in a wave of arrests of potential organizers that successfully pre-vented further anti-regime expressions. Though the regime remains popular in some quarters, it is now clear to all that it stays in power only through violence. The proportion of the public that falls for political tricks like the canal opening will never increase.

Beyond the grand gesture of pretend politics, Trickster politics natural-ly connects to the sort of outlandish stories we call conspiracy theories and is reminiscent of what some call "Post-truth Politics"—a political style that puts emotion above any plausible invocation of fact. It is a new label for an old phenomenon. One thinks of a classic essay about the United States called *The Paranoid Style in American Politics* by the historian Richard Hofstadter, originally published in 1965, shortly after Barry Goldwater won the Republican nomination for the presidency. The Goldwater candidacy was the pinnacle of that particular episode in paranoid American politics; it had emerged initially during the anti-communist hysteria of the McCarthy era. The hallmark of the paranoid style was a sense of betrayal on the part of the right wing of the political spectrum. The idea was that "the old American virtues have already been eaten away by cosmopolitans and intellectuals" (Hofstadter 1996, 23). It was not just that conspiracies sometimes happened but that conspiracies were themselves *the motive force* in historical events (29). Hofstadter quotes Robert Welch, founder of the racist right-wing John Birch Society, making amazingly precise predictions of apocalypse: "Evidence is piling up on many sides and from many sources that October 1952 is the fatal month when Stalin will attack" (Welch in Hofstadter 1996, 30). Change a few details, and Welch morphs into Taufiq 'Ukasha predicting the fateful unfolding of a Masonic conspiracy on the thirteenth day of the thirteenth month of the year 2013. Such discourse may indeed be paranoid, as Hofstadter says, but it is also the hallmark of a Trickster's pretend politics.

'Ukasha inserted the notion of "fourth-generation warfare" into Egyptian political discourse some time in 2011. "4G" warfare was essentially conflict by means other than military action—disinformation in media, funding civil society NGOs, even the simple spreading of rumors. It is the perfect term for a phony expert, because *anything* can be seen as fourth-generation warfare. The idea was later repeated in Egypt by numerous other television personalities and politicians. Once others started stealing "his" idea, 'Ukasha one-upped himself and started talking about "fifth-generation warfare." However, 'Ukasha's 4G warfare idea actually originated, perhaps unsurprisingly, from an American paranoid politician named William Lind, who is a direct descendent of the McCarthy and Goldwater era that Hofstadter was writing about (Lind 2014).

In Egypt 4G warfare became more than talk show fodder. Sisi picked up the term. In early February 2015, he appeared on Egyptian television in a kind of faux-intimate "fireside chat," sitting in an armchair in front of his desk rather than sitting more formally at the desk or standing behind a podium. This particular "conversation" by Sisi was done to counteract damaging leaks of recorded phone conversations in which he derisively talked about his Gulf patrons—on whom Egypt had become utterly dependent—characterizing their money as "rice" and laughing cynically at the Egyptian military's ability to fleece them. Sisi introduced his indirect apology to the Saudis by reference to fourth-generation warfare in order to claim that the leaked conversation had been fabricated by someone stealing his voice from the "thousands of hours" of recorded speech that had been broadcast. "I remind everyone who listens to me: fourth-generation warfare is a generation of the utmost importance which is being used in the entire region, and in Egypt. This generation is used in terrorism as an instrument; it's used in modern media; it's used in psychological warfare. It's a complete system that's used to bring an incredible result. Don't ask about something that was said 'was it said or not?' Ask '*Why* was it said?' What was its purpose?"[20] The purpose, of course, was to get the mark to believe anything the Trickster wanted him to believe. It is entirely possible that by the time Sisi invoked 4G warfare to explain away his embarrassing leaks about the Saudis, the marks were wising up. But by then it was far too late. The Trickster already had the keys to the car and was speeding madly over a cliff.

Conclusion: Events That Structure Tricksters

I know from experience that the idea of 'Abd al-Fattah al-Sisi as a Trickster politician is a hard sell to political scientists, the scholars who probably conjure with revolution the most. They can see it readily in 'Ukasha, but they want to imagine Tricksters as Bugs Bunny tormenting Elmer Fudd. Moreover, the connection between 'Ukasha and Sisi is too circumstantial. The link between them is uncertain (or at least plausibly deniable), and 'Ukasha can, in any case, be seen as a tool rather than as a paradigm. Anthropologists may be equally skeptical, though on different grounds. The nominalist inheritors of the empiricist tradition (Bruno Latour and his many followers; the substantial current of scholarship inspired by Deleuze and Guattari) scarcely leave any space for the sort of shared categories that must be sensed by human beings in order to make liminality real. I am making no claims here about the importance of 'Ukasha to the daily lives of any particular group or in a specific field site, though elsewhere I have noted his insertion into the discourse of daily life (Armbrust 2013). The case for Sisi is admittedly more complicated. In safely private settings, everyone has an opinion about him, and though opinions have become discernably more negative over time (among those who were not opposed to him from the start), negativity is usually expressed in protest of certain acts—the murder of Islamists, his scorched-earth policy against all manner of protest, his ruination of the economy. This is not to say that criticism never takes aim at either his mendacity or his apparent incompetence. He had, after all, become the owner of the fankush by roughly halfway through 2014, and he gladly sold it to gullible buyers. This was duly noted by those who had safe outlets for criticism.

But here, really, the case is primarily about audibility. Liminality makes the Trickster possible, but Tricksters are always part of the cultural field and (though we have rarely noticed) also part of the political field. Yet Tricksters are sufficiently audible to make a difference only in particular circumstances. And so we might ask, when can the Trickster be heard? Revolution, understood as a liminal crisis, is a Trickster moment. There may be others, structured by more "synthetic" forms of liminality—precarious conditions caused by globalized neoliberalism and exacerbated by the capacity of digital media to encyst people within worldviews largely defined by opposition to others (a digital segmentation predicated on agonistic display). But revolution is the salient context for my Tricksters, and revolution, experienced as a moment of violent change, is incomprehensible without reference to a structured "before" and an "after" that may be aspirational at best and may end up being equally structured, if distressingly prone to unintended consequences in most instances.

The Trickster deserves a much greater place in the analysis of politics. Tricksters are salient in particular circumstances, and it must be said that 'Abd al-Fattah al-Sisi has a lot of company. Revolution is not the only incubator of liminality. We live in an "age of the Trickster"—a claim much easier to make in the wake of Brexit and Donald Trump. Trickster tales often end in catastrophe. It was, for example, all too easy to imagine the Trump presidency coming to disaster before his first day in office. The narrative of his excesses, vulgarities, and incompetence was already written, the manner of their unfolding a mere detail. More to the point for present purposes, Western politicians who interpreted Sisi as an unfortunate but necessary bulwark against the chaos of undisciplined freedom grievously misunderstood the nature of his regime. Perhaps Sisi's political style is so close to their own governing strategies that they can no longer tell they've been Tricked.

WALTER ARMBRUST is Associate Professor in the Faculty of Oriental Studies, University of Oxford, and Albert Hourani Fellow of Modern Middle Eastern Studies at St Antony's College. His research focuses on mass media, popular culture, and politics in the Middle East, particularly in Egypt. He is author of *Martyrs and Tricksters: An Ethnography of the Egyptian Revolution*.

Notes

This chapter draws on parts of several chapters in *Martyrs and Tricksters* (Armbrust 2019). My analysis here, however, departs from *Martyrs and Tricksters* by accentuating continuity and discontinuity as productive frames for interpreting the significance of the course of events in a revolution.

1. "Taufiq 'Ukasha Yahdhar min 13-13-2013," 2011, YouTube video, accessed August 2, 2016, https://www.youtube.com/watch?v=8YfVtNxMzTo.

2. "Al-Sisi al-Qatil wal-Nazi wal-Fashi fi Almanya," *Shabakat al-Marsad al-Ikhbariyya*, June 4, 2015, accessed August 13, 2016, http://marsadpress.net/?p=23142.

3. "'Ukasha Yatanaba'u bi-Tai'yin 'Abd al-Fattah al-Sisi Ragil al-Ikhwan fi al-Gaysh," 2012, YouTube video, accessed August 2, 2016, https://www.youtube.com/watch?v=CYrJRWveQTw.

4. For example, Nugent and Vincent's volume on anthropology and politics focuses primarily on long-term social processes such as feminism, globalization, or militarization (D. Nugent and Vincent 2007; see also Thomassen 2008). A review of anthropological writing over the course of 2011 highlights revolution but similarly emphasizes disciplinary work on processes as opposed to events (Dole 2012). Thomassen (2012) discusses the history of anthropology's lack of engagement with political revolutions per se.

5. Ortner used this article as the template for a class I took with her at the University of Michigan in 1986. Dresch was a recent hire at the time and was at first incredulous that an essay he considered so sloppy and in his opinion simply wrong could be so influential. But it was. The article was widely read—it was the topic of a high-profile panel at the American Anthropological Association conference that year. For later iterations of dismissive appraisals of Turner, see Weber (1995, 530) and Caton (1999, 7). An assessment of "History, Structure and Ritual" in anthropology credits Turner significantly for furthering a processual approach to anthropology (Kelly and Kaplan 1990, 136–37) but still criticizes his "implicit functionalisms" (139). Hence he has, until recently, been remembered predominantly as an eclipsed figure of the 1970s and 1980s rather than as a source of ongoing theoretical inspiration. Horvath (2013) and Szakolczai (2009) have elaborated a different and much more positive appraisal of Turner's and van Gennep's work.

6. To be sure, Turner never adopted the theoretical language prevalent during his later years, and he had a tendency to undermine himself by overqualifying his most interesting declarations and insights with caveats that could indeed be seen as tying liminality to social reproduction. For example, the continuation of the passage quoted above is as follows: "'being' to a 'becoming' vocabulary, but with a tender perpetuative regard for the marvelous findings of those who, teachers of the present generation, committed themselves to the discoveries of 'systems' of social relations and cultural 'items' and 'complexes'" (V. Turner 1985, 152). His legacy would certainly have benefited from less "tender perpetuative regard" for his functionalist predecessors.

7. Doctrinaire adherence to nominalist philosophies, particularly those of Deleuze or Latour, both of them prominent in contemporary anthropology, presents the greatest obstacle to conceptualizing boundaries—of objects, categories, structures, or systems. Nominalism dissolves boundaries insofar as it "is in short a claim that only individuals exist, and is . . . a contrasting stance towards ontology which grants that in some way universals, abstractions, and categories can be said to have an existence beyond their mere crafting and use by human beings in ways that have performative social effects" (Bialecki 2012, 302). Without boundaries there can be no in-between. Yet in the end, liminality is as phenomenologically real as the multiple experiences of individuals.

8. The figure of the trickster is well known in the study of literature, folklore, mythology, and anthropology. For a classic study of the phenomenon anchored in folklore, anthropology, and psychology, see Radin (1956).

9. "'Anasir Irhabiyya I'tadat 'ala Wafd al-Fananiyin fi Almanya," 2015, YouTube video, accessed August 13, 2016, https://www.youtube.com/watch?v=pi3W4RNs_Hg.

10. "Al-Sisi al-Qatil wal-Nazi wal-Fashi fi Almanya," *Shabakat al-Marsad al-Ikhbariyya*, June 4, 2015, accessed August 13, 2016, http://marsadpress.net/?p=23142.

11. "Liqa' ma' 'Abd al-Fattah al-Sisi ma' Ibrahim 'Isa wa Lamis al-Hadidi," 2014, YouTube video, accessed August 13, 2016, https://www.youtube.com/watch?v=tKO4bouQPS4.

12. Their presence at the news conference is mentioned in *Radio Sawa* (2014). The most commonly circulated and complete video of the press conference ("Al-Mu'tamar al-Suhufi lil-Quwwat al-Musallaha lil-'Ilaj 'an Jihaz al-Kashf 'an al-Fayrusat," 2014, YouTube video, accessed August 13, 2016, https://www.youtube.com/watch?v=_2Y7t7tQ56E) does not show them (in the video 'Abd al-'Ati comes in at 46:30). A report on the incident ("Taqrir Qanat al-Sharq 'an Liwa' 'Suba' al-Kufta'," 2014, YouTube video, accessed August 13, 2016, https://www.youtube.com/watch?v=4b1TdbyNwKY) does show Mansur and Sisi sitting in a back row, but the image is probably from a different conference.

13. The patent application can be viewed at "WO/2011/116782," 2011, accessed August 13, 2016, https://patentscope.wipo.int/search/en/detail.jsf?docId=WO2011116782&recNum=15. An entirely negative preliminary report on the patentability of the device can also be found online ("International Preliminary Report on Patentability," 2010, World Intellectual Property Organization, accessed August 13, 2016, https://patentscope.wipo.int/search/docservicepdf_pct/id00000018626118/IPRP1/WO2011116782.pdf). For a full debunking of the devices, see Yahia (2014).

14. Some of the many examples are Mazhar Shahin ("Maskharat Mazhar Shahin," 2014, YouTube video, accessed August 13, 2016, https://www.youtube.com/watch?v=arCQd_oXRwU), Sabrin ("Shahid Radd Fi'l Sabrin 'ala Ikhtira' al-Jaysh," 2014, YouTube video, accessed August 13, 2016, https://www.youtube.com/watch?v=J5svgb5aD2g), Mustafa Bakri attacking 'Isam Higgi ("Mustafa Bakri Yuhagim 'Isam Higgi," 2014, YouTube video, accessed August 13, 2016, https://www.youtube.com/watch?v=EdfhVz6UaXg), and Ahmad Musa attacking 'Isam Higgi ("Ahmad Musa 'an 'Isam Higgi," 2014, YouTube video, accessed August 13, 2016, https://www.youtube.com/watch?v=vNTk6VE4Ewg).

15. A central attribute of the project was that the Egyptian public financed it in the short term, through the sale of LE 64 billion (about $8 billion) in bonds that would pay the purchaser 12 percent annual interest over five years. A LE 64 billion loan would ultimately cost the state LE 102 billion—around $13 billion at mid-2015 exchange rates. Since the loan from the public was paid to the state in Egyptian pounds, the repayment cost might diminish, assuming that Egyptian currency would be further devalued over the five-year repayment period, and assuming that none of the bonds collected in Egyptian currency had to be converted to foreign currency to pay for some aspects of the project.

16. Basic parameters of the project included projected "returns and outcome": "Increase the Suez Canal revenues from $5.3 billion at present to $13.226 billion in 2023; an increase equal to 259% that shall positively contribute to Egypt national income of hard currencies" ("New Suez Canal," 2015, *Suez Canal Authority*, accessed August 13, 2016, http://www.suezcanal.gov.eg/sc.aspx?show=69).

17. "Kalimat al-Ra'is 'Abd al-Fattah al-Sisi fi Iftitah Qanat al-Suways al-Jadida," 2015, YouTube video, accessed August 13, 2016, https://www.youtube.com/watch?v=0iBDwbILBGQ.

18. The purchase of the Rafales came in a $5.9 billion package that also included a navel frigate. Sisi's gear was financed by a French bank loan (Lert 2015). Additional military purchases were often rumored, as Egypt sought to both upgrade aging equipment and diversify its sources (*Defense Industry Daily* 2016).

19. About 4 percent of the population of Greater Cairo lives in these glitzy and vast automobile commuter suburbs, and yet they occupy an area roughly three times the size of Greater Cairo. Moreover, 60 percent of the population of Greater Cairo live in *'ashwa'i* (informal) housing built illegally, often on agricultural land.

20. "Al-Gil al-Rabi' min al-Hurub," 2015, YouTube video of a television address by 'Abd al-Fattah al-Sisi on the al-Qahira wal-Nas station, accessed October 16, 2016.

AFTERWORD

Experience and Its Modes

Paul Dresch

> It is surprising ... that this philosophy, which, in almost every instance,
> must be harmless and innocent, should be the subject of so much
> groundless reproach and obloquy. But, perhaps, the very circumstance
> which renders it so innocent is what chiefly exposes it to the public hatred
> and resentment. By flattering no irregular passion, it gains few partizans.
> (Hume, *Enquiry Concerning Human Understanding*, sec. 5, pt. 1)

I FIND MYSELF IN A CORNER, IN THAT colleagues have urged me to discuss current anthropology and thus the alternatives we face. This is not straightforward. We have had the elements of anthropology for a long time, and if we stand back far enough to avoid constraining knowledge—laying down agendas, telling people what to do—then we already know in general terms what analysis requires. Indeed, thought is blocked by pretending otherwise (compare Sahlins 1999). Means to address anthropology's subject matter (the social, briefly put, not the individual's capacities that Kant intended) have been with us for more than a century, and either one accepts that we have these resources or one does not; if one does, then older thinkers, too, take on specific value. The world has changed since Durkheim, let alone since Montesquieu or Hume. We live, year by year, with different problems, not least because literature by non-anthropologists on matters that interest us grows year by year, and it is well to be alert to the times we live in. But the language of "cutting-edge work" seems all too shallow. Do people really believe that reading only new publications allows us to grasp the range of human experience? I cannot find the claim persuasive, and I suspect the contributors to this volume may share my view.

They seem also, in their wider writing, to share a lack of concern with obvious topic boundaries. Nor are they conspicuous for prescribing methods. In one of those sequences of unattributed comment that email produces through "cut and paste," someone else wondered what several of them had in common beyond these patterns of avoidance—whoever it was (I have genuinely failed to guess the mystery person) found in their writing "a sort of obsessive thoroughness and attention to detail that makes use of theory without committing to it and tells stories that have meaning beyond 'illustrating an argument.'" That seems fair. Yet still, the unknown writer said, "it isn't clear what [they're] all cohering around. Similar personality types?" Such questions, in fact, have a fairly straightforward answer.

David Pocock wrote in the early 1970s of a "personal anthropology," and the personal at issue is that of assumptions and ideas.[1] His earlier formulation—whereby a "dialogue of three" among the analyst, the society studied, and literature by anthropologists allows a form of objectivity—makes clear what is going on, for each of us can deduce the position from which colleagues write in a way that we cannot know or share their feelings. None of us will have the same view of anthropology, of course. Nor should we. More generally than in anthropology, there is a difference between making an author one's own and citing "OK names," and the dialogue Pocock speaks of cannot depend in a simple way on approved reading lists. It depends instead on a willingness to engage with others' reading or modes of reading. This in turn takes form within any number of traditions, inside anthropology or not, and people to work with productively can be found almost anywhere.

Some Background

The place to start in my own case is Oxford anthropology in the 1970s, on which Tim Jenkins has written (Jenkins n.d.). Indeed, Tim was part of it. His deeply unusual BLitt thesis, which explored a trajectory of ideas from Bachelard to Althusser, argued that separable "theory" was not an honest option, in anthropology or elsewhere. That was over.[2] It has been a glum experience to see parts of academic life dominated so often in the last forty years by a rhetoric that had lost all excuse for its existence by the time we started. But let us be clear what the implications were. A rejection of theoretical discourse separable from practice did not imply a bluff, unthinking approach to the world. Quite the opposite. Saying anything useful of the social now required questioning each phrase within a sentence, with sad effects on the rate at which one writes, and an indefinitely wide range of reading. If ethnography—very broadly conceived—seemed to be where the magic was, no obvious limits imposed themselves on how to do ethnography, and aids to translation or explanation might come from anywhere. All this before one engaged with an area literature, such as that labeled "Middle East."

If anthropology appeared less a conventional discipline than a space to think from (and, of course, a way of thinking), we were not in an intellectual void. The more earnest kind of student spent as many nights poring over Wittgenstein as poring over, for instance, new books from France. And we learned a lot of anthropology directly by way of anthropology, the Institute being held together by a way of reading Evans-Pritchard (see Pocock 1961; Ardener 1989, 36–37, 55) and of reading the early *Année sociologique*, that provided a common language without much limiting what people worked on or how they did so. Some of this was not honest (I shall give an obvious case below); none of it, however, felt coercive. And the style, if one likes, was as important as anything one could single out as substance, a style or approach one might call "Oxford historicism." Much could be said of what the phrase implies. For the moment let us note that the need to grasp what an author may have had in mind when they wrote is the same need as arises in conducting fieldwork (in neither case does talk of "context" do more than point us in the right direction), and that research on a limited topic, reflection on anthropology in general, and teaching people how to do these things are activities of intellectually the same kind.

Which authors one cites to support such claims, if one wants to cite people, will depend on one's interests, one's friends and age, but in anyone's intellectual life authors can recur; they show up in one's early reading, perhaps fortuitously they show up again later, and later again they appear as on many scores at least not embarrassingly wrong. (To repeat an important point, which authors these are is not crucial.) For my part, I might name Collingwood, who addresses two themes that are intimately linked. One is that thought and action involve suppositions, some more basic than others, that are not, within a form of experience, open to proof or disproof. The other is that seemingly obvious distinctions (oppositions, even) such as that between the knowing subject and the object known turn out, when one pokes at them, not to make sense. The latter point requires, for most of our purposes, simply not saying silly things about, for instance, "epistemology." The former point, about presuppositions, which arises more immediately in anthropologists' work, we learn about as beginning students from, let's say, Azande witchcraft. What we find ourselves learning later is how far the implications extend, although in anthropology we need seldom go far into what Collingwood addressed as "metaphysics." [3] If we wished to go further, we might confront questions of consistency versus wild adventure such that doubting in a radical way what some call "brute" facts (the distance to the moon, for instance) would require a whole, one-off theory of the universe; if we cannot separate the world from the way we know the world, we nonetheless know the world is there. This includes the social world, with its huge variation of localized presuppositions, each set of which may seem to exclude the next.

Most subjects, most of the time, treat presuppositions as given (as suppositions *proprement dit*), and must do so to get their work done. Subjects, one might say, are formed by closure. Anthropology, like certain strands of philosophy, routinely declines that closure (hence the complaints by students and by colleagues in other subjects: what is this *about?*) and then finds itself engaged with "levels" of presupposition among both writers and those written on. The simplest understanding in fieldwork implies grasping the immediate grounds of speech and action, but behind this often lie local assumptions that are more profound. Evans-Pritchard's early opening of the question leads on to such realms of debate as that on Amazonian "perspectivism" and "animism" (Viveiros de Castro 1998, 2012; Descola 2005). Beginning usually with ethnographic perceptions (themselves deeply odd; more of this below), we have no settled idea, or at least should not do, of where we will end up, for the categories that matter first are those that ethnography reveals. Where does anthropological "theory" come into this? If part of what we must do is unpack the grounds of others' common sense and action, then the "cookie-cutter" sense of theory (bang, bang, bang, so many near-identical gingerbread men) prevents us doing anthropology; yet reflection on past anthropology is essential to forming a position of our own.

Schools or paradigms can be set in sequence to provide anthropology's history, and one would not deny the usefulness of diagrams that illustrate this.[4] Those who obsess about the subject, however, soon find that the lists leave out work that matters, and the terms used obscure what is going on. Functionalism, for example, if we can even agree what was meant by the word (see Lowie 1937), is of almost no interest in itself, but it illustrates the more important topic of empiricism, as do any number of schools that thought themselves alternatives to functionalism. In the official descent line of British social anthropology, to take a parochial case, the supposed "transition from functionalism to structuralism" was thus not really that at all. What it marked, or should have done, was the end of empiricism.

All anthropology worth the name is empirical in that it deals with what is in the world, such that axioms are no help to us. Empiricism (or positivism or realism; for the present purpose these are synonyms), however, is the assumption, or the claim, that the world is composed of isolated facts and that knowledge consists in apprehending facts that are, so to speak, given.[5] One cannot pretend this is so in anthropology. "Observation" of such stock characters as a "chief" or a "district officer" (or nowadays the representative of an international NGO) required, and requires, knowing what such terms mean, which implies a level of potentially analytic but usually still tacit knowledge, and knowing which hand goes where in forms of greeting may imply the equivalent of mastering a decision tree (Dresch 2012a, 11). In fieldwork, most obviously, we are asking, "What must be the case to get from this point in what is said or done to that point in what is said or done?" The simpler the formulation here, the happier the prospect. Yet if anthropology is the study by humans of human action and thought, then the realization that fellow anthropologists are human, too, requires the same attitude to what passes as academic authority.

The foundation myth of the place where I learned anthropology was "Evans-Pritchard good, Radcliffe-Brown bad" (here is my example of dishonesty). If Evans-Pritchard said in print something foolish, so orthodoxy ran, "the influence of Radcliffe-Brown" explained it. It took me a long time to wonder, never mind understand, why Radcliffe-Brown, dull though he now seemed, had once been exciting in some quarters, and of course it is something one should understand—if these people had been wearing exotic robes (or, better still, exotic feathers), one would try to grasp what they were doing, and not to try doing so for people in ratty tweed is hubris. The process in the two types of case is much the same. In the case of analytical writers, especially, an attractive formulation is Collingwood's: "What must be the question to which this might have been the answer?" Given what anthropology attempts, we cannot borrow "methods" or "paradigms," yet we cannot dismiss an earlier anthropology as simply wrong.[6] To do so produces what we might call a premature closure, which prevents us both from taking seriously what categories we find in the wider world and from comprehending our own position, as if our views sprang fully formed from nature.

To reduce this to a catchphrase, "theory is only thin ethnography." Authors break into convoluted formulas when they have not thought through their material sufficiently to express themselves clearly (in this sense, "theory" is a refusal of honesty), and what ethnography might teach us is thereby lost; readings of early authors, meanwhile, if attempted at all, are mostly too thin to be useful. Nonetheless, we do, as a subject, learn things. A set of disputes over kinship analysis, which began in the early 1950s, thus culminated at one point in Leach's *Rethinking Anthropology* (1961), from which two lessons emerged. The first was that the harder analysts tried to be objective in the old style, the more they imposed on material their own assumptions (the famous illustration, of course, was "complementary filiation"; behind this lay the common-sense idea that a child's relation to its mother must be of the same kind as its relation to its father). The second was that none of the boxes is real. Kinship, magic, politics, economics, and the like can only be provisional labels, to be discarded when unhelpful. These conclusions seem, or now should seem, obvious. What is less obvious to some is that "theoretical" terms do what supposedly analytical terms once did. *Ontology*, for example, as anthropologists use it, is too grand a term for its purpose and implies a mode of thought that we moderns do not command.[7] Such words, along with for instance *optic* (meaning, I suppose, perspective) or *binary* used as a noun, tend to function as instant clichés. To breathe life into them would need more cunning than most of us command, and in practice they often block analysis by providing the appearance of answers where in fact we require questions. Let me quote, without dropping their name in the mire of controversy, a colleague who, with Pocock in mind, brought the question down to how we teach: "Example: Student tells me they want to use the _____ optic to analyze _____ in _____. First, get rid of the optic. Then get rid of whatever might go in the blanks. Then get rid of the blanks. Then work your way back to what other scholars have put in the blanks, via your own experience with people in fieldwork. You'll probably arrive at a new place; or you'll have confirmed the value of earlier work. But it won't be formulaic." That is one moment of the process, certainly, and an important one, although it is scarcely all we do.

Certain dangers are clear in addressing what is placed in the blanks by others. A feeling of pointless repetition (of the wheel being reinvented with a new name) can blind one to what is new, and mere words can provoke hostility where what matters is how thoughtfully words are used. Yet few can doubt that we live now among clichés that flourish in what Dumont once described as a "climate of competition which favors overbidding" (1986, 203). The odd thing is that bids for sophistication are currently so unsophisticated. Modernism, with its taste for programmatic statements (rather authoritarian statements, one has to say), shows a datable beginning and end in anthropology (Ardener 1989, chap. 13), and "postmodernism" gave the game away in its very name—the highest stage of what it condemned. For at least a generation, claims to be the avant garde have been intellectually naive and morally suspect (Dresch 1992, 23). The damage is less to ethnographic practice than to anthropology's broader self-awareness.

The structure of publishing, meanwhile, has not been helpful. Largely by our own actions—those of us, at least, who have held established posts—we have produced through institutional practice the appearance in print of minds set on autopilot. Too much, indeed, is formulaic. Leave alone books, where newcomers with views of their own are shut out unless provided with established patrons, articles in anthropology have become a scandal; younger colleagues are obliged to bracket their work with discussions of authors not relevant to their own ideas, while major journals (*American Ethnologist* was long a conspicuous offender) display such uniformity that reading the list of contents discourages one from opening the volume.[8] Whatever this may be, it is not really anthropology. Where then does anthropology lie?

Fieldwork

If there is one thing anthropologists have claimed as their own it is fieldwork, and plainly it is something most of us do. It is not the same everywhere, however, as Peter Rivière (2000) explains. The Trio in Amazonia, whom one might, were one a reader of only literary journals, have thought an impenetrably "alien" world, treated him as a failed child and taught him, as best they could, how to be Trio. That produced some notable anthropology. An attempt at fieldwork with cattle ranchers in Brazil produced far less, although Rivière had what human resources administrators would call an "appropriate skill set": his Portuguese was good, he rode well, and learning to read cattle (at least to an acceptable standard) is not all that difficult. But what, asked the *vaqueiros*, could they, as uneducated persons, possibly tell a learned gentleman from England? He found himself stuck on the veranda. The Middle East is not South America any more than Amazonia is the pampas, or one place in Amazonia quite like another, but let us take seriously the specificities of where we work. These are hugely various.

In the 1990s I began some work in the United Arab Emirates. "Are you sure you can *do* anthropology here?" asked a kindly friend in the diplomatic service who had a too common view of the subject. "It's not *Lawrence of Arabia*, you know. It's more like *Blade Runner*." Well, that sounded fun, and he was perfectly right. Abu Dhabi was full of "replicants" who looked like Emiratis, sounded like Emiratis, acted like Emiratis, but (by this local ruling and that) were not Emiratis. Nor was information of repeatable form easy to come by. Supposedly public sources such as statistical yearbooks took weeks of polite coffee-drinking to get hold of. Documents on city planning in Dubai came from a discontented non-Emirati Arab planner who wanted an "educated person" to discuss his work with (the opposite of Rivière's *vaqueiro* problem, but just as uncomfortable), and I would nip around the corner with a pile of reports while his boss was out to lunch and have them photocopied in a nearby shop run by Indians, whose position was as interesting as that of the Arabic-speaking replicants. Here was a world founded on exclusion (Dresch 2006a). If the foreign ethnographer was excluded from much, qua foreigner, those supposedly near the center of affairs were themselves dependent on mobile-phone calls and dreaded having a call unreturned or a number being changed or being passed to a lesser user.[9]

Access problems in the Arab Gulf have changed since then, superficially. Rulers in many Gulf states have decided that a small degree of openness works better than obvious paranoia, and local offshoots of US universities allow sustained engagement. Even the unpromising terrain of Saudi Arabia has seen good anthropology (e.g., Menoret 2003, 2014; Samin 2015). But the smaller Gulf states of the 1990s presented challenges I had not foreseen, such as getting my mind around the global economy of oil and gas, while at bottom was the phenomenon of "small places" that flourish on condition that those who do the work—the sweeping, the cleaning, the plumbing and electrics—are made invisible. (An attempt to present this argument elsewhere, with its inevitable suggestion that US college towns are a lot like Gulf monarchies, went over poorly.) On the conventional-anthropology front, marriage regulation and ideologies of shared descent caught the eye (Dresch 2005) and were plainly not an "ethnographic remnant" but instead something "hypermodern." Indeed, certain forms of exclusion that colleagues dismissed as archaically "Middle Eastern" soon emerged in such places as Denmark, where recent foreign spouses formed a colony at the other end of the bridge to Sweden. In the end, however, I was beaten. Laura Nader's exhortation to "study up" gave no guidance on how to afford hotel rates for sociable coffee or how to keep one's suit pressed while living cheap.

Rural Yemen in the late 1970s had been a great deal easier. For one thing, there was often physical work to do (digging over a field, rebuilding a stone wall, humping sacks of cement or grain off the back of a truck), and, whatever the pressure of totalizing models of the world that locate types of people before one ever meets a person, it is difficult to do tiring work in parallel and not establish fellow feeling. It was anyway a self-consciously rough and ready place. A distinctive phrase that marked eating an unflavored mess of sorghum porridge was thus *al-hasil*, meaning roughly, "Well, that's what there is"; all one had to do was show a willingness to muck in (*al-hasil, ya akhi!*), and there one was for the moment cheerfully distinct from silly people who wanted luxury. Also, one could move from place to place with surprising ease, for in areas north of Sanaa there really was no government, and simple politeness allowed one to move as a temporary guest from one protected space to another within an indefinitely wide tribal system. That in turn highlighted contextual matters of privacy and discretion (Dresch 2000a). We should not get too excited about any of this, but it was an interesting change from the structures of control and anonymity that inform life in most North Atlantic countries. I confess I fell in love with northern Yemen. Only recently has continuing work there become impossible.

The country's position in the world was distinctive, of course, even when I started, but not hard to get one's mind around. Migrant labor in the Gulf was hugely important, which took place, as it were, offstage. If people in the northern parts of Yemen had usually depended, directly or indirectly, on extracting wealth from people further south in Yemen, they were now in the happy position of getting wealth from outside the country. Hard currency was in the pockets of ordinary citizens. That began to turn around in the mid-1980s, and by 1990 hard currency was in the hands of government, the government was of roughly the type that Jean-François Bayart describes in Africa, and new forms of mischief appeared (Dresch 2000b). But even this hardly swamped certain older forms of sociality. Local concerns very obviously outlasted external pressures, informing the sense made of them, and locality was richly various.

Many anthropologists do field research in places other than where their careers are based,[10] and doing this, for however long, does have its uses. Just as Cacambo tells Candide, "*Si nous ne trouvons pas des choses agréables, nous trouverons du moins des choses nouvelles.*" Or at least we should do. If the categories that matter first are local categories (here is the wager on which our subject rests) and we are open to experience, we can hardly fail to rethink our work as we go along, hence the common pattern of anthropologists writing on something different from what had caught their attention when they started. A combination of administrative dullness and intellectual muddle has recently made suspect what Signe Howell (2011, 141) calls "the spirit of adventure." We might better say curiosity. The effect, though, is plain in research proposals: "I often ask myself," she says in despair, "why this particular person wants to investigate his or her particular stated problem, since they already seem to know most of the answers they expect to find" (144). With the spread of postcolonial but "North-centered" NGOs to the back end of almost everywhere, self-validation becomes that much easier. The modern Candide can travel a long way and only confirm the ideas they started with.[11]

Exhortations to keep one's mind open can seem of little help, and most of us will have sympathized with beginning researchers who fear they'll come back from wherever it is having missed a key fact. There are not, though, any facts in that sense. One practical answer, perhaps, is to write as you go along, not drafts of a book but notes that try to summarize some provisional "topic," which is where you discover that your current view is incoherent; either something further needs understanding before you can give a defensible account, or the topic you had set yourself turns out to have been wrong-headed. But intellectual enquiry of a certain kind works that way of its nature. Fieldwork therefore only illustrates, although rather sharply, something far more general.

Earlier I used the phrase "ethnography . . . very broadly conceived," and the point is that all of literature and life can be approached in the same way. Living constantly in "fieldwork mode" is not advisable, for one cannot reflect so intensely and also act in the world, longer term, without becoming more than odd. Also, discussing how one makes analytical sense of life needs a space (perhaps an academic space) set aside from the everyday. If I say in the ordinary course of things that I am listening for what is unsaid in our conversation and analyzing its preconditions, then I will not be easy to be around, although that is what we do in our work and might wish to discuss. Precisely by keeping quiet on this score, anthropologists get along "in the field," be it only a few miles from the office. In the office, of course, there is still some license to spell out the assumptions of published writing (certain problems of engagement here we can touch on later). What an anthropologist brings to the world in either setting is not a "method" or "skill set" but a mode of reading.

Turn this around, and what do we bring to other components of intellectual life? One test of a sound academic, in the humanities at least, is editing, much of which consists, at all levels, very largely—and very simply, it seems at first—of repairing grammar and striking out surplus words; at the next stage, which remains mysterious, one finds oneself moving sections of prose around with the pretense of showing what was "really" meant. The interesting question is why this should work. After all, no one will assert a simple correspondence between words and things. The answer, surely, is that the stripping away reveals overinterpretation, which is anthropology's besetting danger, and its specialized form of false recognition. It is only when we are sure what is being said that we can see, for example, whether "leopard-skin chief" (Evans-Pritchard in *The Nuer*) is or is not a fair gloss for *kuaar muon* or whether "earth priest" (Evans-Pritchard in *Nuer Religion*) is any better. Whatever the *kuaar muon* may have been about, he was not a football referee.

The problem of false recognition is perhaps more pressing with the Middle East than with some areas of the world (see Dresch 1992, 28), partly because of long-term rivalries of Islam and Christendom, with so much of their traditions shared; partly because of current politics and the election of the Middle East by America's empire and its hangers-on as a field in which to exercise their cruelty and incomprehension. A certain effort is required to show Western readers (or readers amenable to Western views, the modernist elites of many places) that people's lives in the region are more than failed versions of their own. Local literature, meanwhile, prevents playing fast and loose with "alterity," for any claim to illustrate the "mind" of the whomever can be met as easily in Arabic, say, as in English or French, by pulling a book off the shelf that says something quite different from the book used to illustrate the claim. (To show what our two imagined books have in common, or do not, requires in its turn serious effort; one must meet the textualists' basic standards before one can do much else, even saying why the book does not matter.) All manner of distinctions—between learned and nonlearned, perhaps town and country, or among different localized traditions—are present before one starts, which it is well to know.[12] And the Middle East has historical depth. Obvious narratives, such as that shared by Edward Said and modernization theorists (see Dresch 2000a, 120), are too parochial a frame of reference.

History, Culture, and the Like

One advantage of taking structuralism seriously as part of the intellectual ambience, if not as a style to follow, was being steeped in the simple idea of *langue* against *parole*. What some would call "high structuralism" ignored the more profound of Lévi-Strauss's insights, and the misrecognition of his work as to do with "symbolism" gave impetus to demands that something like langue be addressed as determining matters other than speech and writing. For a brief moment, "structural Marxism" suggested interesting resources (morally interesting, not least; talk of "speaking from one's position" raised questions of authenticity). Organizationally this evaporated when anthropologists misread such literature as "economic anthropology with wheels on," but one was left, nonetheless, with the insight from which structuralism started. The condition of an utterance or event being intelligible was a set of assumptions that outlasted the event, and one could blunder from unexpected angles, therefore, into problems of historicity.

My own encounter with the topic was through the longevity of tribal names and locations in northern Yemen. Whatever about advanced Marxist theory, the common sense that one started with was really Emrys Peters's (1967) rewarming of Evans-Pritchard. Structural time would reflect structural distance, and accounts of the past would be largely (perhaps merely) reflections of present concerns. Having plowed through a good deal of the tenth-century author al-Hamdani, for lack of much else to do while stuck in Sanaa, I could not help noticing that when the proverbial old men of fieldwork said, "Our tribe and that tribe, the border has been here since the days of Saba and Himyar" (that is, since the Queen of Sheba), they were often much nearer right than they should have been. Whatever tribes were, they were not historical products in the simplest sense (see Dresch 2009, 186–8) but produced a certain type of history, and the nontribal written record that revealed their longevity produced a different kind (Dresch 1989). It felt, I must say, rather lonely to be poring over a millennium's worth of sources. It did not, though, feel intellectually bizarre. In fact, this was something that "happened" to others also (e.g., Jenkins 2010 on households and law in southern France).

So, what to do with this? The temporal depth of the record rubs one's nose in the fact that little of history is apparent to those who make history. Collingwood's language of "re-enactment" thus invites brisk rejection. Nor does a simple wedding of "structure" with "agency" resolve problems of arbitrariness.

A Yemeni example would be the tomb of al-Husayn at Raydah. No one in the immediate area seemed to know who al-Husayn was (a common response when people were pushed was Husayn bin 'Ali; he of course is buried in Iraq, so it cannot be him), yet for as long as anyone can remember the same particular sections—not all the sections—of nearby tribes turn up at the tomb on *yawm al-ghadir* each year in the same order. As learned Yemenis will tell you, the tomb is that of al-Husayn ibn al-Qasim al-'Iyani (d. AD 1013). Rummaging in chronicles suggests that the named elements that meet at the tomb each year correspond to elements that supported al-Husayn.[13] It is unclear when people were meeting at the tomb, in what groupings, and whether or not continuously, but the unsettling possibility comes to mind that they may have been doing so for a long time with little idea or none of why they were doing it save that this is what we do each year.

If continuity can be odd in a brute sense, so it can in a relative sense. What outlasts what, and thus might tempt us to speak of cause and implication? The answer seems to be that we simply don't know until we look. Perhaps the most salient question that spun off from structural Marxism in its day was that of infrastructure somehow determining superstructure, and Jonathan Friedman argued, for example, that in the Kachin case the infrastructure (to simplify somewhat) was the set of assumptions informing Kachin marriage (Friedman 1979). The same sorts of question arise everywhere. If the "vulgar Marxist" view (often caricatured but often real) were sound, then the United States as de Tocqueville depicted it should bear almost no resemblance to the United States as we know it now: a broadly agrarian society of smallholders and a massively urbanized postindustrial seat of empire are very different. Yet de Tocqueville is of more than nostalgic interest. The more one reads, the more it seems that ideology, if that is the word, governs shapes that political economy has taken.

Again, certain dangers are entirely obvious. Braudel's *L'identité de la France* (1986), for instance, may have read well enough in French, but a similar book on America or Britain would have read like the work of a mildly unhinged reactionary. Nonetheless, if certain field patterns are as stable as they seem, then that is something we should know; if certain voting patterns recur in recent times, such that region A tends to go usually the other way from region B, we should not succumb fully, perhaps, to national-level accounts of progress and reaction. Locating forms of continuity, and the illusions that obscure them, is a commonplace of good historiography.[14] No historian worth their salt, meanwhile, would either generalize too freely or limit themselves to the shapes carved out latterly by nation-states, and if historians of early periods write of "outer Europe" (Wickham 2009), it is not only because the Carolingian empire did not reach that far; it is with some awareness that they are dealing with interrelated cases and that such relations might not be found elsewhere. Space must be open to examination as much as continuity through time.

Anthropologists have muddled specificity, often rooted in space, with "culture" and, sometimes eager to disown the latter concept for minor reasons, have denounced the former. Few of us of a certain age will have forgotten a period of people claiming status as anthropologists of the Mediterranean by dissolving the subject of their expertise. The Middle East saw the same frivolity in a minor key.[15] Even now, the kind of comparative work within a region that might be valued elsewhere is not attempted among cases that seem to ask for a broader view, and suggestions that among such cases there may be patterns that, at certain periods, run out at certain places on the map (see Lindholm 1986; Dresch 1998) are ignored—or indeed denounced. The dangers, yet again, are obvious. One's view of the world is not wholly determined by where one lives (among other things, one can always move), and any number of conventionalized views can coexist in a small space, as certainly they do, and always have done, in the Middle East. Nor do "topical" questions that arise make sense in geographical isolation; if anyone thinks "honor," for example, is a concern that, rightly or wrongly, brackets the Mediterranean and Middle East off from other regions, they would be well advised to read Frank Stewart's comparison (1994) with northern Europe.[16] The illusion of familiarity, on the other hand, and with it the problem of false recognition, is often the result of something regional intersecting with foreign writers' unthought assumptions. If proponents of different "paradigms" or "methods" all claim to find calculating individuals in the Middle East,[17] what is it in the region that allows careless writers to feel such conviction? We have to look.

An element of unfamiliarity may encourage us to look, and certainly, if we choose to look, it makes it easier to see that something requires attention. Engseng Ho (2004) thus takes a set of ideas that many of us will have encountered (at the back of them lies, for instance, Harrington's *Oceana*) but will have left in a box marked "history of political thought"; not having grown up with them, Ho treats them as exotic, if we can put it that way, and provides a deep ethnography of why the British, and the Americans after them, have been such a menace in global history. Their particular forms of self-righteousness led to new property regimes and the extension of such regimes by force; the genealogical elite of Hadramawt expanded quietly by becoming parts of local societies. Ho's article, with its important distinction between colonialism and imperialism, was provoked by the attack on New York in 2001 and the baffled violence that would plainly follow.[18] But its power derives from "deep ethnography." Certain assumptions about the world's rightful ordering are so ingrained that "we" (I hold a British passport; my wife is American) are inclined to miss the fact that invocations of historical uniqueness recapitulate all but constant themes of what some would call "our culture." Ho's is very much an anthropologist's approach. Yet all such analyses seem now to disappear in the rush of enforced common sense like twigs down a waterfall, and one feels that something has shifted among our readers that allows this.

Education in the humanities, whatever one's views on its ideal form or content, used to seem directed against parochialism. It is no longer a safe assumption that this is so. Current dramas over cultural appropriation, safe spaces, and trigger warnings present obvious problems to classical anthropology (we cannot study only *choses agréables*), and the broader patterns of neoliberalism, which these dramas only reinforce, are not mysterious. A greater problem for clarity of thought comes from well-meaning attempts to be inclusive, such as Chris Bayly's *The Birth of the Modern World, 1780–1914* (2004). The author wears his heart on his sleeve ("subalterns" are much in evidence; comments on women and the dispossessed are formulaically "correct"), and the aim is to show that modernity is not solely a Western enterprise. Yet the view is entirely Western. It seems not to cross the author's mind that one might provide at least a sample chapter showing what the world looked like from, let us say, the Ottoman Empire or China or some region of India, any of which could be done from secondary literature. If Bayly failed to see a problem here, what hope for lesser authors? Anthropology, with its roster of challenges to suburban normality, is particularly exposed to a confusion of parochial views with evil or righteousness, and anthropology in the Middle East, perhaps, is particularly prone within anthropology.[19] Even to transcribe what people locally say and do may be denounced as wickedness if such people are, so to speak, "off-message" (see Dresch 2000a). These flattening views of the *bien-pensants* have practical effects.

Working as we do in institutional settings, we should distinguish intellectual blockages of thought from practical blockages. The former may be addressed, if not resolved, by commitments to honesty and clarity, while the latter are more intransigent in that few of us possess independent means of livelihood. In the English-speaking world, institutional blockages are oddly uniform despite the fact that, say, British and American university-funding structures are entirely different; the same approved topics appear in both, as does the same list of places in which work is discouraged by insurance provisions, ethics committees, and rhetorics of fieldwork safety (large parts of the Middle East are in effect proscribed at present). But we tend too easily to confuse our career prospects with our duty to get things right. Longer term, there is little excuse to do so. In the British case, at least, academic life as a secular space in which to think and write is scarcely older than Maitland's time, and as a space in which people of no wealth or lineage could easily make an interesting life, it hardly lasted longer than thirty years after World War II. We should face up to the possibility that anthropology may have to be done elsewhere than universities.[20] Almost certainly it will be done somewhere, for, by a series of misadventures that formed the subject, anthropology has hit on something of general worth.

Briefly put, the nineteenth century was the classical age of narrative historiography, bound up with ideas of change as Western progress, to which the complement was a vision of mainly Sanskritic learning as a textual repository of less time-bound truth (Schwab 1950). Anthropology took the residue, the supposed "primitive," an error that packed field-workers off, in due course, to what seemed the back end of nowhere. Once there, however, one faced a choice: either the people one encountered were daft, backward, primitive (choose a dismissive term at random), or the assumptions they were working from were not those one had grown up with. The importance of the social, wherever found (at home or abroad), was revealed by a misfit of expectations in distant places.[21] It was not revealed so starkly to sociologists. Small wonder that even the places where our careers are based look different to us than they do to them, let alone the places that we often write on, very few of which could be mistaken as being less than complex.

If the social is real, although means to think about it systematically are recent, then specialists in the social, such as anthropologists, are stuck with a specific burden, which is the responsibility not to lapse without thinking into individualism. In one form, individualism was what Durkheim and his students tried to think against; in another it may characterize nationally bound traditions of analysis (Varenne 1984); in another still, it may inform "methods" or "paradigms" that superficially look different from each other but in fact are siblings (Werbner 1984). Whatever its form, it lays analysis open to the imposition of categories that explain (superfluously) the fact that people live together. Such categories might, in a given case at given time, be class, ethnicity, gender, or what you will, but a willingness to entertain alternatives to the domestic ordering of life by middle-class persons in the North Atlantic countries has surely lessened as the self-centeredness of this (unstable) class has grown.[22] A growing "professionalization" of anthropology, meanwhile, presents fiercely promoted claims to insight, each jostling the next for precedence and threatening to exclude alternatives.

Shared Experience and Making Sense

We can see, I think, by this stage, the need for a style that our mystery correspondent at the start of this essay said "makes use of theory without committing to it" and attempts more than "illustrating an argument." Obviously one should know what larger arguments are in progress. To take sides in such arguments, however, is usually to adopt a set of academic categories that obscures those categories one wishes to explore, and it is best to treat the former set obliquely. Where that former set, the academic ones, came from deserves thought, and one must consider anthropology's past as one writes. But to spell it all out risks lapsing, again, into a set of assertions that betrays our ambition to engage with other lives and worlds. Indeed, to proclaim a new style of anthropology (often tempting, one must confess) would reproduce the problem one wishes to escape, which is the dominance of academic concerns over free enquiry. This is not the same as wishing to remain where we are at present.

Anthropology, like all such ventures of thought, is cumulative, so what count as questions for whom will shift over time, or should do; one must work out a position for oneself by grasping what others have said and done. But any community of thoughtful readers, provisional and ill-defined as such things may be, will shy away from what Lowie (1937, 234) saw in Malinowski's writing, "battering down wide open doors," a practice that is not only irritating to encounter but that prevents us seeing our own position. Analytical claims do not, as the language of "cutting-edge work" suggests they do, spring solely from our personal brilliance. The recognition that both our own views and those of people we write on spring instead from the social means that no certainty is available sub specie aeternitatis. Small wonder, therefore, that the subject seems perennially to be "in crisis." Rather than fuss about failure to meet criteria that are not our own, however, we should deduce from this what it is that anthropology does, which is to treat seriously the assumptions of lives other than our own and to place contrasting assumptions against each other. In the shorter term, we can ask what sorts of obstacle to this process matter. The answer, surely, is those obstacles that anthropologists do not notice as they think and write.

Howell (2011) refers to a "hyphenated anthropology." Fairly recently a colleague passed on to me an advertisement for experts in "the anthropology of sleep," and Mark Hobart years ago wondered whether what came next might be "the anthropology of premature baldness." Extremes aside, however, we have always needed to be alert to the way our terms can organize our lives. Teaching and conferences have to be ordered somehow (one cannot do everything at once), but categories of convenience, if taken seriously, form precisely that premature closure that anthropology struggles to avoid. One can see all too well why people seeking temporary work to put food on the table must go along with what they know is nonsense. The fact that so many young writers now form part of "the precariat" is intellectually corrosive. "Perhaps more disturbing is that teaching staff tend to identify themselves more and more with hyphenated anthropology and, just like their Ph.D. students, tend to take an interest only in research and writing which corresponds with their own" (Howell 2011, 146). Anthropology "of" threatens always to collapse into not anthropology at all.[23] It may be the anthropology of religion, of kinship, of the Middle East, or of Islam, but if the term is not from the start kept "under erasure," as the friends of Derrida might say, we find ourselves in trouble. None of which is to say the terms are not real or pressing. The question is how to engage with them.

Saba Mahmood thus faced a problem in that powerful North Atlantic rhetorics equate personal development with untrammeled freedom and cast pious young Muslim women as the dupes of oppression, persons in need of saving. In a fine piece of work, she turned this around: the pursuit of a disciplined life has moral value. No analysis is ever complete, of course (life is more complex than representations of life), but something like an ethnographic engagement is needed if we are not to miss the work's value. Too simple an appeal to a general literature can prevent that engagement. Laidlaw (2013) thus situates Mahmood's analysis in "the (new) anthropology of ethics," not in Cairo, and apportions praise and blame; Mahmood herself (2005) and Hirschkind (2006), by comparison with Schielke (2009, also Egypt) and writers on Chitral and Indonesia, lack, in Laidlaw's judgment, due emphasis on the supposedly "self-limiting" nature of piety and on a moral pluralism whose recognition Laidlaw equates in large part with "freedom."[24] There is oddly little interest in who, ethnographically, may be speaking from what position. A difference in position between girls and boys may matter in Cairo as it does elsewhere; the adoption of determined piety may differ in value according not only to one's perceived alternatives at the start but to how far along in pietism one is; and there are surely resources of thought to be drawn from the Islamic world.[25] Beyond this, one must wonder about equating ethics with "self-fashioning." Foucault, once a great exemplar of anti-humanism, is now treated primarily as a prophet of the self in societies where political activity is decried as pointless, "choice" is restricted to preferring one mobile-phone contract over another, and "sexuality" takes the place of *Bildung*. There are no simple answers to the questions that arise. But space must be left to recognize that assumptions constrain the questions.

One could multiply cases of this kind indefinitely, and often we encounter a problem of rhetoric and intended audience; what makes a piece popular is seldom what makes for critical thought. The problem of false recognition, meanwhile ("Ah," one thinks, "I know what *this* is"), requires something in addition to an ethnographer encountering unfamiliar circumstance. Why, then, is anthropology, not something else, the third element of Pocock's dialogue? And anthropology of what kind? I suggested at the start that anthropology of the sort that I find compelling does not (indeed, cannot) limit itself to work written by anthropologists. Nonetheless, the formative errors of the subject make of anthropologists' writing, even nowadays, an unrivalled resource; to approximate its density of encounters with the social (the cultural, if you like; the terms are really not important) would require a vast amount of reading elsewhere and an unusually creative thinker. As it is, half the work has been done for us.

Does anthropology have friends in this regard, or at least neighbors? Historians, perhaps, are closest, but they are interestingly different from anthropologists. In seminars they often refuse to stray outside their own narrow period or place, although discussing topics of vast general interest. Faced with anthropology, one has to say, and with a widespread assumption that we produce "theory," they sometimes throw caution to the winds, and good sense along with it. But in their own domains they disguise their subtlety, which an anthropologist may well find striking, since history has seen at least as many self-proclaimed "turns" as has anthropology—linguistic turns, cultural turns, narrative turns, cognitive turns, critical turns, other turns beyond number. Yet practicing historians seem to continue judging their fellows primarily on the sense they make of Anglo-Saxon England, Renaissance Florence, the Rajput ascendancy, or Berlin at the time of Bismarck. Their professional journals are less febrile than ours, which leads one to ask why anthropology is different.

A laudable search for generality, if not for universality, may place us in a vulnerable position.[26] If at seminars we are freer than historians in questioning categories and looking for unfamiliar connections, we are vulnerable to our immediate colleagues making grandiose claims that some single method or approach is the key to knowledge—and, indeed, to fame. This is not, of course, what most of us spend our lives on. In what anthropologists working elsewhere perhaps still mistake as distinctively "complex" societies, we are likely to be closely engaged with the concerns of geographers, historians, and textualists. We do this as anthropologists, but we do so under particular constraints to "get the spelling right." Most of it is sober, detailed work. But anthropology more generally should be sober (its results are important enough without arm-waving), and, to the extent that it succeeds, it is likely, as Hume said in our epigraph, to be condemned for "flattering no irregular passion." Accusations of colonialism and Orientalism often mark where this occurs. The passions at issue, however, are those of the current moment and of current empire. Under a global regime of unprecedented power, a rising impatience with difference of any but a trivial kind confronts anthropology at every turn, and anthropologists themselves can reproduce such impatience with disturbing ease in too-simple attempts at "engagement" or in claims of theory. Taking too seriously our own imaginings, says Hume, leads to false philosophy. More obviously to us than to him, life is endlessly subdivisible, yet each localized version, with its range of distinct experience, is intelligible to others across time or distance. It is this simple insight that must be preserved if the irregular passions of our own day are not to rule our lives.

PAUL DRESCH is an Emeritus Research Fellow of St John's College, Oxford. He took early retirement from the Institute of Social and Cultural Anthropology in 2013 and is currently working on tribal law manuscripts from Yemen.

Notes

1. The paper saw print years later (Pocock 1994). The earlier (1961) formulation (see just below) recurs almost word for word.

2. The dissertation followed certain arguments of Jacques Rancière and came out, as I remember, reading quite like Rancière; but, as with the man in the Borges story rewriting *Don Quixote*, it was better the second time around. Far more generally, if we can risk a superficial paradox, this was a period of compelling theoretical arguments against abstract theory. The term itself is slippery (Dresch 1992). But when, in the email snippet just quoted, someone says, "makes use of theory," we know that at issue is a certain register of language and a claim to authority.

3. The main points of reference might be Collingwood's *Essay on Philosophical Method* and his *Essay on Metaphysics*, along with the *Autobiography*. There is no need, however, to clutter a bibliography with works not cited in detail. For a guide to the issues and to recent literature see D'Oro and Connelly (2015).

4. The diagram I have particularly in mind is by my one-time supervisor, depicting modernism in anthropology (Ardener 1989, 195). He could not have been more careful to explain what it was and was not worth, or to explain why that way of viewing the subject was of its period and not of ours.

5. What I mean by empiricism is therefore not quite what is meant in, say, conventional accounts of Hume, who himself is a more interesting writer than such accounts suggest.

6. Much of past anthropology has been misrepresented, often in tawdry ways (Lewis 1998; Graeber 2014, 81). The point here is different. Unless we grasp the issues to which earlier authors were responding, we are likely to leave unthought our own assumptions.

7. In general I agree with what Graeber (2015) has to say about parts of this literature. The particular clichés that block analysis are scarcely limited to anthropology, however. In an issue of the *Times Literary Supplement* (January 19, 2018), for instance, one finds two essays, one on Conrad, one on Ann Quin, that each use the phrase "ontological insecurity." In both cases the sentence makes greater sense without the adjective.

8. Go back a while and look at the stereotyped paper titles over stretches of years, whose form has often been that of, say, "Discourse and Desire: The Use of Parrot Feathers on the Lower Orinoco." Even were one interested in parrot feathers, only liquor or a stern sense of duty enabled one to plow through the clichés and excavate what sense there was.

9. The same diplomatic friend said, "What *you* need is network analysis." I was hugely impressed that he seemed to have read Elizabeth Bott or Clyde Mitchell, but it turned out

that was not what he meant. What he had in mind was signals intelligence, deducing the traffic pattern and thus the structure of command. Had such analysis been possible, it would have had to map the practice of members of ruling families passing mobile phones on to their doormen or drivers, and passing their new number only to selected intimates, thus leaving others to supplicate yet again for access.

10. Most fieldwork is these days done "at home," of course. Let us stick, though, to our immediate problems, and let us not forget that the same considerations apply wherever work may be done: a refusal of difference is refusal to understand (see Dresch 2000a, 123–24, with reference to organized incomprehension of the poor). I am also well aware that not all of us are based in North America or Western Europe. But the hope expressed by Pocock, among others, for distinctive anthropologies based elsewhere has so far not come to much. Nor are the claims of identity politics in this way radical, for the language used by each element resembles that used by the next.

11. Not all such organizations are frivolous, and genuinely noble people work for some of them. But the scale of the phenomenon often passes unremarked. To bend a phrase already much bent in the course of two centuries, we confront almost everywhere a vast outdoor relief scheme for the North Atlantic middle classes.

12. Graeber (2014, 82) complains of anthropology being reduced to "area studies" of a kind "encouraged by governing institutions like the State Department or the intelligence establishment." One could wish there *were* such encouragement. In the United States, area centers have in many universities been displaced by "international centers" that show no interest even in Title VI funding to support language learning. Why bother, when local elites speak business English? Nor, one should add, has the State Department been central to America's recent activities in the Middle East. Again, one might wish it had been.

13. The death of al-Husayn forms part of a curious history that is marginalized, if not quite suppressed, in Zaydi tradition. After his death he is seen in company with Jesus and the prophet Khadir (not at all the kind of thing that mainstream Zaydism deals with). Getting further with the problem requires pursuing Ismaili manuscripts.

14. Several pieces reprinted in Hexter (1961), for example, can be read in sequence as exploring where "patterns" in English history might lie. If class often proves a slippery concept, the continual translation of status into landholding shows great persistence.

15. Thus "the Middle East" was a phrase used by American strategists; the British for a long time wrote of "the Near East." But those who cite the fact seem not to argue why this was more or less important than the trivial fact that French writers describe France as a hexagon. Nor is the common accusation that such phrases as "Middle East" imply homogeneity well grounded.

16. Again, if certain principles recur in laws from northern Europe and south Arabia (Dresch 2015), do we have to assume a common ancestry or a commonality imposed only by the analyst? Presumably not.

17. I am thinking here of a remarkable uniformity in the views of, say, Barth, Bourdieu, and Geertz. What all of them reflect unthinkingly may be the product of local structures apparent in, though not reducible to, such domains as kinship (see Dresch 2012a, 11).

18. The place of the Middle East in America's political imagination is explicable, of course; place McAlister (2001) alongside Brands (1993) on the Cold War. But it is symptomatic that people of the most varied political persuasions have for decades sought ulterior explanations, as if it must "really" be about something else (oil, perhaps, or grand strategy). If it were, it would be less disturbing. In fact we confront something far more arbitrary, and that eccentric

but interesting author, Emmanuel Todd (2002, 137), is left to invoke *"une préférence pour l'inégalité et pour l'injustice."*

19. The editors in their introduction single out certain reviews of the field for criticism. There is no need to repeat what they say. But work that claims to be politically and morally engaged with the region does often show a remarkable lack of fit with the interests of people living there. In such cases, anthropology truly is the handmaid of imperialism.

20. I very much hope I am wrong. Graeber (2014, 78) says that "the university, in the original conception of the term, is dead," but there is still, I think, more room in universities than perhaps he credits to get our work done. On the other hand, I have less faith than he does (79) in universities as a source of political progress. Petit-bourgeois intellectuals as a group inspire little confidence.

21. No one "invented" fieldwork. Nor can a simple account be given of the growth of awareness that local categories matter. But this awareness is a feature of the twentieth century as much as historicity, for better and for worse, is a feature of the nineteenth. One's feeling in seminars on, for instance, "cognitive" anthropology is often precisely that the twentieth century never happened.

22. Marshall Sahlins has battled with the problem for years and enjoyed only mixed results. I cannot say I share his interest in distinguishing culture from society. Nor can one miss the way in which his writing often leaves the landmass of Eurasia as a marginal zone. Nonetheless, if one wants an illustration of anthropology's virtues, his work provides it.

23. Is there a difference among areas here? When tiny groups of people in places such as New Guinea appear as illustrating, in rapid succession, the anthropology of this, of that, and then of the next thing, I confess to a feeling of unease.

24. In the same work, Laidlaw cites a piece by Lienhardt on Dinka morality. He does not address Lienhardt's own citation (1973, 111) of Paul Valéry: "Then where did the idea originate that man is free, or the opposite idea that man is not free? I am not sure whether it was philosophy or the police that began it."

25. Good secondary accounts of self-discipline's moral value might begin with Metcalf (1984) and now include Megan Reid (2013) on medieval piety. The point is not that plus ça change. The point is that Islam as much as Christendom has considered Milton's problem: "Licence they mean when they cry liberty; For who loves that, must first be wise and good."

26. For the useful distinction between generality and universality, see Bloch (2008).

REFERENCES CITED

Abbink, Jon, and Tijo Salverda, eds. 2013. *The Anthropology of Elites: Power, Culture and the Complexities of Distinction*. New York: Palgrave Macmillan.

Abélès, Marc. 2007. "Foucault et l'anthropologie politique." *Revue internationales des sciences sociales* 191:67–75.

———. 2014. *Penser au-delà de l'État*. Paris: Belin.

Abrams, Philip. 1988. "Some Notes on the Difficulty of Studying the State." *Journal of Historical Sociology* 1 (1): 58–89.

Abu-Lughod, Lila. 1986. *Veiled Sentiments: Honor and Poetry in a Bedouin Society*. Berkeley: University of California Press.

———. 1989. "Zones of Theory in the Anthropology of the Arab World." *Annual Review of Anthropology* 18:267–306.

———. 1991. "Writing against Culture." In *Recapturing Anthropology: Working in the Present*, edited by Richard G. Fox, 137–62. Santa Fe: School of American Research Press.

———. 2002. "Do Muslim Women Really Need Saving: Anthropological Reflections on Cultural Relativism and Its Others." *American Anthropologist* 104 (3): 783–90.

———. 2005. *Dramas of Nationhood: The Politics of Television in Egypt*. Chicago: University of Chicago Press.

Abu-Lughod, Lila, and Maya Mikdashi. 2012a. "Tradition and the Anti-politics Machine: DAM Seduced by the 'Honor Crime.'" *Jadaliyya*, November 23, 2012. http://www.jadaliyya.com/pages/index/8578/tradition-and-the-anti-politics-machine_dam-seduce.

———. 2012b. "Honoring Solidarity during Contentious Debates: A Letter to DAM from Lila Abu-Lughod and Maya Mikdashi." *Jadaliyya*, December 26, 2012. http://www.jadaliyya.com/pages/index/9249/honoring-solidarity-during-contentious-debates.

Adelkhah, Fariba. 1999. *Being Modern in Iran*. London: Hurst.

Agamben, Giorgio. 1997. *Homo sacer: Le pouvoir souverain et la vie nue*. Paris: Le Seuil.

Ahmed, S. Akbar. 2013. *The Thistle and the Drone: How America's War on Terror Became a Global War on Tribal Islam*. Washington, DC: Brookings Institution Press.

Aklujkar, A. 1996. "*Dharma-Caurya-Rasāyana* as a Text and as a Work of Brahmin Fantasy." In *Amṛtamandākinī: Dr. G. B. Palsule Felicitation Volume*, edited by G. Palsule et al., 239–60. Pune: Dr. Palsule Satkar Samiti.

Alexander, Jeffrey, Bernhard Giesen, and Jason Mast, eds. 2006. *Social Performance: Symbolic Action, Cultural Pragmatics, and Ritual*. Cambridge: Cambridge University Press.

Allen, Nick J. 2000. *Categories and Classifications: Maussian Reflections on the Social*. Oxford: Berghahn.

Alon, Yoav. 2007. *The Making of Jordan: Tribes, Colonialism and the Modern State*. London: I.B. Tauris.

———. 2016. *The Shaykh of Shaykhs: Mighqal al-Fayiz and Tribal Leadership in Modern Jordan*. Stanford: Stanford University Press.

Althusser, Louis. 1969. "Contradiction and Overdetermination." In *For Marx*, 87–128. London: Allen Lane.

Amar, Paul. 2013. *The Security Archipelago: Human-Security States, Sexuality Politics, and the End of Neoliberalism*. Durham: Duke University Press.

Amit, Vered, and Noel Dyck. 2006. "On Claiming Individuality: An Introduction to the Issues." In *Claiming Individuality: The Cultural Politics of Distinction*, 1–21. Chicago: University of Chicago Press.

Anderson, Benedict. 1983. *Imagined Communities: Reflections on the Origin and Spread of Nationalism*. New York: Verso.

Appadurai, Arjun. 1986. "Introduction: Commodities and the Politics of Value." In *The Social Life of Things: Commodities in Cultural Perspective*, 3–63. Cambridge: Cambridge University Press.

——. 1996. *Modernity at Large: Cultural Dimensions of Globalization*. Minneapolis: University of Minnesota Press.

Ardener, Edwin. 1980. "Ten Years of JASO: 1970–1980." *Journal of the Anthropological Society of Oxford* 11:124–30.

——. 1989. *The Voice of Prophecy and Other Essays*. Edited by M. Chapman. Oxford: Basil Blackwell.

Armbrust, Walter. 1996. *Mass Culture and Modernism in Egypt*. Cambridge: Cambridge University Press.

——. 2013. "The Trickster in the January 25th Revolution." *Comparative Studies in Society and History* 55 (4): 834–64.

——. 2019. *Martyrs and Tricksters: An Ethnography of the Egyptian Revolution*. Princeton: Princeton University Press.

Asad, Talal. 1972. "Market Model, Class Structure and Consent: A Reconsideration of Swat Political Organisation." *Man*, n.s., 7 (1): 74–94.

——. 1973a. "Two European Images of Non-European Rule." *Economy and Society* 2 (3): 263–77.

——. 1973b. Introduction to *Anthropology and the Colonial Encounter*, 9–19. London: Ithaca Press.

——. 2009. "The Idea of an Anthropology of Islam." *Qui parle* 17 (2): 1–30. First published 1986.

Austen, Jane. 2003. *Mansfield Park*. Edited by Kathryn Sutherland. London: Penguin. First published 1814.

Al-Azem, Talal. 2017. *Rule-Formulation and Binding Precedent in the Madhhab-Law Tradition: Ibn Qutlubugha's Commentary on the Compendium of Quduri*. Leiden: Brill.

Babb, Lawrence A. 1975. *The Divine Hierarchy: Popular Hinduism in Central India*. New York: Columbia University Press.

Bachelard, Gaston. 1938. *La formation de l'esprit scientifique*. Paris: Vrin.

Balandier, Georges. 1970. *Political Anthropology*. London: Penguin. First published 1967.

Barakat, Salman. 2005. *Al-Qada' al-shar'i al-Ja'fari: Ijtihadat, nusus*. Beirut: Manshurat Zayn al-Huquqiyya.

Baroin, Catherine. 1985. *Anarchie et cohésion sociale chez les Toubou: Les Daza Késerda (Niger)*. Paris: MSH.

——. 1986. "Organisation territoriale, organisation sociale: La logique du système toubou." *Journal des africanistes* 56 (2): 7–27.

——. 2009. "La circulation et les droits sur le bétail, clés de la vie sociale chez les Toubou (Tchad, Niger)." *Journal des africanistes* 78 (1–2): 120–42.

Barth, Fredrik. 1959. *Political Leadership among Swat Pathans*. London: Athlone Press.

———. 1981. *Features of the Person and Society in Swat: Collected Essays on Pathans.* London: Routledge.

Bayly, Chris. A. 1996. *Empire and Information: Intelligence Gathering and Social Communication in India, 1780–1870.* Cambridge: Cambridge University Press.

———. 2004. *The Birth of the Modern World, 1780–1914.* Oxford: Blackwell.

Beeman, William. O. 1986. *Language, Status, and Power in Iran.* Bloomington: Indiana University Press.

———. 2001. "Emotion and Sincerity in Persian Discourse: Accomplishing the Representation of Inner States." *International Journal of the Sociology of Languages* 148:31–58.

Behar, Ruth. 1996. *The Vulnerable Observer: Anthropology That Breaks Your Heart.* Boston: Beacon Press.

———. 1999. "Ethnography: Cherishing Our Second Fiddle Genre." *Journal of Contemporary Ethnography* 28 (5): 472–84.

Benthall, Jonathan. 2007. "Oxford Anthropology since 1970: Through Schismogenesis to a New Testament." In *A History of Oxford Anthropology*, edited by Peter Rivière, 155–70. Oxford: Berghahn.

Ben-Yehoyada, Naor. 2014. "Transnational Political Cosmology: A Central Mediterranean Example." *Comparative Studies Society and History* 56 (4): 870–901.

Bernard, Augustin, and Louis Milliot. 1933. "Les qânûns kabyles dans l'ouvrage de Hanoteau et Letourneux." *Revue des études islamiques* 7:1–44.

Berque, Jacques. 1953. "Problèmes initiaux de la sociologie juridique en Afrique du nord." *Studia Islamica* 1:137–62.

———. 1955. "Les sociétés nord-africaines vues du Haut-Atlas." *Cahiers internationaux de sociologie* 19:59–65.

———. 1970. "Les hilaliens repentis ou l'Algérie rurale au XVe siècle, d'après un manuscrit jurisprudentiel." *Annales: Économies, sociétés, civilisations* 25 (5): 1325–53.

———. 2001. "Qu'est-ce qu'une 'tribu' nord-africaine?" In *Opera Minora*, edited by Gianni Albergoni, 161–70. Paris: Bouchène. First published 1954.

Berry, Maya J., Claudia Chávez Argüelles, Shayna Cordis, Sarah Ihmoud, and Elizabeth Velásquez Estrada. 2017. "Toward a Fugitive Anthropology: Gender, Race and Violence in the Field." *Cultural Anthropology* 32 (4): 537–65.

Betteridge, Anne H. 1985. "Gift Exchange in Iran: The Locus of Self-Identity in Social Interaction." *Anthropological Quarterly* 58 (4): 190–202.

Bhalloo, Zahir. 2015. "Judging the Judge: Judicial Competence in 19th Century Iran." *Bulletin d'études orientales* 63:275–93.

Bhargava, Bhawani Shanker. 1949. *The Criminal Tribes: A Socio-economic Study of the Principal Criminal Tribes and Castes in Northern India.* Lucknow: Universal Publishers.

Bhāsa. 1907. *Avimāraka, Love's Enchanted World.* Edited and translated by J. L. Masson and D. D. Kosambi. Delhi: Motilal Banarsidas.

———. 1930–31. *Thirteen Trivandrum Plays by Bhāsa.* Edited and translated by S. C. Woolner and L. Sarup. 2 vols. London: Oxford University Press.

Bhattacharya, Chanchal A. 1990. *The Concept of Theft in Classical Hindu Law: An Analysis and the Idea of Punishment.* Delhi: Munshiram Manoharlal.

Bialecki, Jon. 2012. "Virtual Christianity in an Age of Nominalist Anthropology." *Anthropological Theory* 12 (3): 295–319.

Bloch, Maurice. 2008. "Truth and Sight: Generalizing without Universalizing." *Journal of the Royal Anthropological Institute* 14:522–32.

———. 2011. "The Blob." *Anthropology of This Century* 1 (May). http://aotcpress.com/articles /blob/.

Bloomfield, Maurice. 1913. "The Character and Adventures of Muladeva." *Proceedings of the American Philosophical Society* 25 (212): 616–50.

———. 1923a. "The Art of Stealing in Hindu Fiction." *American Journal of Philology* 44 (2): 97–133.

———. 1923b. "The Art of Stealing in Hindu Fiction, Part II." *American Journal of Philology* 44 (3): 193–229.

———. 1926. "On Organized Brigandage in Hindu Fiction." *American Journal of Philology* 47 (3): 205–33.

Bourdieu, Pierre. 1965. "The Sentiment of Honour in Kabyle Society." In *Honour and Shame: The Values of Mediterranean Society*, edited by J. G. Peristiany, 191–241. London: Weidenfeld and Nicolson.

———. 1977. *Outline of a Theory of Practice.* Cambridge: Cambridge University Press.

———. 1996. *The Rules of Art: Genesis and Structure of the Literary Field.* Cambridge: Polity Press.

Bousquet, Henri. 1950. "Un culte à détruire: L'adoration de Hanoteau et Letourneux." *Revue de la Méditerranée* 8–9:441–54.

Brands, Henry W. 1993 *The Devil We Knew: Americans and the Cold War.* Oxford: Oxford University Press.

Braudel, Fernand. 1986. *L'identité de la France: Espace et histoire.* Paris: Arthaud-Flammarion.

Bray, Julia. 2010. "Literary Approaches to Medieval and Early Modern Arabic Biography." *Journal of the Royal Asiatic Society* 20 (3): 237–53.

Bromberger, Christian. 2006. "Towards an Anthropology of the Mediterranean." *History and Anthropology* 17 (2): 91–107.

Brookshaw, Dominic P. 2005. "Odes of a Poet-Princess: The Ghazals of Jahān-Malik Khātūn." *Iran* 43:173–95.

———. 2013. "Women in Praise of Women: Female Poets and Female Patrons in Qajar Iran." *Iranian Studies* 46 (1): 17–48.

———. 2014. "Qajar Confection: The Production and Dissemination of Women's Poetry in Early Nineteenth-Century Iran." *Middle Eastern Literatures* 17 (2): 113–16.

Buckingham, James. 1825. *Travels among the Arab Tribes Inhabiting the Countries East of Syria and Palestine.* London: Longman, Hurst, Rees, Orme, Brown, and Green.

Buijtenhuijs, Robert. 2001. "The Chadian Tubu: Contemporary Nomads Who Conquered a State." *Africa* 71 (1): 149–61.

Burckhardt, John. 1822. *Travels in Syria and the Holy Land.* London: John Murray.

Busby, Cecilia. 1997. "Permeable and Partible Persons: A Comparative Analysis of Gender and Body in South India and Melanesia." *Journal of the Royal Anthropological Institute* 3 (2): 261–78.

Candea, Mattei. 2007. "Arbitrary Locations: In Defence of the Bounded Field-Site." *Journal of the Royal Anthropological Institute* 13 (1): 167–84.

Canetti, Elias. 1962. *Crowds and Power.* Translated by Carol Stewart. New York: Farrar, Straus and Giroux.

Caplan, Patricia. 1969. "Cognatic Descent Groups on Mafia Island, Tanzania." *Man,* n.s., 4 (3): 419–31.

Carstairs, G. Morris. 1957. *The Twice-Born.* London: Hogarth Press.

Casares, Aurelia. 2004. "Domestic Service in Spain: Legislation, Gender and Social Practice." In *Domestic Service and the Formation of European Identity: Understanding the Globalization of Domestic Work, 16th–21st Centuries*, edited by Antoinette Fauve-Chamoux, 189–209. Bern: Peter Lang.

Caton, Steven. 1999. "Anger Be Now Thy Song: The Anthropology of an Event." Princeton: Institute for Advanced Study Occasional Papers, no. 5.

Census of India Report. 2001. Indian Census Commission.

Chapelle, Jean. 1957. *Nomades noirs du Sahara: Les Toubous*. Paris: Plon.

Chapman, Malcolm. 1989. Introduction to *The Voice of Prophecy*, by E. Ardener, xv–xxxvi. Oxford: Basil Blackwell.

Chatterjee, Partha. 1993. *The Nation and Its Fragments. Colonial and Post-colonial Histories*. Princeton: Princeton University Press.

Chatterjee, S. 2007. "Disruptions Have Become a Disease." *Times of India*, September 10, 2007, 4.

Clarke, Morgan. 2008. "New Kinship, Islam, and the Liberal Tradition: Sexual Morality and New Reproductive Technology in Lebanon." *Journal of the Royal Anthropological Institute* 14 (1): 153–69.

———. 2010. "Neo-calligraphy: Religious Authority and Media Technology in Contemporary Shiite Islam." *Comparative Studies in Society and History* 52 (2): 351–83.

———. 2012. "The Judge as Tragic Hero: Judicial Ethics in Lebanon's Shariʿa Courts." *American Ethnologist* 39 (1): 106–21.

———. 2014. "Cough Sweets and Angels: The Ordinary Ethics of the Extraordinary in Sufi Practice in Lebanon." *Journal of the Royal Anthropological Institute* 20 (3): 407–25.

———. 2018. *Islam and Law in Lebanon: Sharia within and without the State*. Cambridge: Cambridge University Press.

Clastres, Pierre. 1977. *Society against the State*. Oxford: Blackwell. First published 1974.

Clifford, James. 1986. "On Ethnographic Self-Fashioning: Conrad and Malinowski." In *Reconstructing Individualism: Autonomy, Individuality, and the Self in Western Thought*, edited by Thomas C. Heller, Morton Sosna, and David E. Wellerby, 140–62. Stanford: Stanford University Press.

———. 2012. "Feeling Historical." *Cultural Anthropology* 27 (3): 417–26.

Clifford, James, and George E. Marcus, eds. 1986. *Writing Culture: The Poetics and Politics of Ethnography*. Berkeley: University of California Press.

Cohen, Mark. 2003. "The Foreign Jewish Poor in Medieval Egypt." In *Poverty and Charity in Middle Eastern Contexts*, edited by Michael Bonner, Mine Ener and Amy Singer, 53–72. Albany: State University of New York Press.

Cohen, Ronald and John Middleton, eds. 1967. *Comparative Political Systems: Studies in the Politics of Pre-industrial Societies*. Garden City, NY: American Museum of Natural History.

Cohn, Bernard S. 1996. *Colonialism and Its Forms of Knowledge: The British in India*. Princeton: Princeton University Press.

Collingwood, R. G. 1946. *The Idea of History*. Oxford: Clarendon Press.

Collins, Samuel Gerald, Matthew Durington, and Harjant Gill. 2017. "Multimodality: An Invitation." *American Anthropologist* 119 (1): 1–5.

Collins, Steven. 1985. "Categories, Concepts or Predicaments? Remarks on Mauss's Use of Philosophical Terminology." In *The Category of the Person: Anthropology, Philosophy, History*, edited by M. Carrithers, S. Collins, and S. Lukes, 46–82. Cambridge: Cambridge University Press.

Conder, Claude Reignier. 1881. Eastern Survey, Conder Documents, Collections of the Palestine Exploration Fund, PEF/ES/CON/3a, 8a, and 22b, London.

———. 1883. *Heth and Moab: Explorations in Syria in 1881 and 1882.* London: Richard Bentley and Son.

———. 1889. *The Survey of Eastern Palestine: Memoirs of the Topography, Orography, Hydrography, Archaeology, Etc.* Vol. 1, *The ʿAdwan Country.* London: Committee of the Palestine Exploration Fund.

Cooke, Miriam. 2014. *Tribal Modern: Branding New Nations in the Arab Gulf.* Berkeley: University of California Press.

Crawford, David, 2008. *Moroccan Households in the World Economy: Labour and Inequality in a Berber Village.* Baton Rouge: Louisiana State University Press.

da Col, Giovanni, and David Graeber. 2011. "Foreword: The Return of Ethnographic Theory." *HAU: Journal of Ethnographic Theory* 1 (1): vi–xxxv.

Daṇḍin. 1966. *Daśakumāracarita of Daṇḍin.* Edited and translated by M. R. Kale. Delhi: Motilal Banarsidas.

Das, Veena. 1996. *Critical Events: An Anthropological Perspective on Contemporary India.* Delhi: Oxford University Press.

Das, Veena, and Deborah Poole. 2004. "State and Its Margins. Comparative Ethnographies." In *Anthropology in the Margins of the State*, 3–33. Santa Fe: School of American Research Press.

Daumas, Eugène. 1864. *Mœurs et coutumes de l'Algérie: Tell, Kabylie, Sahara.* Paris: Hachette.

Davids, Tine. 2014. "Trying to Be a Vulnerable Observer: Matters of Agency, Solidarity and Hospitality on Feminist Ethnography." *Women's Studies International Forum* 43:50–58.

Davis, Susan Schaefer. 1983. *Patience and Power: Women's Lives in a Moroccan Village.* Cambridge, MA: Schenkman.

Deeb, Lara. 2006. *An Enchanted Modern: Gender and Public Piety in Shiʿi Lebanon.* Princeton: Princeton University Press.

Deeb, Lara, and Mona Harb. 2013. *Leisurely Islam: Negotiating Geography and Morality in Shiʿite South Beirut.* Princeton: Princeton University Press.

Deeb, Lara, and Jessica Winegar. 2012. "Anthropologies of Arab-Majority Societies." *Annual Review of Anthropology* 41:537–58.

———. 2016. *Anthropology's Politics: Disciplining the Middle East.* Stanford: Stanford University Press.

Defense Industry Daily. 2016. "All Over Again: Egypt Looks beyond the USA for New Arms." April 7, 2016.

Descola, Philippe. 1988. "La chefferie amérindienne dans l'anthropologie politique." *Revue française de science politique* 38 (5): 818–27.

———. 2005. *Par delà nature et culture.* Paris: Gallimard.

de Wilde, Roeland. 2009. "Opium Poppy Husk Traders in Rajasthan: The Lives and Work of Businessmen in the Contemporary Indian Opium Industry." PhD thesis, London School of Economic and Political Science.

Dirks, Nicholas B. 2001. *Castes of Mind: Colonialism and the Making of Modern India.* Princeton: Princeton University Press.

Doeringer, Peter B., Philip I. Moss, and David G. Terkla. 1986. "Capitalism and Kinship: Do Institutions Matter in the Labor Market?" *Industrial and Labor Relations Review* 40:48–60.

Dole, Christopher. 2012. "Revolution, Occupation, and Love: The 2011 Year in Cultural Anthropology." *American Anthropologist* 114 (2): 227–39.

Dornfeld, Barry. 1998. *Producing Public Television, Producing Public Culture.* Princeton: Princeton University Press.

D'Oro, Guiseppina, and James Connelly. 2015. "Robin George Collingwood." In *Stanford Encyclopedia of Philosophy.* https://plato.stanford.edu/archives/sum2015/entries/collingwood.

Dresch, Paul. 1976. "Economy and Ideology: An Obstacle in Materialist Analysis." *Journal of the Anthropological Society of Oxford* 3 (2): 55–77.

———. 1984. "The Position of Shaykhs among the Northern Tribes of Yemen." *Man* 19 (1): 31–49.

———. 1986. "The Significance of the Course Events Take in Segmentary Systems." *American Ethnologist* 13:309–24.

———. 1987. "Episodes in a Dispute between Yemeni Tribes: Text and Translation of a Colloquial Arabic Document." *Der Islam* 64 (1): 68–86.

———. 1988. "Segmentation: Its Roots in Arabia and Its Flowering Elsewhere." *Cultural Anthropology* 3 (1): 50–67.

———. 1989. *Tribes, Government, and History in Yemen.* Oxford: Clarendon Press.

———. 1990. "Imams and Tribes: The Writing and Acting of History in Upper Yemen." In *Tribes and State Formation in the Middle East*, edited by Philip Khoury and Joseph Kostiner, 252–87. Berkeley: University of California Press.

———. 1992. "Ethnography and General Theory or People versus Humankind." *Journal of the Anthropological Society of Oxford* 23:17–36.

———. 1995. "Race, Culture and—What? Pluralist Certainties in the United States." In *The Pursuit of Certainty: Religious and Cultural Formulations*, edited by Wendy James, 61–91. London: Routledge.

———. 1998. "Mutual Deception: Totality, Exchange and Islam in the Middle East." In *Marcel Mauss: A Centenary Tribute*, edited by Nick Allen and Wendy James, 111–33. Oxford: Berghahn.

———. 2000a. "A Wilderness of Mirrors: Truth and Vulnerability in Middle Eastern Fieldwork." In *Anthropologists in a Wider World: Essays on Field Research*, edited by Paul Dresch, Wendy James, and David Parkin, 111–25. Oxford: Berghahn.

———. 2000b. *A History of Modern Yemen.* Cambridge: Cambridge University Press.

———. 2003. "A Pact of Brotherhood from Sufyân (North Yemen)." *Chroniques Yéménites* 10:49–59.

———. 2005. "Debates on Marriage and Nationality in the United Arab Emirates." In *Monarchies and Nations: Globalisation and Identity in the Arab States of the Gulf*, edited by Paul Dresch and James Piscatori, 136–57. London: I.B. Tauris.

———. 2006a. "Foreign Matter: The Place of Strangers in Gulf Society." In *Globalization and the Gulf*, edited by John Fox et al., 200–22. London: Routledge.

———. 2006b. *The Rules of Barat: Tribal Documents from Yemen.* San'â': Centre Français d'Archéologie et de Sciences Sociales.

———. 2009. "Les mots et les choses: L'identité tribale en Arabie." *Études rurales* 184:185–201.

———. 2012a. "Legalism, Anthropology, and History: A View from Part of Anthropology." In *Legalism: Anthropology and History*, edited by Paul Dresch and Hannah Skoda, 1–37. Oxford: Oxford University Press.

———. 2012b. "Aspects of Non-State Law: Early Yemen and Perpetual Peace." In *Legalism: Anthropology and History*, edited by Paul Dresch and Hannah Skoda, 145–72. Oxford: Oxford University Press.

———. 2014. "Outlawry, Exile and Banishment." In *Legalism: Community and Justice*, edited by Fernanda Pirie and Judith Scheele, 97–124. Oxford: Oxford University Press.

———. 2015. "Written Law as Words to Live By." In *Legalism: Rules and Categories*, edited by Paul Dresch and Judith Scheele, 53–78. Oxford: Oxford University Press.

Dresch, Paul, and Wendy James. 2000. "Introduction: Fieldwork and the Passage of Time." In *Anthropologists in a Wider World: Essays on Field Research*, edited by Paul Dresch, Wendy James, and David Parkin, 1–26. Oxford: Berghahn.

Dresch, Paul, and Judith Scheele. 2015. "Rules and Categories: An Overview." In *Legalism: Rules and Categories*, 1–27. Oxford: Oxford University Press.

Dudney, Arthur D. 2013. "A Desire for Meaning: Khān-i Ārzū's Philology and the Place of India in the Eighteenth-Century Persianate World." Unpublished PhD dissertation, Columbia University.

Dumont, Louis. 1964. *La civilisation indienne et nous: Esquisse de sociologie comparée*. Paris: Armand Colin.

———. 1970. *Homo hierarchicus: The Caste System and Its Implications*. Chicago: Chicago University Press. First published 1966.

———. 1986. *Essays on Individualism: Modern Ideology in Anthropological Perspective*. Chicago: University of Chicago Press.

Dupret, Baudouin. 2007. "What Is Islamic Law? A Praxiological Answer and an Egyptian Case Study." *Theory, Culture and Society* 24 (2): 79–100.

———. 2016. *Adjudication in Action: An Ethnomethodology of Law, Morality and Justice*. Translated by Pascale Ghazaleh. Abingdon: Routledge. First published 2011.

Dupret, Baudouin, and Maaike Voorhoeve. 2016. Introduction to *Family Law in Islam: Divorce, Marriage and Women in the Muslim World*, edited by Maaike Voorhoeve, 1–10. London: I.B. Tauris.

Durkheim, Émile. 1991. *Les formes élémentaires de la vie religieuse*. Paris: Livre de Poche. First published 1912.

Durkheim, Émile, and Marcel Mauss. 1903. "De quelques formes primitives de classification." *Année sociologique* 6:1–72.

Early, Evelyn. 1993. "Getting It Together: Baladi Egyptian Business Women." In *Arab Women: Old Boundaries, New Frontiers*, edited by J. Tucker, 84–100. Bloomington: Indiana University Press.

Ehrenreich, Barbara. 2010. *Nickel and Dimed: Undercover in Low-Wage USA*. London: Granta.

Elliott, Henry M. 1859. *Memoirs on the History, Folk-Lore, and Distribution of the Races of the North Western Provinces of India*. London: Trübner.

Ennaji, Mohammed. 1999. *Serving the Master: Slavery and Society in Nineteenth-Century Morocco*. Translated by Seth Graebner. Basingstoke: Macmillan Press.

Etienne, J. 1951. "La vie et les sentiments d'une famille marocaine à Casablanca." In *L'évolution sociale du Maroc*, 5–51. Cahiers de l'Afrique et l'Asie 1. Paris: Peyronnet.

Evans, Anya. 2017. "The Ethnographer's Body Is Gendered." *The New Ethnographer*, February 14, 2017. https://thenewethnographer.org/2017/02/14/gendered-bodies-2/.

Evans-Pritchard, Edward E. 1937. *Witchcraft, Oracles and Magic among the Azande*. Oxford: Clarendon Press.

——. 1951. *Social Anthropology*. London: Cohen & West.

——. 1962. *Essays in Social Anthropology*. London: Faber and Faber.

——. 1973. "Some Reminiscences and Reflections on Fieldwork." *Journal of the Anthropological Society of Oxford* 4 (2): 1–12.

Fabian, Johannes. 1983. *Time and the Other: How Anthropology Makes Its Object*. New York: Columbia University Press.

Fardon, Richard, ed. 1990. *Localizing Strategies: Regional Traditions of Ethnographic Writing*. Edinburgh: Scottish Academic Press.

Faruq, Ahmad. 2015. "20 Fananan Yurafiquna al-Sisi fi Ziyaratuh li-Almanya Dimna Wafd Shaʿbi." *Al-Shuruq*, June 1, 2015. Accessed August 13, 2016. http://www.shorouknews .com/news/view.aspx?cdate=01062015&id=c400e8ef-b56d-4e27-a813-98be420fcb6c.

Fassin, Didier. 2014a. "The Ethical Turn in Anthropology: Promises and Uncertainties." *HAU: Journal of Ethnographic Theory* 4 (1): 429–35.

——. 2014b. "True Life, Real Lives: Revisiting the Boundaries between Ethnography and Fiction." *American Ethnologist* 41 (1): 40–55.

Faubion, J. 2001. "Toward an Anthropology of Ethics: Foucault and the Pedagogies of Autopoesis." *Representations* 74:83–104.

Fenster, Mark C. 2008. *Conspiracy Theories: Secrecy and Power in the American Culture*. Minneapolis: University of Minnesota Press.

Ferguson, James. 1999. *Expectations of Modernity. Myths and Meanings of Urban Life in the Zambian Copperbelt*. Berkeley: University of California Press.

Ferguson, James, and Akhil Gupta. 2002. "Spatializing States: Towards an Ethnography of Neoliberal Governmentality." *American Ethnologist* 29 (4): 981–1002.

Fernea, Robert and James Malarkey. 1975. "Anthropology of the Middle East and North Africa: A Critical Assessment." *Annual Review of Anthropology* 4:183–206.

Finn, James. 1868. *Byeways in Palestine*. London: James Nisbet.

Forge, Anthony. 1967. "The Lonely Anthropologist." *New Society*, August 18, 1967, 221–23.

Forlenza, Rosario, and Bjørn Thomassen. 2016. "Decoding Donald Trump: The Triumph of Trickster Politics." *Public Seminar*, April 28, 2016.

Freed, Ruth S. and Stanley A. Freed. 1964. "Spirit Possession as Illness in a North Indian Village." *Ethnology* 3 (2): 152–71.

Freitag, Sandria. 1998. "*Sansiahs* and the State: The Changing Nature of 'Crime' and 'Justice' in Nineteenth-Century British India." In *Changing Concepts of Rights and Justice in South Asia*, edited by M. Anderson and S. Guha, 82–113. Delhi: Oxford University Press.

Fremlin, Celia. 1940. *The Seven Chars of Chelsea*. London: Methuen.

Friedman, Jonathan. 1979. *System, Structure and Contradiction in the Evolution of "Asiatic" Social Formations*. Copenhagen: National Museum of Denmark.

Fuller, Chris J. 1992. *The Camphor Flame: Popular Hinduism and Society in India*. Princeton: Princeton University Press.

Fuller, Chris J., and John Harriss. 2001. "For an Anthropology of the Modern Indian State." In *The Everyday State and Society in Modern India*, edited by C. J. Fuller and V. Bénéï, 1–30. London: Hurst.

Gabiam, Nell. 2016. *The Politics of Suffering: Syria's Palestinian Refugee Camps*. Bloomington: Indiana University Press.

Gahlouz, Mustapha. 2011. *Les qanouns kabyles: Anthropologie juridique du groupement social villageois de Kabylie*. Paris: L'Harmattan.

Galal, Nadir. 1984. *Wahda bi-Wahda* (film). Cairo.

Gallagher, Sally K. 2012. *Making Do in Damascus: Navigating a Generation of Change in Family and Work*. Syracuse: Syracuse University Press.

Gambetta, Diego. 1996. *The Sicilian Mafia: The Business of Private Protection*. Cambridge, MA: Harvard University Press.

Gandhi, Malli. 2008. *Denotified Tribes: Dimensions of Change*. New Delhi: Kanishka Publishers Distributors.

Garfinkel, Harold. 1984. *Studies in Ethnomethodology*. Oxford: Basil Blackwell. First published 1967.

Garg, R. P. 1965. *Dacoit Problem in Chambal Valley: A Sociological Study*. Varanasi: Gandhian Institute of Studies.

Geertz, Clifford. 1967. "Under the Mosquito Net." *New York Review of Books*, September 14, 1967, 12–13.

———. 1984. "'From the Natives' Point of View': On the Nature of Anthropological Understanding." In *Culture Theory*, edited by Richard A. Shweder and Robert A. LeVine, 123–36. Cambridge: Cambridge University Press. First published 1974.

———. 1988. "I-Witnessing: Malinowski's Children." In *Works and Lives: The Anthropologist as Author*, 73–101. Stanford: Stanford University Press.

Gell, Alfred. 1998. *Art and Agency: An Anthropological Theory*. Oxford: Oxford University Press.

———. 2011. "On Love." *Anthropology of This Century* 2. http://aotcpress.com/articles/love/.

Ghamroun, Samer. 2013. "La communauté sunnite libanaise saisie par les femmes." In *Normes religieuses et genre*, edited by Florence Rochefort and Maria Sanna, 203–15. Paris: Armand Colin.

Giddens, Anthony. 1991. *Modernity and Self-Identity: Self and Society in the Late Modern Age*. Stanford: Stanford University Press.

Gilsenan, Michael. 1976. "Lying, Honor and Contradiction." In *Transaction and Meaning: Directions in the Anthropology of Exchange and Symbolic Behavior*, edited by Bruce Kapferer, 191–219. Philadelphia: Institute for the Study of Human Issues.

———. 1982. *Recognizing Islam: An Anthropologist's Introduction*. London: Croom Helm.

Ginsberg, Faye. 2005. "Media Anthropology: An Introduction." In *Media Anthropology*, edited by Eric W. Rothenbuhler and Mihai Coman, 17–21. Thousand Oaks: Sage.

Gleave, Robert. 2003. "Political Aspects of Modern Shi'i Legal Discussions: Khumayni and Khu'i on *Ijtihad* and *Qada'*." In *Shaping the Current Islamic Reformation*, edited by B. Roberson, 96–116. London: Frank Cass.

Glucklich, Ariel. 1994. *The Sense of Adharma*. New York: Oxford University Press.

Goffman, Erving. 1959. *The Presentation of Self in Everyday Life*. New York: Doubleday.

Gofman, Alexander. 1998. "A Vague but Suggestive Concept: The 'Total Social Fact'." In *Marcel Mauss: A Centenary Tribute*, edited by Nick Allen and Wendy James, 63–70. Oxford: Berghahn.

Goichon, Amélie Marie. 1929. *La femme de la moyenne bourgeoisie Fāsīya*. Paris: P. Geuthner.

Gordon, Stewart N. 1969. "Scarf and Sword: Thugs, Marauders, and State-Formation in 18th Century Malwa." *Indian Economic and Social History Review* 6 (4): 416–29.

———. 1985. "Bhils and the Idea of a Criminal Tribe in Nineteenth Century India." In *Crime and Criminality in British India*, edited by A. A. Young, 128–39. Tucson, Arizona: University of Arizona Press.

Gow, Peter. 2001. *An Amazonian Myth and Its History*. Oxford: Oxford University Press.

Graeber, David. 2004. *Fragments of an Anarchist Anthropology*. Chicago: Prickly Paradigm Press.

———. 2014. "Anthropology and the Rise of the Professional-Managerial Class." *HAU: Journal of Ethnographic Theory* 4 (3): 73–88.

———. 2015. "Radical Alterity Is Just Another Way of Saying 'Reality.'" *HAU: Journal of Ethnographic Theory* 5 (2): 1–41.

Graham, Sandra Lauderdale. 1988. *House and Street: The Domestic World of Servants in Nineteenth-Century Rio de Janeiro*. Cambridge: Cambridge University Press.

Grandguillaume, Gilbert. 1975. "Le droit de l'eau dans les Foggara du Touat au XVIIIᵉ siècle." *Revue des études islamiques* 43 (2): 287–322.

Greene, Graham. 1955. *The Quiet American*. London: W. Heinemann.

———. 1958. *Our Man in Havana*. London: Heinemann Educational Books.

Gudeman, Stephen, 2001. *The Anthropology of Economy*. Oxford: Blackwell.

Guha, Sumit. 1999. *Environment and Ethnicity in India, 1200–1991*. Cambridge: Cambridge University Press.

Guillet, David. 1980. "Reciprocal Labor and Peripheral Capitalism in the Central Andes." *Ethnology* 19 (2): 151–67.

Gupta, Aradhana and Akhil Sharma, eds. 2006. *The Anthropology of the State: A Reader*. Oxford: Blackwell.

Gupta, Dipankar. 1997. *Rivalry and Brotherhood: Politics in the Life of Farmers in Northern India*. Delhi: Oxford University Press.

Gusterson, Hugh. 1997. "Studying Up Revisited." *POLAR: Political and Legal Anthropology Review* 20 (1): 114–19.

Gutelius, David. 2002. "'The Path Is Easy and the Benefits Large: The Nasiriyya, Social Networks and Economic Change in Morocco, 1640–1830." *Journal of African History* 43:27–49.

Haëdo, Diego de. 1998. *Topographie et histoire générale d'Alger*. Paris: Bouchène. First published 1612.

Hall, Bruce. 2013. "Saharan Commerce and Islamic Law: The Question of Usury (*Ribâ*) in the *Nawâzil* Literature of Mali and Mauritania, 1700–1929." *African Economic History* 41:1–18.

Hallaq, Wael. 2009. *Sharī'a: Theory, Practice, Transformations*. Cambridge: Cambridge University Press.

———. 2013. *The Impossible State: Islam, Politics, and Modernity's Moral Predicament*. New York: Columbia University Press.

Hammoudi, Abdallah. 1980. "Sainteté, pouvoir et société: Tamgrout aux XVIIᵉ et XVIIIᵉ siècles." *Annales: Économies, sociétés, civilisations* 35 (3–4): 615–841.

Hann, Chris. 2008. "Reproduction and Inheritance: Goody Revisited." *Annual Review of Anthropology* 37:145–58.

Hannemann, Tilman. 2002. "Recht und Religion in der Grossen Kabylei (18./19. Jahrhundert): Zu rechtskuturellen Wandlungsprozessen des tribalen Gewohnheitsrecht." PhD thesis, University of Bremen.

———. 2005. "Gewohnheitsrecht in einer islamischen Rechtsumgebung: Theoretische Vergleichsperspectiven aus der Grossen Kabylei." In *Rechtspluralismus in der islamischen Welt: Gewohnheitsrecht zwischen Staat and Gesellschaft*, edited by M. Kemper and M. Reinkowski, 47–66. Berlin: Walter de Gruyter.

Hannerz, Ulf. 2010. "Field Worries: Studying Down, Up, Sideways, Through, Backward, Forward, Early or Later, Away and at Home." In *Anthropology's World: Life in a Twenty-First-Century Discipline*, 59–86. London: Pluto.

Hanoteau, Adolphe and Aristide Letourneux. 1872–73. *La Kabylie et les coutumes kabyles*. 3 vols. Paris: Challamel.

Haqqani, Husain. 2005. *Pakistan: Between Mosque and Military*. Lahore: Vanguard Books.

Harris, Marvin. 1967. Review of *Diary in the Strict Sense of the Term*, by Bronisław Malinowski. *Natural History* 76:72–74.

Hasan, Samah, Salwa al-Zughbi, Muhammad Magdi, and Muhammad Shanah. 2014. "Tasrihat 'Isam Higgi lil-Watan haula Ikhtira' al-Jaysh." *Al-Watan*, February 26, 2014.

Hastrup, Kirsten. 2007. "Ultimate Thule: Anthropology and the Call of the Unknown." *Journal of the Royal Anthropological Institute* 13 (4): 789–804.

Haywood, Eliza. 1743. *Present for a Servant-Maid, or The Sure Means of Gaining Love and Esteem*. London: T. Gardner.

Hemavijaya. 1920. *Katharatnakara. Das Märchenmeer. Eine Sammlung Indischer Erzählungen von Hemavijaya*. Edited and translated by J. Hertel. München: Georg Müller.

Henig, David. 2012. "'Knocking on My Neighbour's Door': On Metamorphoses of Sociality in Rural Bosnia." *Critique of Anthropology* 32:3–19.

Hertz, Robert. 1909. "La prééminence de la main droite: Étude sur la polarité religieuse." *Revue philosophique de la France et de l'étranger* 68:553–80.

Herzfeld, Michael. 1987. *Anthropology through the Looking Glass: Critical Ethnography in the Margins of Europe*. Cambridge: Cambridge University Press.

———. 1990. "Icons and Identity: Religious Orthodoxy and Social Practice in Rural Crete." *Anthropological Quarterly* 63 (3): 109–21.

———. 2005. *Cultural Intimacy: Social Poetics in the Nation-State*. New York: Routledge. First published 1997.

Hexter, Jack H. 1961. *Reappraisals in History: New Views on History and Society in Early Modern Europe*. New York: Harper and Row.

Hill, Bridget. 1996. *Servants: English Domestics in the Eighteenth Century*. Oxford: Clarendon Press.

Hirschkind, Charles. 2006. *The Ethical Soundscape: Cassette Sermons and Islamic Counter-publics in Egypt*. New York: Columbia University Press.

Ho, Engseng. 2004. "Empire through Diasporic Eyes: A View from the Other Boat." *Comparative Studies in Society and History* 46 (2): 210–46.

Ho, Karen. 2009. *Liquidated: An Ethnography of Wall Street*. Durham: Duke University Press.

Hobsbawm, Eric, and Terence Ranger, eds. 1983. *The Invention of Tradition*. Cambridge: Cambridge University Press.

Hoffman, Katherine, and Susan G. Miller. 2010. Introduction to *Berbers and Others: Beyond Tribe and Nation in the Maghreb*, 1–12. Bloomington: Indiana University Press.

Hofstadter, Richard. 1996. *The Paranoid Style in American Politics*. Cambridge, MA: Harvard University Press. First published 1965.

Hogbin, Ian. 1968. Review of *A Diary in the Strict Sense of the Term*, by Bronislaw Malinowski. *American Anthropologist* 70 (3): 575.

Hondagneu-Sotelo, Pierrette. 2003. "Blowups and Other Unhappy Endings." In *Global Woman: Nannies, Maids and Sex Workers in the New Economy*, edited by B. Ehrenreich and A. Hochschild, 55–69. London: Granta Books.

Horn, Pamela. 2004. *Flunkeys and Scullions: Life below Stairs in Georgian England*. Stroud: Sutton Publishing.

Hornemann, Friedrich. 1802. *Voyages dans l'intérieur de l'Afrique*. Paris: André.

Horvath, Agnes. 2013. *Modernism and Charisma*. Basingstoke: Palgrave Macmillan.

Howell, Signe. 2011. "Whatever Happened to the Spirit of Adventure?" In *The End of Anthropology?*, edited by J. Holger and K.-H. Kohl, 139–54 Wantage: Sean Kingston.

HRW (Human Rights Watch). 2015. *Unequal and Unprotected: Women's Rights under Lebanon's Religious Personal Status Laws*. Online publication. Accessed November 10, 2016. https://www.hrw.org/sites/default/files/reports/lebanon0115_ForUpload.pdf.

Hsu, Francis L. K. 1979. "The Cultural Problem of the Cultural Anthropologist." *American Anthropologist* 81 (3): 517–32.

Huang, Mingwei. 2016. "Vulnerable Observers: Notes on Fieldwork and Rape." *The Chronical of Higher Education*, October 12, 2016. http://www.chronicle.com/article/Vulnerable-Observers-Notes-on/238042.

Hugh-Jones, Stephen. 2008. "A Courtship but Not Much of a Marriage: Lévi-Strauss and British Americanist Anthropology." *Journal de la société des américanistes* 94 (2): 17–27.

Inhorn, Marcia. 2014. "Roads Less Traveled in Middle East Anthropology—and New Paths in Gender Ethnography." *Journal of Middle East Women's Studies* 10 (3): 62–86.

Iqtidar, Humeira. 2012. *Secularizing Islamists? Jama'at-e-Islami and Jama'at-ud-Da'wa in Urban Pakistan*. Chicago: University of Chicago Press.

———. 2014. "Conspiracy Theories as Political Imaginary: Blackwater in Pakistan." *Political Studies* 64 (1): 200–215. doi:10.1111/1467-9248.12157.

Ivy, Marilyn. 1995. *Discourses of the Vanishing: Modernity, Phantasm, Japan*. Chicago: University of Chicago Press.

Jalal, Ayesha. 2008. *The Partisans of Allah: Jihad in South Asia*. Lahore: Sang-e-Meel Publications.

James, Wendy. 1973. "The Anthropologist as Reluctant Imperialist." In *Anthropology and the Colonial Encounter*, edited by T. Asad, 41–69. London: Ithaca Press.

Jātaka Stories, or Stories of the Buddha's Former Births. 1895. Edited by E. B. Cowell. Translated by R. Chalmers. 6 vols. Cambridge: Cambridge University Press.

Jenkins, Timothy. 1994. "Fieldwork and the Perception of Everyday Life." *Man*, n.s., 29:433–55.

———. 1999. *Religion in English Everyday Life: An Ethnographic Approach*. Oxford: Berghahn Books.

———. 2010. *The Life of Property: House, Family and Inheritance in Béarn, South-west France*. Oxford: Berghahn Books.

———. n.d. "Why Anthropology? Structuralism and Since." Unpublished manuscript.

Johansen, Baber. 1997. "Formes de langages et fonctions publiques: Stereotypes, témoins et offices dans la preuve par l'écrit en droit musulman." *Arabica* 44:333–76.

———. 1999. "Introduction: The Muslim *fiqh* as a Sacred Law. Religion, Law and Ethics in a Normative System." In *Contingency in a Sacred Law: Legal and Ethical Norms in the Muslim Fiqh*, 1–76. Leiden: Brill.

Johnson, Alix. 2017. "Violence and Vulnerability in Anthropology." *Allegralab.net*, October 5, 2017. http://allegralaboratory.net/violence-vulnerability-anthropology/.

Johnson, H. M. 1920. "Rāuhineya's Adventures, the *Rāuhineyacarita*." In *Studies in Honor of Maurice Bloomfield*, 159–96. New Haven: Yale University Press.

Johnson, Paul C. 2002. *Secrets, Gossip, and Gods: The Transformation of Brazilian Condomblé*. New York: Oxford University Press.

Joseph, Suad. 1994. "Brother/Sister Relationships: Connectivity, Love, and Power in the Reproduction of Patriarchy in Lebanon." *American Ethnologist* 21 (1): 50–73.

———. 1996. "Patriarchy and Development in the Arab World." *Gender and Development* 4 (2): 14–19.

———. 2015. "Theory and Thematics in the Anthropology of the Middle East." In *A Companion to the Anthropology of the Middle East,* edited by S. Altorki, 15–49. Oxford: Blackwell.

Kanna, Ahmed. 2011. *Dubai: The City as Corporation.* Minneapolis: University of Minnesota Press.

Kastrinou, A. Maria. 2016. *Power, Sect and State in Syria: The Politics of Marriage and Identity amongst the Druze.* London: I. B. Tauris.

Kasturi, Malavika. 2002. *Embattled Identities: Rajput Lineages and the Colonial State in Nineteenth-Century North India.* Delhi: Oxford University Press.

Kautilya. 1967. *The Kauṭilīya Arthaśāstra.* Edited and translated by Sharma Sastri, Rudrapatna. Mysore: Mysore Printing and Publishing House. Written c. 4th–3rd centuries BCE.

Kelly, John, and Martha Kaplan. 1990. "History, Structure, and Ritual." *Annual Review of Anthropology* 19:119–50.

Kia, Mana. 2014. "Adab as Literary Form and Social Conduct: Reading the Gulistan in Late Mughal India." In *"No Tapping around Philology": A Festschrift in Celebration and Honor of Wheeler McIntosh Thackston Jr.'s 70th Birthday,* edited by Alireza Korangy and Daniel J. Sheffield, 281–308. Wiesbaden: Harrassowitz.

Kolff, Dirk H. A. 1990. *Naukar, Rajput and Sepoy: The Ethnohistory of the Military Labour Market in Hindustan, 1450–1850.* Cambridge: Cambridge University Press.

Kracke, Waud. 1987. "Encounter with Other Cultures: Psychological and Epistemological Aspects." *Ethos* 15 (1): 58–81.

Laidlaw, James. 2013. *The Subject of Virtue: An Anthropology of Ethics and Freedom.* Cambridge: Cambridge University Press.

Lamond, Grant. 2007. "What Is a Crime?" *Oxford Journal of Legal Studies* 27 (4): 609–32.

Lansdown, Richard. 2014. "Crucible or Centrifuge? Bronislaw Malinowski's *A Diary in the Strict Sense of the Term.*" *Configurations* 22:29–55.

Laslett, Peter. 1965. *The World We Have Lost.* London: Methuen.

Latour, Bruno. 1988. *The Pasteurization of France.* Cambridge, MA: Harvard University Press.

Layish, Aharon. 2006. "Interplay between Tribal and *Sharʿī* Law: A Case of Tibbawî Blood Money in the Sharīʿa Court of Kufra." *Islamic Law and Society* 13 (1): 63–75.

Le Cœur, Charles. 1950. *Dictionnaire ethnographique téda: Précédé d'un lexique français-téda.* Paris: Larose.

———. 1953. "Le système des clans au Tibesti." In *In Memoriam Charles Le Cœur,* 11–16. Niamey: IFAN.

Le Renard, Amelie. 2014. *A Society of Young Women: Opportunities of Place, Power, and Reform in Saudi Arabia.* Stanford: Stanford University Press.

Lea, Tess. 2012. "When Looking for Anarchy, Look to the State: Fantasies of Regulation in Forcing Disorder within the Australian Indigenous Estate." *Critique of Anthropology* 32 (2): 109–24.

Leach, Edmund. 1961. *Rethinking Anthropology.* London: Athlone Press.

———. 1970. *Political Systems of Highland Burma.* London: Bell and Sons. First published 1954.

———. 1980. "Malinowskiana: On Reading a Diary in the Strict Sense of the Term, or The Self Mutilation of Professor Hsu." *RAIN* 36:2–3.

Lecocq, Baz. 2015. "Distant Shores: A Historiographic View on Trans-Saharan Space." *Journal of African History* 56 (1): 23–36.

Lert, Frédéric. 2015. "Egypt Officially Signs for 24 Rafales, FREMM Frigate, and Missiles." *HIS Jane's Defence Weekly*, February 16, 2015.

Lethbridge, Lucy. 2013. *Servants: A Downstairs View of 20th-Century Britain*. London: Bloomsbury.

Levinas, Emmanuel. 1969. *Totality and Infinity: An Essay on Exteriority*. Translated by Alphonso Lingis. Pittsburgh, PA: Duquesne University Press. First published 1961.

Lévi-Strauss, Claude. 1963. *Structural Anthropology*. New York: Basic Books.

———. 1964. *Le cru et le cuit*. Paris: Plon.

———. 1966. *The Savage Mind*. London: Weidenfeld and Nicolson.

———. 1983a. "Histoire et ethnologie." *Annales: Économies, sociétés, civilisations* 38:1217–31.

———. 1983b. *Structural Anthropology*. Vol. 2. Chicago: University of Chicago Press.

Lewellen, Ted C. 2003. *Political Anthropology*. 3rd ed. Westport, CT: Praeger.

Lewis, Herbert S. 1998. "The Misrepresentation of Anthropology and Its Consequences." *American Anthropologist* 110 (3): 716–31.

Lienhardt, Godfrey. 1973. "Morality and Happiness among the Dinka." In *Religion and Morality*, edited by G. Outka and J. P. Reeder, 108–22. Garden City, NY: Anchor Books.

———. 1985. "Self: Public, Private. Some African Representations." In *The Category of the Person: Anthropology, Philosophy, History*, edited by Michael Carrithers, Steven Collins, and Steven Lukes, 141–55. Cambridge: Cambridge University Press.

Lind, William. 2014. *The Four Generations of Warfare*. Kouvala, Finland: Castalia House.

Lindholm, Charles. 1982. *Generosity and Jealousy: The Swat Pakhtun of Northern Pakistan*. New York: Columbia University Press.

———. 1986. "Kinship Structure and Political Authority: The Middle East and Central Asia." *Comparative Studies in Society and History* 28 (2): 334–55.

———. 1995. "The New Middle Eastern Ethnography." *Journal of the Royal Anthropological Institute* 1 (4): 805–20.

———. 2008. *The Islamic Middle East: Tradition and Change*. Revised edition. Oxford: Blackwell.

Lindisfarne, Nancy. 1991. *Bartered Brides: Politics, Gender and Marriage in an Afghan Tribal Society*. Cambridge: Cambridge University Press.

Lindisfarne, Nancy, and Jonathan Neale. 2015. "Sing-Along Gender Theory: Sometimes It Takes Balls to Be a Woman." *Anne Bonny Pirate* (blog), March 30, 2015. https://annebonnypirate.wordpress.com/2015/03/30/sing-along-gender-theory-sometimes-it-takes-balls-to-be-a-woman/.

LiPuma, Edward. 1998. "Modernity and Forms of Personhood in Melanesia." In *Bodies and Persons: Comparative Perspectives from Africa and Indonesia*, edited by Michael Lambek and Andrew Strathern, 53–79. Cambridge: Cambridge University Press.

———. 2001. *Encompassing Others: The Magic of Modernity in Melanesia*. Ann Arbor: University of Michigan Press.

Low, Setha. 2011. "Claiming Space for an Engaged Anthropology: Spatial Inequality and Social Exclusion." *American Anthropologist* 113 (3): 389–407.

Lowie, Robert H. 1937. *The History of Ethnological Theory*. New York: Holt, Rinehart and Winston.

Madelung, Wilferd. 1980. "A Treatise of the Sharif al-Murtada on the Legality of Working for the Government." *Bulletin of the School of Oriental and African Studies* 43 (1): 18–31.

Mahdavi, Pardis. 2008. *Passionate Uprisings: Iran's Sexual Revolution*. Stanford: Stanford University Press.

Mahé, Alain. 1993. "Laïcisme et sacralité dans les qanûns kabyles." *Annales islamologiques* 27:137–56.

———. 2000. "Les assemblées villageoises dans la Kabylie contemporaine: Traditionalisme par excès de modernité ou modernisme par excès de tradition?" *Études rurales* 155–56:179–211.

Mahmood, Saba. 2005. *Politics of Piety: The Islamic Revival and the Feminist Subject.* Princeton: Princeton University Press.

———. 2016. *Religious Difference in a Secular Age: A Minority Report.* Princeton: Princeton University Press.

Mair, Lucy. 1980. Letter to the editor: Malinowski's Diary. *RAIN* 40:7.

Major, Andrew J. 1999. "State and Criminal Tribes in Colonial Punjab: Surveillance, Control and Reclamation of the 'Dangerous Classes.'" *Modern Asian Studies* 33 (3): 657–88.

Malinowski, Bronislaw. 1989. *A Diary in the Strict Sense of the Term.* Stanford: Stanford University Press. First published 1967.

Mamdani, Mahmood. 1996. *Citizen and Subject: Contemporary Africa and the Legacy of Late Colonialism.* Princeton: Princeton University Press.

Mandelbaum, David G. 1970. *Society in India,* 2 vols. Berkeley: University of California Press.

Manoukian, Setrag. 2012. *City of Knowledge in Twentieth Century Iran: Shiraz, History and Poetry.* London: Routledge.

Manu. 1886. *The Laws of Manu: Translated, with Extracts from Seven Commentaries.* Edited and translated by G. Bühler. Oxford: Clarendon Press.

Maqsood, Ammara. 2014. "'Buying Modern': Muslim Subjectivity, the West and Patterns of Islamic Consumption in Lahore, Pakistan." *Cultural Studies* 28 (1): 84–107.

———. 2016. "Moving On: Mobility and Spatiality among Tribal Pashtun." *Tanqeed* (January), available on-line https://www.tanqeed.org/2016/01/pashtuns-moving -across-space/.

———. 2017. *The New Pakistani Middle-Class.* Cambridge, MA: Harvard University Press.

Marcus, George E. 1997. "The Uses of Complicity in the Changing Mise-en-Scène of Anthropological Fieldwork." *Representations* 59:85–108.

———. 2012. "The Legacies of Writing Culture and the Near Future of the Ethnographic Form: A Sketch." *Cultural Anthropology* 27 (3): 427–45.

Marriott, McKim. 1976. "Hindu Transactions: Diversity without Dualism." In *Transaction and Meaning: Directions in the Anthropology of Exchange and Symbolic Behavior,* edited by B. Kapferer, 109–42. Philadelphia: Institute for the Study of Human Issues Press.

Marsden, Magnus, and Benjamin Hopkins. 2011. *Fragments of the Afghan Frontier.* London: Hurst.

Marshall, Sandra E., and R. Antony Duff. 1998. "Criminalization and Sharing Wrongs." *Canadian Journal of Law and Jurisprudence* 11:7–22.

Martin, A.-G.-P. 1908. *A la frontière du Maroc: Les oasis sahariennes (Gourara, Touat, Tidikelt).* Algiers: Imprimerie algérienne.

Masqueray, Émile. 1886. *Formation des cités chez les populations sédentaires de l'Algérie: Kabyles du Djurdjura, Chaouïa de l'Aourâs, Beni Mezâb.* Paris: Ernest Leroux.

Massad, Joseph. 2001. *Colonial Effects: The Making of National Identity in Jordan.* New York: Columbia University Press.

Mattson, Ingrid. 2003. "Status-Based Definitions of Need in Early Islamic *Zakat* and Maintenance Laws." In *Poverty and Charity in Middle Eastern Contexts,* edited by

Michael Bonner, Mine Ener, and Amy Singer, 31–52. Albany: State University of New York Press.

Mauss, Marcel. 1985. "A Category of the Human Mind: The Notion of Person; the Notion of Self." In *The Category of the Person: Anthropology, Philosophy, History*, edited by Michael Carrithers, Steven Collins, and Steven Lukes, 1–25. Cambridge: Cambridge University Press. First published 1938.

———. 1990. *The Gift: The Form and Reason for Exchange in Archaic Societies*. Translated by W. D. Halls. London: Routledge. First published 1950.

Mayaram, Shail. 2003. *Against History, Against State: Counterperspectives from the Margins*. New York: Columbia University Press.

McAlister, Melani. 2001. *Epic Encounters: Culture, Media, and US Interests in the Middle East*. Berkeley: University of California Press.

McDougall, James. 2010. "Histories of Heresy and Salvation: Arabs, Berbers, Community, and the State." In *Berbers and Others: Beyond Tribe and Nation in the Maghreb*, edited by K. Hoffman and S. G. Miller, 15–37. Bloomington: Indiana University Press.

McKee, Emily. 2016. *Dwelling in Conflict: Negev Landscapes and the Boundaries of Belonging*. Stanford: Stanford University Press.

Mehrotra, Raja Ram. 1977. *Sociology of Secret Languages*. Simla: Indian Institute of Advanced Study.

Meneley, Anne. 1996. *Tournaments of Value: Sociability and Hierarchy in a Yemeni Town*. Toronto: University of Toronto Press.

Menoret, Pascal. 2003. *L'énigme saoudienne: Les Saoudiens et le monde, 1744–2003*. Paris: La Découverte.

———. 2014. *Joyriding in Riyadh: Oil, Urbanism, and Road Revolt*. Cambridge: Cambridge University Press.

Mernissi, Fatima. 1982. "Zhor's World: A Moroccan Domestic Worker Speaks Out." *Feminist Issues* 2 (1): 3–31.

Merrill, Selah. 1881. *East of the Jordan: A Record of Travel and Observation in the Countries of Moab, Gilead, and Bashan*. London: Richard Bentley.

Mervin, Sabrina. 2000. *Un réformisme chiite: Ulémas et lettrés du Gabal 'Âmil (actuel Liban-Sud) de la fin de l'Empire ottoman à l'indépendance du Liban*. Paris: Karthala.

Messick, Brinkley. 1993. *The Calligraphic State: Textual Domination and History in a Muslim Society*. Berkeley: University of California Press.

———. 2008. "Shari'a Ethnography." In *The Law Applied: Contextualizing the Islamic Shari'a*, edited by Peri Bearman, Wolfhart Heinrichs, and Bernard Weiss, 173–93. London: I.B. Tauris.

———. 2014. "The Judge and the Mufti." In *The Ashgate Research Companion to Islamic Law*, edited by Rudolph Peters and Peri Bearman, 73–91. Farnham: Ashgate.

———. 2017. *Shari'a Scripts: A Historical Anthropology*. New York: Columbia University Press.

Messiri, Sawsan. 1978. *Ibn al-Balad: A Concept of Egyptian Identity*. Leiden: Brill.

Metcalf, Barbara D., ed. 1984. *Moral Conduct and Authority: The Place of Adab in South Asian Islam*. Berkeley: University of California Press.

Milani, Abbas. 2004. *Lost Wisdom: Rethinking Persian Modernity in Iran*. Washington, DC: Mage Publishers.

Milani, Farzaneh. 1992. *Veils and Words: The Emerging Voices of Iranian Women Writers*. Syracuse: Syracuse University Press.

Mills, Amy. 2010. *Streets of Memory: Landscape, Tolerance, and National Identity in Istanbul.* Athens: University of Georgia Press.

Mines, Mattison. 1988. "Conceptualizing the Person: Hierarchical Society and Individual Autonomy in India." *American Anthropologist* 90 (3): 568–79.

———. 1994. *Public Faces, Private Voices: Community and Individuality in South India.* Berkeley: University of California Press.

———. 2006. "In the Aftermath of Death: Presenting Self, Individuality and Family in an Iyangar Family in Chennai." In *Claiming Individuality: The Cultural Politics of Distinction*, edited by Vered Amit and Noel Dyck, 22–50. Chicago: University of Chicago Press.

Mintz, Sidney. 1998. "The Localization of Anthropological Practice from Area Studies to Transnationalism." *Critique of Anthropology* 18 (2): 117–33.

Mir-Hosseini, Ziba. 1993. *Marriage on Trial: A Study of Islamic Family Law: Morocco and Iran Compared.* London: I.B. Tauris.

Mitchell, Timothy. 1991. "The Limits of the State: Beyond Statist Approaches and Their Critics." *American Political Science Review* 85 (1): 77–96.

———. 2002. *Rule of Experts: Egypt, Techno-politics, Modernity.* Berkeley: University of California.

Monroe, Kristin V. 2016. *The Insecure City: Space, Power, and Mobility in Beirut.* New Brunswick: Rutgers University Press.

Montagne, Robert. 1924. "Le régime juridique des tribus du Sud marocain." *Hespéris* 4 (3): 313–31.

———. 1930a. *Les Berbères et le makhzen dans le Sud du Maroc.* Paris: Félix Alcan.

———. 1930b. *Un magasin collectif de l'Anti-Atlas, l'agadir des Ikounka.* Paris: Larose.

———. 1952. *Naissance du prolétariat marocain: Enquête collective 1948–1950.* Cahiers de l'Afrique et de l'Asie. Paris: Peyronnet & Gie.

Montagne, Robert, and M. Ben Daoud. 1927. "Documents pour servir à l'étude du droit coutumier du sud-marocain." *Hespéris* 7 (4): 401–45.

Montgomery, Mary. 2019. *Hired Daughters: Domestic Workers among Ordinary Moroccans.* Bloomington: Indiana University Press.

Moore, M. P. 1975. "Cooperative Labour in Peasant Agriculture." *Journal of Peasant Studies* 2 (3): 276–91.

Mounib, Noura. 2012. "Les nounous venues des Philippines." *L'Observateur*, May 15–June 21, 2012, 20–21.

Muhammad, Dina. 2015. "Hal Tu'awwid 'Rihlat al-Fananiyin' Ziyadat Mu'aradi al-Sisi?" *Wara al-Ahdath*, June 1, 2015. Accessed August 13, 2016. http://tinyurl.com/oyvak2p.

Mullins, Samuel, and Gareth Griffiths. 1986. *Cap and Apron: An Oral History of Domestic Service in the Shires, 1880–1950.* The Harborough Series, no. 2. Leicester: Leicestershire Museums, Art Galleries and Records Service.

Mundy, Martha. 1995. *Domestic Government: Kinship, Community and Polity in North Yemen.* London: I.B. Tauris.

Musa, Suleiman. n.d. *Kitab al-Rahhala.* Amman.

Nader, Laura. 1969. "Up the Anthropologist: Perspectives to Be Gained from Studying Up." In *Reinventing Anthropology*, edited by Dell Hymes, 284–311. New York: Pantheon.

Nafar, Tamer, Suhell Nafar, and Mahmood Jrery. 2012. "Dam Responds: Tradition and the Anti-politics Machine: DAM Seduced by the 'Honor Crime.'" *Jadaliyya*, December 26,

2012. http://www.jadaliyya.com/pages/index/9181/dam-responds_on-tradition-and -the-anti-politics-of.

Nagata, Mary Louise. 2004. "Domestic Service and the Law in Early Modern Japan." In *Domestic Service and the Formation of European Identity: Understanding the Globalization of Domestic Work, 16th–21st Centuries*, edited by Antoinette Fauve-Chamoux, 211–33. Bern: Peter Lang.

Navaro-Yashin, Yael. 2002. *Faces of the State: Secularism and Public Life in Turkey*. Princeton: Princeton University Press.

Nehlil. 1915–16. "L'azref des tribus et qsour berbères du Haut Guir." *Archives Berbères* 1 (1): 77–89; 1 (2): 88–103, 109–34.

Nichols, Robert. 1995. "The Frontier Tribal Areas 1840–1990." Occasional Paper no. 34, University of Pennsylvania.

———. 2001. *Settling the Frontier: Land, Law and Society in Peshawar Valley, 1500–1900*. Karachi: Oxford University Press.

———. 2008. *A History of Pashtun Migration, 1775–2006*. Karachi: Oxford University Press.

Nigam, Sanjay. 1990. "Disciplining and Policing the 'Criminals by Birth,' Part 2: The Development of a Disciplinary System, 1871–1900." *Indian Economic and Social History Review* 27 (3): 257–87.

Ni'ma, 'Abdallah. 1996. *Dalil al-qada' al-ja'fari*. Beirut: Dar al-Balagha.

Noricks, Jay Smith. 1983. "Unrestricted Cognatic Descent on Niutao, a Polynesian Island of Tuvalu." *American Ethnologist* 10 (3): 571–84.

Nucho, Joanne Randa. 2016. *Everyday Sectarianism in Urban Lebanon: Infrastructures, Public Services, and Power*. Princeton: Princeton University Press.

Nugent, David, and Joan Vincent, eds. 2007. *A Companion to the Anthropology of Politics*. Oxford: Blackwell.

Nugent, Stephen. 2012. "Anarchism out West: Some Reflections on Sources." *Critique of Anthropology* 32 (2): 206–16.

Ohlheiser, Abby. 2013. "The Con Man Who Sold Incredibly Fake Bomb Detectors to the Iraqi Government." *Slate*, May 2, 2013. Accessed August 13, 2016. http://www.slate.com /blogs/the_slatest/2013/05/02/ade651_fake_bomb_detector_lands_jim_mccormick_10 _year_prison_sentence.html.

Olmsted, Kathryn. 2009. *Real Enemies: Conspiracy Theories and American Democracy, World War I to 9/11*. Oxford: Oxford University Press.

Olszewska, Zuzanna. 2011. "Afghanistan's Women Poets: A Hidden Discourse." In *Land of the Unconquerable: The Lives of Contemporary Afghan Women*, edited by Jennifer Heath and Ashraf Zahedi, 342–55. Berkeley: University of California Press.

———. 2015. *The Pearl of Dari: Poetry and Personhood among Young Afghans in Iran*. Bloomington: Indiana University Press.

O'Malley, Lewis S. S. 1925. *History of Bengal, Bihar and Orissa under British Rule*. Calcutta: Bengal Secretariat Book Depot.

Ong, Aihwa. 2006. *Neoliberalism as Exception: Mutations in Citizenship and Sovereignty*. Durham: Duke University Press.

Ortner, Sherry. 1984. "Theory in Anthropology since the Sixties." *Comparative Studies in Society and History* 26 (1): 126–66.

———. 1995. "Resistance and the Problem of Ethnographic Refusal." *Comparative Studies in Society and History* 37 (1): 173–93.

———. 2010. "Access: Reflections on Studying up in Hollywood." *Ethnography* 11 (2): 211–33.

———. 2013. *Not Hollywood: Independent Film at the Twilight of the American Dream.* Durham: Duke University Press.

———. 2016. "Dark Anthropology and Its Others: Theory since the Eighties." *HAU: Journal of Ethnographic Theory* 6 (1): 47–73.

Osanloo, Arzoo. 2009. *The Politics of Women's Rights in Iran.* Princeton: Princeton University Press.

Osella, Caroline, and Filippo Osella. 1998. "Friendship and Flirting: Micro-politics in Kerala, South India." *Journal of the Royal Anthropological Institute* 4 (2): 189–206.

Özyürek, Esra. 2002. *Nostalgia for the Modern.* Durham: Duke University Press.

Palmié, Stephan, and Charles Stewart. 2016. "Introduction: For an Anthropology of History." *HAU: Journal of Ethnographic Theory* 6 (1): 207–36.

Panjwani, Imranali. 2012. *The Shi'a of Samarra: The Heritage and Politics of a Community in Iraq.* London: I.B. Tauris.

The Pariśiṣṭas of the Atharvaveda. 1909. Edited and translated by G. M. Bolling and J. von Negelein. Leipzig: Otto Harrassowitz.

Parker, Henry. 1910–14. *Village Folk-Tales of Ceylon.* 3 vols. Dehiwala: Tisara Prakasayako.

Pascon, Paul. 1984. *La Maison d'Iligh.* Rabat: P. Pascon.

Passi, Alessandro. 2001. *Dharmacauryarasāyana (L'elisir del Furton Secondo il Dharma).* Milan: Edizioni Ariele.

———. 2005. "Perverted *Dharma*? Ethics of Thievery in the *Dharmacauryarasāyana*." *Journal of Indian Philosophy* 33 (4): 513–28.

Pellò, Stefano. 2015. "Persian Poets on the Streets: The Lore of Indo-Persian Poetic Circles in Late Mughal India." In *Tellings and Texts: Music, Literature and Performance in North India*, edited by Francesca Orsini and Katherine Butler Schofield, 303–25. Cambridge: Open Book Publishers.

Peters, Emrys. 1967. "Some Structural Aspects of the Feud among the Camel-Herding Bedouin of Cyrenaica." *Africa* 37 (2): 261–82.

Peterson, Mark Allen. 2011. *Connected in Cairo: Growing Up Cosmopolitan in the Modern Middle East.* Bloomington: Indiana University Press.

———. 2015a. "In Search of Antistructure: The Meaning of Tahrir Square in Egypt's Ongoing Social Drama." In *Breaking Boundaries: Varieties of Liminality*, edited by Ágnes Horváth, Bjørn Thomassen, and Harald Wydra, 164–82. New York: Berghahn.

———. 2015b. "Re-envisioning Tahrir: The Changing Meanings of Tahrir Square in Egypt's Ongoing Revolution." In *Revolutionary Egypt: Connecting Domestic and International Struggles*, edited by Reem Abou-El-Fadl, 64–82. London: Routledge.

Peysonnel, Jean-André. 1987. *Voyage dans la régence de Tunis et d'Alger.* Paris: La Découverte. First published 1724–25.

Piliavsky, Anastasia. 2011. "A Secret in the Oxford Sense: Thieves and the Rhetoric of Mystification in Western India." *Comparative Studies in Society and History* 53 (2): 290–313.

———. 2013a. "Borders without Borderlands: On the Social Reproduction of State Demarcation in Western India." In *Borderlands in Northern South Asia*, edited by David Gellner, 24–45. Durham: Duke University Press.

———. 2013b. "The Moghia Menace, or The Watch over Watchmen in British India." *Modern Asian Studies* 47 (3): 751–79.

———. 2015. "The 'Criminal Tribe' in India before the British." *Comparative Studies in Society and History* 57 (2): 323–54.

———. forthcoming. *Nobody's People: Hierarchy as Hope in a Society of Thieves*. Stanford: Stanford University Press.

Pitt-Rivers, Julian. 1971. *The People of the Sierra*. 2nd ed. Chicago: University of Chicago Press.

———. 1977. "The Law of Hospitality." In *The Fate of Shechem or The Politics of Sex: Essays in the Anthropology of the Mediterranean*, 94–112. Cambridge: Cambridge University Press.

———. 1994. "Introduction: Friendship, Honor and Agon. Jus Sanguinis and Jus Soli." In *Les amis et les autres: Mélanges en l'honneur de John Peristiany*, edited by S. Damanianakos, M.-E. Handman, J. Pitt-Rivers, and G. Ravis-Giordani, 25–43. Athens: EKKE.

Platts, John T. 1884. *A Dictionary of Urdu, Classical Hindi, and English*. London: Sampson Low.

Pocock, David. 1957. "'Difference' in East Africa: A Study of Caste and Religion in Modern Indian Society." *Southwestern Journal of Anthropology* 13 (4): 289–300.

———. 1961. *Social Anthropology*. London: Sheed and Ward.

———. 1988. "Persons, Texts and Morality." Marett Memorial Lecture, Oxford.

———. 1994. "The Idea of a Personal Anthropology." *Journal for the Anthropological Study of Human Movement* 8 (1): 11–42.

Postill, John. 2010. "Introduction: Theorising Media and Practice." In *Theorising Media and Practice*, edited by Birgit Bräuchler and John Postill, 1–34. New York: Berghahn.

Powdermaker, Hortense. 1950. *Hollywood, the Dream Factory: An Anthropologist Looks at the Movie-Makers*. Boston: Little, Brown.

———. 1967. "An Agreeable Man." *New York Review of Books*, November 19, 1967, 36–37.

———. 1970. "Further Reflections on Lesu and Malinowski's Diary." *Oceania* 40 (4): 344–47.

Pritchett, Frances W. 1994. *Nets of Awareness: Urdu Poetry and its Critics*. Berkeley: University of California Press.

Rabo, Annika. 2005. *A Shop of One's Own: Independence and Reputation among Traders in Aleppo*. London: I.B. Tauris.

Radhakrishna, Meena. 1992. "Surveillance and Settlement under the Criminal Tribes Act in Madras." *Indian Economic and Social History Review* 29 (2): 171–98.

Radin, Paul. 1956. *The Trickster: A Study in American Indian Mythology, with a commentary by Karl Kerényi and Carl G. Jung*. New York: Philosophical Library.

Radio Sawa. 2014. "Man Yakun al-Liwa' 'Abd al-'Ati Mukhtara' Jihaz "Ilaj' al-Aydz." February 27, 2014. Accessed August 13, 2016. http://www.radiosawa.com/a/244588.html.

Rancière, Jacques. 2006. *Hatred of Democracy*. London: Verso.

Rapport, Nigel. 1997. "'Surely Everything Has Already Been Said About Malinowski's Diary!'" In *Transcendent Individual: Essays toward a Literary and Liberal Anthropology*, 80–92. London: Routledge.

Rashid, A. 2001. *Taliban: Militant Islam, Oil and Fundamentalism in Central Asia*. Yale: Yale University Press.

———. 2008. *Descent into Chaos: The US and Disaster in Pakistan, Afghanistan and Central Asia*. London: Penguin.

Ray, Raka, and Seemin Qayum. 2009. *Cultures of Servitude: Modernity, Domesticity, and Class in India*. Stanford: Stanford University Press.

Reid, Megan H. 2013. *Law and Piety in Medieval Islam*. Cambridge: Cambridge University Press.

Reid, Richard. 2011. "Past and Presentism: The 'Precolonial' and the Foreshortening of African History." *Journal of African History* 52:135–55.

Retaillé, Denis. 1998. "L'espace nomade." *Revue de géographie de Lyon* 73 (1): 71–81.

Richards, Audrey. 1968. "In Darkest Malinowski." *Cambridge Review*, January 19, 1968, 186–89.

Rivière, Peter. 1984. *Individual and Society in Guiana: A Comparative Study of Amerindian Social Organization*. Cambridge: Cambridge University Press.

———. 2000. "Indians and Cowboys: Two Field Experiences." In *Anthropologists in a Wider World: Essays on Field Research*, edited by Paul Dresch, Wendy James, and David Parkin, 27–43. Oxford: Berghahn.

———, ed. 2007. Introduction to *A History of Oxford Anthropology*, 1–20. Oxford: Berghahn.

Roberts, Hugh. 2014. *Berber Government. The Kabyle Polity in Pre-Colonial Algeria*. London: I.B. Tauris.

Rodary, Meryem. 2002. "Argent des femmes et honneur des hommes au Maroc: Un quartier de Marrakech." In *Dissemblances: Jeux et enjeux du genre*, edited by Rose-Marie Lagrave, Agathe Gestin, Eléonore Lépinard, and Geneviève Pruvost, 117–30. Paris: L'Harmattan.

———. 2007. "Le travail des femmes dans le Maroc précolonial, entre oppression et résistance: Droit au travail ou accès aux bénéfices." *Cahiers d'études africaines* 47:753–80.

Rollins, Judith. 1985. *Between Women: Domestics and their Employers*. Philadelphia: Temple University Press.

Rubinoff, A. G. 1998. "The Decline of India's Parliament." *Journal of Legislative Studies* 4 (4): 13–33.

Sahlins, Marshall. 1983. "Other Times, Other Customs: The Anthropology of History." *American Anthropologist* 85 (3): 517–44.

———. 1999. "Two or Three Things That I Know about Culture." *Journal of the Royal Anthropological Institute* 5 (3): 399–421.

———. 2002. *Waiting for Foucault, Still*. Chicago: Prickly Paradigm Press.

———. 2004. *Apologies to Thucydides: Understanding History as Culture and Vice Versa*. Chicago: University of Chicago Press.

———. 2010. "Infrastructuralism." *Critical Inquiry* 36 (3): 371–85.

———. 2013. *What Kinship Is—and Is Not*. Chicago: University of Chicago Press.

Said, Edward. 1978. *Orientalism*. London: Routledge.

Sajdi, Dana. 2018. "In Defense of Damascus: The Genre of Prose Cityscapes (12th and 16th Centuries)." Presentation, seminar series, Dissections: New Directions in Research on the Middle East and North Africa. Middle East and Middle East American Center, the Graduate Center, City University of New York, May 11.

Salahdine, Mohamed. 1988. *Les petits métiers clandestins: "Le business populaire"*. Casablanca: Eddif.

Salamandra, Christa. 1998. "Moustache Hairs Lost: Ramadan Television Serials and the Construction of Identity in Damascus, Syria." *Visual Anthropology* 10 (2–4): 227–46.

———. 2004. *A New Old Damascus: Authenticity and Distinction in Urban Syria*. Bloomington: Indiana University Press.

———. 2006. "Chastity Capital: Hierarchy and Distinction in Damascus." In *Sexuality in the Arab World*, edited by Samir Khalaf and John Gagnon, 48–64. London: Saqi Books.

———. 2010. "Consumption, Display, and Gender." In *Arab Culture and Society*, edited by Samir Khalaf and Roseanne Khalaf, 152–62. London: Saqi Books.

———. 2012. "Prelude to an Uprising: Syrian Fictional Television and Socio-political Critique." *Jadaliyya*, May 17, 2012. http://www.jadaliyya.com/pages/index/5578 /prelude-to-an-uprising_syrian-fictional-television.

———. 2013. "Sectarianism in Syria: Anthropological Reflections." *Middle East Critique* 22 (3): 303–6.

———. 2014. "Reflections on Not Writing about the Syrian Conflict." *Jadaliyya*, February 5, 2014. http://www.jadaliyya.com/pages/index/16290/reflections-on-not-writing-about -the-syrian-confli.

———. 2015. "Syria's Drama Outpouring between Complicity and Critique." In *Syria from Reform to Revolt: Culture, Society and Religion*, edited by Christa Salamandra and Leif Stenberg, 36–52. Syracuse: Syracuse University Press.

———. 2017. "Waiting: The Neighborhood That Eats Its Children." *Drama Critics* 3 (May): 52–63. http://drama-critics.com/?p=987.

Samin, Nadav. 2015. *Of Sand or Soil: Genealogy and Tribal Belonging in Saudi Arabia*. Princeton: Princeton University Press.

———. 2016. "Daʿwa, Dynasty, and Destiny in the Arab Gulf." *Comparative Studies in Society and History* 58 (4): 935–54.

Sanford, Victoria. 2008. "Excavations of the Heart: Reflections on Truth, Memory, and Structures of Understanding." In *Engaged Observer: Anthropology, Advocacy, and Activism*, edited by Victoria Sanford and Asale Angel-Ajani, 19–41. New Brunswick: Rutgers University Press.

Saṇmukhakalpa: Ein Lehrbuch der Zauberei und Diebeskunst aus dem Indischen Mittelalter. 1991. Edited by G. Dieter. Berlin: Dietrich Reimer.

Sawalha, Aseel. 2010. *Reconstructing Beirut: Memory and Space in a Postwar Arab City*. Austin: University of Texas Press.

Schacht, Joseph. 1964. *An Introduction to Islamic Law*. Oxford: Clarendon Press.

Schaeublin, Emanuel. 2016. "Zakat in Nablus (Palestine): Change and Continuity in Islamic Almsgiving." DPhil thesis, University of Oxford.

Scheele, Judith. 2008. "A Taste for Law: Rule-Making in Kabylia (Algeria)." *Comparative Studies in Society and History* 50 (4): 895–919.

———. 2009. *Village Matters: Knowledge, Politics and Community in Kabylia (Algeria)*. Oxford: James Currey.

———. 2010. "Councils without Customs, Qadis without States: Property and Community in the Algerian Touat." *Islamic Law and Society* 17 (3): 350–74.

———. 2012. *Smugglers and Saints of the Sahara: Regional Connectivity in the Twentieth Century*. Cambridge: Cambridge University Press.

———. 2014. "Community as an Achievement: Kabyle Customary Law and Beyond." In *Legalism: Community and Justice*, edited by Fernanda Pirie and Judith Scheele, 177–200. Oxford: Oxford University Press.

Schiefner, Franz Anton von, and William S. Ralston, eds. and trans. 1906. *Tibetan Tales, Derived from Indian Sources*. London: K. Paul, Trench, Trübner.

Schielke, Samuli. 2009. "Ambivalent Commitments: Troubles of Morality, Religiosity and Aspiration among Young Egyptians." *Journal of Religion in Africa* 39:158–85.

Schirazi, Asghar. 1997. *The Constitution of Iran: Politics and the State in the Islamic Republic*. Translated by John O'Kane. London: I.B. Tauris.

Schwab, Raymond. 1950. *La renaissance orientale*. Paris: Payot.

Scott, James. 1998. *Seeing Like a State: How Certain Schemes to Improve the Human Condition Have Failed*. New Haven: Yale University Press.

Searle, John. 1995. *The Construction of Social Reality*. London: Penguin.

Sethi, Aman. 2012. *A Free Man: A True Story of Life and Death in Delhi*. London: Jonathan Cape.

Sethi, N. 2013. "Beyond Hope." *Friday Times*, September 20, 2013.

Shah, Arvind M., and R. G. Shroff. 1958. "The Vahīvancā Bāroṭs of Gujarat: A Caste of Genealogists and Mythographers." *Journal of American Folklore* 71:246–74.

Shah, Popatlal G. 1967. *Vimuktu Jatis: Denotified Communities in Western India*. Bombay: Gujarat Research Society.

Shāh, Waris. 1966. *The Adventures of Hir and Ranjha*. Edited by M. Hasan. Translated by C. F. Usborne. Karachi: Lion Art Press. First published 1766.

Shannon, Jonathan Holt. 2006. *Among the Jasmine Trees: Music and Modernity in Contemporary Syria*. Middletown, CT: Wesleyan University Press.

Sharma, Sunil. 2009. "From ʿĀesha to Nūr Jahān: The Shaping of a Classical Persian Poetic Canon of Women." *Journal of Persianate Studies* 2:148–64.

Shore, Cris, and Stephen Nugent, eds. 2002. *Elite Cultures: Anthropological Perspectives*. London: Routledge.

Shryock, Andrew. 1997. *Nationalism and the Genealogical Imagination*. Berkeley: University of California Press.

———. 1998. "Mainstreaming Arabs: Filmmaking as Image Making in Tales from Arab Detroit." *Visual Anthropology* 10 (2–4): 165–88.

———, ed. 2004a. "The Double Remoteness of Arab Detroit." In *Off Stage/On Display: Intimacy and Ethnography in the Age of Public Culture*, 279–314. Stanford: Stanford University Press.

———, ed. 2004b. *Off Stage/On Display: Intimacy and Ethnography in the Age of Public Culture*. Stanford: Stanford University Press.

———, ed. 2004c. "Other Conscious/Self Aware." In *Off Stage/On Display: Intimacy and Ethnography in the Age of Public Culture*, 3–28. Stanford: Stanford University Press.

———. 2004d. "The New Jordanian Hospitality: House, Host, and Guest in the Culture of Public Display." *Comparative Studies in Society and History* 46 (1): 35–62.

———. 2008. "Thinking about Hospitality, with Derrida, Kant, and the Balga Bedouin." *Anthropos* 103:1–17.

———. 2012. "Breaking Hospitality Apart: Bad Hosts, Bad Guests, and the Problem of Sovereignty." *Journal of the Royal Anthropological Institute* 18 (S1): S20–S33.

———. 2013. "It's This, Not That: How Marshall Sahlins Solves Kinship." *HAU: Journal of Ethnographic Theory* 3 (2): 271–79.

Shryock, Andrew, and Sally Howell. 2001. "'Ever a Guest in Our House': The Amir Abdullah, Shaykh Majid al-ʿAdwan, and the Practice of Jordanian House Politics, as Remembered by Umm Sultan, the Widow of Majid." *International Journal of Middle East Studies* 33 (2): 247–69.

Shryock, Andrew, and Daniel Lord Smail. 2011. *Deep History: The Architecture of Past and Present*. Berkeley: University of California Press.

Siddiqi, Ayesha. 2014. "Climatic Disasters and Radical Politics in Southern Pakistan: The Non-linear Connection." *Geopolitics* 19 (4): 885–910.

Silverstein, Paul. 2010. "The Local Dimensions of Transnational Berberism: Racial Politics, Land Rights, and Cultural Activism in Southeastern Morocco." In *Berbers and Others: Beyond Tribe and Nation in the Maghreb*, edited by K. Hoffman and S. G. Miller, 83–102. Bloomington: Indiana University Press.

Simmel, Georg. 1906. "The Sociology of Secrecy and of Secret Societies." *American Journal of Sociology* 11 (4): 441–98.

———. 1999. "The Stranger." In *Social Theory: The Multicultural and Classic Readings*, edited by G. Lermert, 184–89. Boulder, CO: Westview Press. First published 1908.

Singerman, Diane. 1995. *Avenues of Participation: Family, Politics and Networks in Urban Quarters of Cairo*. Princeton: Princeton University Press.

Singerman, Diane, and Paul Amar, eds. 2006. *Cairo Cosmopolitan: Politics, Culture, and Urban Space in the New Middle East*. Cairo: The American University in Cairo Press.

Singha, Radhika. 1993. "'Providential Circumstances': The Thuggee Campaign of the 1830s and Legal Innovation." *Modern Asian Studies* 27 (1): 83–146.

Sistani, 'Ali al-. 2002. *Minhāj al-sālihīn*. 3 vols. Qom: Maktabat Fadak.

Skaria, Ajay. 1999. *Hybrid Histories: Forests, Frontiers and Wildness in Western India*. Delhi: Oxford University Press.

Sleeman, William Henry. 1836. *Ramaseeana, or a Vocabulary of the Particular Language Used by the Thugs*. Calcutta: G. H. Gutman, Military Orphan Press.

———. 1839. *History of the Thugs or Phansigars of India*. Philadelphia: Carey and Hart.

———. 1844. *Rambles and Recollections of an Indian Official*. 2 vols. London: J. Hatchard and Son.

———. 1849. *Report on Budhuk Alias Bagree Decoits*. Calcutta: J. C. Sherriff, Bengal Military Orphan Press.

Slocum, Karla, and Deborah Thomas. 2003. "Rethinking Global and Area Studies: Insights from Caribbeanist Anthropology." *American Anthropologist* 105 (3): 553–65.

Slyomovics, Susan. 2013. "State of the State of the Art Studies: An Introduction to the Anthropology of the Middle East and North Africa." In *Anthropology of the Middle East and North Africa: Into the New Millenium*, edited by S. Hafez and S. Slyomovics, 3–22. Bloomington: Indiana University Press.

Smail, Daniel Lord, and Andrew Shryock. 2013. "History and the 'Pre.'" *American Historical Review* 118 (3): 709–37.

Smith, John D. 1975. "An Introduction to the Language of the Historical Documents from Rājasthān." *Modern Asian Studies* 9 (4): 433–64.

Somadeva. 1923. *The Ocean of Story: Being C. H. Tawney's Translation of Somadeva's Kathāsaritsāgara (or, Ocean of Streams of Story)*. Edited and translated by C. H. Tawney. Delhi: Motilal Banarsidas.

Spadola, Emilio. 2013. *The Calls of Islam: Sufis, Islamists, and Mass Mediation in Urban Morocco*. Bloomington: Indiana University Press.

Spary, Carole. 2010. "Disrupting Rituals of Debate in the Indian Parliament." *Journal of Legislative Studies* 16 (3): 338–51.

Spencer, Richard. 2014. "Egypt Army Embarrassment after It 'Cures' AIDS." *Telegraph*, February 27, 2014.

Spiro, Melford E. 1993. "Is the Western Conception of the Self 'Peculiar' within the Context of the World Cultures?" *Ethos* 21 (2): 107–53.

Srivastava, Piyush. 2005. "Forget Tigers, Peacocks Are Going Extinct Too." *Indian Express* (Lucknow), August 17, 2005.

Steedman, Carolyn. 2007. *Master and Servant: Love and Labour in the English Industrial Age.* Cambridge: Cambridge University Press.

———. 2009. *Labours Lost: Domestic Service and the Making of Modern England.* Cambridge: Cambridge University Press.

Stewart, Frank. 1994. *Honor.* Chicago: University of Chicago Press.

———. 2006. "Customary Law among the Bedouin of the Middle East and North Africa." In *Nomadic Societies in the Middle East and North Africa: Entering the 21st Century,* edited by Dawn Chatty, 239–79. Leiden: Brill.

Stocking, George. 1968. "Special Review: Empathy and Antipathy in the Heart of Darkness: An Essay Review of Malinowski's Field Diaries." *Journal of the History of the Behavioral Sciences* 4 (2): 189–94.

Strathern, Marilyn. 1988. *The Gender of the Gift: Problems with Women and Problems with Society in Melanesia.* Berkeley: University of California Press.

Śūdraka. 1905. *The Little Clay Cart (Mṛcchakaṭika): A Hindu Drama Attributed to King Shūdraka.* Edited by C. R. Lanman. Translated by A. W. Ryder. Cambridge, MA: Harvard University Press.

Sundararajan, Arun. 2015. "The 'gig Economy' Is Coming. What Will It Mean for Work?" *Guardian,* July 26, 2015, https://www.theguardian.com/commentisfree/2015/jul/26 /will-we-get-by-gig-economy.

Swedenburg, Ted. 1995. "With Genet in the Palestinian Field." In *Fieldwork under Fire: Contemporary Studies of Violence and Survival,* edited by Carolyn Nordstrom and Antonius Robben, 25–40. Berkeley: University of California Press.

Symmons-Symonolewicz, Konstantin. 1982. "The Ethnographer and His Savages: An Intellectual History of Malinowski's Diary." *Polish Review* 27 (1–2): 92–98.

Szakolczai, Arpad. 2009. "Liminality and Experience: Structuring Transitory Situations and Transformative Events." *International Political Anthropology* 2 (1): 141–72.

Szuppe, Maria. 1998. "The 'Jewels of Wonder': Learned Ladies and Princess Politicians in the Provinces of Early Safavid Iran." In *Women in the Medieval Islamic World: Power, Patronage, and Piety,* edited by Gavin Hambly, 325–47. New York: St. Martin's Press.

Tabor, Nathan L. M. 2014. "A Market for Speech: Poetry Recitation in Late Mughal India, 1690–1810." Unpublished PhD dissertation, University of Texas, Austin.

Tanner, Jakob. 2008. "The Conspiracy of the Invisible Hand: Anonymous Market Mechanisms and Dark Powers." *New German Critique* 35, no. 1 (Spring): 51–64.

Taussig, Michael. 1999. *Defacement: Public Secrecy and the Labor of the Negative.* Stanford: Stanford University Press.

The Telegraph (Calcutta). 1998. "Gang of Pardhis Busted." July 31, 1998.

Thomassen, Bjørn. 2008. "What Kind of Political Anthropology?" *International Political Anthropology* 1 (2): 263–74.

———. 2012. "Notes Toward an Anthropology of Political Revolutions." *Comparative Studies in Society and History* 54 (3): 679–706.

———. 2014. *Liminality and the Modern: Living through the In-Between.* London: Routledge.

Tilly, Charles. 2008. *Contentious Performances.* Cambridge: Cambridge University Press.

Tobin, Sarah. 2016. *Everyday Piety: Islam and Economy in Jordan.* Ithaca, NY: Cornell University Press.

Tod, James. 1920. *Annals and Antiquities of Rajasthan, or the Central and Western Rajput States.* Edited by William Crooke. Oxford: Oxford University Press. First published 1832.

Todd, Emmanuel. 2002. *Après l'empire: Essai sur la décomposition du système américain.* Paris: Gallimard.

Todd, Selina. 2009. "Domestic Service and Class Relations in Britain, 1900–1950." *Past and Present* 203:181–204.

Tolen, Rachel. J. 1991. "Colonizing and Transforming the Criminal Tribesman: The Salvation Army in British India." *American Ethnologist* 18 (1): 106–25.

Totah, Faedah. 2014. *Preserving the Old City of Damascus.* Syracuse: Syracuse University Press.

Touati, Houari. 1993. "La loi et l'Ecriture: Fiqh, 'urf et société au Maghreb d'après les Ajwiba d'Ibn Nâsir (m. 1085/1674)." *Annales islamologiques* 27:93–108.

———. 1996. "Le prince et la bête: Enquête sur une métaphore pastorale." *Studia islamica* 83 (1): 101–19.

Trautmann, Thomas. 2006. *Languages and Nations: The Dravidian Proof in Colonial Madras.* Berkeley: University of California Press.

Triaud, Jean-Louis. 1995. *La légende noire de la Sanûsiyya: Une confrérie musulmane saharienne sous le regard français.* Paris: MSH.

Tristram, Henry. 1865. *The Land of Israel: A Journal of Travels in Palestine, Undertaken with Special Reference to Its Physical Character.* London: Society for Promoting Christian Knowledge.

Trouillot, Michael-Rolph. 1991. "Anthropology and the Savage Slot: The Poetics and Politics of Otherness." In *Recapturing Anthropology*, edited by R. Fox, 17–44. Santa Fe: School of American Research Press.

Tsing, Anna. 2005. *Friction: An Ethnography of Global Connection.* Princeton: Princeton University Press.

Tunsi, [al-Mohamed b. Oumar El-Tounsy]. 1851. *Voyage au Soudan oriental: Le Ouadây.* Paris: B. Duprat.

Turner, Ernest Sackville. 1962. *What the Butler Saw: Two Hundred and Fifty Years of the Servant Problem.* New York: St. Martin's Press.

Turner, Victor. 1977. *The Ritual Process: Structure and Anti-structure.* Ithaca, NY: Cornell University Press.

———. 1982. *From Ritual to Theatre: The Human Seriousness of Play.* New York: PAJ Publications.

———. 1985. *On the Edge of the Bush: Anthropology of Experience.* Edited by Edith Turner. Tucson: University of Arizona Press.

———. 1988. *The Anthropology of Performance.* New York: PAJ Publications.

UNEP (United Nations Environment Programme). 2006. *Geo Yearbook 2006.* Nairobi: United Nations Environment Programme.

Vahdat, Farzin. 2002. *God and Juggernaut: Iran's Intellectual Encounter with Modernity.* Syracuse: Syracuse University Press.

van Eijk, Esther. 2016. *Family Law in Syria: Patriarchy, Pluralism and Personal Status Laws.* London: I.B. Tauris.

van Gennep, Arnold. 2004. *The Rites of Passage.* Translated by Monika Vizedom and Gabrielle Caffee. London: Routledge. First published 1909.

Van Nieuwkerk, Karin. 2013. *Performing Piety: Singers and Actors in Egypt's Islamic Revival.* Austin: University of Texas Press.

Varenne, Hervé. 1984. "Collective Representation in American Anthropological Conversations: Individual and Culture." *Current Anthropology* 25 (3): 281–300.

Varisco, Dan. 2005. *Islam Obscured: The Rhetoric of Anthropological Representation*. New York: Palgrave Macmillan.

———. 2007. *Reading Orientalism: Said and the Unsaid*. Seattle: University of Washington Press.

Varzi, Roxanne. 2006. *Warring Souls: Youth, Media, and Martyrdom in Post-Revolution Iran*. Durham: Duke University Press.

Vidal, Denis. 1997. *Violence and Truth: A Rajasthani Kingdom Confronts Colonial Authority*. Delhi: Oxford University Press.

Viveiros de Castro, Eduardo. 1998. "Cosmological Deixis and Amazonian Perspectivism." *Journal of the Royal Anthropological Institute* 4 (3): 469–88.

———. 2012. "Cosmological Perspectivism in Amazonia and Elsewhere: Four Lectures Given in the Department of Social Anthropology, University of Cambridge, February–March 1998." https://haubooks.org/cosmological-perspectivism-in-amazonia/.

Voguet, Élise. 2009. "Islamisation de 'l'intérieur du Maghreb': Les fuqahâ' et les communautés rurales." *Revue des mondes musulmans et de la Méditerranée* 126:141–52.

Wagner, Kim A. 2007. *Thuggee: Banditry and the British in Early Nineteenth-Century India*. Basingstoke: Palgrave Macmillan.

———. 2010. "Confessions of a Skull: Phrenology and Colonial Knowledge in Early Nineteenth-Century India." *History Workshop Journal* 69:27–51.

Walker, Harry. 2013. *Under a Watchful Eye: Self, Power and Intimacy in Amazonia*. Berkeley: University of California Press.

Walzer, Martin. 1983. *Spheres of Justice: A Defence of Pluralism and Equality*. New York: Basic Books.

Warscheid, Ismail. 2017. *Droit musulman et société au Sahara prémoderne: La justice islamique dans les oasis du Grand Touat (Algérie) au XVIIe – XIXe siècles*. Leiden: Brill.

Wartilani, Sidi al-Husayn. 1908. *Nuzhat al-andhār fī fadhl 'ilm al-ta'rīkh w'al-akhbār*. Edited by M. Ben Cheneb. Algiers.

Washbrook, David. 1991. "'To Each a Language of His Own': Language, Culture, and Society in Colonial India." In *Language, History and Class*, edited by P. J. Corfield, 179–203. Oxford: Basil Blackwell.

Watt, Elizabeth. 2018. "Why #MeToo Is Complicated for Female Anthropologists." *Familiar Strange*, March 1, 2018. https://thefamiliarstrange.com/2018/03/01/why-metoo-is-complicated/.

Weber, Donald. 1995. "From Limen to Border: A Meditation on the Legacy of Victor Turner for American Cultural Studies." *American Quarterly* 47 (3): 525–36.

Wellman, Rose. 2014. "Feeding Moral Relations: The Making of Kinship and Nation in Iran." PhD dissertation, University of Virginia.

Werbner, Richard. 1984. "The Manchester School in South-Central Africa." *Annual Review of Anthropology* 13:157–85.

Wetherell, Margaret, and Janet Maybin. 1996. "The Distributed Self: A Social Constructionist Perspective." In *Understanding the Self*, edited by Richard Stevens, 219–80. London: Sage.

Wickham, Chris. 2009. *The Inheritance of Rome: A History of Europe from 400 to 1000*. London: Allen Lane.

Williams, Bianca C. 2017. "#MeToo: A Crescendo in the Discourse about Harassment, Fieldwork, and the Academy." *Savage Minds*, October 28, 2017. https://savageminds.org/2017/10/28/metoo-a-crescendo-in-the-discourse-about-sexual-harassment-fieldwork-and-the-academy-part-2/.

Williams, Richard. 2017. "Printing Out a Virtual Network: Female Poets in Urdu Literary Culture." Paper presented in a seminar on "Online and Offline Forums for Cultural Production," Oxford Comparative Criticism and Translation research program, University of Oxford, March 8, 2017.

Winch, Peter. 1958. *The Idea of a Social Science and Its Relation to Philosophy*. London: Routledge & Kegan Paul.

Wink, André. 1986. *Land and Sovereignty in India: Agrarian Society and Politics under the Eighteenth-Century Maratha Svarajya*. Cambridge: Cambridge University Press.

———. 2002. "From the Mediterranean to the Indian Ocean: Medieval History in Geographic Perspective." *Comparative Studies in Society and History* 44 (3): 416–45.

Yahia, Mohammed. 2014. "The False Science behind Egyptian Army's AIDS and HCV Cure." *House of Wisdom* (blog). March 2, 2014. Accessed August 13, 2016. http://blogs.nature .com/houseofwisdom/2014/03/the-false-science-behind-egyptian-armys-aids-and-hvc -cure.html.

Zayn, 'Arif al-. 2003. *Qawanin wa-nusus wa-ahkam al-ahwal al-shakhsiyya wa-tanzim al-tawa'if al-islamiyya fi lubnan*. Beirut: Manshurat al-Halabi al-Huquqiyya.

Zein, Abdul Hamid El-. 1977. "Beyond Ideology and Theology: The Search for the Anthropology of Islam." *Annual Review of Anthropology* 6:227–54.

Ziegler, Norman P. 1976. "Marvari Historical Chronicles: Sources for the Social and Cultural History of Rajasthan." *Indian Economic and Social History Review* 13:219–50.

INDEX

www.ingramcontent.com/pod-product-compliance
Lightning Source LLC
Chambersburg PA
CBHW030643270326
41929CB00007B/181